UK EARTH LAW JUDGMENTS

This open access book collects 11 reimagined judgments from the UK and challenges anthropocentrism in legal decision-making across a range of legal areas.

It draws from a range of Earth law approaches including rights of nature, animal rights, environmental human rights, well-being of future generations, ecocide and reinterpretations of existing legal principles.

There is an urgent need to transform our legal institutions and cultures to foster healthier relationships between people and planet. The book explores how relationships between people, place, and the more-than-human world are produced, transformed and destroyed through law, the limits of current law and the potential for positive transformation. A paradigm shift towards planetary, ecological and multispecies approaches offers possibilities for envisioning what the future of legal decision-making could look like.

Beyond the judgments, the book critically reflects on the developing field of Earth law and its potential for reshaping legal reasoning in the UK and beyond. It also offers possibilities for the future of Earth law from scholarly, educational, and policy perspectives within legal practice, training and education.

The book is a must read for scholars, students, legal practitioners and activists questioning the role of law and courts as mechanisms for change.

UK Earth Law Judgments

Reimagining Law for People and Planet

Edited by
Helen Dancer
Bonnie Holligan
and
Helena Howe

• HART •
OXFORD • LONDON • NEW YORK • NEW DELHI • SYDNEY

HART PUBLISHING

Bloomsbury Publishing Plc

Kemp House, Chawley Park, Cumnor Hill, Oxford, OX2 9PH, UK

1385 Broadway, New York, NY 10018, USA

29 Earlsfort Terrace, Dublin 2, Ireland

First published in Great Britain 2024

A catalogue record for this book is available from the British Library.

A catalogue record for this book is available from the Library of Congress.

Library of Congress Control Number: 2024934254

ISBN: HB: 978-1-50997-085-8
ePDF: 978-1-50997-087-2
ePub: 978-1-50997-086-5

Typeset by Compuscript Ltd, Shannon

ACKNOWLEDGEMENTS

From beginning to end this project has been highly collaborative. For their guidance in the earlier stages of the project we owe particular thanks to the Hon Justice Brian Preston SC, Chief Judge of the Land and Environment Court of New South Wales, His Honour Jeffrey Burke KC and the academic leads of the Australian Wild Law Judgment Project: Nicole Rogers and Michelle Maloney. We are also grateful to the Society of Legal Scholars for funding, and the Middle Temple for hosting the workshop where the judgments were developed.

Clearly this book could not have happened at all without the contributors, for whose enthusiasm, patience and commitment to the project we are extremely grateful. We are really appreciative of the input and support provided by our colleagues at the University of Sussex, especially Maria Moscati, Donald McGillivray, Nuno Ferreira and Chloe Anthony. We would also like to thank the anonymous peer reviewers for their guidance, although the usual disclaimers apply.

We are grateful to the University of Sussex for generously funding the Open Access publication of the book. We would also like to thank Plum Phillips and Nick Allen for their assistance with copyediting, Ann Barrett for indexing, and Roberta Bassi, Verity Stuart and Linda Goss at Hart for their editorial support and guidance.

Finally, huge thanks go to our respective family and friends, with two legs and four, for their support and motivation.

CONTENTS

PART III
CARE AND OBLIGATION

PART IV
HARM AND RESPONSIBILITY

PART V
KNOWLEDGES

LIST OF CONTRIBUTORS

Julia Aglionby is a Professor of Practice at Cumbria University and was Executive Director of the Foundation for Common Land for ten years. Julia served on the Board of Natural England from 2014 to 2019. Her work focuses on the plural legal systems in England and Indonesia governing protected area management.

Crispin Agnew KC, Honorary Research Fellow, University of Dundee, participated in scientific expeditions to remote regions, firing his environmental enthusiasm. He specialised in rural property and environmental law, developing a special interest in the rights of nature. He is an active member of the UKELA Wild Law Interest group.

Hannah Blitzer is a Policy Officer at Wildlife and Countryside Link, England. She works on English agriculture and chemicals policy and is campaigning for a legal right to a healthy environment. Hannah completed her PhD at the University of Sussex, specialising in UK environmental law and ecological constitutionalism.

Malcolm Combe is a Senior Lecturer in Scots private law at the University of Strathclyde. His main area of research is property law – with particular specialisms including land law reform and public access to land. He also has interests in access to justice and clinical legal education. He practised as a solicitor before his academic career.

Helen Dancer is a Senior Lecturer in Law and Anthropology at the University of Sussex. Her work is interdisciplinary and centres on human–Earth relationships. She has conducted ethnographic fieldwork in ancient English forest landscapes, Ecuador and Tanzania and practised as a barrister in child law before her academic career.

Lucy Finchett-Maddock is an artist and Associate Professor of Law at Bangor University. Her research is concerned with critical legal and contemporary philosophical understandings of law and its materiality, through understandings of aesthetics, property, entropy and resistance, including methodological and practice-based questions around the intersection of art, law, resistance and property.

Johanna Gibson is Herchel Smith Professor of Intellectual Property Law at Queen Mary, University of London. She researches and writes in intellectual property, legal theory and non-human studies. Her most recent book, *Owned, An Ethological Jurisprudence of Property*, establishes the concept of ethological jurisprudence, taking a multispecies approach to property.

Jérémie Gilbert is Professor of Human Rights at the University of Roehampton. His main area of research is international human rights law and, more particularly, the relationship between human rights law, natural resources and environmental issues.

Joanne Hawkins is a Lecturer in Business Law at the University of Leeds. Her research explores regulatory decision-making processes, planning law and policy, democratic rights/public participation, and public trust in the context of development and the environment.

Bonnie Holligan is a Senior Lecturer in Property Law at the University of Sussex. Her research explores the commodification of environment and the role of property rights in the creation of markets in environmental goods and services, such as carbon credit or emissions trading schemes.

Helena Howe is a Senior Lecturer in Law at the University of Sussex. Her research lies at the intersection of property, environmental and animal law, with a particular focus on sustainable agriculture and the legal protection of farmed and companion animals.

Felicity Kayumba Kalunga is a Lecturer of Environmental Law at the University of Zambia and a coauthor of 'Transnational Corporate Liability for Environmental Damage and Climate Change: Reassessing Access to Justice after *Vedanta v Lungowe*'. Her current research studies traditional governance institutions and their regulation under public power.

Rachel Killean is a Senior Lecturer at Sydney Law School and member of the Sydney Institute of Criminology, Sydney Southeast Asia Centre, and Sydney Environment Institute. Her research centres on responses to violence, focusing on transitional justice, victims' rights, sexual and gender-based violence, and harms perpetrated against the natural world.

Karen Morrow is Professor of Environmental Law at Swansea University. Her research interests address theoretical and practical aspects of public participation in environmental, sustainability law and policy, and ecofeminism, gender and the environment. Her current work focuses on ecofeminism and the Anthropocene, with particular reference to climate change.

Andreas Philippopoulos-Mihalopoulos is an artist, theorist and fiction author. He works with performance art, installation, photography, text, sculpture and painting, and has appeared in solo and group shows. He is also Professor of Law and Theory at the University of Westminster and Director of The Westminster Law and Theory Lab.

Chris Rogers is Emeritus Professor of Law at Newcastle University. He has authored several research monographs, including *The Law of Nature Conservation: Property, Environment and the Limits of Law*, and (with collaborators) *Contested*

Common Land: Environmental Governance Past and Present, and *English Urban Commons: The Past Present and Future of Green Space.*

Chris Sangster completed his PhD at Northumbria University on the representation of wildlife in legal proceedings, focusing on the badger cull in England and Wales. His areas of interest are primarily badger-related but extend to all situations of conflict between the interests of wildlife and humans.

Damien Short is Professor of Human Rights and Environmental Justice at the School of Advanced Study, University of London. He has authored several books focusing on the ecocide–genocide nexus, particularly the role of energy production and extractive industries. He is Editor-in-Chief of the *International Journal of Human Rights.*

Anastasia Tataryn is an Associate Professor at St Jerome's University, University of Waterloo, Canada. Her research interrogates the limits of legal frameworks, deeply questioning foundations and categories of modern law and legal subjectivity. Research focuses include labour migration law, labour law, citizenship and social uprising, through feminist, poststructuralist and anarchic approaches.

Saskia Vermeylen is a Reader in Law at the University of Strathclyde. She is a legal phenomenologist with an interest in African legal cultures and embodied understandings of legal placemaking and rituals, which she has studied across Southern Africa using different methodologies ranging from anthropology to photography.

Jo Lindsay Walton is a Research Fellow at the Sussex Digital Humanities Lab. His research explores the role of artistic and creative practice in climate communication and climate policy, with some focus on the role of emerging technologies and their associated sociotechnical imaginaries.

Joe Wills is a Lecturer in Law at the University of Leicester. His research explores the legal status of animals, animal legal personhood and the relationship between animal rights and human rights law. He is working on a project exploring non-anthropocentric modes of common law adjudication.

Ania Zbyszewska is an Assistant Professor at Carleton University in Canada. Her interdisciplinary, socio-legal research focuses on regulation of work as a socio-ecological process, and engages critical, feminist and political ecology approaches to re/consider the interface of work and environmental regulation and explore regulatory alternatives that facilitate more sustainable livelihoods.

LIST OF FIGURES

1

Introduction

HELEN DANCER, BONNIE HOLLIGAN AND HELENA HOWE

Genesis and Genealogy of the Project

The UK Earth Law Judgments Project is the first UK-based project of its kind. Through the methodology of critical judgment-writing, it challenges current anthropocentric paradigms in legal decision-making towards fostering healthier relationships between people and planet. The project builds on the work of other alternative judgment projects, including the Wild Law Judgment Project led by Australian scholars,[1] feminist judgments projects around the world, and critical judgments projects in other areas, including human rights, children's rights and indigenous rights.[2]

The idea for the project grew from the editors' earlier research in the area of Earth law and our conversations at Sussex Law School about an Earth law judgments project for the UK. The project was launched at a conference of the UK Environmental Law Association on the theme of 'Wild Law and Activism' at the University of Sussex in November 2019, to an audience of academics, legal practitioners, third-sector professionals and students. Experts from a range of legal subject areas were then invited to propose an Earth law judgment from their area of specialism. The collection of eleven judgments and their accompanying commentaries was developed through a series of three workshops with co-authors in 2020 and 2021, which included input from guest judges, the Hon Justice Brian Preston SC, Chief Judge of the Land and Environment Court of New South Wales and His Honour Jeffrey Burke KC, and the academic leads

[1] Nicole Rogers and Michelle Maloney (eds), *Law as if Earth Really Mattered: The Wild Law Judgment Project* (Routledge, 2017).

[2] There are over seventeen such critical judgments projects around the world. In the UK context these include: Rosemary Hunter, Clare McGlynn and Erika Rackley (eds), *Feminist Judgments: From Theory to Practice* (Hart Publishing, 2010); Máiréad Enright, Julie McCandless and Aoife O'Donoghue (eds), *Northern/Irish Feminist Judgments: Judges' Troubles and the Gendered Politics of Identity* (Hart Publishing, 2017); Helen Stalford, Kathryn Hollingsworth and Stephen Gilmore (eds), *Rewriting Children's Rights Judgments: From Academic Vision to New Practice* (Hart Publishing, 2017); Sharon Cowan, Chloe Kennedy and Vanessa E Munro (eds), *Scottish Feminist Judgments: (Re)Creating Law from the Outside In* (Hart Publishing, 2019).

of the Australian Wild Law Judgment Project, Professor Nicole Rogers and Dr Michelle Maloney. The final workshop was a two-day event held at the Middle Temple in London in December 2021, which was funded by the Society of Legal Scholars.

Recognising the importance of exploring a plurality of approaches within this emergent legal field, each author was invited to adopt a lens of their choosing for reimagining their judgment, drawing from a range of theoretical and legal framings of Earth law, either that already existed in the United Kingdom or other parts of the world, or which were speculative possibilities for the future. Each of the contributors responded to the overarching theme of relationships between people, place and the more-than-human world, and how such relationships are produced, transformed and destroyed through law. The collection was developed to encompass a variety of contexts around the United Kingdom in which such relationships have been contested.

Aims and Limitations

The central aim of the collection is to explore possibilities for a new more-than-human jurisprudence in the United Kingdom by challenging the limits of existing law. Each judgment presents opportunities to respond more attentively to the interests of 'all lives and life support systems'[3] within recognisable legal frameworks. Only some of the myriad engagements between law and the more-than-human are included in the cases chosen.[4] Yet, the authors bring multiple perspectives on law and strategies for legal transformation in the pursuit of more respectful human–Earth relationships. Creating a body of judicial reasoning, even as an academic exercise, is an 'active' endeavour,[5] one that can contribute to the formation and evolution of new values, principles and even doctrine.[6]

There are, of course, limits to what a collection of reimagined judgments can achieve. The decision to begin from existing case law inevitably shapes how each author constructs the legal landscape, potentially reducing, for example, the opportunity to introduce wholly novel claims or claimants. The choice of private law litigation, made by several contributors, brings difficulties of turning a bilateral claim between individuals into one that reflects the polycentric nature of

[3] Nicole Rogers and Michelle Maloney, 'The Wild Law Judgment Project' in Rogers and Maloney, *Law as if Earth Really Mattered*, 3, 5.

[4] Other natural entities to which Earth law may apply, such as oceans (Irus Braverman and Elizabeth R Johnson (eds), *Blue Legalities: The Life and Laws of the Sea* (Duke University Press, 2020) or space (Emily Ray, 'Outer Space in the Anthropocene' in Peter Burdon and James Martel, *The Routledge Handbook of Law and the Anthropocene* (Routledge, 2023)) are not represented in the collection.

[5] Elizabeth Fisher, 'Afterword: Law in ~~Un~~expected Places' in Brian Preston and Elizabeth Fisher (eds), *An Environmental Court in Action: Function, Doctrine, Process* (Hart Publishing, 2022) 314.

[6] Nicole Rogers, 'Performance and Pedagogy in the Wild Law Judgment Project' (2017) 27 *Legal Education Review* 53.

more-than-human concerns.[7] Although the authors found ways for more-than-human interests to emerge, their freedom was constrained by adopting the mantle of the human judge.

As explained below, the authors were not confined strictly to possible or plausible outcomes but, equally, they could not be wholly 'unrestrained' by the law.[8] This influenced the arguments made. While, in some respects, subduing any urge for normative originality, such constraints also potentially spurred the authors on to more strategic creative imaginings. It certainly shaped the language used. Whilst some authors painstakingly created judgments that would pass as an opinion of the court in the law reports, others delighted in trying to fulfil Lord Rodger's plea for judges to make their judgments more entertaining and memorable.[9]

Crucially, the authors were faced with the complex and diverse interests of non-humans. It is probably inappropriate in this context to refer to the 'elephant in the room', but perhaps the most significant limitation of this exercise lies in the human speaking for a being or entity whose experience they cannot share.[10] The contributors acknowledge the need for epistemic humility[11] in this endeavour but also the vital need for such representation in a human-ordered legal system.[12] The collection proceeds from the premise that sensitive attempts at representation and participation, attentive to difference, are positive steps towards a legal system that can do justice to the more-than-human world.

Methods

There is no template for what it means to write an Earth judgment. Chapter 2 draws out some of the substantive elements of 'Earth law' approaches that informed the collection. In terms of method, authors drew inspiration from feminist judgment scholarship,[13] as well as from Justice Brian Preston's account of wild law judging.[14] At a fundamental level, an alternative judgments project must decide whether to accept the legitimacy of existing court and constitutional structures.[15] As Justice

[7] Elizabeth Fisher, Bettina Lange and Eloise Scotford, *Environmental Law, Text, Cases and Materials*, 4th edn (Oxford University Press, 2019) 87.

[8] Brian Preston, 'Writing Judgments "Wildly" in Rogers and Maloney, *Law as if Earth Really Mattered*, 19, 20.

[9] Lord Rodger, 'The Form and Language of Judicial Opinions' (2002) 118 *LQR* 226, 246.

[10] A challenge similarly acknowledged by Rogers and Maloney, 'The Wild Law Judgment Project', 4.

[11] Lorraine Code, 'Ecological Responsibilities: Which Trees? Where? Why?' (2012) 3 *Journal of Human Rights and the Environment* 84.

[12] Christopher D. Stone, 'Should Trees Have Standing? Toward Legal Rights for Natural Objects' (1972) 45 *Southern California Law Review* 450; Cass R Sunstein, (2000) 'Standing for Animals (with Notes on Animal Rights) 47 *UCLA Law Review* 1333.

[13] Rosemary Hunter, 'An Account of Feminist Judging' in Hunter et al, *Feminist Judgments*, 30.

[14] Brian Preston, 'Writing Judgments "Wildly"' in Rogers and Maloney, *Law As If Earth Really Mattered*, 19.

[15] See here Irene Watson, 'Aboriginal Laws of the Land' in Rogers and Maloney, *Law as if Earth Really Mattered*, 209 and Nicole Watson and Heather Douglas (eds), *Indigenous Legal Judgments: Bringing Indigenous Voices into Judicial Decision Making* (Routledge, 2021).

Preston explains, writing 'wildly' may then involve finding alternative legal authorities, or interpreting the words and aims of authorities differently. New general norms and principles may be recognised. Attention may be paid to a different, or broader, range of facts. Finally, alternative remedies may be offered.

Judgment authors were afforded discretion as to how closely to cleave to existing legal authorities and procedures. Most of the judgments apply existing legal authorities, both case law and statute, in imaginary versions of actually existing courts, while seeking to demonstrate how these authorities could be reinterpreted. Rachel Killean, however, proposes a new international crime via amendments to the treaty establishing the International Criminal Court.[16] While placing emphasis on different facts, and drawing new conclusions, the judgments generally stick to the known facts in the cases that they have chosen. For two of the authors (Killean and Ania Zbyszewska), entirely new decisions were imagined based on fictional factual scenarios that were inspired by real-life incidents of environmental harm.

This flexibility extended to the time at which the judgments are set. Although none of the judgments take place in the future,[17] some authors incorporated authorities and materials not available at the time of the original judgment. For example, Karen Morrow applies the Well-being of Future Generations (Wales) Act 2015 to the early-twentieth-century tort case of *Attorney-General v Cory Brothers*.[18]

The judgments respond primarily to the (geographical and legal) landscapes, communities and concerns of the jurisdictions within the United Kingdom. This does not mean that they neglect international legal contexts; indeed, several judgments draw on formal and informal international norms (in particular, the Universal Declaration for the Rights of Mother Earth).[19] Transnational supply chains, controlled by international corporate actors, raise troubling questions of responsibility but also provide opportunity for English lawyers to learn from other traditions, as Saskia Vermeylen and Jérémie Gilbert highlight in their response to the decision in *Vedanta Resources PLC v Lungowe*, a case about the harms caused by a UK-controlled copper mine in Zambia.[20]

In terms of structure and form, the judgments vary in style. Most adhere more or less closely to conventions of English judicial writing,[21] but Andreas Philippopoulos-Mihalopoulos and Lucy Finchett-Maddock responded to

[16] The Australian Wild Law Judgment project also involved the creation of 'wild' legislation: see eg Benedict Coyne, 'The Fraught and Fishy Tale of Lungfish v the State of Queensland', in Rogers and Maloney (eds), *Law as if Earth Really Mattered*, 56.

[17] Compare Nicole Rogers and Michelle Maloney, 'The Anthropocene Judgments Project: A Thought Experiment in Futureproofing the Common Law' (2022) 0(0) *Alternative Law Journal* 1.

[18] *Attorney-General v Cory Brothers* [1921] 1 AC 521.

[19] garn.org/universal-declaration-for-the-rights-of-mother-earth/.

[20] *Vedanta Resources PLC v Lungowe* [2019] UKSC 20.

[21] For a more detailed examination of what it means to write as a judge, rather than as an academic, see Erika Rackley, 'The Art and Craft of Writing Judgments: Notes on the Feminist Judgments Project' in Hunter et al, *Feminist Judgments*, 44.

Pendragon v United Kingdom[22] with a video installation and a live performance, which are recounted in their text-based contribution to this collection. Bonnie Holligan worked with digital humanities scholar Jo Walton to produce an automated judgment generator alongside the more traditional written judgment. Helen Dancer's judgment also bends established form to address future generations directly.

Each judgment is preceded by an introduction from the author, which sets out the author's motivations and approach. The judgments are followed by a comment from a separate scholar. The commentaries provide a critical appraisal of the approach taken by the judgment writer, reflecting on the contribution made by the reimagined judgment, possible alternative avenues and future prospects for legal development in the area.

Structure of the Book

Time

Part I begins with Helen Dancer's judgment in *R (Packham) v Secretary of State for Transport, the Prime Minister and HS2 Ltd*,[23] and addresses the climate and biodiversity crises that lie at the heart of an application for judicial review to protect ancient woodlands in the path of a proposed high-speed rail line. Her dissenting judgment reinterprets the public law test of 'irrationality' in the face of planetary crisis, based on a legal and ethical duty towards future generations and ecological justice. Foregrounding the rights and well-being of future generations and the ancient woodlands themselves, she draws upon law and emotion scholarship and a child-centred judicial style to write a judgment in the form of a letter to future generations, whose voices are also heard.

Taking a 'view from Wales in 2023', Karen Morrow time-travels the 1921 case of *A-G and others, Kennard and others v Cory Brothers and others*[24] 100 years into the present. Her ecofeminist approach challenges the paradigm of mastery over the environment, reframing the original claims in nuisance to focus on the social and environmental consequences of extractivism in the Welsh Valleys and the community impacted by a disastrous colliery tip landslide. The judgment draws upon innovations in Welsh law that place sustainability and well-being duties on public bodies, including the Well-being of Future Generations (Wales) Act 2015 and the Environment (Wales) Act 2016, bringing attention to excluded voices and reconsidering how human interests and harms to the abiotic environment can be accounted for in law.

[22] *Pendragon v United Kingdom* (1998) 27 EHRR CD 179.

[23] *R (Packham) v Secretary of State for Transport, the Prime Minister and HS2 Ltd* [2020] EWCA Civ 1004.

[24] *A-G and others, Kennard and others v Cory Brothers and others* [1921] 1 AC 521.

Subjectivities

Part II presents the fictional case of *Swale Water v Swale Water Workers for Marshes Coalition*, imagined as a decision of the Employment Appeals Tribunal. Taking a feminist perspective, Ania Zbyszewska envisions an employment law that takes ecological connectedness seriously through exploration of the issue of when an employee can legitimately cease work on the grounds that it poses a danger to 'other persons' under the Employment Rights Act 1996. Zbyszewska's judgment situates her employees within their ecosystem by interpreting 'other persons' to include all beings, casting danger to the environment as one that is inseparable from that posed to humans. Through this relational ontology, Zbyszewska enables glimpses of a labour law framework that is more responsive to social and ecological complexity to emerge.

This is followed by Joe Wills's reimagining of the House of Lords decision in *R (on the application of Countryside Alliance) v Attorney General*,[25] finding the prohibition of hunting wild mammals with dogs by the Hunting Act 2004 compatible with the European Convention on Human Rights. Recentring the fox, Wills highlights the capacity of human rights law to protect animal interests, finding that the rights and freedoms of foxes would provide a legitimate basis for any interference with the rights of the claimants under Article 11. Whilst reaching the same verdict as the majority, Wills takes issue with the anthropocentric framing in the original judgment of the fox as a 'pest', respecting them instead as sentient beings, entitled to pursue their own interests alongside ours.

Care and Obligation

Through a reworking of *Savage v Fairclough*,[26] Helena Howe explores when the operation of an intensive livestock farm should amount to a private nuisance. The hypothetical 'good farmer', against whom the elements of nuisance are to be judged, is reframed as a compassionate and knowledgeable character, more sensitive to risk and their role in a relational web of care. Accordingly, the reimagined judgment enables the range of harms associated with intensive farming to be acknowledged and the perspectives of other beings affected by intensive livestock rearing to be included, particularly the pigs kept by the defendants.

Bonnie Holligan reimagines *R (on the application of Mott) v Environment Agency*,[27] in which the Supreme Court found that restrictions imposed by the Environment Agency on a fisherman's annual salmon catch were an interference with his right to peaceful enjoyment of possessions under Article 1 of Protocol 1

[25] *R (on the application of Countryside Alliance) v Attorney General* [2007] 3 WLR 922.
[26] [1999] Env LR 183.
[27] [2018] UKSC 10.

to the European Convention on Human Rights. She builds on existing European Court of Human Rights and domestic case law to reach a different conclusion, constructing a richer view of property as embedded in a broader social framework of rights and responsibilities that extend over time. This involves more nuanced attention to the obligations connected to ownership. The judgment highlights elements of contingency and dependency within rights-based jurisprudence, and the need to locate human rights, and property rights, within a temporal and ecological context.

Harm and Responsibility

Part IV imagines two new legal approaches to reparation and restorative justice for serious environmental harm caused by the extractive operations of UK companies and their overseas subsidiaries in Africa. In their amicus curiae brief for the case of *Lungowe and Others v Vedanta Resources PLC and Konkola Copper Mines*,[28] Saskia Vermeylen and Jérémie Gilbert urge a future UK court to expand the duty of care of the holding company into a decolonial ethics of care towards the polluted river and its human communities. Their approach integrates Zambian customs and concepts with the rights of the river as a legal entity and proposes a model for restorative justice that moves beyond compensation for past harms suffered, to include a sense of responsibility and preventative action for the future.

In the context of environmental harm caused by oil exploitation in Ogoniland, Nigeria, Rachel Killean steps into the International Criminal Court to imagine what a reparations order for a possible future crime of ecocide could look like. Her imagined judgment against the fictional employee of a UK-registered company, *Mr X*, adopts Polly Higgins's definition of ecocide,[29] bringing attention to the importance of criminal liability for omissions as well as acts associated with interconnected ecological, climatic and cultural loss. As with Vermeylen and Gilbert's brief, the judgment highlights both the large number of victims and the long-term consequences of environmental harm, for which monetary reparations for environmental restitution and human physical, economic and psychosocial rehabilitation can only ever provide partial compensation.

Knowledges

Turning to the theme of knowledge and inclusion in decision making, Sir Crispin Agnew's reimagined *Sustainable Shetland v Scottish Ministers*[30] holds that the

[28] [2019] UKSC 20.
[29] Polly Higgins, *Eradicating Ecocide*, 2nd edn (Shepheard-Walwyn, 2015).
[30] [2015] UKSC 5.

Universal Declaration on the Rights of Mother Earth is relevant to the grant of consent for construction of a windfarm. A balance needs to be struck that 'maintains the integrity, balance and health of Mother Earth'. On this basis, the case is remitted to the Scottish Ministers to hold a public inquiry to consider the scientific and other evidence. The rights of the whimbrel, of other beings, including local human communities, have to be considered in that balance. This alternative approach points to the need to rethink our planning procedures, and legal processes more generally, to give voice to a wider range of knowledges and values.

Julia Aglionby's judgment concerns a challenge to a decision by the Lake District National Park Authority (LDNPA) not to consult on a Traffic Regulation Order restricting the use of four-wheel-drive vehicles in the National Park.[31] Her rewritten judgment emphasises both the designated heritage of the Lake District and the perspective of local communities, their knowledge and wisdom. Greater weight is also placed upon the obligation to address the climate crisis, as reflected in the sustainable travel policies of the LDNPA. On this basis, taking account of the national and international values at stake, the LDNPA is required to reconsider its decision to reject the Traffic Regulation Order.

The collection closes with Andreas Philippopoulos-Mihalopoulos and Lucy Finchett-Maddock's account of their performance 'To Open Up' *Pendragon v United Kingdom*.[32] Under Section 14 of the Public Order Act 1986, a druid, performing a summer solstice ceremony at Stonehenge along with about forty other people, was arrested for trespassing. The case reached the European Court of Human Rights, which held that the arrest interfered with the applicant's right to peaceful assembly, but that such interference was justified as pursuing a legitimate aim and as being necessary in a democratic society. Both authors draw on their creative practice to work outside the text of the law, offering performative rewritings of the decision that they describe as 'stutterings' – a 'poetic undoing' that is never entirely concluded or finished.

[31] *Stubbs (on behalf of Green Lanes Environmental Action Movement) v Lake District National Park Authority* [2020] EWHC 2293 (Admin).

[32] (1999) 27 EHRR CD179.

2

Earth Law Judging: Transforming Legal Reasoning

HELEN DANCER, BONNIE HOLLIGAN AND HELENA HOWE

What is Earth Law?

In many respects, Earth law is an emerging field of theories and legal innovations in response to the planetary crisis with parameters that are still taking shape. We have interpreted its theoretical foundations to include indigenous cosmologies, Earth jurisprudence, Earth system science, animal rights ethics, green criminology, ecofeminism, new materialism and other critical approaches to law. However, it is to be acknowledged from the outset that there is significant contestation between these approaches. Throughout this book, we have chosen to embrace these contestations and diversities in our exploration of what Earth law could become in the United Kingdom. In this introduction to the field, we survey the landscape of theoretical approaches underpinning Earth law and its various legal manifestations explored in this book, including rights of nature, animal rights, environmental human rights, well-being of future generations, ecocide and reinterpretations of existing legal principles.

The Global Response to the Planetary Crisis

The Stockholm Declaration on the Human Environment in 1972[1] was a watershed moment in legal attempts to address the planetary crisis at a global level. These came of age at the 1992 Rio Earth Summit[2] following the publication of the highly influential Brundtland report of 1987, *Our Common Future*.[3] The UN Framework

[1] UN Conference on the Human Environment, Stockholm Declaration on the Human Environment, Resolutions 2994/XXVII, 2995/UVII and 2996/XXII adopted by the UN General Assembly, Stockholm, 16 June 1972 and 15 December 1972.

[2] UN Conference on Environment and Development, Rio de Janeiro, Brazil, 3–14 June 1992.

[3] Gro Harlem Brundtland, *Report of the World Commission on Environment and Development: Our Common Future* (World Commission on Environment and Development, 1987).

Convention on Climate Change and the UN Convention on Biological Diversity, both signed at Rio, and periodic meetings of the Conference of the Parties (COP) that govern these conventions, have become the subject of enormous scientific and public attention as concern has grown over the worsening situation. By 2015, many of the UN Millennium Development Goal targets, including ensuring environmental sustainability, had not been met.[4] Policy-makers have been increasingly urged to take the actions necessary to protect people and planet as scientific evidence shows that we have already exceeded some of the 'planetary boundaries' that keep Earth in 'Holocene-like' stable conditions.[5] Twenty years after the Rio summit, the political outcome document of the UN Conference on Sustainable Development (Rio+20), *The Future We Want*,[6] led to the development of the UN Sustainable Development Goals, adopted by all UN Member States in 2015, which set out a 2030 Agenda for Sustainable Development as a global call to action 'for people, planet and prosperity'.[7] Yet, despite the scientific knowledge, global goals, international environmental agreements and growing pressure on policy-makers to take action, global governance and environmental law has not yet proved effective in turning around the planetary crisis.

The limited effectiveness of environmental law and the concept of sustainable development in tackling environmental, social and economic problems has in part been due to the fact that they do not fundamentally challenge the prioritising of humans over the non-human, private property norms and established capitalist principles of economic growth that have led to increasingly inequitable societies as well as overconsumption of the planet's resources.[8] The language of mainstream environmental economics, including concepts of natural capital and ecosystem services, has become embedded in high-level and national policy agendas on the environment, particularly since the 2001 Millennium Ecosystem Assessment and its influential 2005 synthesis report,[9] entrenching an economic model in environmental governance that maintains rather than transforms business-as-usual. Equally, proponents of 'Earth system law', influenced by Earth system science, point to the gap between law and Earth system governance and in particular, the failures of environmental law and lawyers over the last fifty years, who, by pursuing a 'predominantly mono-disciplinary research agenda' have been unable to respond to the complexities of the Earth system and patterns of socio-ecological

[4] UN Millennium Development Goals un.org/millenniumgoals.

[5] Will Steffen et al, 'Trajectories of the Earth System in the Anthropocene' (2018) 115 *Proceedings of the National Academy of Sciences of the United States of America* 8252.

[6] UN Conference on Sustainable Development, The Future We Want – Outcome Document, UN General Assembly Resolution A/RES/66/288, Rio de Janeiro, Brazil, 20–22 June 2012.

[7] UN General Assembly, Transforming Our World: the 2030 Agenda for Sustainable Development, Resolution A/RES/70/1 adopted by the General Assembly, New York, United States, 25 September 2015.

[8] Compare, for example, Kate Raworth, who proposes a reimagining of economics based on a social foundation and an ecological ceiling: Kate Raworth, *Doughnut Economics: Seven Ways to Think Like a 21st-Century Economist* (Random House Business, 2017).

[9] Millennium Ecosystem Assessment, *Ecosystems and Human Wellbeing* (Island Press, 2005).

change.[10] Earth systems theorists argue that humans in their powerful position as Earth's dominant species have the capacity to govern and regulate to ensure a habitable planet. For these theorists, the agenda centres on how to govern in the face of persistent uncertainties, functional and intergenerational dependencies, the massive anthropogenic harms that have already been caused, and the need to address and increase resilience.[11]

There can be no doubt that business-as-usual is no longer an option and that a paradigm shift in Earth law and governance is urgently needed. Nevertheless, many questions remain to be answered. What theories, norms and values underpin Earth law as an emerging approach, and what are the implications for law and judging in different contexts? These are the core questions at the heart of this collection of Earth law judgments, which seek to address the planetary crisis by reimagining law and judging in the United Kingdom.

The Ecological Turn

It could be said that what is termed here 'Earth law' has been expressed over millennia through the cosmological belief systems and customary practices of many indigenous and First Nations peoples, as well as ancient Celtic paganism in Europe and some Asian religions, including Taoism, Hinduism, Jainism and Buddhism. Although culturally, geographically and historically diverse, they are each grounded in ethical commitments based on interconnectedness between humans and other living and non-living entities and spirit worlds, or as David Abram first conceptualised it, the 'more-than-human world'.[12] Other, secular, theories of environmental ethics and more-than-human relationality have been influenced by the science of ecology, leading to the development of 'ecological law'.[13] In 1949, ecologist Aldo Leopold espoused a 'land ethic' of humans belonging to the land.[14] However, it was not until the 1960s that works by Rachel Carson, Lynn White and Garrett Hardin initiated widespread public debate on the use of pesticides,[15] human dominion over nature,[16] population growth and the need for collective action to curb consumption.[17] By the first Earth Day, 22 April 1970, these roots had grown into what was to become a significant decade for global environmental consciousness and the development of new ethical theories. Chemist

[10] Louis J Kotzé and Kim E Rakhyun, 'Earth System Law: The Juridical Dimensions of Earth System Governance' (2019) 1 *Earth System Governance* 100003, 2.
[11] ibid.
[12] David Abram, *The Spell of the Sensuous: Perception and Language in a More-Than-Human World* (Vintage Books, 1997).
[13] Peter D Burdon, 'Ecological Law in the Anthropocene' (2020) 11 *Transnational Legal Theory* 33.
[14] Aldo Leopold, *A Sand County Almanac and Sketches Here and There* (Oxford University Press, 1972).
[15] Rachel Carson, *Silent Spring* (Houghton Mifflin, 1962).
[16] Lynn White Jr , 'The Historical Roots of Our Ecologic Crisis' (1967) 155 *Science* 1203.
[17] Garrett Hardin, 'The Tragedy of the Commons' (1968) 162 *Science* 1243.

James Lovelock and microbiologist Lynn Margulis's 'Gaia hypothesis' theorised that conditions for life on Earth were self-regulated by the complex systems of interactions between biotic and abiotic forms.[18] At the same time, the 'deep ecology' movement, particularly associated with the works of Arne Næss, was founded on principles of ecological egalitarianism, diversity, symbiosis and interconnectedness between entities.[19]

The global rights of nature movement finds its origins in both indigenous cosmologies and ecological thinking. Rights of nature may be understood as a form of legal hybrid; the result of transnational interactions between indigenous cosmologies and Western rights-based ecocentric philosophy on non-human subjectivity. Christopher Stone's essay on the legal standing of trees[20] and the work of Thomas Berry,[21] Cormac Cullinan[22] and other Earth jurisprudence and wild law scholars is regarded as the Western philosophical starting-point, with a normative foundation that human law must serve the common good of the whole 'Earth community' of human and non-human subjects. Cormac Cullinan has promoted the idea of a Universal Declaration of the Rights of Mother Earth. Earth jurisprudence became influential at a UN level in 2009 when the UN General Assembly proclaimed 22 April International Mother Earth Day, establishing a UN Harmony with Nature programme.[23] At a national level, Ecuador was the first country to enshrine rights of nature in its Constitution in 2008. Rights of nature, often concerned with the rights of rivers and forests, have been legally recognised in countries as diverse as Bolivia, Colombia, New Zealand, Bangladesh, Canada and Spain.[24] At a global level, the inclusion of rights of nature in the Global Biodiversity Framework at COP15 of the UN Convention on Biological Diversity in 2022[25] was an indication of how rights of nature had begun to influence international environmental policy debates from the periphery. In this collection, several judgments explore the potential of rights of nature in the United Kingdom.

The Ontological Turn

The normative theories of Earth jurisprudence discussed above are distinct from the family of critical theories influencing Earth law that have developed since

[18] James E Lovelock and Lynn Margulis 'Atmospheric Homeostasis by and for the Biosphere: The Gaia Hypothesis' (1974) 26 *Tellus A: Dynamic Meteorology and Oceanography* 2.

[19] Arne Næss, 'The Shallow and the Deep, Long-range Ecology Movement. A Summary' (1973) 16 *Inquiry* 95.

[20] Christopher D Stone, 'Should Trees Have Standing? Toward Legal Rights for Natural Objects' (1972) 45 *Southern California Law Review* 450.

[21] Thomas Berry, *The Great Work: Our Way into the Future* (Three Rivers Press, 1999).

[22] Cormac Cullinan, *Wild Law: A Manifesto for Earth Justice* (Green Books, 2002).

[23] UN Harmony with Nature Programme at harmonywithnatureun.org.

[24] Legal developments concerning rights of nature can be followed at the Eco Jurisprudence Monitor at ecojurisprudence.org.

[25] UN Conference of the Parties to the Convention on Biological Diversity, Kunming–Montreal Global Biodiversity Framework, CBD/COP/15/L.25, Fifteenth meeting – Part II, Montreal, Canada, 7–12 December 2022.

the 1980s. An ontological turn in the arts and humanities generated poststructuralist, postmodernist and posthumanist theories of entanglement, materiality and power relations between humans, and between human and non-human. These thinkers explicitly rejected centuries-old normative and monotheistic dualist ideas about nature that were rooted in Aristotelian and Cartesian theories of a nature/culture, human/animal divide. Late-twentieth-century critiques of Western metaphysical dualism, notably Bruno Latour's critique of the nature/culture binary, centred on challenging modernity's artificial attempt to keep separate what were in reality complex systems where nature, culture, politics, science and technology were inextricably bound together.[26] Through Latour and other actor network theorists, a new language emerged to describe more-than-human connections consisting of networks and assemblages.[27]

Alongside the actor network theorists, postmodernists, notably Gilles Deleuze and Félix Guattari, brought attention to the hierarchical effects of dualism and proposed alternative theories of generative processes of becoming.[28] The new materialist thinkers who have followed do not distinguish between living biotic entities and abiotic entities as agents: all matter may be considered vital, entangled and in constant flux.[29] Such approaches underpin a 'critical environmental law', which Andreas Philippopoulos-Mihalopoulos has conceptualised as a space of critique within environmental law (which is itself a space of tension between claims that 'environmental-law-includes-everything' and 'environmental-law-does-not-exist'). In this space, environmental law becomes acentric, fragmented and replaced by a hybridity of connections between human, natural, spatial, artificial and technological.[30]

Ecofeminism has also evolved from its beginnings in the second-wave feminist movement and a focus on care, towards a broader, critical engagement with environmental issues.[31] Karen Morrow, for example, draws upon ecofeminist and new materialist approaches to critique human mastery of the Earth system in the context of debates on climate justice.[32] Ecofeminism has also contributed to critical debates in the field of animal law. Academic interest in the protection of non-human animals had burgeoned initially in the wake of work by Peter Singer[33]

[26] Bruno Latour, *We Have Never Been Modern* (Harvard University Press, 1993).

[27] Bruno Latour, *Reassembling the Social: An Introduction to Actor-Network-Theory* (Oxford University Press, 2005).

[28] Gilles Deleuze and Félix Guattari, *A Thousand Plateaus: Capitalism and Schizophrenia* (University of Minnesota Press, 1987).

[29] For example, Jane Bennett, *Vibrant Matter: A Political Ecology of Things* (Duke University Press, 2010).

[30] Andreas Philippopoulos-Mihalopoulos, 'Toward a Critical Environmental Law' in Andreas Philippopoulos-Mihalopoulos (ed), *Law and Ecology: New Environmental Foundations* (Routledge, 2011), 18–19.

[31] Susan Buckingham, 'Ecofeminism' (2015) *International Encyclopedia of the Social & Behavioral Sciences* 845.

[32] Karen Morrow, 'Ecofeminism and the Environment: International Law and Climate Change' in Vanessa E Munro and Margaret Davies (eds), *The Ashgate Companion to Feminist Legal Theory* (Ashgate, 2013).

[33] Peter Singer, *Animal Liberation* (Random House, 1975).

and Tom Regan,[34] bringing with it vexed questions of the legal status of animals.[35] Ecofeminist animal theorists, such as Josephine Donovan and Carol Adams[36] and their allies have subsequently voiced powerful arguments for recognition of the vulnerability, relationality and diverse capabilities of animals in a way that foregrounds their interests, while accepting that claims for 'personhood' founded on human-like characteristics may be inappropriate.[37]

Scope of Earth Law Judging

There are features of Earth law in some existing environmental law principles, such as the precautionary principle, the public trust doctrine and the Sandford principle for national parks. However, save for the well-being of future generations, which became part of Welsh law in 2015,[38] few legal innovations for Earth law, including rights of nature, the human right to a clean and healthy environment, and ecocide,[39] currently exist in UK legislation. The human right to a clean and healthy environment has its roots in the 1972 Stockholm Declaration and thereafter, its adoption in national legislation by over 150 countries, as well as in regional human rights treaties.[40] A small number of countries now have domestic ecocide laws, and in 2020 the UK campaign group Stop Ecocide convened a panel of international lawyers to draft proposals for an amendment to the Rome Statute of the International Criminal Court to prosecute those who cause widespread or long-term damage to the environment during peacetime.[41] In November 2023, an Ecocide Bill was introduced into the House of Lords as a Private Members' Bill by Baroness Boycott.[42]

Many of the judgments discussed in this book engage with areas of law that might be considered beyond the scope of environmental law as it is conventionally understood. Our aim is to explore Earth law judging in its widest sense – not

[34] Tom Regan, *The Case for Animal Rights* (University of California Press, 1983).

[35] Raffael Fasal and Sean Butler, *Animal Rights Law* (Hart Publishing, 2023).

[36] Josephine Donovan and Carol Adams (eds), *The Feminist Care Tradition in Animal Ethics* (Columbia University Press, 2007).

[37] eg Maneesha Deckha, *Animals as Legal Beings: Contesting Anthropocentric Legal Orders* (University of Toronto Press, 2020); Martha Nussbaum, *Justice for Animals: Our Collective Responsibility* (Simon and Schuster, 2023).

[38] Well-being of Future Generations (Wales) Act 2015.

[39] See eg Richard A Falk, 'Environmental Warfare and Ecocide – Facts, Appraisal, and Proposals' (1973) 4 *Bulletin of Peace Proposals* 80; Mark Allan Gray, 'The International Crime of Ecocide' (1995) 26 *California Western International Law Journal* 215; Polly Higgins, *Eradicating Ecocide*, 2nd edn (Shepheard-Walwyn, 2015).

[40] In 2022, the UN General Assembly declared access to a clean, healthy and sustainable environment a universal human right: UN General Assembly, The Human Right to a Clean, Healthy and Sustainable Environment, Resolution A/76/L.75, New York, United States, 26 July 2022.

[41] Independent Expert Panel for the Legal Definition of Ecocide, *Commentary and Core Text* (Stop Ecocide Foundation, 2021).

[42] Ecocide HL Bill (2023–24) 21.

simply as a replacement for environmental law, but as a range of approaches that could ultimately underpin all areas of law and judicial reasoning. One thing is clear: a plurality of approaches is needed to confront the complex challenges humanity now faces in protecting the planet for the future. The five sections that follow reflect on five interconnected foundational themes that emerged from the process of writing Earth law judgments for this project: time, subjectivities, care and obligation, harm and responsibility, and knowledges. Following the structure of the book, for each theme we tease out the contribution of the judgments to legal reasoning and reflect on the distinctiveness of Earth law approaches to elucidate what Earth law judging could look like in the United Kingdom.

Earth Law Judging: Emerging Themes

Time

The judgments engage with time in multiple ways, from geological time and the agentive capacities of planetary forces to change the climate and abiotic environments, through human histories and legacies of colonialism and cultural heritage in the interpretation of law, to future-oriented debates on sustainability and the well-being of future generations. The importance of connections between past, present and future are often missed in legal reasoning focused on the present. A number of judgments address these connections, some by engaging in time-travel, bringing attention to the significance of changing laws and values in shaping judicial decision-making at any given moment. Through these reimagined temporal narratives, the judgments open up past and future in a way that creates new possibilities for action and responsibility in the present.[43]

Geological Time and the Capitalocene

There is scientific debate as to whether the 'Great Acceleration' in human impacts on the planet since the 1960s marks the beginning of a new Anthropocene epoch in geological time.[44] However, Donna Haraway and others have argued that it is not humans per se, but capitalism that has caused this planetary crisis, with origins that extend back several centuries, even beyond the Industrial Revolution, as part of a much longer 'Capitalocene'.[45] This is a view shared by many ecofeminists

[43] Julia Dehm, 'International Law, Temporalities and Narratives of the Climate Crisis' (2016) 4(1) *London Review of International Law* 16.

[44] Will Steffen, Paul J Crutzen and John R McNeill, 'The Anthropocene: Are Humans now Overwhelming the Great Forces of Nature' (2007) 36 *Ambio* 614.

[45] Donna Haraway, 'Tentacular Thinking: Anthropocene, Capitalocene, Chthulucene' (2016) 75 *e-flux* e-flux.com/journal/75/67125/tentacular-thinking-anthropocene-capitalocene-chthulucene/.

who reject the Cartesian human–nature binary and draw parallels between the role of capitalism and patriarchy in the domination of women and the domination of the environment. Both Helen Dancer's and Karen Morrow's judgments bring attention to the economic forces that have underpinned long-term environmental damage and their enduring legacies for the future. Dancer's judgment focuses on the irreplaceable qualities of ancient woodlands, established over centuries, but lost to a high-speed rail infrastructure project, and the potential contribution of that project to carbon emissions and climate change. Morrow's account of her visit to Wales' 'moving mountains' of coal tips, which were the site of an industrial disaster, reveals a case 'rooted in geological time, in a landscape re-fashioned in historical time, with an afterlife that extends into the present and that will reach into the future'.

Colonial Legacies and Cultural Heritage

As Carol Adams and Lori Gruen point out, responsibility for the planetary crisis is not equally shared by humanity, entwined as it is with legacies of colonial and ecological violence inflicted on some groups by others.[46] The judgments in this collection interrogate not only the legacies of colonialism in terms of environmental harm (discussed under the section on 'Harm and Responsibility' below) but also the influence of colonial legacies on legal processes in the United Kingdom and Africa today. In the context of pollution to the Kafue River in Zambia's copperbelt, Saskia Vermeylen and Jérémie Gilbert argue that neocolonial mercantile practices that have caused environmental damage constitute a provocative act that may aggrieve the ancestors as ultimate arbiters and judges in local religions and cultures. A decolonised English law would need to recognise the importance of ancestors in local customary laws and belief systems as a source of law potentially relevant for adjudicating claims against UK-based parent companies in the English courts.

On English soil, a comparison between the original facts of two cases concerning UNESCO World Heritage Sites – the Lake District and Stonehenge – reveals inconsistencies in the treatment of cultural heritage and legal acknowledgement of the relationships between humans and ancient landscapes. Julia Aglionby's rewriting of a judgment that permitted four-wheel-drive vehicles on green lanes in the Lake District, notwithstanding their environmental impact, provides a striking contrast with Lucy Finchett-Maddock and Andreas Philippopoulos-Mihalopoulos's critique of the ECtHR's decision to uphold the exclusion of druids at Stonehenge on midsummer's evening, despite their ceremonial rituals expressing human connection with the Earth in deep time. Taken together, these three judgments highlight the marginalisation of living cultural values founded in the

[46] Carol Adams and Lori Gruen, *Ecofeminism: Feminist Intersections with Other Animals and the Earth* (Bloomsbury, 2022) 27–28.

past, when balanced against contrasting cultural expectations expressed through capitalist modernity.

Sustainability and Future Generations

Alongside responsibility for the past, concern for future human and non-human generations is a theme present in a number of the judgments. Both Dancer and Morrow's judgments engage with the principle of the well-being of future generations, which became Welsh law through the Well-Being of Future Generations (Wales) Act 2015. Wales' Act enshrines the Sustainable Development Principle as a duty that all public bodies must comply with, both in terms of decisions concerning management of resources, and as a public well-being duty. This principle requires that 'a public body must act in a manner which seeks to ensure that the needs of the present are met without compromising the ability of future generations to meet their own needs'.[47] Both authors draw upon this principle to bring attention to the marginalised voices of future generations. While Morrow reimagines how human interests and harms to the abiotic environment could be accounted for in law, Dancer expands the meaning of 'future generations' to include concern for the rights and interests of the ancient woodlands themselves, as well as future human generations.

The emphasis placed on temporal and physical interconnectedness in sustainability thinking informs the judicial balancing act in Bonnie Holligan's judgment, leading to the finding that interference with the property rights of a salmon fisherman is proportionate in light of the need to ensure the long-term health of the salmon population. Similarly, in Crispin Agnew's judgment, the construction of a windfarm in Shetland as part of a long-term renewable energy policy is balanced against the interests and conservation status of the whimbrel that also inhabit the place. In both reimagined judgments, greater weight is placed on the long-term integrity of ecosystems and species, noting that this is also in the long-term interests of humans.

Dynamism and Time-Travelling Judgments

Several authors engage in time travel to critique the original judgments, either to show how contemporary laws would lead to different outcomes, or to show how little has changed in terms of social and cultural values in judicial decisions. Morrow moves a case from 1921 one hundred years into the present to engage with the Well-Being of Future Generations Act, bringing attention to the 'living legacy of extractivism' and the long-term consequences of short-term profit. Joe Wills relocates his judgment on the fox-hunting ban from 2007 to 2023, putting forward a less anthropocentric approach to human and animal rights that is

[47] Well-being of Future Generations (Wales) Act 2015, s 5(1).

reflective of a shift in moral values since the Hunting Act 2004. By contrast, Helena Howe's reimagining of her judgment over a similar period (from 1999 to 2023) shows that relatively little may have changed in terms of legal expectations of 'the good farmer', which continue to be based on regulatory compliance rather than a relational sense of interconnectedness to other species and to environmental harm. By embracing the contingency and dynamism of legal norms, the judgments create space for future transformation. They also assert the ability of judges, and other legal professionals, to play an active role in transition to Earth law alongside those more obviously advocating for change, connecting hope to responsibility.

Subjectivities

One of the main objectives of Earth law is the decentralisation of the autonomous human person as the subject of law. Standard answers to the question 'Who matters in law?' cast both non-human and some humans outside of the realm of legal concern.[48] The reimagined judgments, however, reject perceptions of the non-human as mere objects liable to ownership and exploitation, protected only where that protection fosters economic interests or the sanctity of private property. They help answer Irus Braverman's call for 'more-than-human legalities' that make visible 'the myriad relational ways of being in the world, their significance to law, and in turn, law's significance to these other modes of existence'.[49] As such, the terms 'legal subject' or 'legal subjectivity' are given expansive meaning. By exploring opportunities for extending legal concern or recognition to the marginalised, the judgments go beyond the question of whether and how to ascribe legal rights to non-humans.[50] They also bring a wider range of human and more-than-human subjectivities and diverse ways of experiencing the world to law's attention.

It is a huge challenge to produce a framework for extending legal subjectivity that is both coherent and flexible enough to accommodate all putative claimants.[51] The aim here is to highlight some of the ways the authors approached the challenges produced by such extension. These include questions about the basis for such extension, the legal mechanisms by which such extension can be undertaken, as well as difficult assessments about the meaning and protection of the 'individual' in an entangled world.

[48] Maneesha Deckha, *Animals as Legal Beings: Contesting Anthropocentric Legal Orders* (University of Toronto Press, 2020) 14.

[49] Irus Braverman, 'Law's Underdog: A Call for More-than-Human Legalities' (2018) 14 *Annual Review of Law and Social Science* 127, 140–41.

[50] Which may be the expected focus: Anna Grear, 'Law's Entities: Complexity, Plasticity and Justice' (2013) 4 *Jurisprudence* 76, 79.

[51] ibid 78.

Extending Legal Recognition and Concern

The judgment writers have extended legal recognition to a much wider range of beings and entities than is traditional in UK law. Other-than-human animals are represented in this collection in the form of foxes (Wills), pigs (Howe), salmon (Holligan) and birds (Agnew), along with other non-human beings who take smaller parts in the production. More-than-human entities and assemblages are captured in the forms of river and delta ecosystems (Zbyszewska; Vermeylen and Gilbert; Killean), forests (Dancer), landscapes (Morrow; Aglionby) and megaliths/ancient sites (Philippopoulos-Mihalopoulos and Finchett-Maddock).

Humans are not left out. Amplifying the voices of marginalised people is central to many judgments. These are people whose existence, culture and livelihood are, to use Morrow's phrase, 'wholly intermingled' with the waterways and landscapes despoiled by anthropogenic activity.[52] Indeed, for many authors it is the connection between human and non-human entity which should itself be one of the main subjects of legal concern.

Unsurprisingly, the normative imperatives for extending legal subjectivity suggested by the authors are varied. Almost all of the judgments highlight relationality and the situated reality of all beings and entities. Such interdependence is well captured by Zbyszewska, who describes employees of a water company as 'of their ecosystem', embedding them within an employment law framework that recognises harm to human and non-human alike. For some, relationality is combined with recognition of the intrinsic value of the more-than-human, whose interests in pursuing species-relevant behaviours should be respected by law and included in any balancing of interests.[53] For Wills, like Howe, the law should be particularly attentive to sentient beings. Extending legal subjectivity solely by reference to characteristics closely associated with humans, such as rationality, agency and suffering, will fail fully to accommodate the more-than-human.[54] However, the capacity for sentience may ground particular ethical and legal considerations, including the legitimate privileging of sentient interests over others who do not share that capacity for embodied suffering.[55] Pushed to the margins, Wills's foxes are hunted down as 'pests', their lives ended in an orgy of pain and terror. These vulnerabilities of the embodied and relational being, discussed further below in the section on 'Care and Obligation', are also exposed by the judgment writers and provide, for Morrow and Killean in particular, a rationale for extending legal concern to underrepresented victims of anthropogenic harms.

[52] Braverman, 'Law's Underdog', 141.
[53] Nussbaum, *Justice for Animals*; Cullinan, *Wild Law*.
[54] Braverman, 'Law's Underdog'.
[55] eg Deckha, *Animals as Legal Beings*, 150–58; Nussbaum, *Justice for Animals*.

Diverse and Plural Methods of Inclusion

The methods by which the judgment writers extend 'our jurisprudential deliberations and practices'[56] to the more-than-human are overlapping and various. They can, however, be grouped loosely into the categories outlined by Justice Preston in his review of the Wild Law Judgment Project.[57] Three of these – 'considerateness', 'duties' and 'rights' – will be considered here, whilst the last – remedies – is discussed in the section below on 'Harm and Responsibility'.

Extending 'considerateness' to the more-than-human is a common approach across all the judgments but takes different forms. Many authors increase consideration of the more-than-human by naming and giving a materiality to the beings and entities so often missing from the 'lawscape':[58] mountains of coal waste loom restlessly over the dwellers below (Morrow), as Stonehenge pulsates with ancient spiritual energy (Philippopoulos-Mihalopoulos and Finchett-Maddock). In their different ways, the judgments also seek to open epistemologies of law to a more responsible and responsive 'hearing' of 'communicative interactions' of all kinds.[59] Like Howe, Wills asks us to put ourselves in the place of the animal and feel its distress. But this attention to other modes of existence also helps reframe our perception of these beings and their relationship with us: Wills's foxes are not 'pests' but 'heroic outlaws'; clever and resilient navigators of contested terrain on which they are as entitled to pursue their species-specific needs as we are. In so doing, the judgments challenge the ontological falsity that the non-human are homogeneous contents of the box marked 'object',[60] and our acceptance of a legal system organised on this basis.

'Considerateness' involves not just acknowledging marginalised beings and entities but providing mechanisms for respecting those diverse forms of flourishing. Zbyszewska, for example, expects the court to consider the interests of the river ecosystem alongside those of humans when assessing the risk of harm. This legal consideration of the more-than-human is combined with expanded duties on employees to ensure protection of all affected beings. The imposition of wider duties of care, discussed further in section 3, is an approach to extending legal subjectivity used by several authors, often in conjunction with the recognition of substantive or procedural rights. Maintaining this pluralist approach, Vermeylen and Gilbert combine recognition of a duty of care for a river ecosystem with rights for rivers.

[56] Braverman, 'Law's Underdog', 128.

[57] Justice Brian Preston, 'The Challenges of Approaching Judging from an Earth-centred Perspective (2018) 35 *Environment and Planning Law Journal* 218.

[58] Nicole Graham, *Lawscape: Property, Environment, Law* (Routledge, 2011); Andreas Philippopoulos-Mihalopoulos, *Spatial Justice: Body, Lawscape, Atmosphere* (Routledge, 2015).

[59] Anna Grear, 'Towards New Legal Futures? In Search of Renewing Foundations' in Anna Grear and Evadne Grant (eds), *Thought, Law, Rights and Action in the Age of Environmental Crisis* (Edward Elgar Publishing, 2015), 301.

[60] Brian Favre, 'Is There a Need for a New, an Ecological, Understanding of Legal Animal Rights?' (2020) 11 *Journal of Human Rights and the Environment* 297, 306.

Although legal rights for the more-than-human remain sparse,[61] several authors find 'rights' approaches to prove a fruitful medium by which to recognise more-than-human interests. Like Dancer, and Vermelyen and Gilbert, Agnew deploys rights of nature approaches to ground rights – the right to life for the whimbrel – in UK law. Whilst the grant of legal standing to the more-than-human to vindicate their rights is a significant part of Earth law,[62] it is a not a central feature in this collection. Nevertheless, Agnew's judgment acknowledges the importance of expanding juridical processes as a vital means by which law can be more attentive to situated subjectivities of human and more-than-human.[63] As Agnew illustrates, process and fora may be crucial in properly understanding and mediating the plurality of interests affected by the proposed wind turbines.

The growing acceptance of animal rights motivates Wills to include foxes within the purview of the European Convention on Human Rights (ECHR). Despite disagreements over whether rights for animals, equivalent to human rights, are possible or desirable,[64] Wills takes foxes to have – at the very least – rights as a corollary of our duties not to hunt them.[65] Like others in the collection, Wills finds human rights frameworks to offer real potential for accommodating the interests of the more-than-human, provided that human rights are not premised on human supremacy.[66] Whilst Wills reinterprets the requirement to protect the 'rights and freedoms of others' in Article 11 ECHR to include animals, Dancer employs the human right to a healthy environment and Articles 2 and 8 ECHR to include the interests of future generations and woodlands in decisions about environmental destruction. Holligan's engagement with human rights, however, is different. Whilst Wills and Dancer use this as a mechanism to expand rights coverage, Holligan reinterprets Article 1 Protocol 1 ECHR to restrict expectations of rights-holders to future unsustainable exploitation of their property.

Several judgments challenge – explicitly or implicitly – the property status of the non-human, acknowledging the contribution of that status to the violence and degradation suffered.[67] Yet, support for the replacing of that status with one of legal 'personhood' is ambivalent. Zbyszewska, alongside Vermeylen and Gilbert, explicitly denominates the more-than-human as 'persons' by including river ecosystems within this category. For Vermeylen and Gilbert, granting legal personhood is fundamental to achieving effective representation and protection for the river.

[61] Preston, 'The Challenges of Approaching Judging', 218–20.

[62] Stone, 'Should Trees Have Standing?'; Cass R Sunstein, 'Standing for Animals (with Notes on Animal Rights)' (2000) 47 *UCLA Law Review* 1333.

[63] Grear, 'Towards New Legal Futures?', 311.

[64] Raffael Fasal and Sean Butler, *Animal Rights Law* (Hart Publishing, 2023).

[65] Drawing on Wesley N Hohfeld, 'Some Fundamental Legal Conceptions as Applied in Judicial Reasoning' (1913) 23 *Yale Law Journal* 16.

[66] Citing Will Kymlicka, 'Human Rights without Human Supremacism' (2018) 48 *Canadian Journal of Philosophy* 763.

[67] Gary Francione, *Animals, Property and the Law* (Temple University Press, 1995); Margaret Davies, Lee Godden and Nicole Graham, 'Situating Property within Habitat: Reintegrating Place, People, and Law' (2021) 6 *Journal of Law, Property, and Society* 1.

Yet, as Anastasia Tartaryn notes in her commentary on Zbyszewska's judgment, the question of whether it is helpful to grant non-humans status as 'persons' is as contested as whether 'rights' akin to human rights should be the vehicle for extending legal subjectivity. Legal 'personhood' is frequently criticised for failing to capture the relational subjectivities and the diversity of interests that require attention from law, even for animals relatively like us,[68] let alone beings and entities that are not. Zbyszewska, however, is not claiming personhood as the ideal legal status for the more-than-human, or employing 'person' to extend fundamental rights to the river. As Wills employs reference to the 'right of others' to include animals, 'person' is used as a vehicle through which to ensure legal recognition of the more-than-human at risk of harm, through existing statutory wording. Yet, in all cases, pragmatism is coupled with a powerful sense in which all beings are united within a legal system that recognises the inseparability of harms and obligations to human and non-human.

Entanglement, Ecosystems and the Individual

In attending to interdependencies and the governance of systems, there is a risk of failing to sufficiently value or protect individual beings or entities within those systems. What Braverman identifies as 'tensions between the individual and ecosystem paradigms'[69] arise over whether the law should prioritise the interest of the biotic community overall or individual members of that community. Whilst the nature of 'the individual' in an entangled world is complex,[70] individual humans and other sentient beings – at the very least – have an ethical claim to legal protection of their fundamental rights and interests, harm to which is experienced qualitatively very differently from that suffered by an ecosystem or species.[71] Whilst traditional environmental or ecological approaches have been charged with privileging 'nature' over animals, women and people of colour,[72] the judgments suggest an awareness of both individual and collective interests.

Although there are no examples in this collection of extensions of legal subjectivity to an individual non-human animal,[73] the judgments propose methods to protect individual animals unfortunate enough to be members of a group subject to a particular harm: that of hunting (Wills) or intensive farming (Howe). Whilst the primary concern for Holligan is the sustainability of salmon populations, this species-level concern is married with consideration of the impacts of fishing on

[68] Deckha, *Animals as Legal Beings*.

[69] Braverman, 'Law's Underdog', 135.

[70] Jennifer Nedelsky, *Law's Relations: A Relational Theory of Self, Autonomy, and Law* (Oxford University Press, 2012).

[71] Nussbaum, *Justice for Animals*.

[72] Adams and Gruen (eds), *Ecofeminism Feminist Intersections*, 21–22.

[73] Contrast Nicole Rogers and Michelle Maloney (eds), *Law as if Earth Really Mattered: The Wild Law Judgment Project* (Routledge, 2017).

the salmon in a particular estuary. Despite recognising rights for the whimbrel and hooded crow, Agnew illustrates the risk that individual interests – of whimbrel and hooded crow – may be required to give way in the pursuit of otherwise beneficial conservation or climate initiatives, even under rights of nature approaches. Yet, by proposing the use of substantive and procedural mechanisms that would involve a careful and knowledgeable balancing of those interests, Agnew reflects what Brian Favre terms 'an ecological approach to animal rights',[74] and a growing awareness of the need to take account of animal lives within ecological contexts.[75]

Insights into issues of scale and fungibility are also provided by those judgments whose locus of concern is entire ecosystems and assemblages. These judgments recognise the interests of individual humans within those ecosystems, reminding us that ecosystems comprise populations of relationally situated beings with both individual and collective interests that need protecting. At the same time, they encourage us to look at these entities as unique in themselves. Whilst a forest, a river or even an individual tree possess a different set of subjectivities from a bird or mammal, and cannot suffer harm in the same way,[76] the judgments encourage us to look at assemblages and entities as comprising unique components and as unique beings, which should therefore not be seen as fungible or replaceable.

Care and Obligation

A commitment to care and to the duties that flow from compassionate and responsive relationships informs many of the reimagined judgments but is central to those of Howe and Zbyszewska. In foregrounding care, Earth law draws heavily on the work of ecofeminists and feminist ethics of care theorists who have long sought to rescue 'feminist relational commitments to empathy and care' from its gendered relegation to the private sphere.[77] Zbyszewska notes, for example, the separation of care-related work from productive labour.[78] The court's expectation, in Howe's judgment, that a farmer should approach land-use risks with care and compassion for her human neighbours, her land and her animals, arguably takes more holistic account of the geographical, temporal and relational dimensions of her position than by asking only whether she had complied with an abstract set of regulatory standards.

Three features of the judgments' engagement with care and obligation are highlighted here. The first is the recognition that care and obligation are vital

[74] Brian Favre, 'Is there a need for a new, an ecological, understanding of legal animal rights?' (2020) 11 *Journal of Human Rights and the Environment* 297.

[75] Werner Scholtz (ed), *Animal Welfare and International Law: From Conservation to Compassion* (Edward Elgar, 2019).

[76] Nussbaum, *Justice for Animals.*

[77] Adams and Gruen (eds), *Ecofeminism Feminist Intersections* 16, 39 et seq.

[78] ibid 11.

components in meeting the needs of a vulnerable and entangled Earth community. The second is the important role of processes that motivate care and foster informed obligations towards diverse entities, whilst the final strand outlines some of the methods by which law can incorporate those obligations, including through extended duties of care and obligation-oriented notions of property.

Relationality and Embodied Vulnerability

For many of the judgment writers, care – and its attendant obligations – is reclaimed as a valuable component in a legal system sensitive and responsive to complex vulnerabilities. In contrast to liberal legal squeamishness about embodiment,[79] the judgments revel in their animality: Howe's pigs are penned into undignified squalor above their own shit; Wills's foxes are ripped limb from limb, whilst Killean's human occupants of a polluted delta sicken and struggle.

Accepting the vulnerability of embodied and relational beings leads both to an ethical imperative to care, and to obligations to provide the required care.[80] Such imperatives extend to the more-than-human[81] with the vulnerabilities of non-human animals appearing particularly stark.[82] Howe's pigs are powerless to escape a violent death at the end of lives which lacked provision of the things a pig needs to flourish. The position in the intensive farming industry illustrates the 'linked oppressions'[83] that cast vulnerable humans alongside their more-than-human counterparts into an intersecting web of harms. In both Howe's and Holligan's judgments, duties to take care arise from the entwined vulnerability and reliance of animal and human for their lives and livelihoods. Holligan's judgment draws on exactly this relational interdependency of salmon populations, river ecosystem and human livelihood to justify limits on a fisher's right to exploit those beings for gain.

Ethics of care approaches seem particularly suitable to accommodating the diverse interests of Earth community members. Whilst not subject to the same capacities for suffering as sentient beings, rivers and landscapes are vulnerable to anthropogenic harms and in need of care. Being sensitive to relationality and complexity, such approaches provide ways to conceive of ecological justice that avoid the problematic rationalist and dualist assumptions that inhabit the notion of rights.[84] As befits the pluralist vision of Earth law, the judgments tend to avoid setting care approaches up in opposition to rights. Approaching care and rights as

[79] Deckha, *Animals as Legal Beings*, 167.
[80] Nedelsky, *Law's Relations*.
[81] ibid.
[82] Ani Satz, 'Animals as Vulnerable Subjects: Beyond Interest-Convergence, Hierarchy and Property' (2009) 16 *Animal Law* 65; Lori Gruen, *Entangled Empathy: An Alternative Ethic for Our Relationship with Animals* (Lantern Books, 2015).
[83] Deckha, *Animals as Legal Beings*, 18 (drawing on feminist animal care theory).
[84] Raffael Fasal and Sean Butler, *Animal Rights Law* (Hart Publishing, 2023) 70.

entwined, Vermeylen and Gilbert draw on rights of nature approaches in combination with Zambian traditional and customary norms to develop an expanded duty of care in negligence owed by a mining company to the more-than-human victims of their activities.

Valuing Practices of Care and Informed Obligation

Embedding ethics of care approaches in law requires attention to practice, ritual and experience that enhance affective more-than-human connections and the development of caring attachments.[85] Embodied experiences of 'enchantment' with the more-than-human are crucial to developing the motivation to understand and empathise with the needs and interests of different others.[86] Whilst the judgments in this collection cannot draw directly on the ontologies of indigenous or First Nation peoples (as could, for example, the Wild Law Judgment Project[87] in Australia), they highlight more local experiential traditions of spiritual and emotional engagement with the natural world, such as the druidic worship at Stonehenge in Philippopoulos-Mihalopoulos and Finchett-Maddock's judgment. Moreover, the judgments suggest that Earth law is alive to the value of these rituals or practices and takes seriously both the facilitation of their performance and the compensation for their loss. In her damning declaration of ecocide, Killean identifies the prevention of rituals of care and connection in respect of sacred waterways as a major source of harm for which both condemnation and compensation are due.

In addition to feelings of empathy and compassion, care is fundamentally an active process through which obligations are performed. For care to be effective and valuable, it must be knowledgeable and attend to the needs of the recipient.[88] Ethical obligations to care for the more-than-human give rise to epistemic responsibilities to understand the needs of multiple beings and to find ways of making these present for law.[89] Holligan and Howe expect both fisher and farmer to exercise their power over the lives of salmon and pig within boundaries of species-specific knowledge. Yet the context of fishing and farming also show that attentive care from the perspective of the Environment Agency or the farmer remains unjustified violence from that of salmon caught or pig incarcerated. Engaging with the 'peculiar enmeshment of care and harm' that bedevil conservationist discourses

[85] Val Plumwood, 'Nature, Self, and Gender: Feminism, Environmental Philosophy, and the Critique of Rationalism' (1991) *Hypatia* 3; Helena Howe, 'Making Wild Law Work – The Role of "Connection with Nature" and Education in Developing an Ecocentric Property Law,' (2017) 29 *Journal of Environmental Law* 19.

[86] Agatha Herman, 'Enchanting Resilience: Relations of Care and People–Place Connections in Agriculture' (2015) 42 *Journal of Rural Studies* 102.

[87] Rogers and Maloney, *Law as if Earth Really Mattered*.

[88] Nel Noddings, 'Moral Education in an Age of Globalization' (2010) 42 *Educational Philosophy and Theory* 390.

[89] Nussbaum, *Justice for Animals*, ch 5.

and practice,[90] Agnew joins the writers of other judgments who propose expanded legal fora through which to more fully understand and mediate between multiple conflicting interests.

Extending Duties of Care and Reimagining Property

In response to the care imperative, many judgment authors extend legal duties of care beyond their present bounds. Dancer and Morrow emphasis such duties to future humans, whilst Zbyszewska, Howe, Vermeylen and Gilbert, and Aglionby include other animals, river systems and landscapes. The authors find legal opportunities for this extension in a variety of locations. In both public and private law, the judgments draw on statute, common law, principles and practice to found obligations to take better care of vulnerable others. As noted above, for Morrow, the duties to care for future generations arise through statutory obligations imposed on public authorities to act in ways compatible with established principles such as 'sustainability' and the well-being of future generations. Vermeylen and Gilbert extend the duty of care in negligence to a river ecosystem, drawing, in part, on local or customary laws, which bring, as Kalunga notes in her commentary, additional duties to care for the more-than-human, not present in colonial systems. For Howe, obligations in private nuisance are widened in response to heightened sensitivity to the risks inherent in intensive farming practices and the principles of responsible land stewardship.

Informed by conceptions of property as relational and responsible,[91] including Earth jurisprudence and 'wild law' framings,[92] both Howe and Holligan seek to reshape expectations of ownership. Despite the capacity of private property to facilitate human domination and harm,[93] these judgments find opportunities within property for expressions of care and the performance of obligations to others. Intrinsic limits on entitlements to exploit our 'property' beyond its ecological capacities is a particular feature of Holligan's judgment. Her reasoning allows the obligation to protect salmon populations to take priority over a property right

[90] Krithika Srinivasan, 'Conservation Biopolitics and the Sustainability Episteme' (2017) 49 *Environment and Planning A: Economy and Space* 1458, 1461.

[91] Kevin Gray and Susan Francis Gray, 'The Idea of Property in Land' in Susan Bright and John Dewar (eds), *Land Law: Themes and Perspectives* (Oxford University Press, 1998) 39–41; William NR Lucy and Catherine Mitchell, 'Replacing Private Property: The Case for Stewardship' (1996) 55 *Cambridge Law Journal* 566; Craig Anthony Arnold, 'The Reconstitution of Property: Property as a Web of Interests' (2002) 26 *Harvard Environmental Law Review* 281; Joseph Singer, *Entitlement: The Paradoxes of Property* (Yale University Press, 2000); Carl J Circo, 'Does Sustainability Require a New Theory of Property Rights?' (2009) 58 *University of Kansas Law Review* 91, with many preferring some form of reference to 'stewardship' or 'guardianship' of land, as opposed to 'ownership'.

[92] Peter D Burdon, *Earth Jurisprudence, Private Property and the Environment* (Routledge 2015); Howe, 'Making Wild Law Work'.

[93] Francione, *Animals, Property and the Law*; Graham, *Lawscape*; and Nicole Graham, 'Owning the Earth' in Peter Burdon (ed), *Exploring Wild Law: The Philosophy of Earth Jurisprudence* (Wakefield, 2011) 259.

to a certain catch quantity; falling fish stocks rendering absurd any expectation that such rights could continue to be exercisable indefinitely. Moreover, property should involve expectations of positive obligations to others. For Holligan, it is legitimate to ask whether the interdependency of salmon population and Mr Mott's right to fish should be interpreted as placing on him a positive duty to take action to protect the salmon. Likewise, Howe requires the 'good farmer' to undertake positive steps to safeguard the interests of their land and animals, alongside others who might reasonably be affected by the exercise of those property rights. Part of recognising property as a multispecies endeavour of shared interests[94] involves owner-stewards facilitating the collective and individual flourishing of the more-than-human in respect of whom they hold power.

Harm and Responsibility

The judgments also address concepts of harm and responsibility across public and private law, including in criminal law, tort law and administrative law. They reframe thinking about harm along three core lines: recognition of interconnectedness, an expansive approach to attribution of responsibility and reimagining of reparative remedies.

Interconnectedness and Harm

All of the judgments emphasise the embeddedness of humans in ecosystems and communities, and several, in particular Morrow's and Zbyszewska's, explicitly reject the abstracted, property-owning subject as the paradigm victim of harm. Our entanglement in, and responsibility to, the world around us requires a concept of harm that better encompasses the more-than-human. One obvious response is expansion of the rules of standing,[95] but this is not a direction that the collection explores in depth.[96] Instead, many of the judgments decentre the subjective approach dominant in existing doctrine. As Wills argues, full legal personhood should certainly not be required in order to be protected from harm. As explored above in the section on 'Subjectivities', a narrow focus on sentient, or even living, beings does not capture damage to complex systems and relationships, and vice versa. Many of the judgments emphasise that harms to the places in which humans live are also harms to humans. This is evident in, for example, Aglionby's judgment regarding landscape protection and Morrow's judgment regarding the harm caused by mine tipping.

[94] Johanna Gibson, *Owned, An Ethological Theory of Property – From the Cave to the Commons* (Routledge, 2020); Sanna Ojalammi and Nicholas Blomley, 'Dancing with Wolves: Making Legal Territory in a More-than-human World' (2015) 62 *Geoforum* 51.

[95] See eg Stone, 'Should Trees Have Standing?'; Sunstein, 'Standing for Animals'.

[96] See the discussion in section 2 above on subjectivities.

The decentring of individual beings in favour of a focus on ecological systems, communities and relationships calls into question the value of bilateral adjudication as a means of redress, particularly private law claims. The judgments wrestle here with the constraints of existing doctrinal form. Without entirely abandoning extant procedural norms, they seek to bring these relationships into judicial sight. Dancer's judgment draws upon the form of a letter to a child, a practice that has been used in the family courts, but not elsewhere.

As attention is drawn to a greater range of harms, the weight that may be afforded to environmental harms changes. Our dependence on ecosystems means that, as Holligan and Zbyszewska emphasise, ecological values cannot simply be dismissed as secondary to economic values. This has important implications when undertaking the kind of balancing exercises necessary in, for example, human rights jurisprudence or judicial review. Ecological thinking also demands consideration of temporal interconnections, and a concept of harm that takes account of processes as well as discrete actions and episodes. The cyclical nature of ecological systems requires a long view that addresses the interconnection between past, present and future human generations, a point that features prominently in Dancer and Morrow's judgments and that was discussed above in the section on 'Time'.

Expanding Responsibility

Our interconnectedness also has implications for the attribution of responsibility. The just imposition of liability, especially in our present context of climate instability, requires the unpicking of complex chains of causation and engagement with harms that are cumulative or have multiple contributors.[97] In the context of climate change and the renewable energy transition, the judgments illustrate the complexity of assessing downstream effects where a project is part of a broader scheme.[98] For example, Agnew's judgment suggests the need for greater attention to harms arising from the enabling effect of the interconnector in question on a broader scheme of energy development. Responsibility must also extend to prevention of future harm, leading to questions of regulation of risk rather than completed harm.[99] The judgments tend towards a strict

[97] In the context of civil law claims, see Monika Hinteregger, 'Civil Liability and the Challenges of Climate Change: A Functional Analysis' (2017) 8(2) *Journal of European Tort Law* 238 and David Bullock, 'Public Nuisance and Climate Change: The Common Law's Solutions to the Plaintiff, Defendant and Causation Problems' (2022) 85(5) *MLR* 1136. For a broader perspective, see Florentina Simlinge and Benoit Mayer, 'Legal Responses to Climate Change Induced Loss and Damage' in Reinhard Mechler et al (eds), *Loss and Damage from Climate Change* (Springer, 2019).

[98] This issue was discussed in relation to wind farms in England in *R (on the application of Substation Action Save East Suffolk Ltd) v Secretary of State for Business, Energy and Industrial Strategy* [2022] EWHC 3177 (Admin). Links could also be made in relation to greenhouse gas emissions and carbon targets. For example, the challenge to oil extraction that was, at the time of writing, being heard in the Supreme Court in *R (on the application of Finch) v Surrey County Council*: www.supremecourt.uk/cases/uksc-2022-0064.html.

[99] See Elizabeth Fisher, *Risk Regulation and Administrative Constitutionalism* (Hart Publishing, 2007) and discussion in section 1, Time.

application of the precautionary principle,[100] calibrating standards of care in tort law to require farmers (Howe) and mine operators (Morrow) to operate in a way that is sensitive to risk.

The operation of international markets in energy and manufactured goods serves to obscure further questions of both legal and ethical responsibility. To what extent are users of oil-based products, or consumers of food grown using fertiliser produced from methane or coal, responsible for the harms caused by mining or oil exploration? New means of accounting for the lifetime impacts of a project, including indirect or 'Scope Three'[101] impacts are needed.[102] *Vedanta Resources PLC v Lungowe and others*,[103] although a decision ostensibly about technical and jurisdictional issues, exemplifies the challenges of accountability raised by the international trade in the products of environmental damage and the role of international corporate actors. Addressing this fully requires liability to be attached to corporations and public authorities, as well as individuals.[104] Both Vermeylen and Gilbert's amicus curiae brief and Killean's reparations order explicitly acknowledge the role of structural inequalities, in particular those produced by colonialism and extractivism, in generating environmental harms; throughout the collection, addressing environmental injustice within and between human communities is assumed to be a core part of Earth law.

Reshaping Reparative Remedies

How, then, can reparative remedies look beyond individual harm to address harm to communities, human and more-than-human? Many of the judgments emphasise the need for reparative mechanisms that speak to the communal as well as the private. This necessitates both seeking alternatives to traditional private law remedies (Morrow) and extending the scope of those remedies to ensure that they include measures targeted at restoration of ecosystems (Vermeylen and Gilbert). Use is also made of the ability of the criminal law to offer moral condemnation, in Killean's application of a novel international crime of ecocide, drawing on the

[100] Principle 15 of the *Rio Declaration on Environment and Development* (United Nations Conference on Environment and Development, 1992). See Nicolas de Sadeleer, *Environmental Principles from Political Slogans to Legal Rules*, 2nd edn (Oxford University Press, 2020) ch 5.

[101] Carbon Trust, *Briefing: What Are Scope Three Emissions?* Available at www.carbontrust.com/our-work-and-impact/guides-reports-and-tools/briefing-what-are-scope-3-emissions.

[102] For example, the idea of the carbon budget explored in Julia Dehm's contribution to the Wild Law Judgment project: Julia Dehm, 'Quantifying the environmental impact of coal mines: lessons from the Wandoan case, *Xstrata Coal Queensland Pty Ltd v Friends of the Earth Brisbane Co-Op*' in Rogers and Maloney, *Law as if Earth Really Mattered*, 143.

[103] *Vedanta Resources PLC v Lungowe and others* [2019] UKSC 20.

[104] See Elisa Morgera, *Corporate Accountability in International Environmental Law*, 2nd edn (Oxford University Press, 2020) and, on the interplay between global, regional and national actors in relation to environmental liability regimes, Emanuela Orlando, 'From Domestic to Global? Recent Trends in Environmental Liability from a Multi-level and Comparative Law Perspective' (2015) 24(3) *Review of European, Comparative and International Environmental Law* 289 and Emanuela Orlando, *Environmental Liability and the Interplay between EU Law and International* Law (Routledge, 2024).

work of Polly Higgins.[105] As Killean's reparation order makes clear, attention must be given to the political and transformative potential of reparative measures, as well as to their local efficacy.

Remedies are required that not only compensate for past harm, but also address future risks. This may require remediation work (Morrow) or changes to entire systems and processes that push the boundaries of private law in setting environmental standards (for example, the move away from industrial farming suggested in Howe's judgment). Ultimately, the changes needed go well beyond the capacity of any judge, or even legal system, and into the realm of political transformation. The judgments in the collection do not address the extent to which ecological harm may justify civil disobedience or even violent acts to protect ecosystems.[106] Some suggest, however, that greater attention should be given to ecological solidarity as a justification for actions that might otherwise breach a legal obligation, eg stopping work (Zbyszewska).

Although, in general, the judgments focus on the impacts of harm, they do take into account a range of perspectives and justifications for harmful activity. These are most obviously economic, although broader environmental and social benefits are hinted at in the renewable energy infrastructure at issue in Agnew's judgment, and in the high-speed rail project questioned by Dancer. Again, our embeddedness in ecological communities provides a means of evading binary oppositions between human and more-than-human interests. In this respect, the challenge to conservation measures based on livelihood in *Mott v Environment Agency* (reimagined by Holligan) makes an interesting counterpoint to the reparation for loss of livelihood due to ecological damage in Killean's reparation order.

Knowledges

Ecological thinking engenders a reimagining, an opening up, of legal knowledge. Transforming ecological relations will both require and produce different kinds of knowledge. The methodology of the judgment project calls into question both the sorts of facts to which a court's attention is drawn and the processes by which those facts are generated.[107] The judgments draw on a body of scholarship that engages with these epistemological questions from a theoretical perspective.[108] They go beyond this, however, in giving doctrinal form to expanded knowledge relations.

[105] Higgins, *Eradicating Ecocide.*

[106] On criminal law and environmental activism, see the contributions collected in part 5 of Rogers and Maloney, *Law as if Earth Really Mattered.*

[107] eg Justice Brian Preston, 'Writing Judgments Wildly' in Rogers and Maloney, *Law as if Earth Really Mattered*, 19; Nicole Watson and Heather Douglas (eds), *Indigenous Legal Judgments: Bringing Indigenous Voices into Judicial Decision Making* (Routledge, 2021) esp ch 1.

[108] Margaret Davies, *EcoLaw: Legality, Life, and the Normativity of Nature* (Routledge, 2022); Ruth Thomas-Pellicer, Vito De Lucia and Sian Sullivan (eds), *Contributions to Law, Philosophy and Ecology: Exploring Re-embodiments* (Routledge: 2016); Grear and Grant, *Thought, Law, Rights.*

Each Earth law judgment occupies a part of the legal imaginary, using alternative pasts to generate new future trajectories. They share several core features captured in Karen Barad's concept of 'ethico-onto-epistem-ology':[109] commitment to plurality, a process-based and relational understanding of knowledge, and an engagement with the ethical and political dimensions of legal knowledge generation.

Diversity and Multiplicity of Knowledges

Central to all of the Earth law judgments is their willingness to recognise plurality and multiplicity, the existence of different *umwelts*, or ways of experiencing the world. It is impossible to separate ways of knowing from ways of being.[110] Ontological pluralism implies a need for pluralism at the normative level,[111] and for legal systems that allow space for multiple human and more-than-human voices.[112] In a world of multispecies entanglements, the conceptual barriers that set apart and privilege human (and particular kinds of human) experience break down.[113] This ontological flattening means that human subjectivity becomes merely one node among other perspectives and knowledges.[114] The Earth law judgments engage, in different ways, with the possibility of horizontal, rather than vertical, relations with the more-than-human world.

One part of this is reimagining how judicial decision-making, and particularly the public law principles governing judicial review, might better reflect the diversity of human knowledge. While a certain plurality is inherent in the common law adjudicative process, and in legal interpretation, this often takes a bilateral rather than multi- or poly (involving non-traditional actors)- lateral form, particularly in the realm of private law. Further, even as a judge opens up normative space by considering different possible interpretations and applications of legal norms, she must ultimately close it down again by reaching a decision. A number of the judgments examine the role of judges in ensuring adequate processes for participation and deliberation. They grapple with familiar questions of scale, and the role of situated, affective and non-expert knowledge claims. Taken together, the judgments suggest that both procedural and substantive changes are needed to maximise opportunities for human participation in decision-making, and to increase the weight afforded to a broader range of ecological knowledges.

[109] Karen Barad, *Meeting the Universe Halfway: Quantum Physics and the Entanglement of Matter and Meaning* (Duke University Press, 2007) 185.

[110] Barad, *Meeting the Universe Halfway*; Osca Monaghan, '*Milirrpum v Nabalco Pty Ltd* (1971) 17 FLR 141' in Watson and Douglas, *Indigenous Legal Judgments*, 25.

[111] Davies, *EcoLaw*, 21.

[112] Grear, 'Towards New Legal Futures', 283, 311.

[113] See section 2 above on subjectivities.

[114] Davies, *EcoLaw*, 18.

The Earth law judgments further attempt to create space for more-than-human voices to be heard; pigs (Howe), foxes (Wills) and megaliths (Philippopoulos-Mihalopoulos and Finchett-Maddock) loom large. The interconnected nature of ecosystems means that the range of facts deemed potentially relevant to a dispute is likely to be radically expanded. Both individual species and broader ecosystem function must be considered.[115] However, as acknowledged in the section above on 'Subjectivities', there are obvious limitations to the use of human-focused legal processes to account for more-than-human concerns. Our legal processes necessarily privilege and reify human subjectivity and knowledge. When considering questions such as the suffering of other beings, human insight is inevitably and intrinsically limited. This may, however, serve as foundation for a richer concept of knowledges as situated, dynamic and produced in relation, rather than fixed.[116]

Knowledge as Embodied and Relational

When knowledge is approached as nexus and relation,[117] attention is focused on the processes by which knowledge is generated, and on the material politics of these relationships. Systems of knowledge are practices of power.[118] Some of the judges (eg Agnew and Dancer) point to the need for more weight to be placed on the knowledge of expert bodies such as nature conservation agencies. Engagement with technical expertise has been argued to be of great value in some areas of environmental adjudication; for example, scientific modelling is critical to the demonstration of causality in climate litigation.[119] There is, however, no neutral scientific (or judicial) stance from which to produce and interpret empirical claims, a point that emerges strongly in Indigenous and decolonial scholarship.[120] As Code argues, any sharp distinction between politics and scientific knowledge is no longer tenable.[121] Western, male-dominated scientific traditions have privileged the individual and abstract, while the experiences of women, Indigenous peoples and other marginalised humans are constructed as embodied and collective, and placed outside the canon.[122] Disciplinary fragmentation presents a further barrier

[115] Preston, 'Writing Judgments 'Wildly', 23.

[116] As suggested by eg Lorraine Code, *Ecological Thinking: The Politics of Epistemic Location* (Oxford University Press, 2006).

[117] Ruth Thomas-Pellicer and Vito De Lucia, 'Introduction' in Thomas-Pellicer et al, *Contributions to Law, Philosophy and Ecology*, 1, 9.

[118] ibid 2.

[119] Sophie Marjanac and Lindene Patton, 'Extreme Weather Event Attribution Science and Climate Change Litigation: An Essential Step in the Causal Chain?' (2018) 36(3) *Journal of Energy & Natural Resources Law* 265; Petra Minnerop and Friederike Otto, 'Climate Change and Causation: Joining Law and Climate Science on the Basis of Formal Logic' (2019–20) 27 *Buffalo Environmental Law Journal* 49.

[120] eg Watson and Douglas, *Indigenous Legal Judgments*; and Irene Watson, 'Aboriginal Laws of the Land: Surviving Fracking, Golf Courses and Drains Among Other Extractive Industries' in Rogers and Maloney, *Law as If Earth Really Mattered*, 201.

[121] Lorraine Code, 'Doubt and Denial: Epistemic Responsibility Meets Climate Change Scepticism' in Grear and Grant (eds), *Thought, Law, Rights*, 25, 44.

[122] A point emphasised by eg Code, 'Doubt and Denial', 35.

to the kind of holistic and connected knowledges necessary to understand ecological relationships and systems.

Many of the judgments open adjudication to ecological knowledge beyond established scientific canons. Morrow's exploration of the impacts of mining in South Wales highlights the need to go beyond natural-science-based approaches to understand the socio-ecological impacts of mining. Dancer's judgment engages explicitly with emotion as a form of knowledge, and advocates for greater respect for affective connection in decision making. Aglionby also suggests that it is the non-expert knowledge of locals that needs to be given greater procedural prominence. These connections may allow the traversing of embodiments[123] between the human and more-than-human worlds.

On the other hand, it should not be assumed that lived experience will always lead to conclusions that are more ecocentric. Relations of power and exploitation nonetheless shape the kinds of knowledge that is produced, and the way that this knowledge informs decision-making. For example, although not discussed in Holligan's judgment, in the case of *Mott v Environment Agency*,[124] a key issue of fact was the extent to which salmon in the Severn Estuary could be identified with a particular spawning river. The lived experience of Mr Mott, a salmon fisherman, conflicted with the conclusions of university scientists on which the Environment Agency relied. Apparently neutral information about the lifecycle of the salmon was deeply embedded in particular relationships to the fish, which inevitably influenced the kinds of facts generated and attended to. A focus on local or affective knowledge cannot be used to evade the difficult work of politics. In this respect, Zbyszewska's judgment is especially interesting. It envisions knowledge beyond technical expertise as communally generated and shared between employees, who are embedded in social and ecological communities.

Knowledge as Responsibility

The rootedness of legal knowledge in societies and ecosystems implies that it is correspondingly freighted with ethical and political responsibility. Writing of the traditional lands of the Tanganekald, Meintangk and Boandik peoples, and the erasure of First Nations laws by colonial violence, Irene Watson cites Boaventura de Sousa Santos's warning of 'epistemicide': laws that are not based in relations of respect and reciprocity close off possibilities of knowing.[125] As Lorraine Code argues, we are responsible for what we know,[126] and knowing may, in turn, oblige us to act.

[123] Thomas-Pellicer and De Lucia, 'Introduction', 9.

[124] See discussion in the High Court, reported at [2015] EWHC 314 (Admin) and in the Court of Appeal, reported at [2016] EWCA Civ 564.

[125] Watson, 'Aboriginal Laws of the Land', 217–18.

[126] Code, *Ecological Thinking*, 4.

The Earth law judgments must, therefore, consider questions such as who is empowered to collect the kind of information that will be recognised by a court? What duties should be placed on corporations or individuals to collect information about harms and risks associated with their business? What is reasonably foreseeable gains an ethical dimension. Howe's rewriting of *Savage v Fairclough* challenges the knowledge claims of the dominant community of farming practice. This is not unproblematic, but points to the possibilities for relationships of respect and care with both human and non-human neighbours to generate alternative knowledges. As Johanna Gibson's commentary highlights, there is no ethically neutral standpoint from which knowledge may be curated or assessed.

Knowledge also imposes responsibilities, as the employees of the polluting water company find in Zbyszewska's judgment. Relationships of care mean not only that our attention is drawn to different kinds of facts, but that these facts may place us under legal or ethical obligations to act. In this respect, the judgments ask legal norms and processes to foster solidarities, in which knowledge is employed not merely to avoid harm, but to nourish connection.

Conclusions

This chapter has identified five distinctive elements of the Earth law approaches adopted by the contributors to this collection. While the judgments are diverse, they share a concern with temporal interconnectedness and obligation to past, present and future human and more-than-human communities. This does not imply, however, that time operates in a linear or entirely predictable way; the collection is methodologically committed to an openness to change according to which both history and prospects are far from fixed and may give rise to shifting possibilities and responsibilities in the here and now. In terms of ontology, the judgments begin from a perspective of entanglement and interconnectedness that demands attention to both individuals and systems. The embedded and relationally constituted subject necessitates engagement with vulnerability, practices of care and extension of duties of care beyond the human. It also requires expanded concepts of harm, responsibility and reparation. On the epistemological level, knowledge is understood as plural, situated and generative of responsibility. These concerns are familiar from existing legal theoretical literature, but, in its articulation between the level of abstract principle and that of the individual case, the chapter, and the collection, provide a novel perspective on the pathways through which Earth law might emerge, and how it might transform legal reasoning.

PART I

Time

3

A Letter to Future Generations: *R (on the application of Packham) v Secretary of State for Transport, The Prime Minister and HS2 Limited*

HELEN DANCER

Generational Roulette

Reflecting on a century of my family history in the United Kingdom, I have been struck by how a generational roulette of war, welfare state, neoliberalism and planetary crisis has brought about existential changes in the direction of individual lives and the legacy that each generation leaves for the next. I belong to a political generation known as 'Thatcher's children', born at 331.92 ppm[1] not long before Margaret Thatcher's rise to become Prime Minister in 1979, and I grew up in a British economy that was transformed through her neoliberal ideology of free markets, privatisation and deregulation.[2] My grandparents, born at 303 ppm, were part of the wartime generation who fought fascism in Europe and founded the welfare state in its aftermath. My parents' generation, born in the postwar era at 310 ppm, were the first to fully benefit from the welfare state, and perhaps will be the last. They were also the first generation of young people to be awake to global concerns about the environment during the 1960s and 1970s. As a university academic in the 2020s, I have witnessed the struggles of young people and the challenges that await them and future generations. This younger generation is facing a future full of uncertainty. Societal support structures, the proximity of social ties, and ethics of care and responsibility have shifted as neoliberalism has superseded the post-World War 2 consensus on the role of the state, employers, family and community in caring for each other.

[1] Parts per million (ppm) of carbon dioxide measured in the atmosphere.

[2] Maria Teresa Grasso et al 'Thatcher's Children, Blair's Babies, Political Socialization and Trickle-down Value Change: An Age, Period and Cohort Analysis' (2019) 49 *British Journal of Political Science* 17.

These are not even the greatest challenges facing young and future generations. According to Earth systems scientists, since the 1950s carbon dioxide levels in the Earth's atmosphere have been rising dramatically at rates not seen for over 800,000 years.[3] In 2016, for the first time in millions of years, carbon dioxide levels exceeded 400 ppm,[4] and in 2022 they reached a record high of 418.56 ppm. There are many uncertainties in predicting changes in the Earth system over the next century and beyond, but there is widespread scientific consensus that a global temperature rise of 3°C would be a tipping point towards an uninhabitable planet, and that, if the rich biodiversity of life on Earth is to continue similar to now, carbon dioxide levels would need to reduce to at most 350 ppm,[5] with global temperature rise limited to 1.5°C. Even in this best-case scenario, the UN Intergovernmental Panel on Climate Change predicts that temperature rises will disproportionately affect low- and middle-income countries, the poor and vulnerable, and there is a real risk that the world will heat by 3°C within the lifetime of current younger generations.[6] It is hard to come to terms with the fact that we are now witnessing climate and biodiversity crises that may be the start of the Sixth Mass Extinction on planet Earth.[7]

The planetary crisis is shaping new intergenerational priorities and attitudes to security and risk. In response to the recommendations of the UN Intergovernmental Panel on Climate Change, the Paris Agreement of 2015, adopted by 196 State Parties to the 1992 UN Framework Convention on Climate Change (UNFCCC) set a goal to hold 'the increase in the global average temperature to well below 2°C above pre-industrial levels' and to pursue efforts 'to limit the temperature increase to 1.5°C above pre-industrial levels'.[8] The UNFCCC's sister Convention on Biological Diversity has obliged contracting states to stop and reverse biodiversity loss since it entered into force in 1993. Three decades later, States Parties had failed to meet this requirement, although in 2022 the Kunming–Montreal Global Biodiversity Framework set new goals towards ecosystem and species health, including to halt human-induced species extinction by 2050.[9] Since

[3] Dieter Lüthi et al, 'High-Resolution Carbon Dioxide Concentration Record 650,000–800,000 Years before Present' (2008) 453 *Nature* 379.

[4] Nicola Jones, 'How the World Passed a Carbon Threshold and Why It Matters' (2017) *Yale E360*, 26 January, e360.yale.edu/features/how-the-world-passed-a-carbon-threshold-400ppm-and-why-it-matters.

[5] James Hansen et al, 'Target Atmospheric CO_2: Where Should Humanity Aim?' (2008) 2 *Open Atmospheric Science Journal* 217.

[6] Valérie Masson-Delmotte et al (eds), *Global Warming of 1.5°C. An IPCC Special Report on the Impacts of Global Warming of 1.5°C Above Pre-industrial Levels and Related Global Greenhouse Gas Emission Pathways, in the Context of Strengthening the Global Response to the Threat of Climate Change, Sustainable Development, and Efforts to Eradicate Poverty* (IPCC, 2018).

[7] Robert H Cowie, Philippe Bouchet and Benoît Fontaine, 'The Sixth Mass Extinction: Fact, Fiction or Speculation?' (2022) 97 *Biological Reviews* 640.

[8] Paris Agreement under the United Nations Framework Convention on Climate Change, adopted at COP21, Paris, France, 12 December 2015, entered into force on 4 November 2016.

[9] UN Conference of the Parties to the Convention on Biological Diversity, Kunming–Montreal Global Biodiversity Framework, CBD/COP/15/L.25, Fifteenth meeting – Part II, Montreal, Canada, 7–12 December 2022.

the Paris Agreement, a discourse of 'net-zero by 2050' has become a policy touchstone for reducing and offsetting carbon emissions as a mitigation strategy. In one sense, this is a clear and laudable goal, although the focus on carbon has somewhat eclipsed concerns about other greenhouse gases, biodiversity and water. A further concern is that in the implementation of net-zero, policies and methods for calculating emissions reductions and the markets for carbon and biodiversity offsetting that have emerged can lack transparency, often treating living entities including forests as fungible assets or generating practices and outcomes that cause environmental and social harm in other ways.[10]

According to UNICEF, 'The climate crisis is the defining human and child's rights challenge of this generation, and is already having a devastating impact on the well-being of children globally.'[11] No wonder then, that this has become an age of eco-anxiety, with young people particularly affected.[12] Young people are becoming increasingly vocal about the impact of the planetary crisis on their future. Growing movements of young activists have been making their voices heard around the world through 'Fridays for Future' school strikes, other forms of environmental protest and, increasingly, climate litigation. Successful youth climate justice cases include the 2018 ruling of the Colombian Supreme Court of Justice in favour of the young plaintiffs' rights to a healthy environment, life, food and water in the Amazon, which was itself recognised as a subject of rights;[13] and the 2021 decision of the German Federal Constitutional Court that the protection of life and health under Article 2 of the German Basic Law gave rise to an objective duty to protect future generations against the risks posed by climate change. The court struck down parts of the country's 2019 Federal Climate Protection Act as incompatible with these fundamental rights for failing to spread out environmental burdens for emissions cuts between different generations.[14] Initial attempts by youth in the United States under state constitutions and the public trust doctrine were largely unsuccessful;[15] but, in August 2023, in the United States' first constitutional climate trial, a group of sixteen Montana young people aged five to twenty-two years old were granted injunctive relief against state officials for violating their constitutional right to a clean and healthful environment.[16] Building on the momentum of human-rights-based approaches, in September 2023, the Grand Chamber of the European Court of Human Rights heard the claims of

[10] James Fairhead, Melissa Leach and Ian Scoones. 'Green Grabbing: A New Appropriation of Nature?' (2012) 39 *Journal of Peasant Studies* 237.

[11] United Nations Children's Fund, *The Climate Crisis is a Child Rights Crisis: Introducing the Children's Climate Risk Index* (UNICEF, 2021).

[12] Hailie Brophy, Joanne Olson and Pauline Paul, 'Eco-anxiety in Youth: An Integrative Literature Review' (2023) 32 *International Journal of Mental Health Nursing* 633.

[13] *Future Generations v Ministry of Environment and others* STC 4360-2018, 5 April 2018.

[14] *Neubauer and others v Federal Republic of Germany* 1 BvR 2656/18, 1 BvR 78/20, 1 BvR 96/20, 1 BvR 288/20, 24 March 2021.

[15] Including the long-running case of *Juliana and others v United States of America and others* 6:15-cv-01517-AA, filed in 2015. On 1 May 2024 the Ninth Circuit Court of Appeals directed the lower court to dismiss the case for lack of standing.

[16] *Held and others v State of Montana and others* CDV-2020-307, 14 August 2023.

six Portuguese young people brought against thirty-two European nations, including the United Kingdom, arguing their rights under Articles 2, 3, 8 and 14 ECHR were being violated by state failures to cut emissions fast enough.[17] These youth-led cases join a growing wave of other climate cases brought around the world calling on governments to be held accountable for their climate commitments.[18]

The rights of non-human entities, including forests, have also gained legal recognition in some countries, particularly in South America and New Zealand. They include the rights of the Te Urewera Forest in New Zealand,[19] and the 2021 Constitutional Court decision in Ecuador, which upheld the rights of the Los Cedros cloud forest against mining activities.[20] In the United Kingdom, however, legal innovations in Earth law have primarily concerned the well-being of future human generations. In 2015 the Welsh Assembly passed the ground-breaking Well-being of Future Generations (Wales) Act. This act began as the Sustainable Development Bill around the time of the Rio+20 conference. However, following a national conversation on 'The Wales We Want', the title of the bill was changed. This reflected public concern to solve long-term problems for future generations, particularly climate change, and encompassed all aspects of human well-being interdependent with the health of the planet.[21] A UK-wide Well-being of Future Generations Bill inspired by the Welsh Act was introduced in the House of Lords as a Private Members' Bill by Lord Bird in May 2021.[22]

Summary of the Case

It is against this backdrop that I chose to reimagine the 2020 case of *R (Packham) v Secretary of State for Transport, The Prime Minister and HS2 Limited*,[23] an application for judicial review brought by the well-known television broadcaster and

[17] *Duarte Agostinho and others v Portugal and 31 other States*, 39371/20. The case was later declared inadmissible, but the ECtHR found a violation of Articles 8 and 6 ECHR in the linked case of *Verein KlimaSeniorinnen Schweiz and Others v Switzerland* [GC] 53600/20.

[18] In Europe: *The State of the Netherlands (Ministry of Economic Affairs and Climate Policy) v Urgenda* ECLI:NL:HR:2019:2007, *Friends of the Irish Environment v Government of Ireland and others* [2020] IESC 49, *Commune de Grande-Synthe and another v French Republic* 427301, 1 July 2021, *R (Friends of the Earth Ltd) v Secretary of State for Business, Energy and Industrial Strategy* [2022] EWHC 1841 (Admin), and *VZW Klimaatzaak v Kingdom of Belgium and others* Brussels Court of Appeal 2021/AR/1589, 2022/AR/737 and 2022/AR/891, 30 November 2023.

[19] The Te Urewera Act 2014 declared the forest to have inalienable title to itself as part of a treaty settlement between the Crown and the local Māori people.

[20] Collateral Review Case Ruling 1149-19-JP/21, Constitutional Court of Ecuador, 10 November 2021.

[21] Eleanor Messham and Sally Sheard, 'Taking the Long View: The Development of the Well-being of Future Generations (Wales) Act' (2020) 18 *Health Research Policy and Systems* 33.

[22] The UK Bill was passed by the House of Lords and sent to the House of Commons in February 2022. The Bill was due for Second reading in May 2022 but failed to complete all its stages by the end of the parliamentary session.

[23] *R (Packham) v Secretary of State for Transport, The Prime Minister and HS2 Limited* [2020] EWHC 829 (Admin); [2020] EWCA Civ 1004.

environmental campaigner, Chris Packham. The case concerned the UK government's decision to continue with the controversial High Speed Two (HS2) rail project in England, and the clearance of six ancient woodlands along phase 1 of the route between London and the West Midlands. The rail project and the company in charge of it, HS2 Ltd, were set up in 2009 under the then Labour transport secretary, Lord Adonis, who later became a non-executive director of HS2 Ltd in 2015. The project continued under successive Conservative governments and in 2017 the High Speed Rail (London–West Midlands) Act was passed, allowing phase 1 of the project to proceed. The promise of the fastest high-speed rail links in Europe connecting London, Birmingham, Manchester and Leeds became part of the government's 'levelling-up' agenda to create jobs and prosperity throughout the country and improve public transport links, particularly for the north of England. However, the project remained politically contentious over its environmental and community impacts and cost to the public purse and became the subject of sustained protest.[24]

In August 2019, the Department for Transport commissioned a review by Sir Douglas Oakervee, former chairman of HS2 Ltd, to decide 'whether and how' to proceed with HS2.[25] Chris Packham's application was made in response to the government's decision to continue with HS2 following publication of the Oakervee Review report in February 2020, despite a dissenting report by the deputy chairman, Lord Berkeley, who resigned in objection. The application for judicial review was refused and the works continued, including the clearance of the ancient woodlands. However, from November 2021 the government began to progressively scale back the project, and, by October 2023, amid reports of whistleblowing, a *Sunday Times* investigation into escalating costs, and HS2 Ltd's launch of an internal fraud investigation, Prime Minister Rishi Sunak axed what remained of the Birmingham to Manchester leg and removed HS2 Ltd from construction of the new London terminus.[26] This left only the phase 1 London–Birmingham leg still going ahead at an estimated cost of at least £50 billion, although independent analysts have projected the final cost to be double this amount.[27] Government decisions to axe the entire northern part of the project amid a public cost controversy happened over a year after the application for judicial review in 2020. In reimagining the judgment, I have chosen to stay with the law and facts as they were known to Parliament and the courts at the time of the original judgment, particularly since environmental concerns rather than economic arguments formed the main basis of the application for judicial review.

[24] Gwyn Topham, 'HS2 Asks Government to Help it Deal with Rising Number of Protests', *The Guardian*, 24 June 2021.

[25] Oakervee Review of HS2, Department for Transport, 11 February 2020 gov.uk/government/publications/oakervee-review-of-hs2.

[26] Jonathan Calvert and George Arbuthnott, 'HS2: The Secret Files that Expose a Multibillion-Pound Cover-up', *The Sunday Times*, 5 November 2023.

[27] ibid. This compares with HS2 Ltd's original 2011 estimate of £37.5 billion.

In the High Court, after initial procedural issues as to promptness of the application and the relevant public law test to be applied,[28] the substantive grounds considered by the Court were first, whether the Oakervee Review process had departed from the published terms of reference, particularly in light of a dissenting report produced by the panel's deputy chair, Lord Berkeley; second, whether there was a legal requirement for the Oakervee Review and the defendants to give a full account of the local environmental impacts of HS2; third, the consideration given by the Review report to carbon emissions and the government's decision to proceed in light of the Paris Agreement and Climate Change Act 2008; fourth, the public's legitimate expectation of the nature, scope and extent of the Oakervee Review; and finally, whether an interim injunction should be granted to prevent irreversible damage to the six ancient woodlands in question. The application was rejected on all grounds and the application for an interim injunction was refused. The Court stated: 'In these circumstances, not even the irreversible damage and other harm upon which the Claimant relies could possibly justify the grant of the interim injunction sought.' The Court based its decision not to intervene on the fact that Parliament had already judged that the project should proceed 'in the national interest'.[29]

The Court of Appeal also refused permission to appeal. The substantive issues were narrowed to the second ground concerning local environmental concerns and the third ground concerning the government's obligations under the Paris Agreement and Climate Change Act 2008. As to the environmental effects, the Court concluded that 'there was nothing to show that the Government failed to understand the limited scope it had given the Oakervee review to deal with environmental effects, or to grasp what the review report said about such effects. Nor did it err in failing to ask the review panel to investigate environmental effects more fully, or to do so itself at this stage.'[30] On climate change the Court of Appeal agreed with the conclusions of the High Court that the submissions made did not 'amount to a viable argument that the Government's decision was irrational, or otherwise unlawful'.[31] The Court restated the public law test that 'where the decision is one of political judgment on matters of national economic policy, the court would only intervene on grounds of "bad faith, improper motive and manifest absurdity"'.[32]

Reimagining the Case for Future Generations

At this time of planetary crisis, the courts' reasoning brought into sharp focus the narrow scope for challenging government decision-making on the environment

[28] *Associated Provincial Picture Houses Ltd v Wednesbury Corporation* [1948] 1 KB 223.
[29] *Packham* [2020] EWHC 829 (Admin), paras 118, 125.
[30] *Packham* [2020] EWCA Civ 1004, para 82.
[31] ibid para 104.
[32] ibid para 48.

through traditional public law tests, and substantive weaknesses in UK law concerning environmental protection of ancient woodlands and enforcement of the government's climate commitments. Judicial review of a macropolitical decision concerning the existential issue of climate change was done with the conventional 'light touch'. In the context of a large infrastructure project authorised by parliamentary legislation, UK law seemingly placed no duty on government to ensure that irreplaceable ancient woodland should be protected and respected whether for its own existence or for the benefit of future human generations. In reimagining the case through an Earth law lens, I wanted to reinterpret the legal test of 'irrationality'[33] in light of the urgent need to preserve a habitable planet. As part of this, I wanted to bring attention to the importance of time and generation in legal principles concerning the human rights and the well-being of present and future generations, as well as the rights of non-human entities. These principles did not form the basis of the legal arguments that were made in the original case of *Packham*, although they have become increasingly significant globally and in the United Kingdom.

A striking feature of the Divisional Court judgment in *Packham* was its refusal to engage with the significant level of public concern and emotion in the case, despite acknowledging the 'strongly held views for and against the HS2 project' and witness statements against the conduct of HS2 Ltd filed by nature conservation groups including the Woodland Trust and the Royal Society for the Protection of Birds (RSPB).[34] Courts in the tradition of liberal legalism, particularly in public law cases, are generally cautious about engaging with moral sentiments in their decision-making. Yet, as scholarship in the field of feminist judgments[35] and law and emotion[36] has demonstrated, there is no clear separation between reason and emotion in law. Law and emotion scholar Terry Maroney has argued that 'emotional common sense' is necessary in judging. To consign emotion-relevant legal questions into an 'epistemological blank space' destabilises law, rendering it 'unmoored' and idiosyncratic.[37] This is all the more important when judges communicate their findings to audiences on the losing side of their decisions, such audiences often extending well beyond the litigants in the case. In a study of judicial drafting in Australian public law judgments titled 'A Letter to the Loser', Sarah Murray has argued that whether or not the judgment literally takes the form of a letter, the device of a 'letter to the loser' in judging has multiple functions and advantages: it focuses on the psychological well-being of the unsuccessful party, speaks to their perception of fairness, sense of participation in the process and

[33] *Associated Provincial Picture Houses Ltd v Wednesbury Corporation* [1948] 1 KB 223.

[34] *Packham* [2020] EWHC 829 (Admin) paras 5 and 34.

[35] Rosemary Hunter, Clare McGlynn and Erika Rackley (eds) *Feminist Judgments: From Theory to Practice* (Hart Publishing, 2010).

[36] eg Kathryn Abrams and Hila Keren, 'Who's Afraid of Law and the Emotions?' (2010) 94 *Minnesota Law Review* 1997; Robin West, 'Law's Sentiments' in Susan A Bandes et al (eds), *Research Handbook on Law and Emotion* (Edward Elgar, 2021).

[37] Terry A Maroney, 'Lay Conceptions of Emotion in Law' in Bandes et al, *Research Handbook*, 16.

confidence in the legal system. As such, 'a letter to the loser would go beyond the standard explanation of the facts and ultimate legal resolution. It would also acknowledge or attest to the significance of the matter for the losing party. In so doing, the court's judgment becomes a permanent record that the party's story has been heeded.'[38]

In approaching the task of reimagining the judgment from the perspective of young and future generations, I drew inspiration both from this body of law and emotion scholarship and from the child-centred judicial style of Mr Justice Peter Jackson (as he then was, subsequently Lord Justice Jackson) sitting as a Family Division judge in *Re A: Letter to a Young Person*,[39] in which his judgment took the form of a letter to a fourteen-year-old boy. A letter to a young person is a powerful but challenging medium for legal writing. Although apparently simple in language, stripped of obfuscating legalese it lays bare the logic and morality underpinning a legal decision about their future in the simplest terms and holds it up to scrutiny by the person who is most impacted. There is no room to hide behind procedural technicality in a letter to a young person. Holding oneself directly accountable to future generations in this way requires emotional insight, empathy and connection with a sense of intergenerational justice.

My reimagined judgment in *Packham* takes the form of a letter to future generations, both to expose law's sentiments in the case and to acknowledge and respond to the fear and anger that surrounds the planetary crisis, the future of human generations and the fate of the ancient woodlands themselves. The commentary to this judgment takes the form of a conversation with two young people about the reimagined judgment and the planetary crisis. Instead of turning away from moral sentiments, I wanted to explore how in such grave circumstances law could transform to meet the need for intergenerational equity and ecological justice. How different might the results be in an environmental public law case if courts wrote their judgments directly to those most affected, whose voices are often marginalised or unheard in court, and not simply the legal parties in the case? What might we learn and how might decision-making change if courts listened to those voices?

Rather than rewrite the original decision, I chose to position myself in time and space alongside the judges sitting in the Court of Appeal on 31 July 2020 and to write the letter to future generations as a dissenting judgment on the basis of the law and facts as they were known at that time. On a practical level this enables points of comparison and contestation to be made explicit. Dissenting judgments also have jurisprudential value in other ways: they may signal the need for change in legislation, lay the foundation for shaping future directions in judging, and offer alternative perspectives on the law, the position of powerful actors and broader social context.[40] As the late US Supreme Court Justice Ruth Bader Ginsberg, who

[38] Sarah Murray, '"A Letter to the Loser"? Public Law and the Empowering Role of the Judgment' (2014) 23 *Griffith Law Review* 545, 547.

[39] *Re A: Letter to a Young Person* [2017] EWFC 48.

[40] Orit Gan, 'I Dissent: Justice Ginsburg's Profound Dissents' (2021) 74 *Rutgers University Law Review* 1037.

was known for her profound dissenting opinions in the interests of social justice, famously remarked:

> Dissents speak to a future age. It's not simply to say, 'My colleagues are wrong and I would do it this way.' But the greatest dissents do become court opinions and gradually over time their views become the dominant view. So that's the dissenter's hope: that they are writing not for today but for tomorrow.[41]

[41] Interview by Nina Totenberg with Ruth Bader Ginsburg, *Morning Edition*, 2 May 2002, seamus.npr.org/programs/morning/features/2002/may/ginsburg/index.html.

Court of Appeal (Civil Division)

R (on the application of Christopher Packham) v Secretary of State for Transport, The Prime Minister and High Speed Two (HS2) Limited

JUDGMENT

31 July 2020

Lady Justice Dancer, dissenting

Dear future generations

I have chosen to write my judgment in the form of a letter directly to you because, when I considered the nature of the environmental issues in this case, I felt that it is you who would be most affected by the consequences and I wanted to recognise that reality. I have written this letter separately from the other judges because I disagree with the court's decision in this case. While I cannot change that decision, my intention in writing this letter is to give a different perspective, putting the issues that were raised in this case into the context of the rights and interests of future generations and the irreplaceable ancient woodlands that will be affected. I also wanted to express my view on legal change for the future.

This case is about the environmental and climate change impacts of the High-Speed Two (HS2) rail project. If completed, the new railway would enable high-speed trains to travel between London, Birmingham, Manchester and Leeds. This is a very large infrastructure project that will cost billions of pounds of public money and take decades to complete, so Parliament has to give approval for the construction of each phase of the railway. It is then for the Government to keep the project under review.

This case is about the first phase of the railway to be built between London and Birmingham, which Parliament approved in 2017. The claim in this case was brought to the High Court by the well-known naturalist, television personality and environmental campaigner, Christopher Packham, against the Secretary of State for Transport, Grant Shapps, the Prime Minister, Boris Johnson, and the rail company, HS2 Ltd.

There has been a lot of political debate about this project. This is not simply due to concerns about the high cost of the project, but also because of its impact on the environment and local communities. These environmental concerns include the impacts on protected species of wildlife and the destruction of ancient woodland along the route of the railway. Local authorities, local and national Wildlife Trusts and the Woodland Trust brought petitions to Parliament objecting to HS2. People have physically protested the removal of trees and woods along the route and there have been several court cases challenging decisions over the rail project.

In 2019 Mr Shapps announced that the project would be reviewed by a panel chaired by Sir Douglas Oakervee, who was a former Chairman of HS2 Ltd, to decide 'whether and how' the rail project should go ahead. During this period the Government asked HS2 Ltd to stop clearance of ancient woodland, which it recognised was 'irreplaceable', unless this was absolutely necessary. In response HS2 Ltd paused the clearance of eleven ancient woodland sites until the report was concluded. A further six sites that were the subject of Mr Packham's claim were paused until early 2020. Five other sites were paused until autumn/winter 2020.

Sir Douglas Oakervee produced his report (known as the Oakervee Review report) on 11 February 2020 and recommended that 'on balance' the project should still go ahead. There was also a second unofficial Dissenting Report produced by the Deputy Chair of the review panel, Lord Berkeley. He took a different view and resigned from the panel. His concerns included whether the costs involved in building HS2 had been properly considered. However, on the basis of the official Review report, the Prime Minister, Mr Johnson, announced to Parliament that HS2 would still go ahead.

It was in response to this decision by the Prime Minister that Mr Packham made his claim to the High Court. He challenged the Government's decision to allow HS2 to continue, taking into account the Oakervee Review report and the 'open mind' that the Government had said it would take in deciding on the future of the rail project. He also asked the court to make an order to prevent the clearance of six of the ancient woodlands that was about to happen in Warwickshire and Staffordshire. The High Court rejected Mr Packham's claim and the woodland clearance works were allowed to continue. Mr Packham appealed to this court.

Issues

Mr Packham's case in this court concerns two main issues:

1. The first issue is whether the Government made a legal error by misunderstanding or ignoring local environmental concerns and failing to examine the environmental effects of HS2.
2. The second issue is whether the Government made a legal error by failing to take account of the effect of HS2 on greenhouse gas emissions and the importance of reducing carbon emissions during the period leading up to 2050.

Issue 1 – Environmental Impacts

Part of Mr Packham's claim about local environmental concerns was the loss of ancient woodland. Officially, a woodland is considered 'ancient' if the area has been wooded continuously since at least 1600 AD. Ancient woodland covers around 2 per cent of the United Kingdom. Unlike newly planted woodlands, ancient woodland is recognised as 'irreplaceable' due to its rich wildlife communities, including a high proportion of rare and vulnerable species, undisturbed soils, which lock away large amounts of carbon, and a 'treasure trove' of historical woodland features (The Woodland Trust, *Position Statement, Ancient Woodland*, January 2017). In 1994 the Government's UK Biodiversity Action Plan noted: 'Given time, perhaps centuries, new woods may be able to achieve the same level of biodiversity as ancient woodland' but 'the full suite of communities and features associated with ancient woodland can never be replicated'.

As part of the original planning process, HS2 Ltd was required to make statements and produce assessments of the environmental impact of the project before Parliament allowed each phase of the project to go ahead. The Oakervee Review report was written in a short period of time and the Government did not ask the Review panel to carry out or consider new environmental impact assessments of HS2. However, the Review report did briefly consider local environmental issues. For example, it noted that HS2's Environmental Policy included aims of 'no net biodiversity loss' and minimising its carbon footprint. It also recognised the loss of wildlife habitats, including ancient woodland, and potential impacts on species such as barn owls (Review report 6.15–6.16).

The target of 'no net biodiversity loss' makes it legally possible for the destruction of natural habitats in one area to be offset by the creation of new natural habitats in another area. This idea of offsetting means that, unlike the way that we value human life, plants, animals, fungi and their habitats are treated as exchangeable instead of important in their own right, or having rights themselves.

The Government was aware of the importance of ancient woodland as irreplaceable because it asked HS2 Ltd to put clearance works on pause during the Oakervee Review. The Review report noted that under the practice of offsetting, HS2 Ltd had agreed to plant 112.5 hectares of new woodland to compensate for the loss of 29.4 hectares of ancient woodland along the London to Birmingham route. However, the Review panel also recognised that 'planting new woodland is not a direct replacement for removing areas of ancient woodland' (Review report 6.17).

Part of the evidence provided to the High Court by Mr Packham were witness statements from the Woodland Trust and the RSPB concerning the way works had been carried out by HS2 Ltd to date. The High Court described this evidence as 'wholly irrelevant to the legal basis of the claimant's challenge or the application for the interim injunction. It seems to have been included for prejudicial purposes' (para 34), in other words, the Court did not think the evidence should be taken into account. I disagree with the High Court's view of this evidence and consider that this information was relevant. In the wider context, according to the 2019 State of Nature report on wildlife in the United Kingdom, between 1970 and 2017 UK woodland bird indicator species fell by 25 per cent. Overall, the United Kingdom will not meet most of the 2020 targets of the UN Convention on Biological Diversity. In the context of a national and global biodiversity crisis, such evidence is vital for both the Court and the Government to consider.

Issue 2 – Climate Change

In June 2019, after the Paris Agreement on climate change, the UK government committed to bring all greenhouse gas emissions to net zero by 2050. The Climate Change Act 2008 was updated to reflect this. It requires a reduction in greenhouse gas emissions by at least 80 per cent by 2050 compared to 1990 levels. To achieve this, UK governments must set five-yearly carbon budgets which are designed to limit carbon emissions and meet the national target of net zero by 2050. However, the UK Committee on Climate Change's 2019 report *Net Zero: The UK's Contribution to Stopping Global Warming*, has already noted that the United Kingdom is struggling to meet its carbon budgets and, therefore, its legal commitment under the Paris Agreement.

The Oakervee Review looked at the environmental case for and against HS2, 'particularly in the light of the Government's recent commitment to net zero carbon emissions by 2050 and the impact of the construction of HS2 itself on the environment' (Report 2.2). The Oakervee Review considered the carbon emissions that HS2 was predicted to produce, both during the construction process and in the sixty years of operation after it had been completed. The Review report concluded that 'it is not clear whether overall HS2 is positive or negative for greenhouse gas emissions'. Whether the project would reduce carbon emissions by an estimated 3–4 million tonnes of CO_2 or contribute a further 1–3 million tonnes of CO_2 would largely depend on the level of emissions during the construction process (Report 5.37).

The Review report noted that, in 2018, transport contributed 33 per cent of UK CO_2 emissions and that rail travel emits less carbon than road and air travel. However, the report also concluded that 'the whole rail network needs to be decarbonised if the Government is to deliver its net zero target. HS2 should be considered carefully in the role it could play in helping meet this target' (Report 5.33).

There was uncertainty in the Review report about the long-term impacts of HS2 on carbon emissions. However, the report gave a clear conclusion that, for much of the time leading up to 2050, the construction of HS2 was expected to add to UK carbon emissions (Report 5.31).

How Should the Court Judge the Government's Decision?

It is a long-established rule that governments must not act unlawfully or irrationally. This means that governments cannot make a decision that is so unreasonable that no one who was acting reasonably could have made such a decision. If a claim is brought to court challenging a government decision on the basis that it was irrational, the court can intervene if the decision did not take into account something that was 'obviously material', that is to say, obviously relevant. This legal test has been applied by the courts since the case of *Associated Provincial Picture Houses Ltd v Wednesbury Corporation* [1948] 1 KB 223. It is not the role of courts to make laws or to take political decisions themselves. When courts are asked to review large (or 'macro-political') decisions as in this case, they have traditionally taken a 'light touch' approach to whether a decision was irrational and they have allowed governments a wide amount of discretion.

We are living at a time of planetary crisis and, taking into account the large amount of scientific evidence on climate change and biodiversity loss, I consider that justice and what is 'irrational' and 'obviously material' must now include a concern for future generations and for ecological justice. This means that doing justice includes serving more than the interests of today's adults. It also includes the interests of young people, future generations and other living beings and their habitats, all of which are important for the future of a healthy planet.

Mr Packham, Mr Shapps, Mr Johnson and HS2 Ltd as parties to this case have moral and professional interests in whether or not HS2 continues. They have the legal right to be included in this case and to make their voices heard. But ultimately, their interests in the case are not existential, as yours are. They are not the ancient trees that will be cleared or the woodland species whose habitat will be destroyed. They are not the young people and the yet-to-be-born who will have to adapt to an increasingly unstable climate, rising sea levels and escalating rates of species extinction during their lifetime.

UK law does not yet allow for the voices and interests of future generations and non-human living beings to be heard or considered directly in cases such as this. The Well-being of Future Generations Act has been part of Welsh law since 2015, so if the route of HS2 had passed through Wales, then the government, the rail company (HS2 Ltd) and this Court would have been legally required to act, as the law puts it, 'in a manner which seeks to ensure that the needs of the present are met without compromising the ability of future generations to meet their own needs' (s 5(1)).

However, this duty to act sustainably and meet your future needs does not yet exist in the law covering England. UK law also does not recognise the human right to a clean and healthy environment, although this right has been recognised in the laws of more than 80 per cent of United Nations Member States around the world (*Right to a Healthy Environment: Good Practices. Report of the Special Rapporteur on the issue of human rights obligations relating to the enjoyment of a safe, clean, healthy and sustainable environment.* A/HRC/43/53 UN General Assembly, 30 December 2019).

There is a European Convention which includes the right of every person 'to live in an environment adequate to his or her health and well-being' (Aarhus Convention on Access to Information, Public Participation in Decision-making and Access to Justice in Environmental Matters 1998, Article 1). However, when the UK Government signed the Convention, it declared that this right was an 'aspiration'. In other words, this right has no legal force in UK law.

I regret that I am unable to consider your well-being and right to a healthy environment as stand-alone rights under UK law. I also regret that I am unable to consider the rights of the ancient woodlands and the species that live there under UK law. To allow something irreplaceable in terms of its biological diversity to be destroyed impacts the ability of future generations including future non-human generations to meet their own needs. These are important issues for your future and for the future of the planet. They are rights and needs that are being increasingly recognised around the world, and there is an urgent need for legal reform in this area in the United Kingdom.

We are now seeing cases being brought against governments in other countries to fulfil their climate commitments on the basis of environmental human rights. Often, these cases are being brought by young people themselves, and their voices are being heard. For example, in 2018 the Colombian Supreme Court ruled in favour of claims made by young people concerning their rights to a healthy environment, life, food and water in the Amazon. The Court also recognised that the Amazon itself had rights (*Future Generations v Ministry of Environment and others STC* 4360-2018, 5 April 2018).

Another important case was the decision of the Supreme Court of the Netherlands in December 2019 which required the Dutch government to urgently and significantly reduce greenhouse gas emissions on the basis of the human right to life (Article 2) and the right to private and family life (Article 8) of the European Convention on Human Rights (*The State of the Netherlands (Ministry of Economic Affairs and Climate Policy) v Urgenda* ECLI:NL:HR:2019:2007).

These rights also exist in UK law under the Human Rights Act 1998. The preamble to the Paris Climate Agreement acknowledges that states 'should, when taking action to address climate change, respect, promote and consider their respective obligations on human rights'. In my view your right to life and to private and family life are relevant and important for the Court to consider to decide whether the Government's decision to proceed with HS2 was proportionate.

Conclusions

The Court has to decide whether in light of the local environmental concerns and the government's climate commitments, the Government's decision to proceed with HS2 was irrational and did not take account of something obviously material. I disagree with the other judges in this case, who have concluded that the Government had discretion to allow the project to continue.

When the Prime Minister confirmed that the project would go ahead the main justification was to increase rail capacity and faster journey times. I have concluded that the government's decision was irrational because it failed to take account of the obviously material biodiversity and climate interests of future generations and its human rights obligations under the Paris Agreement on Climate Change.

Reducing carbon emissions significantly over the next few years will be essential for the future of a habitable planet. Crucially, the Review report stated that the construction process of HS2 would *add* to UK carbon emissions during the period up to 2050. There was real uncertainty about whether or not in the long term the project would increase or decrease carbon emissions. In my view it was irrational for the government to allow the project to continue knowing this, at a time when the United Kingdom is already struggling to meet its climate targets.

Combined with concerns over the project's climate impact, in the midst of a biodiversity crisis and the country's failure to meet its global biodiversity commitments, it is irrational to allow the project to continue to destroy the irreplaceable habitat of woodland species that are already at risk.

For these reasons I also consider that proceeding with the project in these circumstances interferes with the right to life and right to private and family life of future generations.

Change is happening around the world and it is often young people who are showing leadership in the face of the planetary crisis. It is my sincerest hope that legal change will come soon for the sake of your future and for the sake of the rights and well-being of non-human beings, all of which are vital to the future of our home, planet Earth.

Kind regards

Lady Justice Dancer

Commentary

Young Voices

This commentary takes the form of extracts from two short interviews between the judgment writer and two young people, both aged fourteen, who responded to a call to participate in this project via their school Eco Club. The interviews have been abridged for reasons of space but their words are presented as spoken. Both young people had the opportunity to read the judgment in advance of the interview and to express their opinions on the issues.[42]

Young Person 1

What action do you think should be taken around climate change and biodiversity?

Well, connecting it to the generations I know when you were writing the judgment, in the conclusion … you said about how young people are taking action. And I think in some cases, our generation are doing more. We're learning more because it's something that's going to affect us. So having our generation's voices heard. I think that's a step that will really help see different views and different perspectives of the problem. You have then the actions you can take to cut down CO_2 emissions like reducing the use of fossil fuels.

Had you been aware of the HS2 rail project before you read the judgment?

Actually, I've heard quite a bit about it. … Do you want my opinion? I thought it was, I mean, it's traumatic to hear what they've done to create this path for humans. By cutting down all these ancient forests and decreasing the biodiversity. I think personally, I don't know all the economic and kind of impacts the railway will have, and I know it will obviously have connections. But in my personal opinion, that's not the priority. At the moment the priority is to tackle climate change. And well, the railway is literally doing the complete opposite. … So I feel quite strongly that it shouldn't have been done at all. It's stopped now. But the first part, that still destroyed so many habitats.

What do you think about the idea that if you cut down, or partially cut, an ancient woodland to make a path for the railway that you compensate for that by planting trees or creating a new woodland somewhere else?

[42] I wish to thank the two young people for taking the time to engage with this project so thoughtfully; and to acknowledge the support of my colleague, Maria Moscati at the University of Sussex, for our invaluable exchanges of ideas on research design, ethical issues and full participation of young people as commentators to this judgment. My thanks also go to Kirsty Shakespeare of the Trust for Sustainable Living for her assistance with the call for participants and for facilitating contact with schools, the children and their parents. The young people's identities have been anonymised at their own request.

It's not the same is it? Because those woodlands have been there for hundreds, possibly even thousands, of years. They hold so much history and nutrients in the ground. And you can't really replicate that again. We can't wait another few hundred years. Yes, I don't think that compensates, because obviously, you want as many trees as possible. And new woodlands are great, because it does increase biodiversity and wildlife. But that does not mean that you can cut down ancient woodlands.

If you had the opportunity to speak to the court that made this decision, what would you want to say to the court about these environmental issues?

I think the main thing is just listen, stop and look around at what you're doing. It's irresponsible, I think. They're adults, obviously, and what they're doing is destroying habitats that will affect future generations for generations. And to, really, be more caring to our environment, because you can't replace it. It's not something that you can build a new forest for. You know, what we have is what we have. And to listen to the young people that have these passionate opinions that really could save this planet. So, I think these are the main points.

What would you like to say to the court about reducing carbon emissions?

To also think about if they're kind of setting these goals to then say right, well, we then need to think about what our plans were and what our plans are now going to be. The railway line HS2 may have been decided before these goals. But the goals are the priorities. The reduction of carbon emissions is a priority. So yes, things like HS2, which will emit more carbon into the atmosphere, to think about it and to basically stop projects that you can physically stop now. It's not something … that they really need, you know. And to think about it for the environment. Many projects haven't been started. So, if they think about it beforehand, they won't do as much damage. And then, therefore, cutting down on the CO_2 emissions. And then that goes for many other things. Cars are a huge problem as well. And use of water, within that area of using carbon. So, I think you have to start somewhere, and starting somewhere where you can easily stop. That's, I guess, at the moment the easiest or the thing that they need to do.

Was there anything else that you wanted to add that we haven't already talked about on this subject?

I think there'd only be one thing, and that was what they're doing is irreplaceable. They cannot undo what they've done. And yes, I think your judgment definitely was emphasising that as well. … But yes … think of what they're doing and the impact on the environment. Like, really have a moment to take it in and realise that they can't undo, they can't undo the section of railway they've just laid down or prepared, and can't undo the chopping down of ancient woodland. However, they can stop the reckless behaviour and start to come up with solutions to these serious problems.

Young Person 2

What action do you think should be taken around climate change and biodiversity?

Well, I think, firstly, I think the governments need to kind of step up a bit, because obviously a lot of people care. But it's just the government, some of the governments they'll promise things, and then they might not do it. Or they'll yeah, they're kind of doing whatever gets the majority of votes. So if you've got … less people who … care about climate change, less people who are gonna vote, then, obviously, the people who are running, they're gonna be less worried about that. So I think governments need to kind of step up and do a bit more and get involved and collaborate 'cause, we're not very good at collaborating at the moment. I think we don't do a lot of that. I think we need to, the governments need to do more and work a bit harder.

Had you been aware of the HS2 rail project before you read the judgment? Is that something you'd ever heard about before?

I think it might have been … I'm kind of vaguely familiar. But yeah, I think this is the first time.

What were your thoughts then, when you heard about this idea of a high-speed train being built that would pass through ancient woodland?

I think it's really sad because it's, a lot of the wildlife that's lived there, they're not going to have a home any more, they can't be there and it's destroying a lot of that. But again, it's kind of really hard, because obviously you've got a train, 'cause trains are much better than cars. And it's really hard to decide, you know, do you put a train in that's going to be much better for the environment than loads of people taking cars, but it's gonna cut through the woodland? And I think yeah, but I think it's really sad that they did that, I think, 'cause … it's destroying a lot of the woodland and a lot of old, because … you can't just replace it instantly.

If you had the opportunity to speak to the court that made this decision, what would you want to say to the court about these environmental issues?

Well, it's really hard, 'cause obviously the train, because it's like, do you build it? 'cause in the long term obviously we don't really know, but it could be really good, but it could also be. I think governments sometimes they might not think as much about the long term because they're, you know, they're older, they're not gonna live. … I think they might need to think about the future generations 'cause obviously what they do, what they decide, whatever they do is gonna have an effect for future people and they need to think a bit more about that.

4

Attorney-General and Others and Kennard and Others v Cory Brothers and Company, Limited, and Others: A View from Wales in 2023

KAREN MORROW

Introduction: Contexts

Hindsight is a wonderful thing: the judgment to follow re-examines an early case engaging with the environmental and human consequences of extractivism in the Welsh Valleys through the lens of innovative modern Welsh law. When I was asked to take part in this project, I wanted to bring a Welsh case to the table, as Wales was early to experience both the benefits and burdens of industrialisation and its legacies. With that in mind I selected the *Cory Brothers* nuisance case, which provides an early example of judicial consideration of (at least some) of the ramifications of extractivism. While the claims in the original case were framed in nuisance and negligence, for reasons of space the former, including liability under the rule in *Rylands v Fletcher*, provides the principal focus here. For the same reason, other claims – not least those based on human rights law, which are also potentially arguable on the facts – will not be considered.

When reading around the case, I was astonished to find that, in 1909, some six years before the incident that prompted the litigation,[1] the Cory Brothers' Pentre tip had caused a (conspicuously unreferenced) disastrous landslide. This destroyed five homes, several rented by colliers and their families, who would not have been in a financial position to litigate, and killed five-year-old James Williams.[2] Contemporaneous press reports reveal that the incident was regarded as novel in the area and that, while the aesthetic impact of tipping was widely appreciated,

[1] *Attorney-General and Others and Kennard and Others v Cory Brothers and Company, Limited, and Others* [1921] 1 AC 521.

[2] 'The Pentre Disaster', 13 February 1909 article, transcribed from the *Rhondda Leader*, online at www.pentre-rhondda.org.uk/tip-slides/.

the dangers involved were not.[3] The 1909 landslip indicated that reshaping the abiotic environment above Pentre in the service of mining not only detrimentally altered the landscape, but in so doing posed significant ongoing threats to the village below. In the aftermath of the 1909 disaster, the human impacts were addressed through community self-help initiatives and ex gratia payments by Cory Brothers. A coroner's inquest was held for James Williams, and recorded a verdict of accidental death.[4] In omitting these salient issues, the original judgment exhibits the still typical, artificially truncated, focus of a common law *inter partes* dispute, stripping the contested issues of social and environmental context. In many ways, it points to the self-imposed limits of this species of framing, failing to do justice as fully as required to address all the interests implicated. Nevertheless, the judgment does represent an early attempt to address what would now be termed a hybrid disaster, 'where forces of nature are unleashed as a result of technical failure or sabotage'.[5]

The 1916 landslide, like its predecessor, wrought havoc on the community of Pentre, though this time litigation ensued, framed in negligence and nuisance. The first claim was a relator action brought by the Attorney General on behalf of the Rhondda Urban District Council, (hereafter the District Council); and an action brought by the District Council its own right, as highway authority, in respect of interference with the road running through Pentre. The second claim was an action by the trustees of the Crawshay Bailey Estate (hereafter the Estate) for damage to houses and other property sustained in consequence of the landslide. Both claimants originally sought damages for harm already caused and an injunction against future harm to their assets. The District Council's claim centred on whether or not Cory Brothers had taken reasonable precautions to ensure the stability of the soil heap; the Estate's claim focused on whether Cory Brothers tipped 'to an unreasonable extent and in an unreasonable manner'. Cory Brothers argued in its defence that the landslide was 'a purely natural phenomenon'[6] ascribed to the geology of the area or, in the alternative, caused by a pre-existing quarry tip created by earlier leased or licensed activity on the site.

Ultimately, liability was found by a majority in the District Council's action in negligence, as well as under the rule in *Rylands v Fletcher*[7] (which was treated in effect as a specialised species of nuisance) and in the Estate's claim in negligence. However, arriving at this destination proved controversial. At first instance, Sarjant J attributed the landslide to Cory Brothers' activities and gave a decision for the claimants, awarding damages and a perpetual injunction to the District Council and the Estate, with additional (oddly favourable, to modern eyes, given

[3] ibid.
[4] ibid.
[5] Igor Boyarsky and Amiram Schneiderman, 'Natural and Hybrid Disasters – Causes, Effects, and Management' (2002) 24 *Advanced Emergency Nursing Journal*, 1.
[6] *Cory Brothers*, 524.
[7] *Rylands v Fletcher* (1868) LR 3 HL 330.

that they had both sanctioned the mine and profited from rent for it) provision for the latter of an indemnity against any liability they might be found to owe to District Council.[8]

The Court of Appeal arrived at a majority verdict attributing the landslide to natural causes and reversing the first-instance decision. Scrutton LJ's minority judgment agreed with Sarjant on the District Council's claim, though, insofar as the Estate's claim was concerned, he attributed the landslide to both the Cory Brothers' tips and previously deposited quarry spoil which had been permitted by the Estate, precluding its claim for damages as a joint tortfeasor.[9]

A further appeal to the House of Lords also resulted in a split decision. Viscount Haldane, who led the majority, described the main issue to be determined thus, 'whether … Cory Brothers & Co, Ltd, were responsible for bringing about a landslide … or whether anybody else, or nobody at all, could be held responsible for what happened'.[10]

In reaching his decision, and quite remarkably for an early case of its kind, Haldane considered the local geology, hydrology, prevailing weather conditions and the manner in which they interacted with one another in some detail.[11] He considered that either actual or constructive knowledge on Cory Brothers' part of the risks that the site posed following heavy rainfall sufficed to establish negligence.[12] Interestingly, Haldane observed that although the precipitation 'was no doubt unusually heavy, … it was of no unique character, nor … such as ought not to have been foreseen as possible. It could not be contended that it amounted to an "Act of God"'.[13] His Lordship concluded that the weight imposed by the colliery tips, in placing undue pressure on the unstable hillside, was the cause of the landslip.

Re-examining *Cory Brothers* opened up a whole range of possibilities, prompting consideration of the complex and continuing legacies of extractivism in Wales and beyond. The modern people of Wales inhabit a landscape shaped and scarred by mining and briefly prosperous communities long left behind by the industries they powered and the capital they generated. In the former mining areas of Wales people are habituated to the uncertainties of living on 'moving mountains',[14] and haunted by the spectre of Aberfan.[15] The already complex living legacy of extractivism is now being further compounded by climate change, as increasing rainfall sees more frequent flooding from defunct mine workings,

[8] ibid.
[9] ibid.
[10] ibid 530.
[11] ibid 530–32.
[12] ibid 536–37.
[13] ibid 537.
[14] Steve Mellen, 'Swansea Valley Landslides: Living on a "Moving Mountain"', www.bbc.co.uk/news/uk-wales-49099510, 26 August 2019.
[15] Gaynor Madgwick, *Aberfan: A Story of Survival, Love and Community in One of Britain's Worst Disasters* (Y Lolfa Cyf, 2016).

and landslides caused by shifting spoil tips, being visited on former mining communities.[16] Welsh Government research carried out in 2021 makes the extent of the problem clear: 2,456 coal tips remain in Wales, 303 in the Rhondda Cynon Taf Council area, where Pentre, the village where the *Cory Brothers* case took place, is located. Of the latter, 75 fall into categories, posing a 'potential risk to safety'.[17] The Law Commission has reviewed current legislative provision for coal tips and found it wanting on several fronts.[18] The problem remains: mining may bring profit in the short term; in the long term it brings human and environmental costs. Who will pay?

A reconsideration of *Cory Brothers* must also be viewed in the context of Welsh law. This is profoundly shaped by the unique central role of the sustainable development duty placed on the Welsh Ministers (and now applicable to the Welsh Government) under the devolution settlement.[19] In consequence, modern Welsh law has the potential to address broader conceptions of intersecting harms involved to the local community and to the environment. For present purposes, key provisions include the Well-being of Future Generations (Wales) Act 2015 and the Environment (Wales) Act 2016. The former is particularly significant as it extends sustainability and well-being duties more broadly than hitherto, applying them to public bodies in Wales. Local authorities and Cyfoeth Naturiol Cymru/Natural Resources Wales, the prime environmental regulator, fall within this category. The distinctive law and policy milieu in Wales means that even the shared provisions of the Environmental Permitting (England and Wales) Regulations 2016 (SI 2016.1154) have a distinctive Welsh cast. The combination of sustainable management of natural resources provided for in the Environment (Wales) Act and the sustainability and well-being provisions of the Well-being of Future Generations (Wales) Act place Welsh law at the vanguard of attempting to actualise sustainability in the activities of public bodies. This framing facilitates reconsideration of the *Cory Brothers* case both to extend the view of human interests to be accounted for, and to seek to address harm to the environment in its own right.

As an academic, case law is usually simply fuel for research and teaching – in a way a form of intellectual extractivism, mining primary sources for meaning. This project, however, provided an opportunity to take a more fully (figuratively and literally) grounded approach, looking at local archives and taking a field trip to see what marks remain on the landscape of the catastrophic events of a century ago. I thought this would be interesting: it was, and more. Although the tips above Pentre were removed in the 1980s and extensive remedial works were

[16] See Rhondda Cynon Taff Council: 'Tylorstown landslip – Remediation Process' (undated) www.rctcbc.gov.uk/EN/GetInvolved/TylorstownLandslip/Tylorstownlandslipremediationprocess.aspx.

[17] Welsh Government Coal Tip Data (updated version) 30 March 2022, gov.wales/coal-tip-safety#section-72291.

[18] Law Commission No 406: Regulating Coal Tip Safety in Wales: Report 23 March 2022.

[19] Now contained in s 79(1) of the Government of Wales Act 2006, originally found in s 121 of the Government of Wales Act 1998.

undertaken at public expense by the local council to avert future threats, the scar left on the landscape is still clearly visible. It takes the form of a ribbon of hillside, cleared of buildings, and now largely repopulated by a linear woodland. I took the opportunity to speak to one friendly local resident in a row of terraced houses adjacent to the site and asked him what he thought about the now distant disaster. He told me that his grandmother had lived in the same street at the time and remembered the noise of the landslide throughout her life. He added that, on wet nights, he lies and listens to the water rushing down through the heavily engineered drainage channel that is now in place and that the sound makes him feel safe. Setting foot on the ground brought the case to life for me in new ways, reaching beyond the law reports, academic commentary, and even the contemporary newspaper reports and photographs. I could now see the case rooted in geological time, in a landscape refashioned in historical time, with an afterlife that extends into the present and that will reach into the future, continuing to shape the land and the people who live in it. What more could be asked of the subject of an Earth law judgment?

The Supreme Court

Attorney-General and Others and Kennard and Others v Cory Brothers and Company, Limited, and Others

18 August 2023

Lady Morrow

This judgment stems from an appeal against the imposition of liability, in the form of a perpetual injunction and damages, on the defendants, Cory Brothers. To summarise the facts provided in argument by the parties: prompted by global demand for Welsh steam coal, Cory Brothers, a colliery company, developed the Pentre mine, its coal seams being worked under a lease from the Crawshay Bailey Estate from 1870 onward. In 1908, under licence from the trustees of the Estate, Cory Brothers began to dump spoil from the Pentre Colliery.

The current claims take place against the factual background of the 1909 disaster, and this is germane to the Court's consideration of the nature of the defendants' subsequent conduct. Cory Brothers continued to dump spoil across two undrained tips which eventually combined in a single mass. By late 1916 the accumulated spoil amounted to approximately 500,000 imperial tons/508,023.454 metric tonnes. In the autumn of that year, after a drought, a period of 'excessive' rainfall led to an enormous landslide causing considerable damage (and threatening more) over a large section of the valley, including to the main road. In the local context it was entirely foreseeable that further consequences of ongoing damage to the environment were visited on local people. The District Council argues that Cory Brothers' actions perpetuated and intensified what had become a foreseeable risk not only to property and human life and well-being, but to the environment itself.

Ownership or, alternatively, holding the tenancy of, an affected house in principle (affordability considerations notwithstanding) allows recourse to proceedings in private nuisance for property damage incurred. This is confirmed in *Hunter v Canary Wharf* [1997] 2 All ER 426. However, by virtue of the same case, the majority of those affected by the Pentre landslip, who called these houses home but lacked a proprietary interest in them, have no cause of action in nuisance. In any case, for this group, even were such a course available, it would not be viable given the disconnect between its resources and the high costs of litigating and modest sum of damages that would be recoverable. Nevertheless, the population of Pentre remains vulnerable to future landslips.

Directly preceding the instant case, and in light of immediate needs on the ground, the District Council, Cory Brothers and the Estate agreed upon remedial drainage works, accompanied by an injunction indicating that who would ultimately bear the costs associated with the incident was to be determined by this Court (*AG v Cory Brothers* 535). However, activities to date notwithstanding, the District Council contends that the local community in Pentre remains in the unenviable position of 'living on a moving mountain' with all the insecurity that entails for their physical safety, mental well-being and quiet enjoyment of their homes. All of this is in consequence of Cory Brothers' activities and is not adequately addressed by damages after the event for property damage and personal injury. Likewise, private law does not provide redress for damage to the environment in its own right. There are however statutory provisions in place in Wales that require the District Council to argue for a more holistic legal approach towards the impacts of Cory Brothers' actions and its responsibility for them that can encapsulate damage to community interests and damage to the environment itself. The Court will now consider the various lines of argument that they have made to this end.

I look first at the arguments raised by the District Council in common law, in nuisance, under the rule in *Rylands v Fletcher* and (to a lesser extent) negligence. I will then consider key public law provisions in Wales that are raised as significant in regard to addressing the broader public and environmental impacts of Cory Brothers' activities, namely the Environmental Permitting (England & Wales) Regulations 2016, the Environment (Wales) Act 2016 and the Well-being of Future Generations (Wales) Act (2015). I will further consider the Council's argument as to the persuasive value of the Council of Europe, Council of Ministers Recommendation Rec (2004)3 on conservation of the geological heritage and areas of special geological interest in the context of this case. I will also dispose of the Estate's claim for damages in negligence.

Initially though, it is clear that the question of factual responsibility for the damage caused by the landslip is a fundamental issue that must be resolved at the outset.

Factual responsibility for the landslip is the central question in this case and, with that in mind, this Court has a number of options to consider. First, did Cory Brothers alone cause the landslip? Second, was anyone else responsible, either alone or in combination with Cory Brothers? And third, as Cory Brothers has argued in previous proceedings and continue to maintain, was the landslip an act of Nature, for which no one can be held responsible? I note that the latter argument was also made by the defendants in separate nuisance proceedings arising from these facts where damages were awarded to the individual owners of affected houses and business premises. I note in passing that this defence, summarised in the local press of being to the effect that 'it was the mountain that moved, effectively dislodging the tip' and further described as 'rather amusing', was not successful.[20]

In determining the issues, I adopt a science-grounded approach. I have considered evidence adduced by both claimants and the defendant relating to

[20] Summary of court reports on successful proceedings by house and business owners following the 1916 landslide from the *Cambrian and Western Mail*, online at www.pentre-rhondda.org.uk/tip-slides/.

which the geology, hydrology and prevailing weather conditions in the Rhondda Valley and the way they interacted with each other in the Pentre area. I conclude that the weight imposed by the colliery tips, in placing undue pressure on the unstable hillside, was the cause of the landslip. In addition to the natural science material in play, the District Council also argues that the social sciences raise relevant considerations for the Court in terms of the human dimensions of events of this kind. It argues that the Pentre landslip is a compelling example of a 'hybrid disaster'. In the case of the coal tips, more precisely, human activity has altered the speed and scale of natural geological processes imposing externalities on the environment and the local community (and taxpayers) at the time, now, and in future.

In summary, it is clear, drawing on the scientific evidence, that the prime cause of the Pentre landslides was human agency. Furthermore, given the 1909 landslide, Cory Brothers knew – or ought to have known – that its activities posed a continuing risk of damage to the environment and the community of Pentre.

Common Law

(i) District Council's Claims – Nuisance, the Rule in Rylands v Fletcher *(and Negligence)*

(i.i) Nuisance

The claim against Cory Brothers is brought in the interests of the people of Pentre by the District Council for harm caused to the main road through the village, and is pursued under s 222 of the Local Government Act 1972, which empowers it to bring civil proceedings where it considers it appropriate to do so to protect the interests of those living in its area. While an action in public nuisance in its capacity as the highway authority (at common law and preserved under s 333 of the Highways Act 1980 to address interference with the highway) would also be viable, the District Council favours the former route as it represents an established avenue to take wider community concerns into account.

The District Council further argues that the disjuncture between rights on paper and the ability of ordinary citizens to pursue and realise claims in private nuisance makes recourse to action by public authorities acting in the public interest centrally important in cases of this nature. It posits that pursuing an expansive action in public nuisance, prompted by the duties imposed by the Well-being of Future Generations Act (considered below) provides a potentially significant avenue to consider harms to the community of Pentre as a whole, both at the present time and from a long-term perspective. In consequence, the District Council, pursuant to its responsibilities as a public authority, claims in public nuisance for damage to the highway, which is vested in it, and seeks damages for interference with it to date.

Furthermore, given the continuing and long-term impact of the tip on the geology of the hillside, the District Council seeks a perpetual injunction against further tipping by Cory Brothers and a mandatory injunction to compel Cory Brothers to carry out such works as might be necessary permanently to protect the highway and the village of Pentre more widely, a complex and costly endeavour, but one where, it argues, responsibility should lie with the defendant as the author of the damage, rather than ultimately falling on the public purse at some future date. The Council points to the extreme pressure that subsequent remediation of mine legacy pollution imposes on public finances, citing the initial clearance of the recent mining tip landslip at Tylorstown in the Rhondda costing £2.5 million and the estimated total cost of dealing with the displaced waste alone at £13 million referred to in Law Commission Report No 406 (2022) as an example. The future protection of the highway and the village will certainly require remediation of the affected environment, comprising clearing residual tipped material to a more suitable location, and substantial engineering works to ensure effective drainage and stabilise the mountainside.

While works focused on the highway will likely also resolve much of the ongoing threat to the village as these issues are inextricably linked, the District Council argues that more substantial action will likely be required to fully address the interests of the local community. These interests include their property rights, but extend more broadly to their health, well-being and enjoyment of their homes. The District Council argues that, as demonstrated by Sean Coyle and Karen Morrow in their book *A Philosophical Foundation for Environmental Law* (Hart, 2004), long-established innovative use of nuisance and remedies for it allows this branch of the common law to both rise to new environmental challenges and new societal understandings of the same, and to provide appropriate injunctive relief where required.

The central arguments in the nuisance claims relate to the reasonableness or otherwise of Cory Brothers' actions, the District Council's claim centring on whether or not reasonable precautions had been taken to ensure the stability of the soil heap. In response to the nuisance claims brought against it, Cory Brothers argue (in an extension of its unsuccessful approach in separate proceedings brought by property owners in the village pursuant to this incident) that the landslide was a purely natural phenomenon, attributable to the geology of the area or, in the alternative, to a pre-existing quarry tip created by earlier leased or licensed activity on the site.

However, insofar as reasonableness is concerned, both geology and the 1909 disaster indicate that the risk of a catastrophic landslide was by 1916 no longer novel but known; and this necessarily altered what amounted to reasonable behaviour around tipping and management on the site as per *Overseas Tankship (UK) Ltd v The Miller Steamship Co Pty, The Wagon Mound (No 2)* [1967] 1 AC 617. This court finds Cory Brothers' behaviour to have been unreasonable and the consequences of its actions to be foreseeable, grounding liability in nuisance. Furthermore, in not only failing to address the issues arising from its previous tipping but continuing to add to the problem, Cory Brothers profited from passing the consequences of its activities on to the immediate environment and by extension to the local community.

The District Council's claim in respect of public nuisance on the highway is allowed and it does vindicate one important community interest in this area. Damages are awarded in respect of clean up and repair costs incurred regarding the highway due to the landslip. However, if (as has happened before) Cory Brothers' poor tipping practices are not addressed and efficacious remedial works are not carried out, the tip poses an ongoing threat to the highway and the village community, and to this end a perpetual injunction prohibiting tipping is granted in the terms requested. The content of a mandatory injunction requiring remedial works is however necessarily a more complex matter, both in its own right and in meshing with other relevant legal provision and will be considered further below. While not raised in this instance, the Court notes that any future personal injury claims by the inhabitants of Pentre will be actionable in public nuisance under *Corby Group Litigation Claimants v Corby BC* [2008] EWCA Civ 463.

Finally, in light of the known risk of a landslide at the time of the 1916 incident, the District Council rightly raised the possibility of proceedings in nuisance against the Estate as Cory Brothers' landlord on the basis that it authorised the nuisance. The District Council points out that, while the threshold to be met is *per Coventry v Lawrence* (2015) AC 106 a high one, this was not a case wherein the Crawshay Bailey Estate as landlord merely knew of the risk and failed to act on it; but rather, one that arguably satisfies the requirement of it being highly probable that the letting of the property would result in 'inevitable or nearly certain' (*Coventry v Lawrence*, para 22) nuisance, thus attracting liability in principle as a joint tortfeasor. However, having taken advice, the District Council regards this element of the claim as more speculative than the case against Cory Brothers and has ultimately opted against pursuing it here. I note in passing that, had the District Council chosen to proceed with this head of argument, on the facts adduced, the Court would have considered it arguable.

(i.ii) *Rylands v Fletcher*

The District Council also attempts to argue a claim against Cory Brothers under the rule in *Rylands v Fletcher* (1868) LR 3 HL 330. Under the law as restated in *Transco Plc v Stockport MBC* [2004] 2 AC 1 and *Stannard v Gore* [2012] EWCA Civ 1248, the requirements of that rule include the defendant engaging in an extraordinary and unusual use of the land, which cannot, given the evidence, apply to mine tipping in the Rhondda. Furthermore, the harm suffered must result from something that is brought on to land from elsewhere. Thus, Cory Brothers argue that the case of *Willis v Derwentside DC* [2013] EWHC 738 (Ch) should apply here. That case held that the rule in *Rylands v Fletcher* could not be applied to an escape of gas naturally occurring in mine workings and the same approach would appear to apply to mine waste generated on site and this the claim must fail.

However, while *Stannard v Gore* confirms that an Act of God constitutes a defence to liability under the rule in *Rylands v Fletcher* (*Stannard v Gore*, para 22), in the instant case it must be observed that, as the District Council argues, while the precipitation involved was unusually heavy, it was well within the usual parameters for weather in the Rhondda Valley and was therefore foreseeable and does not qualify as an Act of God. This argument is persuasive and the weight that must be given to it is already increasing as climate change renders the incidence of what would in the past have been deemed unusually heavy rainfall a much more common occurrence. However, *Willis v Derwentside* disposes of this issue in Cory Brothers' favour.

(i.iii) Negligence

I simply touch on this issue to observe that either actual or constructive knowledge on Cory Brothers' part of the risks that the site posed following heavy rainfall were sufficient to establish negligence. The decision in *The Wagon Mound (No 2)* also pertains to a claim in negligence, insofar as the damage sustained was undoubtedly foreseeable.

(ii) Crawshay Bailey Estate Claims

The second claim against Cory Brothers is a nuisance action by the trustees of the Crawshay Bailey Estate for damage to houses and other property owned by it. This was an issue that generated some discomfort in the lower courts but one that can now be disposed of expeditiously. The Estate played a role in authorising the nuisance by issuing a lease which allowed tipping, referred to above, and continued to allow it to proceed unchallenged despite knowing that the tip was unstable. This claim must therefore fail either on the basis of consent, or of contributory negligence. Consent would apply here as the claimants, knowing of the danger to their property following the 1909 landslip, by failure to intervene thereafter, showed themselves to be willing to accept the danger that ongoing tipping posed, as noted by Megaw LJ in *Leakey v National Trust* [1980] 1 All ER 17. In the alternative, the Estate's own conduct could be regarded as contributing to the damage the estate sustained.

Public Law

The District Council persuasively argues that Welsh public law facilitates the consideration of broader social and environmental issues here, allowing the Court to do justice fully to all of the interests concerned. In particular the District Council raises the obligations incumbent on it and Natural Resources Wales in exercising their roles and responsibilities as public bodies under the Well-being of Future Generations (Wales) Act 2015. S 6 of the Act places public bodies under a duty to pursue sustainable development in their functions; s 4 of the Act requires them to pursue sustainable development by seeking to achieve the seven well-being goals; and s 5 requires them to pursue the sustainable development principle and to 'act in a manner which seeks to ensure that the needs of the present are met without compromising the ability of future generations to meet their own needs'. S 5 gives further content to the sustainability principle, identifying the 'five ways of working' that must be considered by public bodies, namely: balancing short-term and long-term needs; the need to take an integrated approach to the well-being goals; promoting wide participation in well-being decisions; considering the possibilities of collaboration in assisting it or another body to meet well-being objectives; and considering how deploying resources to prevent problems from occurring or getting worse may contribute to it or another body meeting well-being objectives.

There are multiple considerations in play here. Firstly, Natural Resources Wales applies stringent regulation to mining waste disposal under the Environmental Permitting (England & Wales) Regulations 2016 and active mine tips are regulated under the Quarries Regulations 1997 and the Mines Regulations 2014, as recently considered in Law Commission Report No 406. The District Council correctly argues that compliance with statutory regimes gives defendants only limited protection from proceedings in nuisance and that these do not apply here. They point out that a statutory authorisation defence covers only nuisances which are the inevitable result of authorised activities, see *Allen v Gulf Oil Refining* [1981] AC 1001. The tipping practices in the instant case would not meet even minimum statutory requirements and any nuisance not the inevitable consequence of authorised activities attracts liability in the usual way.

The District Council seeks a mandatory injunction to compel Cory Brothers to carry out necessary remedial work to stabilise the hillside and the content of such an injunction raises additional public law considerations. It argues that what I will term for convenience 'environmental factors' (in the shape of damage to the environment through detriment to geology and ecology), 'human factors' (rooted in the ongoing legacy of living with unstable tips and including, but extending far beyond property damage, extending to the impact of living with risk on the enjoyment of one's home and on mental health and well-being), and the interactions between them must be considered. The District Council has acted in collaboration with Natural Resources Wales to inform its argument regarding what is required to comply with Welsh environmental and sustainable development law.

Natural Resources Wales points out that the environment is now regarded as worthy of consideration in its own right in a plethora of legal provisions. In terms of the injunction sought here, the District Council seeks to fulfil its obligation under s 6 of the Well-being of Future Generations Act in its action for mandatory injunctive relief requiring Cory Brothers to address not only the highway nuisance but the broader community impacts consequent on its tipping at Pentre. In this the District Council is subject to the s 5 sustainable development principle, which requires it to act not just in the interests of current inhabitants of the area, but also of future generations.

This provision, alongside the long temporal impact of Cory Brothers' mine tipping activities alluded to above, it is argued, justify seeking the novel future-proofing element in the injunctive relief requested by the District Council.

The Well-being of Future Generations (Wales) Act also requires public bodies to pursue the statutory well-being duty contained in s 3 and to set well-being goals in six areas outlined in s 4 and Table 1. Of the latter, the District Council argues that the resilient Wales goal (which promotes maintaining and enhancing 'a biodiverse natural environment with healthy functioning ecosystems that support social, economic and ecological resilience and the capacity to adapt to change (for example climate change)'); the healthier Wales goal (focused on maximising people's physical and mental well-being now and in future); and the cohesive communities goal (centred on 'attractive, viable, safe and well-connected communities') all speak to the matters before the Court. The District Council points out that the five ways of working in sub-ss 5(2)(a)–(e) of the Well-being of Future Generations (Wales) Act are also relevant here. It argues that all five are relevant in the context of public bodies' functions around mining tips with their ongoing legacy issues; intractability and difficulty (favouring prevention over cure); complex cross-cutting and cross-agency implications; and the high level of public concern they generate. In using its statutory power to seek injunctive relief, the District Council has worked in collaboration with Natural Resources Wales, seeking to optimise its case for relief and ensure its harmony with other legal provision in this area.

In particular, the District Council points out that Natural Resources Wales's expertise pursuant to the sustainable management of natural resources under the Environment (Wales) Act 2016 is significant in the context of this case. S 3(2) of that act states the objective of sustainable management of natural resources as:

> to maintain and enhance the resilience of ecosystems and the benefits they provide and, in so doing –
>
> (a) meet the needs of present generations of people without compromising the ability of future generations to meet their needs, and
> (b) contribute to the achievement of the well-being goals in section 4 of the Well-being of Future Generations (Wales) Act 2015

The District Council compellingly argues that the demands of sustainable management of natural resources tie the consideration of ecosystem and human impacts together, which offers an approach well-suited to disposing of the situation arising in the instant case. Furthermore, it adds that the expansive definition of natural resources provided in sub-ss 2(c)–(f) of the Environment (Wales) Act, in explicitly including minerals, geological features and processes, physiographical features and climatic features and processes, helps here. Additionally, and uniquely in the post-Brexit context in the United Kingdom, the prevention and precautionary principles have legal status as principles of sustainable management of natural resources, enshrined in s 4 of the Environment (Wales) Act (sub-ss 4(e) and (h), respectively) and are highly relevant to the matters in hand. Finally, and importantly giving cognisance to the damage wrought to the hillside above Pentre, s 4(f) identifies the 'benefits and intrinsic value of natural resources and ecosystems' as one of the principles of sustainable management of natural resources. All these factors support the District Council's arguments for an expansive approach to injunctive relief here.

Remedies

To this end, in addition to awarding damages to the District Council in regard to damage to the highway, injunctive relief to protect the highway is also required and this must engage with the environmental and human impacts of the tips. In addition to geology, hydrology, weather conditions and the interaction between them, this Court must look in the round at the multiple dimensions of the interface between these natural systems and their human counterparts. Furthermore, the District Council contends that emerging thinking that seeks to account for the linkage of human and abiotic nature concerns is incorporated in Welsh legal provision. To flesh out the content of this argument, the Council refers to soft law coverage in international law, notably the Council of Europe, Council of Ministers Recommendation Rec (2004)3 on conservation of the geological heritage and areas of special geological interest. The District Council argues that this cutting-edge recommendation recognises that we cannot protect biotic entities (humans included) without acknowledging that geodiversity (as defined by John E Gordon and Hugh F Barron (2012): 'Valuing Geodiversity and Geoconservation: Developing a More Strategic Ecosystem Approach', 128 *Scottish Geographical Journal*, 297):

> forms the foundation of ecosystem services through its influence on landscape, habitats and species, economic activities, climate change adaptation, sustainable management of the land, river catchments and the coast, historical and cultural heritage, and people's health and well-being. (298)

This type of systems thinking on the intertwined nature of human and environmental concerns must be to the fore in dealing with the adverse impacts of extractive industries. Without careful and conscious consideration, the abiotic environment is, as in this case, particularly vulnerable to being viewed in a narrowly instrumental and economics-dominated light, as a profit-generating resource and a dumping ground for spoil – ultimately at significant cost to the biotic elements of ecosystems and neighbouring humans. Read together, the

Environment (Wales) Act and Well-being of Future Generations (Wales) Act offer legal avenues to recognise the intrinsic and instrumental value of abiotic entities and human/institutional responsibility to respect and protect it. This Court attributes the landslides and the consequent damage to Cory Brothers' indiscriminate and profligate tipping in a location that was already known to be risky. Cory Brothers has profited hugely from its cavalier business practices at the expense of the natural environment and the neighbouring community (landowners or not) and damningly, it continued to act without due regard to the consequences of its activities, despite the 1909 disaster.

At the same time, Cory Brothers has unilaterally imposed the costs of its actions on the environment, creating an unstable hillside, and on neighbouring property owners, and the community of Pentre as a whole, where the population lives in the knowledge of the landslides associated with the mine. In consequence, upholding the approach adopted by Sarjant J at first instance, this Court confirms the perpetual injunction against further dumping awarded at first instance) and extends its scope to the entire area of the Estate above the Pentre. It also awards a further injunction, mandating an independent survey and remedial works be carried out by Cory Brothers, requiring it to stabilise, and where this is not possible, remove, previously dumped material in order to ensure the stability of the mountainside in the long term. These measures are required given the scale and nature of the changes that Cory Brothers has wrought on the mountain, their dangerous interaction with topography and local weather conditions, and the evident and continuing threat posed to the road and the community of Pentre by this site, now and stretching far into the future. The works in question must, as far as is practicable, remedy damage to the mountainside, giving due consideration to both its intrinsic and instrumental value. The outcome will protect the mountain, and in turn the interests of the whole local community of Pentre now and for future generations.

Commentary

Joanne Hawkins

Introduction

'The past is a foreign country: they do things differently there.'[21] Climate change and ongoing environmental degradation are drawing ever-increasing attention to the intertwined relationship between human activity and the environment and nature. Yet surprisingly little change is visible in our approach to tortfeasors' actions and the environment since the *Cory Brothers* judgment was handed down more than a century ago. Against this backdrop, the rewriting of the judgment offers a timely opportunity to consider, very much live, questions about how we engage with tortfeasors' acts or omissions and their impact on both the environment and affected humans. In reimagining the case, we are offered the chance to explore and interrogate the underpinnings and assumptions (the dominance of economics and privileging of private property rights) that shape how we deal with this interplay.

The Judgments

Original Judgment

As outlined in Lady Morrow's introduction, the case concerned the Cory Brothers' liability under negligence, and *Rylands v Fletcher*,[22] in relation to its colliery in South Wales, following a 1916 landslide caused by deposits of mining spoil. The House of Lords' decision establishes a clear link between the environment, and human (extractive) activities in the context of a tort law claim. Throughout the judicial reasoning, there is visible use of scientific evidence, Viscount Haldane explicitly discussing the geological formation, and Lord Shaw noting the insufficient study, on the part of the colliery, of relevant geological and climatic circumstances.[23]

Yet, in considering the extent to which the original case truly engages with the interplay between environmental issues and human activity, there are four key limitations. First, whilst the original judgment indicates a willingness to engage with scientific evidence, the framing of this consideration is highly technocratic and reductionist.[24] This framing risks furthering the paradigm of mastery and exploitation that we often see in the context of extractives, to the detriment of the environment. Second, utilising this common law approach for environmental protection presents practical challenges. Such action depends on affected

[21] Leslie Poles Hartley, *The Go-Between* (Hamish Hamilton, 1953) 1.
[22] *Rylands v Fletcher* UKHL 1, (1868) LR 3 HL 330.
[23] *Attorney General v Cory Brothers & Co Ltd* (n 13) paras 530, 546.
[24] ibid.

individuals with privileged property interests to bring the relevant claims. Third, these cases are focused on current and past damage, limiting the scope of protection to damage already done, and failing to offer any guarantee that financial compensation will actually be used to rectify damage done to the environment.[25]

Fourth, and most fundamental, these limitations are situated within a system where an economic approach to harm dominates. The underlying individualised approach, where entitlement through property is key to accessing the law, restricts how we engage with the impacts of tortfeasors' actions on both the environment and affected humans.[26] This overarching dominance of economics and privileging of private property rights in the original judgment is a state of affairs that, despite the passing of more than a century, has seen little change.[27] This limitation, which privileges select groups, and oppresses both the non-privileged humans and the environment, is an underpinning theme that is challenged in the reimagined judgment.

Reimagined Judgment

Lady Morrow's reimagined judgment offers a refreshing approach. At a time when the climate crisis is drawing ever-greater attention to the intersection of humans and the environment, this offers an opportunity to shift the way that both the law, and we as lawyers, engage with this relationship. The rewritten judgment, and its ecofeminist approach (an approach that focusses on the intrinsic value of the environment and the inclusion of excluded human voices) draws to the fore the factors that were notably absent from the original judgment: damage to the environment, exposing the existing community to risk, and exposing future generations to risk. In highlighting these absences, the judgment redraws the boundaries of the relevant debates, offering ecofeminist insights into how to address the gaps exposed.

The recognition of the problematic link between extractive industries and the exploitation of nature is visible throughout the reimagined judgment and is key to addressing the four limitations identified (above) in the original judgment. First, Lady Morrow's inclusion of additional voices (ie not just property and economic interests) helps in moving beyond a highly technocratic and reductionist framing by rendering alternative framings explicitly visible within the judicial process. Further, it helps in moving beyond the second original limitation: reliance on a privileged group of voices to act. It achieves this by removing the exclusionary effect of a focus solely on property, creating space within the process for the voices of previously non-privileged humans (ie those without property or economic interests) and the environment, and expanding the pool who can take action.

[25] *Attorney General v Cory Brothers & Co Ltd* (n 13) para 524; J Steele 'Private Law and the Environment: Nuisance in Context' (1995) 15(2) *Legal Studies* 236, 241.

[26] Steele, ibid.

[27] *Anthony and others v The Coal Authority* [2005] EWHC 1654.

The reimagined judgment shows that this inclusion is not an abstract concept and evidences how existing principles, and practices, can help in making this move – for example, principles of sustainable resource management (enshrined in s 4 Environment (Wales) Act 2016 requiring sustainable management of natural resources and public participation in decision-making), and duties placed on public bodies under the Well-being of Future Generations (Wales) Act 2015 (to pursue, and involve a diverse range of people in, sustainable development, which promotes not only economic well-being, but also social, environmental and cultural well-being).[28] These mechanisms call for inclusion of a wider range of voices in decision-making (opening up potential for future legal challenges where public bodies fail to do so) and allows for an expansive approach to injunctive relief as seen in this case.

Third, in moving beyond the focus upon past damage, the issue of legacy in the reimagined judgment is of particular note. Whilst active large-scale coal mining may no longer dominate the Welsh, or British, landscape, the legacy of these activities very much remains. Engagement with this issue of legacy is neglected in the original judgment. Genuine engagement with, and reflection on legacy as seen in the reimagined judgment, has significant benefits. First, it considers ongoing risks to current and future local communities (acknowledging the centrality of affected human communities)[29] and to the environment, and how to safeguard against this. Second, it allows for engagement with the ongoing structural implications of extractive developments.

These structural implications can materialise in a number of forms, for example natural resource dependence. This occurs where resource-rich areas (which are paradoxically poor economically) become locked into ongoing acceptance of reinvestment in extractive (or associated) industries even when they, and the environment, have been negatively impacted. Whilst those with property or economic interests may be offered protection through private law claims, as seen in the original *Cory Brothers* judgment, the original approach perpetuates the impacts on excluded voices and interests (ie non-privileged humans, future generations and the environment) through its economic approach to harm.[30] Arguably, legacy is a challenging issue to address.

However, Lady Morrow's judgment shows how we can address future generations, and their exposure to risk, in a less speculative way. Her approach utilises the legally binding common purpose, the seven well-being goals, under the Well-being of Future Generations (Wales) Act 2015.[31] Although subject to potential

[28] Future Generations (Wales) Act 2015 ss 4–5.

[29] Charles Roche et al, 'A Mining Legacies Lens: From Externalities to Wellbeing in Extractive Industries' (2021) 8(3) *Extractive Industries and Society*, 3.

[30] Stephanie A Malin, Stacia Ryder and Mariana Galvao Lyra, 'Environmental Justice and Natural Resource Extractions' (2019) 2(5) *Environmental Sociology* 109.

[31] This duty applies to public bodies: national government, local government, local health boards and other specified public bodies.

institutional culture challenges, ensuring that not only is space made for, but that weight is attached to previously excluded voices is key to making sure they are not simply dominated again by traditional economic approaches.[32] Whilst this promising approach currently only applies in Wales, this novel statutory approach to legacy extends beyond property to encompass the well-being and rights of affected communities and, crucially, future communities. This provides an opportunity to lift the oppressive and exclusionary approach that dominates the original judgment, in an effort to include excluded voices and interests utilising currently available, and established, legal mechanisms in Wales. Further, it presents the opportunity to work on embedding local frames and developing notions of local resilience.

Fourth, and underpinning much of the above, the reimagined judgment draws out the intertwined relationship between human activity and the environment and nature, and the artificiality of privileging economic and property voices. Exploitation of extractives, in particular coal, presents very clear conflicts in the dual role that human activities play in being driven by, and affecting, the environment and nature.[33] This generates complexity and unpredictability, prompting calls, both here and more widely, for active reflection on existing legal frameworks, and the nature of the legal reasoning embedded within them and associated legal disputes.[34] Given this, the dominance of economics and privileging of private property rights is ever more problematic, and the need for inclusion of previously excluded voices, as seen in Lady Morrow's reimagined judgment, is ever more pressing.

The reimagined judgment offers a potential avenue through which to engage with, and move past, this current artificiality in the context of tortfeasors and the environment and affected humans.

Final Remarks

Re-engagement with the *Cory Brothers* case reminds us that the environment is not a passive object simply available for exploitation at our whim. Lady Morrow's judgment, and her ecofeminist approach, provides us with an opportunity to elevate the presence of the environment, and previously non-privileged humans, in judicial reasoning.

Lady Morrow's judgment prompts us to engage with some of the deeper underlying challenges associated with the way in which we currently treat the

[32] See eg Suzanna Nesom and Eleanor MacKillop 'What Matters in the Implementation of Sustainable Development Policies? Findings from the Well-Being of Future Generations (Wales) Act, 2015' (2021) 23(4) *Journal of Environmental Policy and Planning* 432.

[33] Brita Broham, *Legal Design for Social-Ecological Resilience* (Cambridge University Press, 2021) 1.

[34] Elizabeth Fisher, Eloise Scotford and, Emily Barritt, 'The Legally Disruptive Nature of Climate Change' (2017) 80(2) *MLR* 173.

environment in tort law claims: our ongoing exploitation of nature. With the challenges posed by climate change, and ever-growing need for resilience, we cannot continue to treat the environment as an incidental. Our historic and continued privileging of a narrow range of property and economic interests in cases such as the original *Cory Brothers* litigation demands re-evaluation. This may require what appear to be radical shifts in underpinnings and approaches, yet with the pressing importance of the intertwined relationship between human activity and the environment, perhaps the time is ripe for a shift away from a human-centric economic approach to one that privileges care of (previously non-privileged) communities and the environment, encompassing previously excluded voices, over capitalism and the paradigm of mastery.

PART II

Subjectivities

5

Swale Water v Swale Water Workers for Marshes Coalition: Dangerous Work Through the Lens of Earth Law

ANIA ZBYSZEWSKA

The fictional judgment of the UK Employment Appeals Tribunal (EAT) that follows builds on and expands case law relating to employee refusal to perform work that they deem dangerous to their or other persons' health and safety. Specifically, the decision reinterprets the protections against detrimental treatment, including dismissal, which are available to employees (and workers) who refuse to work or who take other 'appropriate' steps to protect themselves because they believed they or other persons were in 'serious and imminent danger' (ss 44 and 100 Employment Rights Act 1996 (ERA)). These statutory protections suspend the implied common law duty to obey the employer's directions, and the breach of that duty as the basis for summary dismissal. Crucially, unlike 'normal' dismissal claims which require employees to have sufficient length of service with the employer, the section 100 protection operates from the first day of employment.

The protections provided by sections 44 and 100 are relatively untested, albeit health and safety hazards ensuing from the COVID-19 pandemic led to more claims utilizing these provisions. Thus far, Employment Tribunals (ETs) and EATs have interpreted these non-detriment provisions in a relatively expansive way. Most recently, those in the wider category of workers, rather than employees, were found to benefit from these provisions.[1] In earlier rulings, tribunals have also adopted a wide definition of danger[2] and interpreted the category of persons to whom serious and imminent danger is posed to include members of the broader public.[3] My fictional judgment continues along this trajectory to expand the right not to be subject to detrimental treatment or dismissal to circumstances where

[1] *R (on application of the IWGB) v Secretary of State for Work and Pensions and others* [2020] EWHC 3050.

[2] *Harvest Press Limited v McCaffrey* [1999] IRLR 778.

[3] *Masiak v City Restaurants* [1999] IRLR 780.

the work refusal is linked to a belief that the work poses serious and imminent danger to *all beings* and the *local ecosystem*. It should be noted that the whistleblowing provisions under ERA already protect workers who disclose information about environmental harms. These provisions are not at issue here. Notably, however, even these whistleblowing provisions enumerate environmental risks and breaches of health and safety as separate, rather than interconnected, categories of harm. This, as I explain below, relates to the broader disconnect between legal regimes that regulate labour and employment, on the one hand, and environmental matters (including those that stem from business activities), on the other. The ERA provisions at issue do not make any references to environmental danger or harm, nor have they been interpreted in that way so far. Contra this, my judgment casts danger to the environment as inseparable from the dangers posed to a worker's (or other persons') corporeal health and safety, and vice versa. Namely, it interprets 'other persons' – a term already understood to encompass the broader public – to include all beings within the ecological system, encompassing human and non-human, biotic and abiotic, life. In so doing, my judgment subverts labour and employment law's anthropocentrism and reimagines what our approach to danger at work might look like through the lens of Earth law. The relational ontology that underpins this move is also applied to another aspect of the judgment – namely, its acknowledgement that the relevant legal protections should apply to workers acting collectively, not merely to an individual worker's actions. An employment law that takes ecological interconnectedness seriously must also recognise plurality of voices, actions and subjectivities alongside, or instead of, the autonomy and singularity it tends to prioritise.

Labour and Employment Law in an Ecological Key

What might it mean to think of labour and its regulation ecologically, as a constitutive element of Earth law? My own ecological perspective is influenced by feminist political ecology, as well as critical and feminist engagements with work and labour.

My work reflects on the enduring legacy – and gendered consequences – of the once-dominant models of work regulation; a legacy that is visible also in their post-Fordist reregulation. From the perspective of legal scholarship informed by feminist political economy, the crucial starting point for thinking about modern labour law's exclusionary operation is the historically specific separation of spaces of so-called 'productive' and social reproductive activity.[4] From that, feminist

[4] Adelle Blackett, *Everyday Transgressions: Domestic Workers' Transnational Challenge to International Labor Law* (Cornell University Press, 2019); Ania Zbyszewska, 'Regulating Work with People and 'Nature' in Mind: Feminist Reflections' (2018) 40 *Comparative Labour Law and Policy Journal* 101; Judy Fudge, 'Feminist Reflections on the Scope of Labour Law' (2014) 21 *Feminist Legal Studies* 1; Joanne Conaghan and Kerry Rittich, 'Introduction: Interrogating the Work/Family Divide'

scholars have shown, follows the devaluing or outright exclusion of some forms of work from labour and employment law's consideration – often women's work, or work gendered female, carried out within the home, the work of care, and so on.[5] And this is not to say that labour law produces exclusions only along gender lines: class, race, location in colonial matrix of power,[6] but also ability, age and sexuality in their various intersections are other key relations on the basis of which exclusions are (re)produced. Thinking about the relationship between production and social reproduction helps illuminate that the normative separation of what are in fact interconnected activities of supporting and reproducing life is labour and employment law's core feature. From this perspective, which foregrounds instead the material interconnection and entwining of these activities, treating them as separate is also labour and employment law's core problem.

My feminist ecological perspective builds on, and further expands, these insights by drawing on the conceptual contributions of feminist political ecology, which centres the inherent linkages between Earth's ecology and the labour of producing and reproducing life. It also draws attention to their simultaneous exploitation under patriarchal, capitalist and colonial forms alike. Like social reproduction, Earth's ecology is the condition of possibility for what are deemed 'productive' activities.[7] Yet, the same rapacious and extractive logic that subordinates and exploits labour, including that of social reproduction, for economic gain and to fuel capitalism, devours natural resources and spews waste back at a rate that threatens the viability of life on the planet, albeit with more immediate and severe consequences to some bodies and lives than others.[8] As such, these spheres are already entwined, even if the relations between them are under conditions of capitalism, colonialism and patriarchy ones of domination, extraction and depletion, rather than sustenance, care and enlivenment.

Despite these material interconnections, much like the taken-for-granted work of social reproduction, ecological concerns have for the most part been excluded

in Joanne Conaghan and Kitty Rittich (eds), *Labour Law, Work, and Family: Critical and Comparative Perspectives* (Oxford University Press, 2005).

[5] Blackett, *Everyday Transgressions*; Lydia Hayes, *Stories of Care: A Labour of Law* (Palgrave Macmillan, 2017); Nicole Busby, *A Right to Care?* (Oxford University Press, 2011); Judy Fudge and Rosemary Owens, *Precarious Work, Women, and the New Economy: The Challenge to Legal Norms* (Hart Publishing, 2006).

[6] Daniela Muradas and Flavia Souza Maximo. 'Decolonial Thinking and Brazilian Labour Law: Contemporary Intersectional Subjections' (2018) 9 *Direito e Praxis* 4.

[7] Silvia Federici, *Caliban and the Witch. Women, the Body and Primitive Accumulation* (Autonomedia, 2004); Silvia Federici, *Revolution at Point Zero: Housework, Reproduction, and Feminist Struggle* (Autonomedia, 2012); Nancy Fraser, 'Behind Marx's Hidden Abode: For an Expanded Conception of Capitalism' in Penelope Deutscher and Cristina Lafont (eds) *Critical Theory in Critical Times: Transforming the Global Political And Economic Order* (Columbia University Press, 2017).

[8] Maria Mies, *Patriarchy and Accumulation on a World Scale: Women and the International Division of Labour* (Zed Books, 2014); Ariel Salleh, *Eco-sufficiency and Global Justice: Women Write Political Ecology* (Pluto Press, 2009); Maria Lugones, 'Towards a Decolonial Feminism' (2010) 25 (Special Issue: Feminist Legacies/Feminist Futures) *Hypatia* 742; Mary Mellor, 'Ecofeminist Political Economy. Integrating Feminist Economics and Ecological Economics' (2005) 11 *Feminist Economics* 120.

from modern law's approach to regulation of work.[9] As others have argued, modern legal frameworks have engendered and juridically reproduced Enlightenment-era logics that position humans as *apart* from 'nature' rather than as a part of the living Earth.[10] This anthropocentric (and androcentric) bias informs employment law too;[11] indeed, critical environmental scholars have levelled the same critique at environmental law itself.[12] Thus, while legal frameworks extend protections to both workers and 'environments', the jurisdictional division of labour that characterises modern law's approach to social and environmental matters tends to maintain each field's autonomy and reach. This is despite the underlying material entanglements between human labour, its more-than-human collaborators, and their mutual environmental conditions and socio-ecologies they enact together. This is consequential in that it obscures and impedes closer scrutiny of labour and employment law's tethering to unsustainable economic models associated with modernity and capitalism.[13] A key exception is the area of occupational health and safety, which does address environmental conditions, albeit drawing a fairly tight boundary around workplace environment.[14] Given this affinity between health and safety and environment, the fictional judgment focuses on protections pertaining to danger at work understood as a risk to health and safety.

When our starting point is interconnection, interdependence, relationality, and recognition that the labour process and the employment relation are possible only because of webs of more-than-human life in its various forms, it becomes impossible to detach an employee from their community or their local ecosystem of beings. Embracing the recognition that each worker, and workers collectively, are socio-ecologically embedded relational beings has implications for how we are to understand what workplace health and safety entails; what it means for work to be dangerous; and what steps might be appropriate and available in a situation

[9] Zbyszewska, 'Regulating Work'.

[10] Fritjof Capra and Ugo Matei, *The Ecology of Law: Toward a Legal System in Tune with Nature and Community* (Berrett-Koehler, 2015); Anna Grear, 'Vulnerability, Advanced Global Capitalism and Co-symptomatic Injustice: Locating the Vulnerable Subject' in Martha A Fineman and Anna Grear (eds), *Vulnerability: Reflections on a New Ethical Foundation for Law and Politics* (Ashgate, 2013).

[11] Anastasia Tataryn, *Law, Migration and Precarious Labour: Ecotechnics of the Social* (Routledge, 2021); Supriya Routh, 'Embedding Work in Nature: Anthropocene and Law' (2018) 40 *Comparative Labour Law and Policy Journal* 29; Zbyszewska, 'Regulating Work'.

[12] Margherita Pieraccini, 'Rethinking Participation in Environmental Decision-Making: Epistemologies of Marine Conservation in South-East England' (2015) 27 *Journal of Environmental Law* 45; Andreas Philippopoulos-Mihalopoulos, 'Looking for the Space between Law and Ecology' in Andreas Philippopoulos-Mihalopoulos (ed) *Law and Ecology: New Environmental Foundations* (Routledge, 2011).

[13] Stefania Barca, 'The Labor(s) of Degrowth' (2017) 30 *Capitalism Nature Socialism* 207; JB Foster and B Clark, 'Marx's Ecology and the Left' (2016) 68 *Monthly Review* 1; Capra and Matei, *Ecology of Law*.

[14] Kerrie Blaise and Nadia Ibrahim, *Workers' Environmental Rights in Canada.* A Project with Adapting Canadian Work and Workplaces to Respond to Climate Change (ACW, 2021) cela.ca/wp-content/uploads/2021/07/Workers-Environmental-Rights-in-Canada_Full-Report.pdf, 202; Alexis Bugada and Cohen-Donsimoni, '"Green" Collective Bargaining in France' (2021) 10 *E-Journal of International and Comparative Labour Studies* 4.

where work harms or poses danger to health, safety and life. Ecologically attuned labour and employment law must refuse the fiction of a bounded, autonomous subject of rights.[15] The speculative judgment that I have written attempts to give effect to this perspective.

The Fictional Judgment

Unlike the majority of other contributions in this book, the EAT judgment in *Swale Water v Swale Water Workers for Marshes Coalition* is not a result of rewriting an existing case but rather an exercise is 'speculative' judgment writing. This decision was taken in part for pragmatic reasons: finding an appropriate employment law case that tackled environmental concerns proved difficult. Instead, while the case and the judgment I produced are themselves fictional, the factual matrix underpinning them is inspired by a real case, albeit one not dealing with employment law directly.

Specifically, the starting point for the judgment was the sentencing remarks delivered on 9 July 2021 by Justice Johnson in the case of *Environment Agency v Southern Water Services Limited*,[16] in which he ordered Southern Water to pay a fine of £90 million.[17] The case stemmed from an investigation and prosecution by the Environment Agency, with Southern Water Services Limited (Southern Water) pleading guilty to fifty-one counts of discharging untreated sewage into controlled coastal waters. These offences were committed at seventeen separate wastewater treatment sites over a six-year period from January 2010 to December 2015. In that period, there were a total of 6,971 discharges of untreated sewage into controlled waters, amounting to an estimated total 16–21 billion litres of sewage. All seventeen sites are located along the north Kent coast and the Solent; and all are in proximity to or within areas of special protection as 'precious and delicate ecosystems'.[18]

As Justice Johnson observes in his remarks, this was not the first time that Southern Water had been indicted and fined for pollution.[19] In this particular investigation, the Environment Agency had faced significant resistance from the company, and several employees convicted of obstructing an investigation cited 'instructions from managers or the Defendant's solicitors' as reasons for interfering with the Agency's efforts.[20] Justice Johnson noted that – and this point is key in

[15] Sara Seck, 'Transnational Labour Law and the Environment: Beyond the Bounded Autonomous Worker' (2018) 33 *Canadian Journal of Law & Society* 137.

[16] The sentencing remarks are available from Courts and Tribunals Judiciary website: judiciary.uk/judgments/environment-agency-v-southern-water-services-limited/.

[17] ibid para 1.

[18] ibid para 2.

[19] ibid para 10.

[20] ibid para 11.

my fictional judgment – Southern Water employees knew of the company's practices. At the Eastchurch Wastewater Treatment Works, for example, 'employees were well aware'[21] of the operational irregularities that led to multiple discharges of untreated sewage into nearby Windmill Creek. In fact, many different employees – both technical and lower management – reported these problems to management but were ignored.[22] As Justice Johnson notes, 'The number and the nature of these reports is such that it is inconceivable that the company, at the highest level, was unaware of the problems.'[23] These findings suggest that at least some of the company's employees refused to passively 'turn a blind eye'. While it is possible that those workers who did not complain simply lacked care, another plausible explanation is that they were concerned about the consequences of complaining. They may not have felt that the legal frameworks intended to protect them in challenging their employer's practices were sufficiently robust to actually do so in their specific circumstances.

The fictional case below imagines a different scenario. It involves a group of technical employees of Swale Water, a fictional water treatment company located in south-east England, and their efforts to challenge their employer's illegal practices. Rather than act individually, the employees act collectively. Leaving their usual work positions, these workers organised to inform the public by setting up a picket in front of the Swale Water Wastewater Treatment Works. Swale Water suspended all employees involved without pay, and subsequently terminated their employment. The judgment that follows pertains to Swale Water's partial appeal of the ET decision in the original claim that the Coalition brought under sections 44 and 100 ERA, in which the Tribunal found the company to have subjected the employees to detrimental treatment and unfair dismissal for their actions.

The judgment is speculative in that it uses a fictional scenario but builds on previous jurisprudence to reinterpret these ERA sections, focusing on the meaning of 'other persons' and 'appropriate steps'– both of which are elements that are central to making out relevant claims. The reinterpretation of the category of 'other persons' to highlight relationality and interconnectedness is the linchpin of the judgment's ecological approach. Rather than engage in discussion on expanding legal personhood to encompass all beings as rights-bearing subjects, the judgment interprets the phrase 'other persons' to convey that human workers or employees are *of their ecosystem*: that is, they are not just embedded within an ecosystem but rather a part of it, and as such, enmeshed in relations with all other beings that comprise that ecosystem. Furthermore, the judgment critically engages with the individualist conception of rights by recognising the right to act collectively as an expression of mutual care and relational species-being. From this perspective, the legal protections at issue can be understood as facilitating the reproduction of

[21] ibid para 24.
[22] ibid paras 24, 25.
[23] ibid para 32(2).

relationality; through granting protection for workers acting not just for their own sake, but also in solidarity with each other and all other beings, human and non-human alike. In so doing, the judgment challenges the normative assumptions about liberal law's ideal subject, which are reproduced in labour and employment law too, despite its avowedly distinct (including collective and emancipatory) orientation.

Concluding Thoughts: On the Challenges and Possibilities of Speculative Legal Fiction

The exercise of drafting a speculative judgment was a challenge, not least given my misgivings about the corrosive effects of the dominant (liberal) legal form. Would channelling ecological thinking through a form with particular origin and enduring legacy not undermine the very exercise of rethinking employment law anew, as one that is broadly relational and ecologically attuned? Would another form, or methodology, not be more appropriate given the different ontological starting point? In some ways, the tension between the formality of a legal judgment, and the speculative case-making and subversive interpretation of the technical legal provisions have produced an outcome that does not appear all that far-fetched; on the contrary, it appears plausible. At the same time, modern law, including norms that pertain to regulation of work, remains embedded in, and reproductive of, capitalist modernity and thus of hierarchical power relations as opposed to relations of mutual care, connectedness and sustenance. I am not sure that a Tribunal judgment that is not imagined, as the one I have written is, can realistically foreground and prioritise the latter so long as subordination (of humans and non-humans alike) is a normatively accepted, even if ameliorated, status quo.

Appeal No UKEAT/9999/15/ZZ*

Employment Appeals Tribunal

Some House, Some Square, Somewhere

At the Tribunal
On 22 April 2015

Before

HER HONOUR JUDGE ZBYSZEWSKA

(SITTING ALONE)

SWALE WATER	APPELLANT
SWALE WATER WORKERS FOR MARSHES COALITION	RESPONDENT

JUDGMENT

HER HONOUR JUDGE ZBYSZEWSKA

1. This is an appeal by Swale Water (the Appellant) against a judgment of the Employment Tribunal (ET). The Respondent is a Coalition composed of four former employees of the Appellant company, acting collectively.

2. In its judgment, the ET accepted the Coalition's claims of unlawful detriment pursuant to s 44 (health and safety) Employment Rights Act 1996 ('the ERA') and unfair dismissal pursuant to s 100 ERA (health and safety).

3. The Appellant company is challenging the ET's decision, in part, on the basis that it erred in its interpretation and application of these statutory provisions. At issue is the ET's interpretation of the terms 'other persons' and 'appropriate steps' in ss 44(1)(e) and 100(1)(e) ERA.

The Background Facts

4. The Appellant company provides water treatment and sewage disposal services and has numerous facilities located across southeastern United Kingdom. Many of these facilities are located along the coast.

5. The Respondent Coalition is composed of four former employees who worked for the Appellant in its facility located in the town of Swale. All four employees commenced their employment between October 2011 and May 2012.

6. All four employees gave evidence that they personally observed numerous instances, going back to at least 2012, of the facility's storm tanks overflowing and being flushed into Winding Creek, which flows through protected marshlands and into the local river, and in turn into the sea.

7. In early 2013, one of the employees learned from a friend working as a marine biologist that her research station had observed high E-coli counts in the coastal waters and a significant decline in the local oyster and shellfish population. Shortly after this, she read news reports of faecal contamination of beaches along the Long coast and of the Wistful oyster beds. She raised the issue with her line managers and the company's health and safety committee on several occasions in 2013 and 2014. She states that her concerns were dismissed, and that she was repeatedly told that these incidents occurred only during storms and heavy rainfall and were within the scope of the permitted discharges and in compliance with regulatory standards.

8. The Respondent Coalition was formed in September 2014, following one of Swale Water's annual Corporate Social Responsibility shoreline clean-up campaigns, in which the four former employees participated. During this clean-up, the four employees learned of each other's concerns about the company's practices pertaining to discharges of untreated sewage. All four, on various occasions, took their concerns to senior management but were ignored.

9. On 20 January 2015, after observing another episode of wastewater spillage, all four employees approached their line manager. As before, they were told that the discharge complied with regulatory standards and were reprimanded for taking time away from their work. At that point, the four employees refused to continue working, citing danger to their own health and safety, and to the health and safety of the local community, the local marshlands, and the broader marine ecosystem. After leaving their positions, the coalition members set up an information picket in front of the treatment works and called the local press with the aim of drawing the community's attention to Swale Water's discharges of untreated water into Winding Creek.

10. The company suspended all four employees without pay on 20 January 2015. They remained at the picket during the following week. On 27 January 2015, the company sent them dismissal letters, citing insubordination and unauthorised absence as cause for dismissal.

The ET Claim and the Decision

11. The Coalition's claim of detrimental treatment, in the form of suspension without pay, and unfair dismissal, pursuant to ss 44(1)(d) and (e) and 100(1)(d) and (e) ERA, respectively, was upheld by the ET. These provisions create protections against detrimental treatment, including dismissal, for employees who refuse to work or who take other appropriate steps to protect themselves because they believe they or other persons are in serious and imminent danger stemming from work-related activity.

12. The ET received oral evidence and the facts recited above draw on its findings.

13. The burden of proof is on the employer to demonstrate that the principal reason for detrimental treatment or dismissal did not fall within the scope of the protections in ss 44 and 100 ERA, respectively. The ET observed that the employer's reason for detrimental treatment or dismissal is a set of facts known to the employer, or beliefs that they held, which caused them to dismiss the employee (*Aberenthy v Mott, Hay and Anderson* [1974] ICR 323). It noted that identification of the employer's reason should be approached in light of the context and purpose of the legislative provisions.

14. In dealing with both sections, the ET pointed out that the test to be applied is not only whether the employee genuinely feared for their safety, but whether that fear was based on reasonable grounds. This is a question of fact, to be determined not only by the nature of the potential danger (ie whether it is 'serious and imminent') but by the steps that the employee could have taken to follow any procedures laid down by the employer that would mitigate against the danger (*Kerr v Nathan's Wastesavers Ltd* EAT 91/95).

15. In assessing the reasonableness of the employee's belief that there was serious and imminent danger, the ET noted that it must look to the specific circumstances of the case and the conditions of the workplace, including any guidance and policies that the employee has received from the employer in relation to dealing with danger at work. It followed *Kerr v Nathan's Wastesavers Ltd*, where the EAT held, albeit with respect to s 100(1)(c), that 'in considering what is reasonable, care should be taken not to place an onerous duty of enquiry on the employee'. The ET noted that there is no reason why this standard should not be applied to inquiry under ss 100(1)(d) and (e).

16. The ET observed that, provided the employee had a reasonable belief that there was serious and imminent danger and acted in response to that belief, they will be covered by ss 44 and 100. The employer cannot avoid the protection merely because they disagreed with the employee about the danger in question (*Oudahar v Esporta Group Limited* [2011] IRLR 730 EAT).

17. The ET found the original Claimants (Respondents in this appeal) individually and collectively to be believable and sincere. Conversely, it found the company's management representatives who testified to be evasive and unable to provide a good explanation for their unresponsiveness to the employees' concerns and failure to follow the company's safety procedures.

18. The ET accepted that the Coalition's members acted in response to what they perceived to be a significant threat or danger that was not only imminent but already ongoing, in light of their knowledge of prior incidents of waste spillage. Given the well-publicised dangers associated with faecal contamination of local waterways that the Coalition members had observed, and which was also within the knowledge of Swale Water management, the Coalition's belief that a danger was present or imminent was found to be reasonable. The ET also agreed that the reasonably held belief in this case pertained to danger affecting health and safety of the workers, as well as that of the local community and the ecosystem at large. Furthermore, the ET accepted the Coalition's evidence on their previous efforts to address the problem with management, and found that, given the latter's unresponsiveness and its failure to follow its own safety procedures, it was also reasonable to conclude, as the employees did, that it was impossible to avert the danger in any other way than by refusing to return to work, and by alerting the public to the danger.

19. The ET found that the employer's decision to suspend and terminate the Coalition members was directly related to the latter's actions. The Tribunal held that, in the circumstances at hand, engaging in work refusal was a protected action within the meaning of ss 44(1)(d) and 100(1)(d), because it was taken by the employees on the basis of a reasonable belief that there was serious and imminent danger to their own safety and the safety of other persons, which they could not otherwise avert. Similarly, the ET found that the information picket organised by the employees fell within the meaning of 'reasonable steps' for the purpose of ss 44(1)(e) and 100(1)(e). As such, the ET held that the decision to suspend the employees without pay amounted to detrimental treatment (s 44 ERA), while their terminations constituted unfair dismissal (s 100 ERA).

The Appeal

20. The Appellant company argues that the ET erred in law in its interpretation and application of ss 44(1)(e) and 100(1)(e) ERA.

21. The Appellant accepts the ETs findings pertaining to the employees' belief that the untreated wastewater spillage they observed constituted a serious and imminent danger and agrees with the ET's finding that this belief was reasonable in the circumstances.

22. However, the Appellant challenges the ET's interpretation of the law on two grounds. First, it questions the Tribunal's interpretation of the term 'other persons' in ss 44(1)(e) and 100(1)(e) to include the local ecosystem. Second, the Appellant disputes the ET's interpretation of 'appropriate steps' within the meaning of these provisions to include workers acting collectively and engaging in an information picket.

The Relevant Legal Principles

23. S 44 ERA 1996, which pertains to detriment, provides as follows:

> (1) An employee has the right not to be subjected to any detriment by any act, or deliberate failure to act, by his employer done on the ground that –
>
> …
>
> (d) in circumstances of danger which the employee reasonably believed to be serious and imminent and which he could not reasonably have been expected to avert, he left (or proposed to leave) or (while the danger persisted) refused to return to his place of work or any dangerous part of his place of work, or
>
> (e) in circumstances of danger which the employee reasonably believed to be serious and imminent, he took (or proposed to take) appropriate steps to protect himself or other persons from the danger.
>
> (2) For the purposes of sub-s (1)(e) whether steps which an employee took (or proposed to take) were appropriate is to be judged by reference to all the circumstances including, in particular, his knowledge and the facilities and advice available to him at the time.

Sub-ss 100(1)(d), 100(1)(e) and 100(2) are identical in terms to sub-ss 44(1)(d), 44(1)(e) and 44(2) set out above.

S 100 ERA 1996, which pertains to unfair dismissal, additionally provides that:

> (1) An employee who is dismissed shall be regarded for the purposes of this Part as unfairly dismissed if the reason (or, if more than one, the principal reason) for the dismissal is that –
>
> …
>
> (3) Where the reason (or, if more than one, the principal reason) for the dismissal of an employee is that specified in sub-s (1)(e), he shall not be regarded as unfairly dismissed if the employer shows that it was (or would have been) so negligent for the employee to take the steps which he took (or proposed to take) that a reasonable employer might have dismissed him for taking (or proposing to take) them.

24. To benefit from the protections afforded by either s 44(1)(d) and (e) or s 100 (1)(d) and (e), the employee must have acted in response to 'circumstances of danger which the employee reasonably believed to be serious and imminent'. This requirement encompasses three questions, to be determined on the facts, namely: (1) whether there were circumstances of danger, (2) whether the employee

believed the circumstances of danger were serious and imminent, and (3) whether the employee's belief was reasonable? (*Edwards and Others v Secretary of State for Justice* [2014] 7 WLUK 909).

25. Following *Harvest Press Limited v McCaffrey* [1999] IRLR 778, the danger in question need not refer to the workplace specifically. Considering s 100(1)(d), the EAT found that the term 'danger' is used without limitation, meaning that the 'Parliament was likely to have intended those words to cover any danger however originating.' In that case, abusive and threatening behaviour by a co-worker was found to constitute danger within the meaning of that legislative provision.

26. There is a related question of whether the circumstances of danger must pertain to health and safety of the *employee*, or whether it can be more widely understood. We note that in both ss 44 and 100, sub-s (1)(e) is wider, as it refers to a situation where an employee acts or proposes to act to protect themselves or 'other persons'. In *Masiak v City Restaurants* [1999] IRLR 780, the EAT interpreted 'other persons' in s 100(1)(e) to extend beyond other employees to include members of the public.

27. Ss 44(1)(e) and 100(1)(e) incorporate additional requirement that the steps taken (or proposed to be taken) by the employee be 'appropriate'. In *Oudahar v Esporta Group Limited* [2011] IRLR 730 EAT, the EAT held that the steps taken by the employee are 'to be judged by reference to all circumstances including, in particular his knowledge and the facilities and advice available to him at the time'. The latter language is the language of ss 44(2) and 100(2).

28. The protections set out in s 100(1)(e) are further circumscribed by s 100(3), which provides the employer with the defence against an employee's s 100(1)(e) claim where 'the employer shows that it was (or would have been) so negligent for the employee to take the steps which he took (or proposed to take) that a reasonable employer might have dismissed him for taking (or proposing to take) them'. It should be noted, however, that the language of the section clearly imposes on an employer an elevated burden of showing that the steps were 'negligent' as opposed to simply inappropriate. The concept of negligence signals that the employee has or would have acted below a reasonable standard of care, with the latter being dependent on the circumstances of the case, including the nature of the work in which the employee engages and the position they hold in the workplace.

Submissions

29. The Appellant company argues that the provisions in question are intended for the benefit of human beings – be they employees or members of the broader human community. They argue that the ET erred in expanding the meaning of 'other persons' to include all beings and the wider ecosystem. Such an interpretation, the Appellant argues, is inconsistent with the purpose of these provisions

which are intended to protect actions stemming from concern about human health and safety. On the issue of appropriate steps, the Appellants rely on *Balfour Kilpatrick Limited v Acheson* [2003] IRLR 683 to argue that the ET erred in finding that collective action by members of the Coalition could be considered appropriate in circumstances such as those present here. The Appellants argue that collective action of the sort in which the workers here engaged constitutes 'unofficial' industrial action as per s 237 Trade Union and Labour Relations (Consolidation) Act (TULRCA). By virtue of s 237, employees taking part in such actions cannot benefit from protections of s 100(1)(e), and by extension s 44(1)(e).

30. The Respondent Coalition maintains that the ET's interpretation was correct with respect to both issues. It asks us to uphold the ET's ruling.

Discussion

31. I disagree with the Appellant that the ET erred by adopting an expansive interpretation of the relevant provisions. The case law interpreting ss 44 and 100 ERA is not very extensive, which is curious given that these provisions provide important protections for employees. Nonetheless, previous cases suggest that tribunals have tended to interpret these provisions in a purposive and generous way, resulting in gradual expansion of their application to incorporate a wider definition of workplace-related danger to which the employees might be responding.

32. This trajectory is unsurprising when we take account of the fact that the non-detriment and unfair dismissal provisions sit alongside duties pertaining to health and safety at work that legislation imposes on employees. Most notably, s 7(a) ERA creates a legal duty to take reasonable care for the health and safety of themselves and of others who may be affected by their acts or omissions at work, which gives effect to Article 13 of EC Directive 89/391/EEC. Commenting on the relationship between employee duties created by these provisions and the right to be protected from detrimental treatment at work, the EAT, in *Balfour Kilpatrick Limited v Acheson* [2003] IRLR 683, observed that 'an employee exercising his obligations under Article 13 of the Directive – and we emphasise that they are obligations – cannot conceivably be lawfully dismissed under English Law on that account'. It follows that a similar relationship exists between s 7(a) duties and s 44 non-detriment provisions.

33. In the present case, we are faced with the question of whether further expansion of the meaning of 'danger' is consistent with the purpose of the legislation. Specifically, at issue is whether the term 'other persons' – as in persons to whose health and safety risk the employee seeking the protection of ss 44 or 100 responded – can be plausibly interpreted to mean other *beings*, and thus incorporate non-human life and the wider ecosystem. This is the interpretation adopted by the ET at first instance, which is now being challenged by the Appellant company.

34. I find unsatisfactory the reasoning that the relevant legislative scheme anticipates employees to be only concerned with and responsible for themselves and to their human communities, as the Appellant proposes: such reasoning carries the anthropocentric bias that ignores relational and ecological dynamics. Contrary to the Appellant's argument, humans do not exist in a vacuum. They are embedded in an ecosystem: a broader complex of living organisms that coexist and interrelate in a specific space (environment, which includes abiotic life). Not only does the broader ecosystem provide the conditions of possibility for humans, individually and collectively, but humans (and so, employees) are an inherent part of the web of beings and relations that constitute the ecosystem itself. It follows then that detrimental impacts on the employee's health and safety have wider implications, much as the impacts on the wider ecosystem of which the employee is a part (including other living organisms and abiotic life that comprise it) are going to also affect the employee's own health and safety. As such, while it is true that interpreting 'other persons' to mean a wider ecosystem of beings who are in relation with the worker(s) seeking the benefit of ERA provisions expands previous interpretations, we find that such an interpretation is not only plausible but in fact unavoidable in light of ecological dynamics. From a perspective that recognises socio-ecological embeddedness and relationality, the legal protections at issue here can be understood as granting protection for workers or employees acting not just for their own sake, but also in solidarity with each other and all other beings, human and non-human alike.

35. The second question in this appeal is whether or not the employees acting collectively as the Coalition took 'appropriate steps' within the meaning of sub-ss 44(1)(e) and 100(1)(e). The Appellant argues that the ET erred in finding that leaving work, refusing to return and engaging in an information picket with assistance of the press outside the Company gates were appropriate steps in light of the reasonably held belief in serious and imminent danger. The Appellant's contention is that the employees acted *collectively*, whereas the ERA protections in question here are only available to individuals.

36. The Appellant relies on *Balfour*, in which the EAT held that an action of work refusal and walk out by a group of workers who deemed their work circumstances dangerous did not benefit from protections under the ERA because it constituted an illegal industrial action, as per s 237 TULRCA. The Appellant contends that the ET erred by failing to follow the EAT in its decision.

37. I disagree with the Appellant's interpretation of *Balfour*. The EAT in that case did find that industrial action does not constitute 'reasonable means' for the purpose of s 100(1)(c); namely, engaging in industrial action is not a way to draw employers' attention to the matter of health and safety with which the employees are concerned. However, we are not dealing with a situation in which the workers were acting as members of a recognised union, although they were indeed acting collectively as members of a Coalition. In *Balfour*, the EAT made a distinction

between employees who were members of the recognised union and those who were in non-recognised union or who did not belong to a union. The EAT held that those employees in the latter category were not caught by the provisions of s 237 and could bring claims for general unfair dismissal. Furthermore, the provisions at issue in the present case pertain not to 'reasonable means' but rather 'appropriate steps'. Namely, at issue here is whether the actions of walking off the job, refusing to return, and engaging in an information picket by a group of employees acting together constitutes 'appropriate steps' within the meaning of s 100(1)(e). Accepting and applying the ecological and relational reasoning of the ET and put forward by the Respondents in this appeal, our conclusion is that these actions indeed fall within the meaning of 'appropriate steps'.

38. In *Oudahar*, the EAT held that the steps taken by the employee are 'to be judged by reference to all circumstances including … his knowledge and the facilities and advice available to him at the time'. A wide range of steps will be considered to be appropriate, and the employer's belief in whether the steps were appropriate is irrelevant (*Oudahar*). Further, employees responding to a belief in a danger that is serious and imminent should not be expected to concern themselves with electing the best route to act or communicate with the employer (*Balfour*).

39. While ss 44 and 100 are not intended to be a shortcut to industrial action, there is no express prohibition on multiple employees leaving the workplace at the same time citing these provisions (as was the case in *Balfour*; *Edwards*). Here, the employees acted as they did in response to what they perceived to be a serious and imminent danger – an issue that is not in dispute in this appeal – and they responded in the way they did in part due to the culture of silence surrounding the employer's illegal and harmful practices, including a lack of responsiveness by the company's health and safety committee. As was established during the proceedings before the Tribunal at first instance, each of these employees had individually unsuccessfully attempted in the past to draw management's attention to the danger inherent in the discharges of untreated wastewater that they observed. They each perceived these discharges to be hazardous to their own health and safety, given that they themselves reside in Swale and use its various bodies of water, and to the health and safety of others (ie the broader community and the local ecosystem of beings). Their work refusal was congruent with a refusal to perform work that was dangerous and harmful to themselves and each other. In acting together, they wished to express and enact solidarity with, and care for, their own and each other's health and safety. Similarly, the information picket, especially in light of Swale Water's culture of silence, was a means to enact the same care towards, and solidarity with, the broader Swale community and the local ecosystem of beings in which it is embedded and of which it is a part.

40. As we observed above, employees (or humans generally) are embedded and relational beings. This means that acting together in response to what employees recognise as a common danger is just as appropriate as if the employees individually

responded. To find otherwise would be to hold onto and further perpetuate the legal fiction that is the autonomous, individual, dis-embedded subject of rights. Labour law already recognises that rights can be vested in collectives of workers acting together, as in the case of the rights to associate, collectively bargain, engage in strike action (although this has been contested), or have 'voice at work' through information and consultation. Ecological and relational thinking pushes us even further, urging us to think of legal subjectivity as relational and multiple, wherein autonomy and collectivity are not mutually exclusive. Through this prism, collective action in response to serious and imminent danger may constitute appropriate steps within the meaning of s 100(1)(e).

41. Two final points have to be made, which relate to the qualifications that are imposed on s 44(1)(e) and 100(1)(e) claims. The first of these is set out by ss 44(2) and 100(2), namely that the appropriateness of the employee's steps is to be assessed with the view to all relevant circumstances, 'in particular his knowledge and the facilities and advice available to him at the time'. Furthermore, s 100(3) limits s 100(1)(e) protections by imposing on the employee a duty of care to not act negligently in exercising their protected rights under the latter section. The Tribunal held that, in light of the employer's historic unresponsiveness and the culture of silence and condonation of dangerous practices that appeared to dominate this specific workplace, the employees acted appropriately. The Tribunal also held that there was nothing negligent about the employees' actions in this case; indeed, it would have been potentially negligent for them to ignore the problems and do nothing about them. While the Appellant did not raise either of these issues in the present appeal, I agree with the ET's interpretation on this.

42. I conclude that there was no error in ET's application of the law, and thus I reject the present appeal on both grounds. The ET's expansive interpretation of the provisions in question reflects its appreciation of relational and ecological dynamics that characterize human and more-than-human interactions.

Commentary: What is it about Work that is Particularly Attentive to Ecology?

Anastasia Tataryn

The catastrophic, devastating effects of the climate crisis are irrefutable. Regular reports from scientists, the IPCC and former UN leaders remind us of the urgency to change consumption habits to avoid irreversible destruction.[24] Yet, the structures and systems of modern law and governance move slowly. This judgment contributes an example of how, working within the frame of modern law, Employment Tribunals (ETs) *could* take the step of reinterpreting existing employment law in the Employment Rights Act (ERA). Reinterpretation would challenge modern law's fixation on the individual human as the locus of law and legal subjectivity, and the reification of autonomous, independent personhood.

Scholars have for decades, if not centuries, illuminated how the individual – white, European male – has enjoyed normative status at the expense of, and through the exploitation of, women, the poor, the colonised and the 'non-human'. Capitalism, colonialism and patriarchy sustain and maintain power for a select 'person' through established, ostensibly universal, law and legal frameworks.[25] Environmental injustice, moreover, cannot be disentangled from this 'matrix of power':[26] capitalism, colonialism and patriarchy. Neither can the assessment of law's anthropocentrism – anthropocentrism being a 'crisis of human hierarchy, of global unevenness, of deepening interdependencies, of Earth system decay, of species extinction, of temporary inter- and intra-species injustices, and of intensifying patterns of human/non-human vulnerability'[27] – deny the dominance of capitalist, colonial and patriarchal values embedded in modern law.

Given that 'the Earth is an adaptive and multi-faceted system comprising human-social *and* ecological elements',[28] ecological jurisprudence welcomes a pluralistic approach to law.[29] From ETs to community-based decision making, Supreme Court rulings to employment and work contracts, ecological jurisprudence urges us to make the interconnectedness of being the starting point of law.

[24] Fiona Harvey, 'Current Policies Will Bring "Catastrophic" Environmental Breakdown, Warn Former UN Leaders', *The Guardian*, 2 June 2022, theguardian.com/environment/2022/jun/02/current-policies-will-bring-catastrophic-climate-breakdown-warn-former-un-leaders; Fiona Harvey, 'The IPCC Issues the "Bleakest Warning Yet" on Impacts of Climate Breakdown', *The Guardian*, 28 February 2022, theguardian.com/environment/2022/feb/28/ipcc-issues-bleakest-warning-yet-impacts-climate-breakdown.

[25] Elena Blanco and Anna Grear 'Personhood, Jurisdiction and Injustice: Law, Colonialities and the Global Order' (2019) 10 *Journal of Human Rights and the Environment* 86; Johanna Oksala, 'Feminism, Capitalism, and Ecology' (2018) 33 *Hypatia* 216.

[26] Anibal Quijano, 'Coloniality and Modernity/Rationality' (2007) 21 *Cultural Studies* 168.

[27] Louis J Kotzé, 'Earth System Law for the Anthropocene' (2019) 11 *Sustainability* 6796.

[28] Liam Phelan, Ann Henderson-Sellers and Ros Taplin, 'The Political Economy of Addressing the Climate Crisis in the Earth System' (2013) 18 *New Political Economy* 198, 219.

[29] Erin O'Donnell, A Poelina, A Pelizzon and C Clark, 'Stop Burying the Lede: The Essential Role of Indigenous Law(s) in Creating Rights of Nature' (2020) 9(3) *Transnational Environmental Law* 403–27.

What would this look like? Ecological relational being is awareness of the more-than-human world. Being, as an ontological state, necessarily involves more than human species.[30] Human persons cannot exist without ecologies of beings materially interacting and relating in the world and atmosphere. Human persons cannot work without ecologies of being relating in the world, as the world. Our work, our labour, and therefore our interactions of/as employment, vitally depend on ecologies of being. Workplace safety, and health and safety at work, involve complex webs of relationality beyond-the-human that depend on a healthy, functioning, ecosystem.

It may seem, for some, that to remove ourselves from modern law's anthropocentrism, we must deny the modern legal form all together. This judgment demonstrates that reinterpretation is not only possible within the frame of modern law, but accessible. The limited interpretation of personhood is outdated.[31] Personhood reinterpreted can encompass being in a wider ecosystem, especially in work and labour relations which, as inherently relational, are reliant on the circulation of human and non-human life. The claim that personhood may extend beyond human creatures may seem radical under sections 44 and 100 ERA, but is not radical when we think firstly, of the constructed, historically contingent nature of the idea of 'the human'.[32] Secondly, but not less importantly, it is not radical when we think of what is vital to facilitate our ability to work, to breathe, to eat, to produce; to be alive. This judgment does not separate the rights of nature from the rights of humans, as is the case in some interpretations and uses of Earth law.[33] Neither does it pursue a rights-based approach, which suffers repeating the same human-centric (male, European, colonial) hierarchical framework that fails to recognise ecology as a living, breathing, complex web itself.[34] Rather, the starting point of this judgment is that human beings will only have health and safety if the Earth has health and safety: the Earth is the workplace that must be protected and honoured because without its health, no one is healthy.

Attention to healthy ecosystems as a foundation of employment law is, however, neglected in modern legal frameworks. This is due to how value is attributed, and denied, in our globalised capitalist market economy. That work forms a key part of daily life may be acknowledged, yet only where work facilitates participation in capital accumulation: we hear about 'economic health' rather than 'ecological health'. Employment law reinforces a hierarchy of privilege where economically productive labour that contributes to capital growth is legally recognised at the negation of both ecological connectivity and work that is not valued as 'productive'

[30] Tataryn, *Law, Migration and Precarious Labour* 7.

[31] Erin O'Donnell, *Legal Rights for Rivers: Competition, Collaboration and Water Governance* (Routledge, 2018).

[32] Joanna Bourke, *What it Means to be Human: Historical Reflections from the 1800s to the Present.* (Virago, 2011).

[33] earthlawcenter.org/river-rights.

[34] Anna Grear, 'It's Wrongheaded to Protect Nature with Human-style Rights' (2019) *HumansandNature.org* humansandnature.org/its-wrongheaded-to-protect-nature-with-human-style-rights/.

or 'economically mobile'. The Swale Water Workers for Marshes Coalition illustrates how one's employment involves much more than the specific work of applying technical expertise, in this case within a water treatment facility. Employment and employee status do not override one's responsibility as a citizen in a community, or a resident of a locale. Responsibility to community, to protect the well-being of that community, cannot be antithetical to law, especially since law is responsive to sociality. And yet the individualistic conceptions of legal subjectivity and legal recognition under modern law privileges employer-led employment contracts over community and communal well-being. In doing so, law privileges capital accumulation and furthers the exploitation and expropriation of all bodies and beings that are 'othered' by capitalism, patriarchy and colonial expansion. We see this most clearly exemplified in law's treatment of care and domestic work, often unpaid and carried out within domestic, private, homes; in other words, 'unproductive labour'. The ambiguous commodification of care and domestic work mirrors the ambiguous treatment of ecology in labour and employment law.[35]

Feminist labour law scholars[36] have drawn attention to the labour of care, caring, sustaining and reproducing. I have referred to this as 'ecological labour'.[37] To *have to care* is a burden that is placed onto women, primarily, and/or global supply chains of foreign workers who supply care work in ostensibly 'economically productive' or 'economically active' (meaning, neoliberal) countries. Care is relevant to this judgment's expanded interpretation of personhood both because the Swale Water Workers for Marshes Coalition *cared* enough to protest their employer's neglectful and dangerous practices, and because care responsibilities typically are seen as an individual burden that is emancipated through the market. Care's integration into the market economic system, the commodification of care, provides a normative dilemma because to care means to go beyond contractual obligation or job description. In exceeding the frame, care illustrates the limits of employment law, and of market recognition. Increased legal recognition together with market incorporation has not necessarily improved a person's experience in work and labour, especially where they are marginalised due to race, gender, immigration or economic status.[38] Indeed, the extension of legal recognition, in this case a reinterpretation of legal personhood to include the web of ecological relationality, can 'end up entrenching pre-existing narratives of human dominance'.[39] Ecological relationality, when used to serve capital accumulation or the reinstatement of patriarchal hierarchies of knowledge or the subjugation of non-European knowledges, will deny the pluralism at the core of ecological jurisprudence. Recognition through the modern legal frame of legal personhood may

[35] Tataryn, *Law, Migration and Precarious Labour* 75.

[36] Zbyszewska, 'Regulating Work'; Routh, 'Embedding Work'; Hayes, 'Stories of Care' (2017); Fudge, 'Feminist Reflections' (2014).

[37] Tataryn, *Law, Migration and Precarious Labour* 75.

[38] ibid.

[39] O'Donnell, *Legal Rights*.

mean little unless it is accompanied by a shift in *how* and *what* is given value. For ecological labour, and ecological jurisprudence more broadly, this would mean a shift in value away from the triumvirate of capital, colonialism and patriarchy.

Such a shift may not seem to be forthcoming in ET decision-making. This is a shift in value that embraces complexity and plurality, and places interconnection and relationship to all beings at the centre of conflict resolution and judgment. It is a horizontal mode of thought that fundamentally denies the vertical hierarchies of modern law, employment contracts and obligations. Nevertheless, such a context-driven interpretation of being is possible.

6

Of Pests and Privilege: Re-examining *R (on the application of Countryside Alliance) v Attorney General*

JOE WILLS

> [The view] that humans are detached from the rest of the natural world, and anything that might challenge manmade harmony needs to be taken out … is damaging to human–animal relations – and the wider environment. It also forgets that foxes living in the post-war suburban sprawl, in the space that is deemed 'human', the space where they 'didn't belong', probably lived there before the cement mixers arrived.[1]

The Original Ruling

In October of 2007 the UK House of Lords delivered its decision in *R (on the application of Countryside Alliance) v Attorney General*.[2] The case was part of a series of failed litigation attempts by the pro-hunting lobby to challenge the fundamental lawfulness[3] and effectiveness[4] of the Hunting Act 2004, which criminalised hunting wild mammals with dogs.[5]

The appellants, headed by the Countryside Alliance, contended that the Act was incompatible with, amongst other things,[6] several of their rights under the

[1] Lucy Jones, *Foxes Unearthed: A Story of Love and Loathing in Modern Britain* (Elliott and Thompson, 2017) 271.

[2] *R (on the application of Countryside Alliance) v Attorney General* [2007] 3 WLR 922 (hereafter *Countryside Alliance v Attorney General*).

[3] *R (on the application of Jackson) v Attorney General* [2005] UKHL 56. Challenges were also brought against the Protection of Wild Mammals (Scotland) Act 2002: *Adams v Scottish Ministers* 2004 SC 665; *Whaley and another v Lord Advocate (Scotland)* [2007] UKHL 53.

[4] See eg *DPP v Wright* [2009] EWHC 105 (Admin); *DPP v Exeter Crown Court* [2008] EWHC 2399 (Admin).

[5] Hunting Act 2004, s 1.

[6] They also argued that the Act was incompatible with EU free movement of goods principles; I do not address that part of the case.

European Convention on Human Rights (ECHR). These included their right to respect for their private life under Article 8; their right to freedom of peaceful assembly and freedom of association under Article 11; their right to enjoy Convention rights without discrimination under Article 14; and their right to peaceful enjoyment of possessions under Article 1 of Protocol 1 (A1P1) of the Convention, all provisions which domestic courts are required to give effect by the Human Rights Act 1998.

The Attorney General and the Secretary of State for the Environment, Food and Rural Affairs, supported by the Royal Society for the Prevention of Cruelty to Animals as interveners, contended that the 2004 Act was not incompatible with the ECHR. They unanimously prevailed before the House of Lords.[7]

In five separate judgments the Lords dismissed all the appellants' human rights challenges. First, Article 8 was inapplicable because hunting is a public, not a private activity. Second, Article 11 was inapplicable[8] because it does not extend to sporting or recreational gatherings and, in any event, the 2004 Act did not prevent those who hunted from continuing to assemble and associate with each other. Third, Lord Bingham and Baroness Hale held, obiter, that even if Articles 8 and 11 were engaged, the interferences with those rights would have been justified and proportionate under the legitimate aim of 'protection of morals' under Articles 8(2) and 11(2) of the Convention.[9] Lord Brown disagreed on this point. Had he been of the view that the appellants' Article 8 rights were engaged – which he was not – he 'would have declined to find the hunting ban justifiable' on the basis that 'the ethical objection of the majority' is not 'a sufficient basis for holding the ban to be "necessary"'.[10] Fourth, Article 14 was not engaged because the appellants' complaint could not be linked to any personal characteristic constituting a protected 'status' under the article. Finally, the Lords found that A1P1 was engaged but the Hunting Act constituted only a comparatively slight interference with the appellants' property rights. This interference was not unlawful because the Hunting Act struck a fair balance between the demands of the general interest in protecting wild animals from unnecessary suffering and the interests of the appellants.

My Rewritten Judgment

My judgment is rewritten as a separate, partially dissenting opinion. The only detail of the case I have altered is the date. I imagine the case is being heard in

[7] The appellants subsequently applied to the European Court of Human Rights, complaining that their Art 8, 11, 14 and A1P1 rights were violated by the criminalisation of hunting with dogs in England, Wales and Scotland. All of their complaints were found to be 'manifestly ill-founded'. See *Friend and Others v the United Kingdom* 16072/06 and 27809/08.

[8] Lord Bingham dissented on this point, *Countryside Alliance v Attorney General* (n 1) [18].

[9] ibid [44]–[46] per Lord Bingham and [122]–[127] per Baroness Hale. Lord Brown disagreed on this point.

[10] ibid [159] (concerning Art 8). Lord Brown's views on the proportionality of an Art 11 interference were somewhat more opaque. See [161].

2023 rather than 2007. The House of Lords has thus become the UK Supreme Court and the United Kingdom is no longer a member of the European Union. The reason that I decided to change the date was because developments in human rights law and animal law since the case offer rich resources to draw upon for a less anthropocentric human rights jurisprudence.

In my judgment, I concur with the Law Lords in dismissing the appeals, albeit for different reasons. First, while agreeing that Article 11 is not applicable, I arrive at this conclusion on a different basis, namely that Article 11 requires assembly to be 'peaceful', which fox hunting patently is not. Here I aim to draw attention to the violence hiding in plain sight in conventional legal reasoning. If animals and their lives are not invisible, then having them torn apart for recreational purposes cannot be considered peaceful.

Second, whilst not conceding that Articles 8 and 11 are engaged, my judgment suggests that if they were, the legitimate aim that could justify interference ought not be 'the protection of morals' but rather 'the protection of the rights and freedoms of others'; the 'others' here being the foxes themselves. The 'protection of morals' framing does not fully avoid anthropocentrism. What justifies interfering with rights is not the protection of animals as such, but rather protecting the moral concern that humans have *about* animals. This approach, I suggest, is not only misguided from an animal protection perspective but also undesirable from a human rights perspective. As Lord Brown rightly observes, permitting the criminalisation of minority practices on the sole basis that the majority finds them unethical carries obvious and worrying authoritarian implications.[11]

The better approach, which would both vindicate the moral worth of animals and offer a firmer basis for a tolerant and pluralistic human rights framework, would be to locate the appropriate basis for interfering with hunting rights (to the extent they exist) in the rights of the foxes. I use legal theory and case law to demonstrate that animals can and do have legal rights that can justify interferences with Convention rights.

In addition to these substantive disagreements, the tone of my judgment differs from those of the other Lords, which at times are rather sympathetic to the appellants' hunting interests and occasionally portray a class bias.[12] My judgment, by contrast, describes fox hunting as 'a blood sport involving the violent spectacle of a live animal being torn limb-from-limb by a pack of trained hounds'. This is a value judgment, of course, but no more so than those presented by Lord Bingham and Baroness Hale.

My alternative judgment serves on the one hand to demonstrate the Lords' anthropocentric approach, which views humans as the only relevant stakeholders

[11] Baroness Hale too expressed misgivings about basing the legitimacy of the interference with Arts 8 and 11 on protection of morals for this very reason. See *Countryside Alliance v Attorney General* (n 1) [122].

[12] ibid, see eg [123] (per Baroness Hale).

in the dispute. On the other, it attempts to demonstrate a jurisprudential approach to human rights that does not assume 'human supremacism'.[13]

Reflections

I seek to show in my rewritten judgment that even an anthropocentric domain of law such as human rights can be interpreted in a suitably animal-friendly way, without involving any radical departure from existing legal doctrine.

There is, however, one area I wish I could have interrogated more, but for reasons of space was unable to. In the original case, both the appellants and respondents agreed that foxes are 'pests' that need to be 'culled', ie slaughtered in large numbers. The disagreement between the parties concerned which methods of pest control were deemed humane and which ought to be legal.

It is interesting to note that there is no legal definition of a pest in English law, although some statutes classify particular species as 'pests' for various reasons.[14] The notion of a 'pest' – taken for granted by the parties and the Court – is a social classification. On what basis are foxes viewed as 'pests'? Their predation on chickens is no match for the industrial slaughter of chickens by humans. The diseases foxes carry pose a negligible threat compared to the numerous deadly global pandemics spread by human activity. The harm caused by foxes rummaging through bins pales in comparison to the catastrophic and existential environmental vandalism the human species has unleashed.

When the pestiferous activities of foxes are contrasted to those of humans, a more sympathetic picture of the fox is available. An alternative narrative of the fox, alluded to in the introduction of my judgment and captured in myth and legend, is the fox as heroic outlaw, a Robin Hood-type figure who uses their wits and cunning to reappropriate small parts of the global commons being hoarded by humanity. A non-anthropocentric jurisprudence would begin from an acknowledgement that all species are entitled to live and flourish on this Earth and would strive to develop ways of living together as harmoniously as possible, rather than simply exterminating anything that gets in humanity's way.

[13] See Will Kymlicka, 'Human Rights without Human Supremacism' (2018) 48 *Canadian Journal of Philosophy* 763.

[14] See eg Prevention of Damage by Pests Act 1949 (defining rats and mice and pests for pest control measures), Protection of Wild Mammals (Scotland) Act 2002, s 10(1) (defining 'pest species' as 'foxes, hares, mink, stoats and weasels').

The Supreme Court

R (on the application of Countryside Alliance and others (Appellants) and others) v Her Majesty's Attorney General and another (Respondents)

JUDGMENT

1 June 2023

Lord Wills

Introduction

1. The fox has come to represent a thorny and emotional array of characters for different people. For some, the fox is a particularly devious and dastardly pest. Aristotle described the fox as 'cunning and evil-disposed'. Aristotle, *History of Animals* (Richard Cresswell tr, George Bell and Sons, 1883) 6. In *Aesop's Fables* the fox repeatedly demonstrates elusiveness, craftiness and trickery. In the Middle Ages, the popular stories of *Reynard the Fox* portray a Machiavellian villain, albeit one we are invited to have begrudging respect for.

2. This vision of the fox as a cunning enemy has undoubtedly left its imprint on the law. The Preservation of Grain Act, passed in 1532 by Henry VIII, made it compulsory for every man, woman and child to kill as many creatures characterised as 'vermin' as possible, including foxes. William Blackstone described foxes as 'noxious animals' and 'ravenous beasts of prey', explaining that the common law authorises their hunting even without the consent of the landowner, on the grounds that 'destroying such creatures is said to be profitable to the public'. William Blackstone, *Commentaries on the Laws of England Volume 3* (Clarendon Press, 1768) 213–214. In short, foxes were 'the "outlaws" of the animal world, unprotected by the Game Laws or the property rules pertaining to *ferae naturae* [wild animals]'. Andrea McDowell, 'Legal Fictions in *Pierson v Post*' (2007) 105 *Michigan Law Review* 735, 748.

3. In the infamous US case of *Pierson v Post* 3 Caines 175, 180 (1805), Judge Livington described the fox as a 'wild and noxious beast' regarded by both parties 'as the law of nations does a pirate, "*hostem humani generis*," (the enemy of all humanity)'. In near hysteria, he continued:

> His depredations on farmers and on barn yards, have not been forgotten; and to put him to death wherever found, is allowed to be meritorious, and of public benefit. Hence it follows, that our decision should have in view the greatest possible encouragement to the destruction of an animal, so cunning and ruthless in his career. (ibid).

4. In nineteenth-century England, when blood sports like bear baiting and dog and cock fighting were proscribed, hunting continued to be permitted; a double-standard many at the time regarded as stemming from class privilege and anti-poor bias. See Mike Radford, *Animal Welfare Law in Britain: Regulation and Responsibility* (Oxford University Press, 2001) 57–59. Hunting and coursing were later, at the insistence of the House of Lords, expressly excluded from the prohibitions in the Wild Animals in Captivity Act 1900.

5. Yet an alternative narrative of the place of the fox in our culture exists; one that presents the fox as a hero, a rebel, a symbol of resistance to class power and greed. The image of the fox as hero is perhaps most iconically captured in Roald Dahl's *Fantastic Mr Fox* in which the protagonist is a noble and sympathetic creature relentlessly hunted by three mean-spirited farmers. Then there is Disney's 1973 animated feature film *Robin Hood* where the legendary heroic outlaw assumes vulpine form. Finally, in Colin Dann's *The Animals of Farthing Wood* a group of forest animals dispossessed by human activity are led to a nature reserve by a brave and kindly fox.

6. These duelling visions of the fox as – on one side – a noxious and vicious pest to be exterminated and – on the other – a proletarian hero to be admired and coexisted with have shaped and reshaped the law. What appears on its surface a narrow dispute concerning the legality of a blood sport in fact addresses itself to the millennia-long fraught relationship between *Homo sapiens* and *Vulpes vulpes*. More broadly still, this case raises profound questions about the place of non-human animals and ecological balance in modern human rights jurisprudence. Are human rights exercised to the exclusion, and at the expense, of our fellow creatures or should they be interpreted in a manner that is consistent with the inherent value of other sentient beings?

7. I agree with Lord Bingham, Lord Hope, Lord Brown, Lord Rodger and Baroness Hale that in the present case the claims based on Articles 8, 11 and 14 of the European Convention on Human Rights (ECHR) and Article 1 of protocol 1 (A1P1) to the ECHR must fail. Nonetheless I depart from my fellow Lords in two respects. First, I offer an alternative, and in my view more fundamental, reason why Article 11 is inapplicable. Second, even assuming that the claimants' Article 8 and 11 Convention rights are engaged, I believe that Lord Bingham and Baroness Hale erred with respect to the basis of the justification for interfering with such rights.

The Applicability of Article 11

8. The text of Article 11(1) holds that '[e]veryone has the right to freedom of peaceful assembly and to freedom of association with others'. The appellants maintain that, as a result of the prohibition on hunting mammals with hounds in the Hunting Act 2004 Act, their right to assemble and associate for such purposes was effectively restricted. With the exception of Lord Bingham, my noble and learned

friends find Article 11 inapplicable because, they believed, it does not extend to sporting or recreational gatherings and, in any event, the 2004 Act does not prevent those who hunted from continuing to assemble and associate with one another. My noble and learned friend Lord Bingham was dissatisfied with this line of reasoning, observing that a right to assemble is of little value if people are prohibited from participating in the type of activity whose purpose they assembled for.

9. I agree with my noble and learned friend Lord Bingham that such an unduly narrow interpretation of Article 11 is undesirable. I would further warn against placing sporting and recreational gatherings wholly outside the scope of Article 11. The Strasbourg organs have recognised that Article 11 extends beyond political gatherings to assemblies of an essentially social character (*Emin Huseynov v Azerbaijan*, Application no 59135/09 (unreported), 7 May 2015, para 91) as well as to cultural gatherings (*The Gypsy Council and Others v the United Kingdom* (2002) 35 EHRR) and religious and spiritual meetings (*Barankevich v Russia* (2008) 47 EHRR 8, para 15). As I will outline below, whilst both the purpose of the assembly and the existence of viable alternatives for its participants are relevant for determining whether an interference with Article 11(1) is justified and proportionate under Article 11(2), they are not, I suggest, always in and of themselves reasons to find Article 11 inapplicable.

10. The reason Article 11(1) is best thought to be inapplicable in the present instance, I suggest, is that Article 11(1) applies only to *peaceful* assembly. The adjective qualifier 'peaceful' – or *pacifique* in the official French text – is critical to the scope of Article 11. As the Strasbourg Court has made abundantly clear, the notion of 'peaceful assembly' does not cover demonstrations where the organisers and participants act violently, incite violence or have violent intentions. See *Kudrevičius and Others v Lithuania* (2016) 62 EHRR 34, para 92; *Gülcü v Turkey* [2016] ECHR 87, para 97; *Shmorgunov and Others v Ukraine*, para 491 (Application Nos 15367/14 and 13) (unreported) decision of 21 January.

11. Whatever position one takes on the ethics of fox hunting, it stretches the bounds of credulity to suggest that this activity could be appropriately categorised as 'peaceful', either in law or ordinary language. Fox hunting is a blood sport involving the violent spectacle of a live animal being torn limb from limb by a pack of trained hounds. As fox hunting involves non-peaceful assembly, it falls outside the scope of Article 11.

12. Whilst unlikely that the drafters of the ECHR gave any consideration to animal protection when formulating Article 11, the meaning of that provision is not frozen in time. The Convention is a 'living instrument which … must be interpreted in light of present-day conditions' (*Tyrer v The United Kingdom* (1979–80) 2 EHRR 1, para 31). It is undeniable that the moral, political and legal landscape concerning non-human animals has shifted dramatically since 1950. In his separate judgment in *Herrmann v Germany* (2013) 56 EHRR 7, Judge Pinto De Albuquerque argues that there is 'clear and uncontested evidence of a continuing international trend' in the practice of European states that is 'in favour of the

protection of animal life and welfare' (para OI-9). As evidence of this international trend, Judge Albuquerque notes the overturning of animals' status as 'things' (*res*) in European civil law jurisdictions; the extension of constitutional protections to animals in several European countries; the tendency to legally recognise the sentience of animals; and a variety of European and international treaties aimed at ensuring the welfare, protection and preservation of animals (paras OI-2 to OI-8).

13. This international trend, Judge Albuquerque says, is 'reflected in the application of the Convention' (para OI-9), noting, for example that '[t]he clear public interest in various matters concerning animal welfare has … been frequently stressed in the light of the Convention guarantee of freedom of expression' (para OI-2). He also observes that 'the Court has unequivocally rejected the existence of a Convention right to hunt or a right to take part in person in the performance of ritual slaughter' (ibid). As such:

> [A]nimals are viewed by the Convention as a constitutive part of an ecologically balanced and sustainable environment, their protection being incorporated in a larger framework of intra-species equity (ensuring healthy enjoyment of nature among existing humans), inter-generational equity (guaranteeing the sustainable enjoyment of nature by future human generations) and inter-species equity (enhancing the inherent dignity of all species as 'fellow creatures'). (para OI-9).

14. In light of these social and legal developments that have, over the course of the last four decades, extended greater protections to non-human animals, we should not hesitate to interpret the rights contained in the Convention non-anthropocentrically. At the very least, this means reading Convention rights in ways that do not come at the expense of the inherent dignity of other sentient creatures. Accordingly, we should be loath to accept acts of violence against animals, especially those done for purely recreational purposes, as falling within the ambit of the Article 11.

15. I have argued it is erroneous to include violence to animals within the purview of the right to peaceful assembly. In the alternative, assuming Article 11 is engaged, I agree with my noble and learned friends Lord Bingham and Baroness Hale that the interference with that right under the Hunting Act 2004 can be justified on the basis that it is prescribed by law, is necessary in a democratic society and advances a legitimate aim pursuant to Article 11(2). By parallel reasoning, I also agree with them that, to the extent there is any interference with Article 8, it can also be justified on the basis of Article 8(2). I disagree, however with my noble and learned friends on what the legitimate aim that justifies those interferences is. I turn to this question in the next section.

The Basis for Interferences with Articles 8 and 11

16. Lord Bingham and Baroness Hale believe that, even if the appellants' Article 8 and 11 rights are engaged, the interference with those rights by the Hunting Act 2004

is justified on the basis that it is 'necessary in a democratic society' in order to protect morals under Articles 8(2) and 11(2). Lord Brown expresses notable consternation with allowing the protection of morals to permit such an interference. His concern is entirely understandable. Denying a social minority the ability to participate in a tradition or pastime merely because the majority finds it morally objectionable runs contrary to the spirit of 'pluralism, tolerance and broad mindedness' the ECHR exists to uphold (*Handyside v The United Kingdom* (1979–80) 1 EHRR 73, para 49).

17. Yet, the prohibited activity in question is neither victimless nor harmless. As *The Report of Committee of Inquiry into Hunting with Dogs in England & Wales* (2000) (hereafter the Burns Report) noted, this practice 'seriously compromises the welfare of the fox' (para 6.49). On this basis I submit that it is the 'protection of the rights and freedoms of others' under Articles 8(2) and 11(2) that is the appropriate legitimate aim to consider here – the 'others' here being the foxes themselves.

18. Can Convention rights be limited to protect the rights and freedoms of animals *themselves*? As noted above, the Convention is a 'living instrument which … must be interpreted in light of present-day conditions' (*Tyrer v The United Kingdom*, above, para 31). The evolving legal norms of our treatment of animals impact how the Convention rights are interpreted and applied. As Judge Albuquerque puts it: 'Under the Convention, "animal rights" … correspond to obligations imposed on the Contracting Parties as part of their commitment to full, effective and practical enjoyment of human rights' (*Herrmann v Germany*, above, para OI-11). This entails that 'the safeguarding of the environment and animal life constitutes an implicit restriction on the exercise of human rights' and is 'an inherent obligation on the Contracting Parties bound by the Convention' (ibid). A non-anthropocentric reading of the 'rights and freedoms of others' is warranted in light of the clear international trend across Europe in recognising animals as possessing intrinsic value in need of legal protection.

19. The claim that animals can possess rights and freedoms recognised by the Convention requires justification. Some may wonder whether animals are the sorts of entities that can even possess legal rights in the first place. To answer this we need to take a brief foray into legal theory. A highly influential account of legal rights was offered by Wesley Newcomb Hohfeld in the early twentieth century. What Hohfeld called a 'right in the strictest sense' involves the possession of a legal entitlement that places another under a duty, either to act or refrain from acting (Wesley Newcomb Hohfeld, 'Some Fundamental Legal Conceptions as Applied in Judicial Reasoning' (1913) 32 *Yale Law Journal* 16, 30). Plainly, under this common definition of a right, we can talk of animals possessing legal rights. Under the Hunting Act 2004, foxes are entitled not to be hunted with hounds and all legally competent persons are placed under a duty not to hunt them with hounds. To assert that animals have legal rights is by no means a novel claim; numerous legal scholars have already pointed this out. See Joel Feinberg, 'The Rights of Animals and Unborn Generations' in Joel Feinberg, *Rights, Justice and the Bounds of Liberty*

(Princeton University Press, 1980); Cass R. Sunstein, 'The Rights of Animals: A Very Short Primer' (John M. Olin Program in Law and Economics Working Paper No 157, 2002); Matthew H Kramer, 'Do Animals and Dead People Have Legal Rights?' (2001) 14 *Canadian Journal of Law and Jurisprudence* 29.

20. Courts likewise have recognised animals as bearers of legal rights. In *R (on the application of Cruelty Free International (formerly the BUAV) V SSHD and Imperial College London (Interested Party)* [2015] EWHC (Admin) [60] the High Court described the Animals (Scientific Procedures) Act 1986 as serving to, amongst other things, 'protect the rights of animals'. Other common law courts have similarly recognised animal protection law as conferring rights on animals. In *Cetacean Community v Bush*, 386 F3d 1169, 1175 (9th Cir 2004), the US Ninth Circuit Court of Appeals stated that 'Animals have many legal rights, protected under both federal and state laws.' See also *Tilikum v Sea World Parks & Entm't, Inc*, 842 F Supp 2d 1259, 1264 (SD Cal 2012). The Indian Constitutional Court likewise noted that the duties in India's Prevention of Cruelty to Animals Act 1960 'confer corresponding rights on animals' (*Animal Welfare Board of India v A Nagaraja and Ors* (2014 7 SCC 547) para 27). See also *Islamabad Wildlife Mgmt Bd through its Chairman v Metropolitan Corp Islamabad through its Mayor & 4 others* (WP No 1155/2019) 25 (Islamabad High Court Judicial Dep't, 25 April 2020) 7: 'Do the animals have legal rights? The answer to this question, without any hesitation, is in the affirmative.'

21. Currently, the Strasbourg Court has not recognised animals as entitled to the substantive rights contained within the ECHR. In *Balluch v Austria* application no 26180/08 (unreported) application lodged on 4 May 2008 and *Stibbe v Austria* application no 26188/08 (unreported) application lodged on 6 May 2008, claims bought on behalf of a chimpanzee were rejected by a committee of the First Chamber for incompatibility *ratione materiae*. However, the Convention's own jurisprudence on abortion suggests an individual's direct protection under the Convention is unnecessary for the courts to consider their rights and freedoms as a legitimate basis for interfering with a Convention right. Whilst the Strasbourg Court has held that 'the unborn child is not regarded as a "person" directly protected by Article 2 of the Convention' (*Vo v France* [2015] ECC 32, para 80), it has also stressed the need to weigh a pregnant woman's Article 8 rights against 'the rights and freedoms of others including the protection of pre-natal life' (*A, B and C v Ireland* (2011) 53 EHRR 13, para 181). This shows that animals do not need to be applicants before the Court for the Court to take their rights into account in weighing the legitimacy of an interference with a Convention right.

22. Nor do the 'rights and freedoms' mentioned in Articles 8(2) and 11(2) have to correspond to the substantive rights outlined in the Convention. A number of commentators have noted that the Court typically fails to spell out with precision who constitute the relevant 'others' and which of their 'rights' or 'freedoms' have been interfered with. Consequently, the phrase has been described as 'something of a catchall' that the Strasbourg organs have invoked in a 'perfunctory'

and 'highly casuistic' manner. See respectively: Malcolm Evans, *Religious Liberty and International Law in Europe* (Cambridge University Press, 1997) 328; William Schabas, *The European Convention on Human Rights: A Commentary* (Oxford University Press, 2015) 437; Stephen Greer, *The Exceptions to Articles 8 to 11 of the European Convention on Human Rights* (Council of Europe Publishing, 1997) 35. At the very least, it is evident that the Court has interpreted the phrase as protecting a range of rights and freedoms that are significantly broader than those enumerated in the ECHR and its protocols.

23. In light of the above considerations, I conclude that it is appropriate to consider the rights and freedoms of the foxes and other mammals targeted by hunting with hounds as the basis for any purported interferences with Articles 8 or 11 of the Convention in this present case.

Justification

24. In order to justify an interference with a qualified Convention right, it must be shown that the interference in question is prescribed by law, pursues a legitimate aim and is necessary in a democratic society. The ban on hunting wild mammals with hounds is plainly prescribed by law and, as the previous paragraphs have argued, it pursues the legitimate aim of protecting the rights and freedoms of wild mammals. We therefore turn to whether the interference is necessary in a democratic society.

25. The well-established four-stage test to determine whether an interference with a qualified Convention right can be justified was clearly summarised by Lord Wilson in *R (Aguilar Quila) v Secretary of State for the Home Department* [2011] UKSC 45; [2012] 1 AC 621, para 45: (a) is the legislative objective (legitimate aim) sufficiently important to justify limiting a fundamental right; (b) are the measures which have been designed to meet it rationally connected to it; (c) are they no more than are necessary to accomplish it; and (d) do they strike a fair balance between the rights of the individual and the interests of the community?

Legitimate Aim

26. First, we consider whether the legitimate aim of protecting animal welfare was sufficiently important to justify limiting Articles 8 and 11. The Strasbourg Court has noted that animal protection is a significant area of deliberation across Europe, pointing out that 'it cannot be denied that in many European societies there was, and is, an ongoing general debate on the protection of animals and the manner in which they are reared' (VgT *Verein gegen Tierfabriken v Switzerland*, Application (2002) 34 EHRR 4 para 70). The Strasbourg Court has recognised the significance of such concerns in relation to the killing of animals on several occasions. In a case relating to the media's ability to report on the controversial

practice of skinning seals alive, the Grand Chamber described the matter as a 'vital public interest' (*Bladet Tromsø and Stensaas v Norway* (2000) 29 EHRR 125, para 73). In *Friend & Others v The United Kingdom* (2010) 50 EHRR the Court found evidence relating to animal suffering was sufficient to ground a 'public interest to ban hunting' (para 56). The Grand Chamber has even acknowledged that objections to hunting have the required level of 'cogency, cohesion and importance' to be 'worthy of respect in a democratic society' (*Herrmann v Germany*, above, para 20). In light of these pronouncements, I conclude that protecting animal welfare is indeed sufficiently important to justify interferences with Articles 8 and 11.

Rational Connection

27. As Lord Brown pointed out, the ban on hunting with hounds had two aims: (1) to reduce unnecessary suffering to animals; (2) to give effect to the view of those opposed to hunting that causing suffering to animals for sport is unethical. As Lord Bingham and Baroness Hale discussed in in their judgments, the Hunting Act clearly has a rational connection to the second of these objectives.

28. The appellants dispute that the first of these objectives has been shown. They maintain that there is no evidence that the prohibition of hunting has reduced the overall level of suffering endured by foxes as compared to the situation which pertained before the Act. They point out that other methods of 'culling' foxes – such as shooting and snaring – cause just as much, if not more, suffering to foxes as hunting them with hounds.

29. The comparison between the different welfare impacts of different methods of killing is fraught with empirical challenges. As the Burns Report noted, 'there is very little by way of scientific evidence to help us in establishing the facts on these issues' (para 6.42). Nevertheless, the Report suggests that lamping using rifles, if carried out properly and in appropriate circumstances, would have 'fewer adverse welfare implications than hunting' (para 6.60). In areas where lamping is not possible – such as upland areas – the adverse impacts on fox welfare could be avoided if 'dogs could be used, at least to flush foxes from cover' (para 6.61). In short, the Burns Report indicated that there are methods of controlling the fox population that cause less suffering than hunting with hounds.

30. I concur with Baroness Hale that the mere fact that animal welfare considerations could have justified a wider ban than the one contained in the Hunting Act 2004 does not indicate a narrower ban cannot be justified. See further *R (on the application of Petsafe Ltd) v The Welsh Ministers* [2010] EWHC 2908 (Admin), para 65 (rejecting 'selectivity' arguments against the proportionality of animal welfare measures).

31. It strikes me as plainly obvious that hunting foxes with hounds causes them significant suffering. Given both the paucity of evidence concerning the comparative welfare impacts of different fox population control methods and the

inherent limitations of judicial bodies making determinations about such issues, Parliament's intention to prohibit hunting mammals with hounds was warranted to prevent unnecessary animal suffering. I therefore conclude that there is a rational connection between the Hunting Act 2004 and its objectives.

Less Intrusive Means

32. Next, we consider whether a less intrusive interference with the Appellants' purported Convention rights was possible. Perhaps rather than prohibit hunting mammals with dogs, Parliament should have considered regulating it.

33. Other human rights cases involving animal welfare are instructive here. *R (The Electronic Collar Manufacturers Association and Petsafe) v DEFRA* [2021] EWCA Civ 666 concerned DEFRA's ban on the use of remote-controlled hand-held electronic collar devices ('shock collars') for cats and dogs in England for animal welfare reasons. The Appellants – who had commercial interests in the sale of shock collars – argued that the ban violated their property rights under A1P1 on the grounds that, inter alia, less intrusive measures could have been imposed. In particular, they argued that the regulation of shock collars could have prevented abuse. In rejecting this line of argument Lady Justice Elisabeth Laing DBE noted:

> 102. … the less intrusive means must be capable of achieving the legitimate aim which is at issue … the concern about e-collars is that, if they are not banned, no system of regulation will prevent a cruel owner from using one to inflict unnecessary suffering on an animal.

This reasoning applies with even greater force in the present case. It seems unlikely that any lesser measure than a ban of hunting with hounds could have achieved the Hunting Act's objectives as effectively. Hunting is, by its very nature, almost impossible to regulate. Even if the hunters themselves can be placed under certain legal duties in theory, a pack of dogs trained to kill cannot.

34. The European Court of Justice's (ECJ) ruling in *Centraal Israëlitisch Consistorie van België e.a. and Others* (2020) C-336/19 also provides instructive, if non-binding, precedent on this matter. The ECJ considered whether the Flemish legislature's prohibition of religious non-stun slaughter was compatible with Article 10 of the Charter of Fundamental Rights of the European Union, which protects freedom of thought, conscience and religion. In determining whether such a prohibition exceeded the limits of what is appropriate and necessary in order to attain the animal welfare objectives pursued by that legislation, the ECJ examined whether recourse had been made to the least onerous interference with freedom to manifest religious beliefs. It observed:

> 73. … the Flemish legislature stated … that 'the gap between eliminating animal suffering, on the one hand, and slaughtering without prior stunning, on the other, will always be very considerable, even if less radical measures were taken to minimise the impairment of animal welfare'.

> 74. It follows that the Flemish legislature was entitled … to consider that the limitations placed by the decree at issue in the main proceedings on freedom to manifest religion, by requiring prior stunning which is reversible and cannot result in the animal's death, meet the condition of necessity.'

In the present case, similar reasoning can be applied. Even if it were possible to regulate hunting with hounds, it would still cause more suffering than if it were banned outright.

35. Indeed, for many opponents of fox hunting, the prohibitions did not go far enough. Schedule 1 of the Hunting Act 2004 sets out nine forms of hunting that are exempted from the hunting ban. Furthermore, the 2004 Act does not touch 'trail hunting' – the practices of using artificial scent trail in hunts rather than chasing and killing live animals. Again, hunt opponents have claimed trail hunting has often merely served as a ploy for hunters to take part in 'real' hunts of live animals. There were 550 reports of illegal hunts taking place during the hunting season in 2018 alone ('Hundreds of Illegal Hunts Took Place in British Countryside Last Autumn, Animal Rights Group Says', *The Independent*, April 3 2018). These concerns prompted the National Trust membership in 2021 to vote to end the issuing of trail hunt licences on National Trust property and the Scottish Parliament to pass the Hunting with Dogs (Scotland) Act 2023, which prohibits trail hunting entirely.

36. I conclude that there was no less intrusive means for Parliament to achieve its objective of reducing animal suffering.

A Fair Balance

37. Lastly, we turn to the issue of whether a fair balance between the rights of hunters and the need to protect animal welfare has been struck. Granting, *arguendo*, that Articles 8 and 11 are engaged by the Hunting Ban, we must ask two questions: first, how significant are the interferences with these rights; and second, how significant are the benefits of interfering with these rights to secure the rights of wild animals?

38. Even granting that Articles 8 and 11 are engaged, the interferences with them are minor. Starting with the right to a private life under Article 8, if it is engaged at all, it will be at the very periphery of the right. The notion of a private life is not restricted to an individual's 'inner circle' (*Denisov v Ukraine* (Application No 76639/11) (unreported) 25 September 2018, para 96) and encompasses the right for each individual to approach others in order to establish and develop relationships with them and with the outside world (*Bărbulescu v Romania* [2016] IRLR 235, para 71; *Botta v Italy* (1998) 26 EHRR 241, para 32). However, 'there is nothing in the Court's established case-law which suggests that the scope of private life extends to activities which are of an essentially public nature' (*Nicolae Virgiliu Tănase v Romania* [2019] ECHR 491, para 129). Thus, even if

hunting does fall within the scope of Article 8, it is very far from the 'core' of the right.

39. Turning next to Article 11, as I already discussed, the right to freedom of assembly has been construed broadly by the Strasbourg organs to include not only political gatherings, but also to assemblies of an essentially social character. Nonetheless, 'the primary or original purpose Article 11 was and is to protect the right of peaceful demonstration and participation in the democratic process' (*Friend & Others v UK*, above, para 50). As fox hunting does not concern participation in the democratic process, it cannot be considered part of the core of Article 11.

40. To the extent that Articles 8 and 11 are interfered with, these interferences do not strike at the core of the rights, but rather at the periphery. This is compounded by the fact that the Hunting Act 2004 provides nine exemptions for the general prohibition on hunting and the general ban only prevents a hunt from gathering for the aim of killing a wild mammal with hounds. Accordingly, it does not restrict the right to associate with others but only the goals they can collectively pursue. Hunters remain free to participate with one another for the purposes of drag or trail hunting, which preserve the wider public or social dimensions of a traditional hunt.

41. Next we turn to the strength of the rights and freedoms of the foxes that the Hunting Act 2004 attempts to protect. As noted above, the Strasbourg organs have identified a 'vital public interest' in matters relating to the killing of animals (*Bladet Tromsø and Stensaas v Norway*, above, para 73) and acknowledged that objections to hunting have the required level of 'cogency, cohesion and importance' to be 'worthy of respect in a democratic society' (*Herrmann v Germany*, above, para 20). In his separate judgment in *Herrmann*, Judge Pinto de Albuquerque notes a 'clear and uncontested evidence of a continuing international trend in favour of the protection of animal life and welfare is reflected in the application of the Convention' (para OI-9, internal quotes removed). This extends to making proportionality assessments with respect to restricting qualified Convention rights to protect animal welfare. As the ECJ notes in *Centraal Israëlitisch Consistorie van België and Others*, above:

> 77. … like the ECHR, the Charter is a living instrument which must be interpreted in the light of present-day conditions. … Animal welfare, as a value to which contemporary democratic societies have attached increasing importance for a number of years, may, in the light of changes in society, be taken into account to a greater extent in the context of ritual slaughter and thus help to justify the proportionality of legislation such as that at issue in the main proceedings [internal citations omitted].

42. If animals are to count for anything, their interest in not being ripped up alive by a pack of trained dogs must be considered as a very weighty and serious interest.

43. I too would dismiss these appeals.

Commentary

Chris Sangster

Political Context of the Hunting Act 2004

Hunting has long been an emotive, controversial subject, and the passing of the Hunting Act 2004 was the end result of a long and difficult process. The Act was passed in the face of significant protest, with pro-hunting activists invading the House of Commons chamber to disrupt a debate, whilst a demonstration of up to 10,000 people amassed outside Parliament to protest against the Bill.[15] The Act was eventually passed only through the use of the Parliament Acts 1911 and 1949 to override the House of Lords.

However, in some respects the hunting ban appears to have become less controversial. Although at the 2017 election Theresa May pledged to hold a free vote on repealing the Hunting Act if the Conservative Party won a majority, this pledge was scrapped in January 2018, and at the 2019 election the Conservatives under the leadership of Boris Johnson announced that they would no longer seek to make changes to the Act.[16] This falls short of promises made by other parties to strengthen the ban under the Act, but suggests that there is now substantial cross-party support for retaining the ban. Of course, as detailed in this rewritten judgment, it is not appropriate to use the law to impose the morality of a majority on a minority.

The Burns Report found evidence of a feeling amongst farmers that their interests were not understood by central government and the urban majority.[17] However, it would be overly simplistic to reduce the issue of hunting to a manifestation of the urban–rural divide. The Burns Report found a diversity of opinion in rural communities, with a significant rural minority opposed to hunting.[18] One reason for this lack of unanimous support is the significant number of cases of trespass, disruption and disturbance caused by hunts. This difference of opinion has caused social tension within communities, rebutting the assertion that hunting is necessary for social cohesion.

[15] Matthew Tempest, 'Protests as MPs Vote for Hunt Ban', *The Guardian*, 15 September 2004, theguardian.com/uk/2004/sep/15/hunting.ruralaffairs.

[16] Jane Dalton, 'Animal Lovers Hail Conservative Manifesto Pledge to Abandon Revival of Fox-hunting', *The Independent*, 24 November 2019, independent.co.uk/news/uk/politics/fox-hunting-conservative-manifesto-legal-carrie-symonds.

[17] Her Majesty's Stationery Office, *Report of Committee of Inquiry into Hunting with Dogs in England & Wales* (9 June 2000) Dd 5067685 6/00 521462 19585, para 4.10.

[18] ibid para 4.12.

The Social Role of Hunting

Although the Burns Report stated that the traditional hunt did make a significant contribution to the cultural and social life of rural communities, other community hubs such as village churches and pubs were found to be more important.[19] Although several social events were previously carried out to support the costs of hunting, such as dances, barbecues and competitions, many were not directly linked with hunting and could equally be carried out by other groups in those communities, with the funds raised being diverted instead to more worthy causes.[20]

Trail hunting – an alternative that involves following the scent of a live animal – has increased in popularity following the introduction of the hunting ban. This carries the risk that hounds may pick up the scent of a live animal, and there have been accusations that this is commonly used as a 'smokescreen' for the continuation of traditional hunting. By contrast, drag hunting does not pose a direct threat to wildlife if carried out correctly according to the RSPCA. This is because an artificially laid scent not derived from animals is followed. It therefore provides a less harmful alternative for those who still wish to engage in hunting.

There is a separate argument regarding whether foxes are 'pests' and whether some control of fox populations is necessary to protect other wildlife and livestock predated by foxes. The pro-hunting lobby tends to conflate such issues with those surrounding hunting for 'sport'. The alternative judgment and this commentary contend that this argument for pest control must not be conflated with arguments concerning tradition, community and rights to peaceful assembly. Lethal control must be carried out as a last resort when other control measures have been proven ineffective. However, farmers who are not able to rely on hunting as a form of 'free pest control' may still turn to other methods of culling foxes, potentially employing those who do not have sufficient expertise to ensure that culling is carried out humanely.[21] It is therefore vital to consider how we may change the narrative away from viewing foxes as 'pests'.

Changing Societal Values and Non-human Sentience in UK Law

By including foxes within the scope of 'others' to be protected, the alternative judgment allows us to reimagine the narrative that has established the fox as a 'pest' to be dealt with through lethal control. Conceptual framings of foxes as

[19] ibid para 4.41.
[20] ibid paras 4.15–4.16.
[21] ibid para 5.37.

pests serve as distancing mechanisms that allow people to feel more inclined to dislike and even kill members of a species in accordance with the generally accepted view of that species.[22] The term 'pest' betrays a strong anthropocentric bias, labelling a species in relation to its perceived value to humans as a natural resource to be exploited.[23]

Wills's decision to rewrite this case in 2023 allows us to consider legislation that has been passed in the intervening years, in particular the Animal Welfare (Sentience) Act 2022. This Act requires legislators to consider sentience when making and amending laws and created an Animal Sentience Committee to review government policy on non-human animal welfare. Although this Act does not force the government to make decisions in favour of non-humans or overturn existing cruel practices, it clearly indicates growing recognition of animal sentience and the capacity of animals to experience feelings such as pain and joy.

Arguments made at the time the Hunting Act was passed in 2004, that emotions such as fear attributed to the victims of the hunt could be dismissed as mere anthropomorphism, are no longer tenable in the face of this statutory recognition that animals are sentient beings capable of experiencing pain and fear. Recognition of sentience would be practically meaningless if cruel practices allowing foxes to be chased and torn apart by hounds for the purpose of recreation were permitted to continue.

While these statutory developments in animal welfare reflect changing attitudes towards nature as valuable in its own right, in the less than two decades since this case was originally decided the state of the UK countryside has degraded further. The United Kingdom is now often referred to as one of the most nature-depleted countries in the world.[24] In this context, it is reasonable to suppose that there would be even greater opposition to any activity that seeks to persecute a native UK species at a time when protecting our remaining wildlife has become even more essential. The fox is neither a pestilential marauder determined to ruin the lives of farmers, nor a cunning, Robin Hood-esque hero; the fox is merely another species with just as much right to enjoy life on Earth as us, free from persecution by humans on horseback with hounds.

[22] Colin Jerolmack, 'How Pigeons Became Rats: The Cultural-Spatial Logic of Problem Animals' (2008) 55 *Social Problems* 72, 86.

[23] Fred H Besthorn, 'Restorative Justice and Environmental Restoration, Twin Pillars of a Just Global Environmental Policy: Hearing the Voice of the Victim' (2004) 3 *Journal of Societal & Social Policy* 33, 41.

[24] 'Environment Agency Report Sets Out Urgent Need to Work with Nature' (12 July 2022) gov.uk/government/news/environment-agency-report-sets-out-urgent-need-to-work-with-nature.

PART III

Care and Obligation

7

Who Let the Pigs Out? Rooting for the 'Good Farmer' in *Savage v Fairclough*

HELENA HOWE

Why Savage *Savage*?

In many ways, this case[1] is completely unremarkable. The defendants were not liable in private nuisance for polluting their neighbours' watercourse by applying nitrates and pig manure to their own land during the late 1970s and 1980s. Their fertiliser use was within accepted limits for the time, and so the court found they could not reasonably have foreseen any harm to the claimant's land. Intensive pig and arable production was a reasonable use of land. It looks like a simple application of *Cambridge Water Co Ltd v Eastern Counties Leather Plc*[2] to farming pollution. Yet, in its normalisation of these harms lies its significance.

It has bothered me for years.[3] For a start, the neighbours were complaining from an early stage about pollution to their spring and continued to do so. Despite ignoring these complaints and failing to inform their advisors of a problem, the defendants were held to be 'good farmers', unable to foresee any harm to the land of these long-suffering neighbours. It is true that their farming practices were the same as other intensive farmers of the period and their application of fertiliser was not unduly high. The legal obligations at the time were few and the defendants were not breaking any rules. We knew less about the negative impacts of intensive agriculture on the environment and on the animals involved. Hindsight can be a cruel judge.

But I have never found the approach satisfactory. I have a particular issue with the courts' representation of the 'good farmer' as someone who follows basic legal rules, completely divorced from the needs and interests of their wider community. How could it be 'good farming' to ignore the 'distress' of your neighbours for years,[4] even if you are complying with your legal obligations? And whilst we

[1] *Savage and Another v Fairclough and Others* [1999] Env LR 183.

[2] *Cambridge Water Co Ltd v Eastern Counties Leather Plc* [1994] 2 AC 264.

[3] Thanks are due to Chloe Anthony and Alastair Hudson for helpful discussion.

[4] *Savage* 189.

undoubtedly have more evidence now of the myriad harms resulting from intensive farming, we cannot pretend the potential for harm was not widely known at the time in question. The Soil Association was established three decades earlier, in 1946, Compassion in World Farming in 1967 and Friends of the Earth in 1969. As counsel for the claimants argued in the original judgment,[5] the specific issue of pollution by nitrates was understood well beyond the scientific community and one of which farmers and their advisors were becoming aware during the relevant period. Yet, despite this context, there was no expectation that the 'good farmer' ought to be responsive to risks outside their explicit legal obligations in a way that might give rise to a duty to – at least – investigate their practices. Even when coupled with complaint of that very harm occurring.

The Care-full 'Good Farmer'

From an Earth law perspective, this failure to see the 'good farmer' as embedded in their community and sensitive to risk seems particularly stark. And this is not *just* a case about pollution of one individual's property by another. It is a case about what it means to produce food ethically, sustainably and with care for other lives. It is a case about the untapped potential of private law and the courts to help us achieve this.

As a result, my aim in rewriting this judgment was to do three things. The first was show how the law could present a much more relational and compassionate picture of the 'good farmer'. This is the 'good farmer' as a knowledgeable and caring land steward, whose intimate connection with human and non-human nature gives rise to greater regard for the needs and interests of others than shown in the case. Rather than a passive recipient of regulation, this is someone who actively creates their farming practice to care for the natural environment. This construct is not just more compatible with Earth law principles but, I would argue, better reflects the expectations set by the wider law and policy on farming.[6] It is also more representative of the identity of the 'good farmer' held, increasingly, by farmers themselves.[7] The 'good farmer' identity matters because it influences farmer attitudes and behaviour[8] and thus plays a key role in promoting – or resisting – the transition to a farming system that cares for vital ecosystems and the beings

[5] ibid.

[6] eg DEFRA, *The Path to Sustainable Farming: An Agricultural Transition Plan 2021 to 2024* (DEFRA, 2020).

[7] Mark Riley, 'How Does Longer Term Participation in Agri-environment Schemes [Re]shape Farmers' Environmental Dispositions and Identities?' (2016) 52 *Land Use Policy* 62; George Cusworth, 'Falling Short of Being the "Good Farmer": Losses of Social and Cultural Capital Incurred through Environmental Mismanagement, and the Long-term Impacts Agri-environment Scheme Participation' (2020) 75 *Journal of Rural Studies* 164.

[8] Rob Burton et al, 'Exploring Farmers' Cultural Resistance to Voluntary Agri-environmental Schemes' (2008) 48 *Sociologia Ruralis* 16.

who inhabit them.[9] I wanted this judgment to support this emergent, ecologically responsible identity, rather than stifle it under the narrow and technical approach of the original decision.

The second was to bring a wider range of the beings affected by the defendant's activities into the judgment, particularly the pigs kept by the defendants and the animals living on the claimants' land. They are almost completely absent from the original judgment. Like other 'nuisance' animals they are a conversational footnote: merely the source of smell, noise or offensive waste.[10] Yet Gibson's 'ethological jurisprudence' reveals the glorious disruptive potential of animals for our legal discourse.[11] It might be dogs who bring the greatest capacity for resocialising humans and reorienting us towards a cooperative, interactional, property of shared interests. But the potential for what Gibson calls the 're-invigoration of multi-species relationality'[12] spurred me on to let the pigs out to see what kind of nuisance they could make in nuisance law.[13] There is much more that they could have contributed on their view of a good life, if properly represented.[14] Nevertheless, I have tried to at least make them present, both in their own right and as part of a system. The latter point has become particularly relevant as we become aware of how animal and human welfare intersect. I have drawn on the US nuisance case of *McKiver*,[15] in which the court is explicit about the relationship between poor farmed animal welfare, harms to humans and environmental harms, in ways that ours have not yet been. As such, the pigs are integral to that judgment, as I have tried to make them here.

The third – related to both points above, yet also distinct – was to highlight how narrow the original judgment was. I see this case as illustrative of a tendency to avoid acknowledging the full range of harms associated with intensive farming. The courts have distanced themselves from the impacts through euphemistic language to describe animals' suffering,[16] or downright refusal to allow 'legal consideration of the issues to be heightened by the stark reality of the position and status animals have in the human food chain'.[17] As we each must confront our food choices, the courts should be encouraged to address other lives and our exploitation of them. I see this as relevant to questions of foreseeability – and perhaps fault – in nuisance, but it appears particularly important in establishing

[9] Rob Burton et al, *The Good Farmer Culture and Identity in Food and Agriculture* (Earthscan, 2021) ch 8.

[10] *Wheeler v Saunders* [1996] Ch 19.

[11] Johanna Gibson, *Owned, An Ethological Theory of Property: From the Cave to the Commons* (Routledge, 2020).

[12] ibid 13.

[13] ibid 18.

[14] eg Martha Nussbaum, *Justice for Animals: Our Collective Responsibility* (Simon and Schuster, 2023) 273–78.

[15] *McKiver v Murphy-Brown, LLC*, No 19-1019 (4th Circuit 2020).

[16] eg *R (on the application of Squire) v Shropshire County Council* [2019] EWCA Civ 888, para 17, using the term 'crop cycles' to refer to the animals' short lives.

[17] *R (on the application of Compassion in World Farming Ltd) v Secretary of State for Farming, Food and Rural Affairs* [2003] EWHC 2850 (Admin) para 55.

the boundaries of 'reasonable' land use. We know that we are living – and farming – beyond the Earth's ecological limits.[18] Yet, my fear is that, even today, this case could be heard without any mention of the pigs' interests or the potential alternatives to intensive agriculture. This is not a suggestion that the court should impose its own ethical agenda on complex issues; it is concern about the continued normalisation of an extremely harmful set of practices by treating intensive agriculture as an entirely acceptable – indeed the only – way to produce food.

There is a role for private nuisance in contributing to environmental protection and arguably animal welfare, alongside regulatory regimes.[19] But this can only evolve effectively if the courts acknowledge the broader scientific evidence driving shifts in policy and practice, and interpret important concepts such as the 'good farmer' or 'reasonable user' in accordance with this evidence. Or, ideally, begin to push these even further towards an Earth law interpretation. Regulations – such as those governing welfare and water pollution – and incentive schemes like those provided for by the Agriculture Act 2020 are positive steps towards balancing food production and ecological needs of the more-than-human. But they are insufficiently radical and holistic.[20] An Earth law approach requires a transition to a system of agroecology that ensures food production alongside the health of vital ecosystems.[21] Nuisance could begin to play a part in facilitating a transition to agroecology by recognising the responsibilities of a farmer to all the beings affected by the use of land for agriculture.

The Perils of Time Travel

I was torn between rewriting this judgment at the time it was handed down in 1999 or bringing it up to date. The former was attractive because I believe that the court should have found, even then, that the 'good farmer' ought to have responded more sensitively to their neighbours. We would surely be further forward if the court in 1999 had begun to grapple with the damaging role of intensive farming and questioned how the 'good farmer' could take better care of their human and

[18] Tim G Benton et al, 'Food System Impacts on Biodiversity Loss: Three Levers for Food System Transformation in Support of Nature' (Research Paper, Chatham House, 2021) 16.

[19] See Ben Pontin, *Nuisance Law and Environmental Protection: A Study of Nuisance Injunctions in Practice* (Lawtext Publishing, 2013). Despite Lord Goff's insistence in *Cambridge Water* (305) that environmental issues should be dealt with by legislation, rather than developments in the common law, it is clear that nuisance plays a part in shaping land use obligations, albeit working alongside regulations; see Lord Neuberger in *Coventry v Lawrence* [2014] UKSC 13 [92] citing Lord Carnwath in *Barr v Biffa Waste Services Ltd* [2013] QB 455, para 46(ii) and Maria Lee where she states: 'the property rights protected in private nuisance are not clearly pre-defined; as well as protecting property rights, private nuisance (with regulation) shapes, or "constitutes", those rights.' See Maria Lee, 'The Public Interest in Private Nuisance: Collectives and Communities in Tort' (2015) 74 *Cambridge Law Journal* 329, 356.

[20] IPES-Food, *From Uniformity to Diversity: A Paradigm Shift from Industrial Agriculture to Diversified Agroecological Systems* (International Panel of Experts on Sustainable Food Systems, 2016); Food and Agriculture Organization, *Report of the Regional Symposium on Agroecology for Sustainable Agriculture and Food Systems for Europe and Central Asia* (FAO, 2017).

[21] Rob Amos, *Advancing Agroecology in International Law* (Routledge, 2023).

more-than human community. However, I decided to set the case at the date of writing (2023), as I think there is a risk that a court would still take a very narrow and impoverished interpretation of the 'good farmer' and look only at what the regulatory framework requires, without full consideration of their interconnectedness and capabilities. I also think it unlikely that the court hearing a private nuisance case on intensive pig farming would bring those pigs into the judgment or reflect on the interconnected nature of the resulting harms. This means that these remain live concerns. Bringing the case up to date meant I can address these concerns using current knowledge.

However, it also meant a slightly uncomfortable updating of the legal matrix. Whilst the law of private nuisance has not advanced substantially, the regulation of agricultural pollution has. I have imagined the defendants farming between 2011 and 2018. This means their activities are covered by a Code of Good Agricultural Practice, but that they ceased farming as the mandatory requirements under the 2018 Regulations were brought in.[22] This echoes the pattern of the original case. I have drawn on the relevant regulatory context but limited the detail because the important point is that harm was occurring despite the defendants complying with their basic regulatory obligations of the time. The first-instance judgment has been transplanted to 2022 using the law as described in the reimagined judgment. Regardless of this updated legal framework, the approach of the original judge at first instance remains sadly plausible and it was possible to summarise[23] very similar findings of fact and conclusions of general legal principle as quoted in the original decision.[24]

Factually, I have stayed close to the original. Clearly, water pollution from nitrate application is no longer an emerging risk but a well-known one. As such, pollution by nitrates is likely to be more easily foreseen now than then. Yet, the approach taken by the court to assessing risk and how the 'good farmer' reacts to reports of harm, remain live concerns, and it is on this that the judgment turns. Given the distance from the original judgment, the names of the parties have been changed so as not to unfairly hold them to standards of a different age or embroil them in the issue of whether intensive farming is a reasonable use of land. That question played no part in the original judgment and is entirely a frolic of my own.

Desire Lines

Rewriting a judgment also presented the opportunity to imagine the law through a range of creative possibilities. Inspired by Michelle Lim,[25] I toyed with radical approaches that fictionalised the legal framework or the process. But I kept

[22] Outlined in paras 10 and 11 of the reimagined judgment.
[23] Paras 3 and 4 of the reimagined judgment.
[24] *Savage*, 187–88.
[25] Michelle Lim, 'Fiction as Legal Method – Imagining with the More-than-Human to Awaken Our Plural Selves' (2021) 33 *Journal of Environmental Law* 501.

returning to Justice Brian Preston's advice about using judgments to build on existing 'flashes' of Wild law.[26] And, in the end, I felt the greatest value lay in sketching out a route from where we are to a place closer to Earth law. Anything else was to risk the legal equivalent of the old joke about the person who, when asked directions, replies that there are various routes to the desired location but none of them start from here. And, in some ways, it felt as though fiction wasn't needed. An Earth law approach to the 'good farmer' and even 'reasonable user', is in view, just over the next (agroecologically farmed) field.

[26] Brian Preston, 'The Challenges of Approaching Judging from an Earth-centred Perspective. A Book Review.' (2018) 35 *Environmental and Planning Law Journal* 218, 218, drawing on Cormac Cullinan, *Wild Law* (Siber Ink, 2002) 10.

In a Court of Appeal

Salvage and Another v Fairburn and Others

19 February 2023

JUDGMENT

Lady Justice Howe

Introduction

1. The land that forms the claimants' home lies in a part of the Kent countryside designated an Area of Outstanding Natural Beauty. The defendants operated an intensive pig and arable farm on neighbouring land. Between 2011 and 2018, the defendants applied inorganic nitrogen and pig manure to that land.

2. The application of these fertilizers polluted the spring running through the claimants' land. The water supply has been rendered permanently undrinkable for the claimants, their companion animals and other beings living on the land. The claimants seek a remedy that takes full account of the harm caused by the defendants' activities.

The Judgment at First Instance

3. In 2022, the judge made some findings of fact, which I summarise as follows:
    1. The application of inorganic fertilizer and pig manure was a major cause of the pollution.
    2. The defendants' application of fertilizer and manure was within accepted standards (and the relevant Code of Good Practice was likely to have come to their attention).
    3. The defendants were aware from 2013 of the claimants' concerns about pollution of their watercourse, when fish in their pond died.
    4. The defendants farmed in accordance with good agricultural practice at the time.

4. The judge concluded that:
    1. The use of the farm land by the defendants was in accordance with the practices of the day and was prima facie reasonable.
    2. The defendants could not have foreseen that their application of pig manure and chemical fertiliser would give rise to a real risk of contamination of

> the claimants' water supply. The judge had regard to good agricultural practice and applied the test of the hypothetical 'good farmer'.

The action for damages therefore failed.

The claimants appeal on the grounds a) the pollution ought to have been foreseeable by the hypothetical 'good farmer' and b) use of land for intensive agriculture is not reasonable.

The Role of the 'Good Farmer'

5. The 'good farmer' lies at the heart of this case. It is by reference to this hypothetical person that the two key – interlinked – questions of whether the harm was reasonably foreseeable and whether the use of the land was reasonable are judged.

6. In this case, the judge at first instance explained that the notional person by whom the reasonable foreseeability of harm is to be assessed is:

> the hypothetical good farmer, competent to run an intensive pig operation and arable farm such as that in question.

7. The 'good farmer' is also the touchstone for reasonable user. The judge described the use of land for intensive pig and arable production as reasonable because the defendants followed good agricultural practice for the time. In other words, the defendants met the standard of care expected of the 'good farmer', despite the harm caused.

8. We must therefore establish the characteristics of the notional 'good farmer' if we are to stand the defendants in her shoes. Or, perhaps more accurately, in her wellies. This should be done with great care. Farming is a vital and difficult endeavour, but farmers have a huge impact – for good or ill – on many lives. The standards expected of the 'good farmer' must reflect that.

Who is the 'Good Farmer' in Law?

9. The judge defined the 'good farmer' as someone who follows 'good agricultural practice'. This meant compliance with existing regulatory requirements coupled with accepted practice in industry, such as taking agronomist and Natural England advice. But nothing further.

10. The regulatory requirements for avoiding diffuse nitrate pollution from the application of fertilisers, in place during the time when the defendants were farming, were limited. As the defendants' land was not in a Nitrate Vulnerable Zone, they were not subject to the Nitrate Pollution Prevention Regulations 2015

or its predecessor. All farmers are subject to the obligations introduced by the Reduction and Prevention of Agricultural Diffuse Pollution (England) Regulations 2018, which came into force April 2018. But, as the judge highlighted, the 2018 requirements came in just as the defendants were finishing their pig and arable operation. As such, they could not have been expected to comply with them.

11. These rules were supplemented by those associated with cross-compliance for farmers in receipt of certain rural payments under the Common Agricultural Policy but, as this did not apply to the defendant, I shall not go into further detail. A Code of Good Agricultural Practice was published in 2011 and updated in 2018: *Protecting our Water, Soil and Air*, DEFRA, 2018. Although the judge found the defendants were likely to have been aware of this Code, it is unclear whether they fully abided by it.

12. It is beyond dispute that the regulatory framework forms the foundations of the 'good farmer' in law. The standards contained therein, coupled with relevant guidance, provide a baseline set of obligations which shape our expectations of this character. An ambitious Code of Good Practice may prove a valuable supplement. But this is not enough by itself. As Lord Carnwath stated in *Barr v Biffa Waste Services Ltd* [2012] EWCA Civ 312 [76]: 'Sticking to the rules is an aspect of good neighbourliness, but it is far from the whole story – in law as in life.'

13. The construction of the 'good farmer' should not be a narrow, technical exercise. Focus on the regulatory 'rules' led the lower court to disregard aspects of the defendants' behaviour that are highly relevant to the question of whether they were acting as 'good farmers'. It allowed the judge to ignore the significance of their relationships with their land, animals and human neighbours, and to downplay the responsibilities flowing from these relationships. It enabled the uncomfortable finding that the defendants were acting as 'good farmers', despite causing the claimants years of avoidable distress.

14. Farmers form part of a web of interconnected relationships linking them to the wider human and non-human community through their land. Like other landowners or managers, the 'good farmer' has an obligation to be aware of risks within her control that might harm neighbouring land: see *Network Rail Infrastructure Limited v Williams* [2018] EWCA Civ 1514. Farmers are taken to have such understanding of how to protect the environment – and promote animal welfare – that they may be paid solely for providing these 'public goods', under s 1 Agriculture Act 2020. The 'good farmer' takes her ecological responsibilities seriously.

15. Indeed, I have been urged in argument to go further and recognise that landownership should be conceptualised as a form of stewardship, with inherent duties to care for the ecological health of the land (see, for example, James Karp, 'A Private Property Duty of Stewardship: Changing our Land Ethic' (1993) 23 *Environmental Law* 735). I agree that such duties should inform the land management standards expected of the 'good farmer', in addition to those imposed by regulation.

16. But how far can we expect the 'good farmer' to respond to potential harms that do not form part of the regulatory requirements, or which arise despite compliance? On the one hand, it is unfair to impose expectations based on hindsight: see Lord Denning in *Roe v Ministry of Health* [1954] 2 QB 66 (CA), 84. Nevertheless, the 'good farmer' is entirely capable of adopting a more precautionary and proactive approach to risk than proposed at first instance. Farmers have long been expected to identify risks of injury, disease and pollution and to maintain systems for managing these. The 'good farmer' is an innovative and entrepreneurial character, able to meet the challenges of running a successful business: see for example, *Moore v Moore* [2016] 2202 EWHC (Ch) [36]. Indeed, post-Brexit payment schemes have been co-designed with farmers. This is not the picture painted at first instance of a passive recipient of legal obligations who is poorly equipped to manage emerging risk.

17. This does not mean that the 'good farmer' will identify and mitigate all novel or unexpected risks. However, it does mean that she is expected to be aware of serious risks that are known to the public, even before such risks are incorporated into regulatory standards. This is particularly so where the risk itself – or harm associated with such a risk – is drawn to her attention.

18. This brings us to the neighbours. One of the starkest features of the 'good farmer', as portrayed by the judge, is her isolation. She appears as a lone dweller in her landscape, able to disregard the impacts of her activity on other members of her human community. Yet the 'good farmer' is, in fact, a highly connected being. Even the most introvert farmer is likely to benefit from the help and camaraderie of neighbours (see *Thorner v Major* [2007] UKHC 2422 (Ch) [35]–[37]). Delivery of conservation, recreation and climate goals has long been premised on farmers' relationships with other landowners, advisors and even the public. Far from being alone, the 'good farmer' is deeply embedded in her human community. As such, she should be expected to show care and compassion for the interests of that community when making decisions about her farming practice.

19. Finally, we must ask what the 'good farmer' looks like from the perspective of the animals in her care. Animal welfare is an essential component of the 'good farmer', in part because welfare is a systemic issue. Poor animal welfare suggests practices liable to cause wider environmental harm: see UN Environment Assembly 5 2022, Resolution 1. Welfare also matters because it has a profound effect on the lives of the animals themselves. Who is the 'good farmer' in their eyes? We may think that there can be no such thing. But, whilst animals are kept for food, the law must require they experience the best quality of life – and death – possible. The behaviour of their human handler is a key component of welfare: see DEFRA, *Code of Practice for the Welfare of Pigs*, 2020, para 9. In addition to providing high standards of accommodation, food and health provision, the good farmer must ensure kind and species-appropriate care. The good farmer in the eyes of their animals needs to be the same knowledgeable, aware, and compassionate character needed by the wider Earth community.

20. The question now is whether this 'good farmer' would have foreseen the harm at issue.

Reasonable Foreseeability

21. As laid down by the House of Lords in *Cambridge Water Co Ltd v Eastern Counties Leather Plc* [1994] 2 AC 264 (HL) 300B, 301C, the defendant must be able to foresee harm of the relevant type for the claimant to recover damages in nuisance.

22. Here, the defendants were applying nitrates in accordance with the law and the practice of other conventional farmers. In so doing, the judge found they were following good agricultural practice of the time. On this basis, he held that they could not have foreseen substantial risk of harm to the claimants' watercourse.

23. It is difficult to accept that the 'good farmer', in the defendants' position, could not reasonably foresee the harm to the claimants. Counsel for the claimants rightly points out that the question is not only what the defendants actually knew, but what they ought to have known.

24. It is highly significant that concerns were raised over the defendants' farming practices repeatedly and from an early stage in their farming career. It cannot be right that the 'good farmer' is permitted to ignore direct reports of serious harm to neighbouring land brought to her attention again and again. This is particularly relevant where a defendant is engaged in an activity – such as intensive or 'conventional' farming – known to be capable of causing serious ecological damage.

25. The case at hand is very different from *Cambridge Water*. There, the defendant could not have foreseen that the chemicals from the tannery process would seep into the ground and contaminate the claimant's borehole many miles away. Pollution of the borehole only became known after the defendants had ceased the polluting activity (pp 291–292 of the judgment). A scientific report on water pollution by inorganic chemicals was only published long after the harm had occurred.

26. In contrast, harm of the type caused by the defendants was known during the period the defendants were farming. Whilst the exact site of the spring on the claimants' land might not have been known until 2017, its existence was known. The claimants began complaining in 2013 about the defendants' activities and the statutory water authority also raised concerns about resulting water pollution. The defendants knew by 2015 that they were causing 'anxiety and distress' to their neighbours, who had made several reports of water pollution by this time.

27. I accept that the defendants' application of nitrates and fertilisers was not unduly high and was in accordance with advice from Natural England and their agronomist. Nevertheless, water pollution was a known risk of nitrate application. The complaints should have alerted the defendants to the fact that their level of use was problematic.

28. The defendants cannot rely on the evidence from their agronomist or Natural England (NE) advisor that they saw no improper level of nitrate or manure use, because the defendants did not disclose the claimants' complaints to these advisors. Had they been informed of those complaints they would almost certainly have considered a reduction in nitrate and manure application. Moreover, the defendants were aware that waste from the pig unit was an environmental concern, hence keeping their true plans for expansion from the planning department. Taken overall, this suggests that the defendants either knew, or at the very least ought to have known, of a risk that required investigation.

29. In conclusion on this issue, I find that harm was reasonably foreseeable to a 'good farmer' in the defendants' position. This applies from the date of the initial complaints in 2013.

30. Given that finding, it is necessary to assess whether the defendants' use of the land was reasonable. This will be dealt with in two stages: (1) whether the defendants met the standards of the 'good farmer'; and (2) whether intensive farming should be treated as a reasonable use of land given the likelihood of harm.

Reasonable User and the 'Good Farmer'

31. As stated by Lord Millett in *Southwark LBC v Mills* [2001] 1 AC 1 at 20:

> The law of nuisance is concerned with balancing the conflicting interests of adjoining owners. … For this purpose, it employs the control mechanism described by Lord Goff of Chieveley in *Cambridge Water Co Ltd v Eastern Counties Leather Plc* [1994] 2 AC 264 at 299 as 'the principle of reasonable user – the principle of give and take'.

32. Reasonable user is assessed by reference to all the material circumstances: see *Clerk and Lindsell on Torts*, 24th edn (2023) para 19-34. If the activity could have been conducted in a less harmful manner, then this will point towards the user being unreasonable: see *Coventry v Lawrence* [2014] UKSC 13 [181]. However, taking all reasonable care will not necessarily absolve the defendant from liability if the activities still cause foreseeable harm to their neighbour, see Lord Goff in *Cambridge Water* at 300.

33. Regulatory compliance is an important component in assessing reasonableness, although there can be no expectation of compliance with future obligations. Yet meeting regulatory requirements is not necessarily enough by itself to avoid liability in nuisance. In *Barr v Biffa*, [76], Lord Carnwath stated: 'An activity which is conducted in contravention of planning or environmental controls is unlikely to be reasonable. But the converse does not follow.' In that case, waste disposal practices were unreasonable because the defendants failed to take mitigating action in the face of a neighbour's complaints, despite compliance with their regulatory permits.

34. Where there is evidence that harm is occurring despite operating within regulatory obligations, the 'good farmer' must take appropriate steps to investigate and mitigate any harm. Their actions are more likely to be reasonable where they have taken active steps to become aware of risks and taken prompt action in response to complaints: *Network Rail* [56]. Following codes of good practice, cooperation with conservation advisors and engagement with environmental stewardship schemes will contribute to a finding of 'reasonable care'. Determined adherence to harmful, intensive agricultural practices and failure to engage with knowledge outside that intensive sector will not.

35. The judge at first instance found that the defendants' use of their land appeared reasonable on the basis that they had complied with 'good agricultural practice' by meeting regulatory obligations and accepted practices of the intensive farming industry. Albeit that he observed that, if they had known that they were polluting the claimants' land, this would not have enabled them to carry on regardless.

36. I have found that the defendants knew or ought to have known of the pollution risk. Had they informed their advisors of the complaints and responded in a considerate and timely fashion, this would have been the actions of a good farmer and have rendered their actions reasonable. Clear compliance with the 2011 Code would have reinforced this finding. Continuing the same farming practices in the face of their neighbours' distress, without any investigation, did not meet the standards of the 'good farmer'. As such, the requirements of reasonable user are not met.

Can Intensive Livestock Farming be a Reasonable Use of Land?

37. I would, however, like to say more about the land use in this case. The judge found the use of land as an intensive pig and arable farm to be a 'prima facie' reasonable use of land, at least where the farm was run in accordance with the practices of the day. This is not a position I find easy to endorse given the disastrous environmental and animal welfare impacts of intensive farming. The intensity of the land use is highly relevant in assessing reasonableness: *Fearn v Board of Trustees of the Tate Gallery* [2023] UKSC 4 (SC) [74]. Counsel for the claimant submitted that intensive farming should be prima facie an unreasonable use of land. There is force in this submission. The court must question ecologically harmful activities and be ready to include the voices of those who have hitherto gone unheard.

38. What is reasonable is understood to change with the times. This includes the need to adapt to environmental concerns. In *Coventry v Lawrence*, Lord Carnwath [180] drew, with approval, on the words of Lord Cooke in *Hunter v Canary Wharf Ltd* [1997] AC 655, where he highlighted these changes:

> [T]he lineaments of the law of nuisance were established before the age of television and radio, motor transport and aviation, town and country planning, a 'crowded island', and a heightened public consciousness of the need to protect the environment. All these are now among the factors falling to be taken into account in evolving the law. (711D–E)

39. Whilst some farming practices work with nature to promote ecological health, intensive farming does not. It does quite the opposite. These practices damage the health of ecosystems and contribute to atmospheric carbon, see for example, the *State of Nature Report* 2023, 50–56. Such practices also harm the health and well-being of human neighbours. On this basis alone, it must be right for the court to consider the general reasonableness of this activity. But these practices also harm other animals that we do not usually name in a nuisance suit: wildlife, companion animals and the farmed animals themselves. I would like to return to one of the sources of the nuisance: the pigs.

40. If animals are a nuisance, it is because we make them so. It is not just a 'pig in the parlour' that causes trouble if we make the barnyard just as unsuitable. In *Wheeler v Saunders* [1996] Ch 19, 39 the Court of Appeal notes that intensification of production by housing pigs on slatted floors under which their waste collects, rather than on straw bedding, is bound to have greater negative effects on the locality. The problem is captured clearly by Judge Wilkinson in the US case of *McKiver v Murphy-Brown, LLC*, No 19-1019 (4th Circuit 2020), where he explained that:

> The warp in the human–hog relationship, and the root of the nuisance in this suit, lay in the deplorable conditions of confinement prevailing [on the defendant's farm], conditions that there is no reason to suppose were unique to that facility. Confinement defined life for the over 14,000 hogs. (71)

41. What of the pigs here or in *Wheeler*? Does this land use look 'reasonable' from their perspective? Pigs are highly intelligent, sociable and empathic creatures. Yet the vast majority of pigs in the United Kingdom are reared in intensive systems which, according to organisations such as Compassion in World Farming, restrict beneficial natural behaviours, increase stress and end in distressing deaths: Compassion in World Farming, *Pigs*. Confinement causes aggressive interactions and a range of painful physical mutilations: Farm Animal Welfare Committee, *Opinion on Mutilations and Environmental Enrichment in Piglets and Growing Pigs*, 2011. It is hard to see how any level of care by the farmer could make life in this system 'reasonable', never mind the good life to which they should be entitled.

42. Counsel for the defendants questioned whether we can speak for other animals in any legitimate sense. In my view, it is better that we try to represent those who have traditionally been voiceless, than avoid doing so for fear of getting it wrong. Modern ethology provides a rich source of evidence from which to make informed guesses about animals' experience. Unthinking anthropomorphism should be

avoided. But so should the opposite. Anthropodenial reinforces the narrative of human separation and dominance and leads to a refusal to recognise as equivalent behaviours and emotions that appear to reflect our own, see: Frans de Waal, *Mama's Last Hug* (Granta, 2019) 47–51. Communication lies well beyond speech. The well-being or otherwise of a pig is embodied in its movements, sounds and smell. Just because they cannot speak our language is no reason not to listen to theirs.

43. The pigs' experience is important of itself. As recognised by the Sentience Act 2022, pigs are sentient beings and deserve lives and deaths that, at the very least, meet the highest standards of welfare. This is something more likely to be achieved outside of the intensive sector, as illustrated by the farmer Helen Browing in her book *Pig* (with Tim Finney (Wildfire, 2018)). Indeed, there are many who would argue for recognition of non-human animals as legal subjects with rights that would constrain our use of them; for example, Maneesha Deckha, *Animals as Legal Beings: Contesting Anthropocentric Legal Orders* (University of Toronto Press, 2020). Moreover, the pigs of whom we speak were individuals, with their own characters, motivations and preferences; they are not a homogenous mass of the genus *Sus* (*domesticus*).

44. But the pigs' experience is also important because, as Judge Wilkinson in *McKiver* presents so vividly, poor pig (hog) welfare is part of the 'interlocking dysfunctions' shared between animal, human and the wider environment (76). The harm to the pigs is fundamentally entwined with wider injuries to people and the land. The potential for harm coupled with the virtual impossibility that any level of care can avoid these harms occurring makes it more appropriate to treat intensive farming as prima facie an unreasonable use of land than a reasonable one.

45. The counter argument is, of course, that intensive agriculture is in the public interest. It claims to provide large quantities of cheaper food than more ecologically sustainable alternatives and to support the livelihoods of many farmers. These are obviously vital considerations, but they do not dispose of the matter.

46. We should take account of whether the activity could be performed in another, less harmful, manner and still provide the public benefit: see Lord Carnwath in *Coventry* [181]. We should not be too quick to accept the necessity of intensive farming techniques. Significant evidence was provided that agroecological production methods can provide substantial quantities of nutritious food, without the ecologically harmful impacts. Moreover, liability in nuisance may still be found where an activity has a public benefit; that benefit being addressed at the remedies stage, see *Coventry*.

47. Nevertheless, we must remain sensitive to the interconnected realities of the system. It is difficult for the courts to treat intensive farming as an unreasonable use of land until farmers can be paid a fair price for their produce and enabled to transition to more sustainable and higher welfare practices. Pushing our own farmers out of business may mean even heavier reliance on imports from countries whose standards of ecological and animal welfare may be well below our own.

48. However, it remains my view that the courts have a far greater role to play in challenging the acceptability of intensive farming by being explicit about the harms caused by these practices and the availability of plausible alternatives.

Conclusions and Remedies

49. A restorative remedy is appropriate as the defendants have ceased the harmful activities. Damages should reflect the harm to all the beings whom the defendants could reasonably foresee would be affected, not only the human claimants. It is recognised that compensation may include harm to other beings on the land, such as trees and shrubs, see *St Helen's Smelting Co v Tipping* (1865) HL Cas 642. The award should look to restoring, as far as possible, the health of the land, including the claimants' spring. This takes fuller account of the harm flowing from an activity and is more compatible with the principle that the polluter should pay for harm caused, as enshrined in, for example, the 1992 Rio Declaration on Environment and Development.

50. Nuisance law seeks to ensure my actions do not unreasonably interfere with a neighbouring landowner's use and enjoyment of their land. To enhance the tort's role in environmental justice, scholars have argued for its scope to include non-property-owning human claimants; see Sam Porter, 'Do the Rules of Private Nuisance Breach the Principles of Environmental Justice? (2019) 21 *Environmental Law Review* 21. But why extend this only to my human neighbour? Surely nuisance should have a role in regulating my impact on my non-human neighbour too.

51. In future I would like to see claims on behalf of sentient beings who treat the land as a home. Domesticated animals have an argument for inclusion within the purview of nuisance that is analogous to children housed on the land. Wild animals have an interest in the land as a means of providing food, water and shelter. Both groups possess, arguably, a concept of the land as a 'home'; a place of safety that meets their own needs and those of their young. In this way, nuisance could provide a more effective private law mechanism for enforcing human obligations to care for land. Including when there is no directly affected human claimant.

Judgment for the claimant. And for all the others.

Commentary

Johanna Gibson

Whither the Pigs?

Helena Howe's judgment in *Savage v Fairclough*[27] brings all parties to the table, scrutinising the contact in nuisance, both physical and cultural, through the relationships at stake. In so doing, the judgment respects boundaries as points of contact and relation in the constitution of property, as distinct from a contrived objectivity of individual powers. The dynamic relationship in nuisance is articulated in the judgment through attention to the concepts of the 'good farmer' as 'reasonable user' and the 'foreseeability' of harm.[28] The characterisation of 'good', the nature of 'use' and the 'foreseeability' of the reasonable are critical to the Earth law of obligations in this present case.

The technical legal meaning of 'good' is understood most fully through the law of contract – that is, a good consideration is one that is both valuable and real.[29] Thus, the concept of 'good' in and of itself necessarily entails a relationship and the 'good' is always already a value perceived through relation. Importantly then, as far as the law is concerned, to be 'good' is always to be in contact, to be in a relationship, to be connected. And in this context, the 'good' relationship is one of valuable consideration and therefore obligation. The concept of 'good' arguably therefore includes an appreciation of the provision of that 'good' to the public.[30] In the case of *Savage v Fairclough*, rewilding the law of nuisance necessitates the affirmation of this relationality of the 'good farmer'. The fundamental question then remains – who are the parties in this relationship? Where are 'all the others'? Whither the pigs?

The conventional approach to nuisance as characterised in the original judgment persists with a notion of separate spheres in order to effect the objectivity of property supposed in the decision. Howe describes this approach to the good farmer as that of 'a lone dweller in their landscape', but fundamentally refutes this, arguing compellingly that the 'good farmer' is, in fact, 'a highly connected being.' This connectedness is central to Howe's judgment and to an ethological jurisprudence[31] – that is, approaching the co-constitution of property through the

[27] *Savage v Fairclough* [2000] Env LR 183.

[28] *Cambridge Water Co Ltd v Eastern Counties Leather Plc* [1994] Env LR 105.

[29] *Davies v Bolton* [1894] 3 WLR 678.

[30] For instance, see the discussion of the relationship between public goods and good farming in George Cusworth and Jennifer Dodsworth, 'Using the "Good Farmer" Concept to Explore Agricultural Attitudes to the Provision of Public Goods: A Case Study of Participants in an English Agri-environment Scheme' (2021) 38 *Agriculture and Human Values* 929. In their field research, the authors note that certain goods, including animal welfare, were raised by only a few interview subjects (933).

[31] Gibson, *Owned.*

relations of farmers, neighbours, pigs and 'all the others'. The question of contamination is one of not only the shared suffering of 'interlocking dysfunctions',[32] but also the shared interests[33] of accountability to the Earth and to all others. Indeed, this is fundamental to the understanding of foreseeability in terms of futures, both as actual agricultural commodities, and as times to come, as distinct from always already too late reactions.

It is in this respect that Howe's introduction of 'knowledge' as part of the concept of 'good' is not only relevant but also entirely consistent with animal welfare science and policy. Howe's judgment re-orientates the question of knowledge to account for an ethological sensibility towards the 'systemic issue' of welfare, asking 'what the "good farmer" looks like from the perspective of the animals in her care,' in order to fulfil the value of 'good' as farmers. After all, to be reasonable is, quite simply, to know what you ought to know.[34] Indeed, the 1965 *Brambell Report* into animal welfare in intensive farming identified explicitly the importance of stockpersonship training to the welfare of animals in their care.[35] And before this, the emergence of the study of stress in animals introduced a discourse of connectedness in early welfare science.[36] In the context of animal welfare law, this relationship of 'use' in intensive farming motivates a wider interpretation of the users of the system itself. What is the pig's perspective on the concept of a good farmer? Animal welfare law arguably requires us to try to answer this question, not only in terms of determining the fulfilment of obligations to welfare under animal welfare legislation,[37] but also in terms of acknowledging the animals as users of the system, as having an interest in the answer, by reason of their 'welfare property'.[38]

To understand the relevance of 'welfare property' in this context, the concept of 'suffering' is critical. Suffering is a key concept in animal welfare and in interpreting welfare offences, and is thus crucially important in answering this question of the 'good farmer' from the pigs' perspectives. As Howe acknowledges, the original judgment avoids the term altogether, at best using 'euphemistic language to describe the animals' suffering'. This is perhaps unsurprising as an inevitable

[32] *McKiver v Murphy-Brown* 980 F.3d 937, 981 (4th Cir 2020).

[33] Gibson, *Owned.*

[34] *Re a Solicitor* [1945] KB 368, 371.

[35] FW Rogers Brambell and the Technical Committee, *Report of the Technical Committee to Enquire into the Welfare of Animals kept under Intensive Livestock Husbandry Systems* (Her Majesty's Stationery Office, 1965).

[36] Robert GW Kirk 'The Invention of the "Stressed Animal" and the Development of a Science of Animal Welfare, 1947–86' in David Cantor and Edmund Ramsden (eds), *Stress, Shock and Adaptation in the Twentieth Century*, (University of Rochester Press, 2014) 241–63.

[37] Both under the Protection of Animals Act 1911 which was in force at the time of the offence and judgment, and under the current Animal Welfare Act 2006, which repealed part of the Protection of Animals Act 1911, leaving in force provisions pertaining to traps and poisons.

[38] Johanna Gibson 'Animals and Property: A Person Possessed' in *The Routledge Handbook of Property, Law and Society* (Routledge, 2022) 297–311.

consequence of the limiting interpretations of the conventional relationships initiated through nuisance. Nevertheless, this silence on suffering somewhat artificially contrives a relationship of nuisance as purely inter-human, while at the same time diminishing the 'good' that is to be delivered (and indeed foreseen) by the 'good farmer', including animal welfare and environmental integrity.

The derivation of the 'good farmer' from the concept of reasonable user is critically significant in addressing this silence. The understanding of good as pertaining to knowledge, that is, knowledge in relation to certain (foreseeable) ends, reinforces the relational nature of the legal concept of 'good'. In other words, the 'good' of that knowledge is concerned with certain purposes and, thus, public goods, returning to the foreground the interconnectedness of the 'good farmer' with animal welfare and the environment. In fact, the concept of the 'good farmer' as 'reasonable user' actually demands it. Instead of their reduction to vessels of contamination, Howe's rewriting gives the pigs wings.

Are there good farmers? Perhaps only when pigs fly.

8

Property Rights and Environmental Regulation on the Estuary: *R (on the application of Mott) v Environment Agency*

BONNIE HOLLIGAN

Capturing Conflict

A putcher is a conical basket woven from willow. Since medieval times, rows of putchers mounted on wooden frames have been used to capture Atlantic salmon as they migrate up the Severn Estuary towards their river of birth.[1] In *R (on the application of Mott) v Environment Agency*,[2] a putcher rank fisherman, Mr Mott, successfully claimed that restrictions imposed by the Agency on his annual salmon catch interfered with his peaceful enjoyment of possessions, protected under Article 1 of Protocol 1 to the European Convention on Human Rights (A1P1 ECHR). Positing an apparently straightforward conflict between property rights (in the form of Mr Mott's lease of salmon fishing rights)[3] and environmental regulation, the case also speaks to how decisions are made, and how the costs of ecological and social transition are allocated.

While leaving open the question of whether the restrictions amounted to a regulatory 'taking' or deprivation, as opposed to a control on use,[4] the Supreme

[1] See Caroline A Buffery, 'The Rivers of Law: A Historical Legal Geography of Fishing on the Severn Estuary' (2017) 25 *Water Law* 263, 264. For photographs, see the Living Levels website, livinglevels.org.uk/stories/2019/8/12/putcher-fishing.

[2] *R (on the application of Mott) v Environment Agency* [2018] UKSC 10.

[3] The nature of salmon fishing rights as a distinct form of property is obscure. A right to fish may be an incorporeal hereditament that can be sold or leased separately from the ownership of the land. See Kevin Gray and Susan Francis Gray, *Elements of Land Law*, 5th edn (Oxford University Press, 2009) 5.1.14–5.1.15 and 4.2.5. Although s 11 of the Salmon Fishery Acts 1861 prohibits the trapping of salmon using 'fixed engines', including putcher baskets such as those at issue in *Mott*, rights exercised by virtue of a pre-existing grant, charter or immemorial usage are preserved, and this appears to be the basis of the rights leased to Mr Mott.

[4] See here Douglas Maxwell, 'Reeling in Classifications of Interferences under Article 1 of the First Protocol and the Fair Balance Test. *R (on the application of Mott) v Environment Agency*' (2018) 6 *Journal of Planning and Environment Law* 639.

Court decided that the catch limitations did amount to an interference with Mr Mott's A1P1 rights, due to the individual and excessive burden placed on him, and the effect of the restrictions on his livelihood. This result fits with Douglas Maxwell's characterisation of A1P1 as often being employed in support of conservation of existing entitlements.[5] The case has been argued to be a missed opportunity to explore the ecological embeddedness of property, and the existence of ecological obligations, as well as rights.[6] The decision can also, however, be located within a longer history of conflict over legal regulation of fishing in the Estuary, and concern that the human communities who rely on fishing for livelihood are unfairly asked to bear the burden of the broader damage wrought by industrialisation of rivers.[7]

Reordering, Diverting and Expanding

The reimagining of *Mott* took multiple forms, elaborated further in Jo Walton's contribution to this chapter. The version presented in this book is not a radical one. The idea of a private property right that allowed the killing of salmon could have been rejected altogether, or the rights of the river and its ecosystem to integrity recognised.[8] Instead, the legal principles and authorities applied are largely identical to those in the original judgment. While ultimately reaching a different result, the reimagined judgment follows the original very closely in its conclusion that fair balance may sometimes require payment of compensation in respect of environmental measures, but that this will turn on the individual facts of each case. Its aim is to work within what Ricketts refers to as the 'adjacent possible',[9] opening up small gaps in the existing order through which transformative ideas might enter.

The reimagined judgment attends to an expanded range of facts that were nevertheless available to the Court at the time of the original decision.[10] These

[5] Douglas Maxwell, *The Human Right to Property: A Practical Approach to Article 1 of Protocol No 1 to the ECHR* (Hart Publishing, 2022) para 12.18.

[6] See Bonnie Holligan, 'Human Rights and the Moralities of Property: Participation, Obligation and Value in *R (on the application of Mott) v Environment Agency*' (2019) 11 *Journal of Property, Planning and Environmental Law* 176.

[7] See Buffery, 'Rivers of Law', 272; and Carl J Griffin and Iain JM Robertson, 'Elvers and Salmon: Moral Ecologies and Conflict on the Nineteenth-Century Severn' in David Worthington (ed), *The New Coastal History* (Springer International, 2017) 99.

[8] See eg Erin O'Donnell, *Legal Rights for Rivers: Competition, Collaboration and Water Governance* (Routledge, 2019); and Erin Ryan, Holly Curry and Hayes Rule, 'Environmental Rights for the 21st Century: Comparing the Public Trust Doctrine and the Rights of Nature' (2021) 42 *Cardozo Law Review* 2447.

[9] Aidan Ricketts, 'Exploring Fundamental Legal Change through Adjacent Possibilities: The Newcrest Mining Case', in Nicole Rogers and Michelle Maloney (eds), *Law as if Earth Really Mattered: The Wild Law Judgment Project* (Routledge, 2017) 178, 180.

[10] An invaluable resource here was the archive recording of the Supreme Court hearings: supremecourt.uk/cases/uksc-2016-0148.html.

include the conclusion that the total sustainable salmon catch, according to the Agency, was incompatible with continued livelihood on the scale previously enjoyed by Mr Mott, even if all allocated catch were transferred to him. Moreover, the catch limitations were imposed on an annual basis and, in theory, could increase again over the remaining duration of the lease, if stocks recovered. There was also evidence of the Agency's long-standing policy to end 'mixed-stock' fishing and prior negotiations to purchase the lease, which the reimagined judgment argues diminish any expectation of indefinite livelihood.

In terms of legal principle, the reimagined judgment again sidesteps reliance on a distinction between deprivation and control. The crucial question remains that of proportionality, and whether the interference struck the required fair balance between Mr Mott's rights and those of others. As several of the contributions to this volume make clear,[11] reference to 'others' leaves space for recognition of the interconnectedness of the human and more-than-human world. The environmental purpose of the restrictions is afforded much greater weight in the assessment of whether a fair balance has been struck. There is support for this approach in the jurisprudence of the European Court of Human Rights (ECtHR).[12] The connection to fair decision-making procedure[13] is also given further consideration. The extent of any individual and excessive burden imposed by regulation remains central, but factors such as the availability of time to adapt, the existence of consultation processes, the general applicability of the regulation and the existence of rights of challenge or review are explored more fully than in the original judgment.[14]

Embedded Property

What emerges from the Earth law judgment is a version of private property that views rights as dynamic and situated within a web of social and ecological relations.[15] The rights protected under A1P1 are re-embedded in space and time[16] to comprehend the links between past and future, as well as ecological benefit and burden. The interference complained of in the case was with future value, and this value is contingent on the health of the salmon, and the rivers in which

[11] eg chs 5 and 6.

[12] See eg *Depalle v France* (2012) 54 EHRR 17; Maxwell, *Human Right to Property*, para 7.18.

[13] See Maxwell, *Human Right to Property*, paras 8.158–8.159.

[14] See ibid paras 8.151; *R (on the application of British American Tobacco UK Ltd) v Secretary of State for Health* [2016] EWHC 1169 (Admin); [2016] RPC 22, para 783.

[15] The judgment here draws on a rich seam of property scholarship including Nicole Graham, *Lawscape: Property, Environment, Law* (Routledge, 2011); Joseph Singer, *Entitlement: The Paradoxes of Property* (Yale University Press, 2000); Peter Burdon, *Earth Jurisprudence: Private Property and Environment* (Routledge, 2014); and Margaret Davies, Lee Godden and Nicole Graham, 'Situating Property within Habitat: Reintegrating Place, People, and Law' (2021) 6 *Journal of Law, Property and Society* 1.

[16] See Nicole Graham, 'Owning the Earth' in Peter Burdon (ed), *Exploring Wild Law: The Philosophy of Earth Jurisprudence* (Wakefield Press, 2011) 259.

they live. Past profits obtained from the exploitation of natural resources should arguably be taken into account when determining whether an individual has been asked to bear an excessive burden. Moreover, individual claims cannot be valued in isolation from their systemic context, a point accepted in the context of banking and financial crises.[17] Through this lens of connectivity and interdependence, the ways in which all kinds of relationships are managed come to the fore, and the possibilities for using A1P1 to navigate, rather than entrench, conflict may begin to surface.

[17] See Maxwell, *Human Right to Property*, paras 8.114–8.122, discussing the litigation arising from bank nationalisation following the 2007–08 financial crisis.

Judgment of the Supreme Court
R (on the application of Mott) v Environment Agency
14 February 2018

Lady Holligan

Background

1. The respondent, Mr Mott, holds a leasehold interest in a 'putcher rank' fishery at Lydney on the north bank of the Severn Estuary. A putcher is a conical basket used to entrap salmon as they return from the open sea to spawn. Mr Mott has operated the putcher rank under successive leases since 1975. Since 1979, salmon fishing has been his full-time occupation. Before the limitations that are the subject of this appeal were imposed, he estimates that his average catch was 600 salmon per year, at a value of about £100 per salmon, giving him a gross annual income of around £60,000.

2. The right to operate the rank derives from a 'Certificate of Privilege' dated 14 May 1866, issued by the Special Commissioners for English Fisheries and owned by the Lydney Park Estate. In 1998, the current 20-year lease was granted jointly by the Estate to Mr Mott and a Mr David Merrett, expiring on 31 March 2018. The lease affords the right to fish two stop nets and 650 putchers. In return for this, Mr Mott and Mr Merrett must pay an annual rent in two parts: a 'monetary rent' of (at present) £276, and a 'fish rent" equivalent to 65 pounds in weight of salmon. Tenants are required to operate the putcher rank during each fishing season unless circumstances make this impossible. They may not assign, sublet or part with the fishery during the term of the lease, save in the case of death or disability, when they may, with the written consent of the landlord, assign to another family member.

3. In order to exercise the rights granted under the lease, s 25 of the Salmon and Freshwater Fisheries Act 1975 ('the 1975 Act') requires the operators of historic fishing installations such as the putcher rank to obtain an annual licence from the Environment Agency ('the Agency'). The Agency's power to impose limitations on the number of fish caught by such installations was introduced by s 217(7) of the Marine and Coastal Access Act 2009. This added a new paragraph 14A of Schedule 2 to the 1975 Act, allowing the Agency to impose such conditions where considered 'necessary … for the protection of any fishery'.

4. The Severn Estuary is considered by the Agency to be a 'mixed-stock' fishery, with salmon travelling through the Estuary to spawn in the rivers Severn, Wye, Usk, Rhymney, Taff and Ely. It has long been government policy to phase out mixed-stock fisheries due to the challenges that the intermingled fish

populations present in terms of conservation and management. The rivers Wye and Usk are designated as Special Areas of Conservation ('SAC') under European Council Directive 92/44/EEC (the 'Habitats Directive'), currently given effect to in domestic law by the Conservation of Habitats and Species Regulations 2017 ('the Habitats Regulations'). It is accepted by the parties that the ecological impact of fisheries in the Estuary has been a long-standing concern of the Agency. Prior to the entry into force of the Marine and Coastal Access Act 2009, it was not within the Agency's power to impose compulsory catch limitations. A number of unsuccessful attempts have been made to end the putcher rank operation via negotiated settlement. Between 2003 and 2005, the Agency entered negotiations to purchase the Certificate of Privilege from the Lydney Estate. In 2011, an offer was made to purchase the then-remaining seven-year term of the respondent's lease. In 2004, 2010 and 2011 respectively, compensation of between £30,000 and £35,000 was paid to the respondent not to operate the putcher rank.

5. A Habitats Regulations Assessment carried out in 2012 concluded that unrestricted catch of salmon in the Severn Estuary was threatening the integrity of the River Wye SAC and recommended that limits be placed on the use of the historic installation fisheries, including putcher ranks. These recommendations were justified by reference to the impact of the installations on the numbers of salmon returning to the Wye to spawn, the stock in that river having long been identified as having an 'at risk' or unfavourable conservation status. A 2012 report from the University of Exeter, commissioned by the Agency, was relied upon to establish the mixed-stock nature of the fisheries. Mr Mott contested the findings of the Assessment and commissioned his own expert report from a Professor Fewster of the University of Auckland, New Zealand. This challenge was the object of detailed study in the courts below, and, although not the subject of this appeal, forms part of the context in which the Agency's actions must be assessed.

6. On the basis of the 2012 Assessment, on 1 June 2012 Mr Mott was served with a notice under para 14(a) of Schedule 2 of the Salmon and Freshwater Fisheries Act 1975. This limited his annual catch for 2012 to a total of 30 fish. The catch was set by reference to 'the lowest catch by any of the historic installation fisheries that had sought a licence in the preceding ten-year period', balanced against the need to avoid 'reduction in licence uptake and failure to maintain possible heritage'. It was proposed that further reductions would be applied for the 2013 and 2014 fishing seasons.

7. In the judgment of the court below, it was suggested that the lease might have retained 'some small value' if sold for leisure rather than commercial use. Whether or not this is correct, given the strict limits on the power to assign the lease, it is apparent that the restrictions had a significant effect on Mr Mott's ability to obtain a livelihood. He alleges that the effect of the restrictions has been to render his leasehold interest worthless and that, in the absence of compensation, this breaches his right to peaceful enjoyment of possessions under Article 1 of Protocol 1 to the European Convention on Human Rights (A1P1).

8. The rationality of the catch restriction and its scientific basis were also challenged in the lower courts. At first instance, the judge held that the analysis in the University of Exeter report did not provide a rational justification for the Agency's actions. The Court of Appeal allowed the Agency's appeal on this point. Although the existence of a reasonable foundation for the restrictions is of some relevance when considering whether an interference with A1P1 rights has taken place, it is the extent to which the Agency's actions constitute such an interference that is now the sole subject of this appeal.

A1P1 Principles

9. In the leading case of *Sporrong and Lönnroth v Sweden* (1982) 5 EHRR 35, the European Court of Human Rights (ECtHR) set out three general principles that can be derived from A1P1: the right to peaceful enjoyment of property, the right not to be deprived of possessions apart from under certain conditions provided for by law, and the principle that a state may impose controls on the use of property in the general interest. These three rules are not 'distinct' in the sense of being unconnected: the second and third rules are concerned with particular instances of interference with the right to peaceful enjoyment of property and should therefore be construed in the light of the first rule (*Bäck v Finland* 40 EHRR 1184, para 52 and *AXA General Insurance Ltd v HM Advocate* [2011] UKSC 46; [2012] 1 AC 868, para 107 per Lord Reed).

10. It was accepted by the parties that the benefit conferred under the lease is capable of being a 'possession' for the purposes of A1P1. The main points on which this court must decide are, therefore, the existence and nature of any interference with the respondent's 'possessions', and whether any interference can nevertheless be justified in the public interest. It is not essential here to categorise the measure as either a deprivation or a control on use. As Lord Reed explained in *AXA General Insurance Ltd* at para 108:

> [T]he test is in substance the same, however the interference has been classified. If an interference has been established, it is then necessary to consider whether it constitutes a violation. It must be shown that the interference complies with the principle of lawfulness and pursues a legitimate aim by means that are reasonably proportionate to the aim sought to be achieved. This final question focuses upon the question whether a fair balance has been struck between the demands of the general interest of the community and the requirements of the protection of the individual's fundamental rights.

11. It was argued on behalf of the Agency that a deprivation will usually presume the payment of compensation, while a control does not. However, it is well established that the public interest may sometimes justify a deprivation of property rights without full compensation, as set out in *James v United Kingdom* (1986) 8 EHRR 123 at para 54:

> Article 1 does not, however, guarantee a right to full compensation in all circumstances. Legitimate objectives of 'public interest', such as pursued in measures of economic reform or measures designed to achieve greater social justice, may call for less than reimbursement of the full market value.

12. Conversely, a control on use may sometimes require the payment of compensation where this is necessary to maintain a fair balance between the rights of an individual and the public interest, a point explored by the Court of Appeal in *R (Trailer and Marina (Leven) Ltd) v Secretary of State for the Environment, Food and Rural Affairs* [2005] 1 WLR 1267; [2004] EWCA Civ 1580, paras 44–58. That case concerned a challenge to the legislative scheme governing Sites of Special Scientific Interest (SSSIs) designated under s 28 of the Wildlife and Countryside 1981 ('the 1981 Act'). Ss 75(1) and 76 of and Schedules 9 and 11 to the Countryside and Rights of Way Act 2000 had amended the 1981 Act and introduced the new sections 28–28Q. The effect of these provisions was to permit restrictions on the claimant's land use without compensation. Previously, the claimant had entered into a management agreement with English Nature under which it had voluntarily agreed to restrict its use of the canal in exchange for an annual payment of £19,000.

13. In determining that the claimant's A1P1 rights had not been breached, Neuberger LJ, as he then was, noted that the distinction between deprivation and control is not always clear-cut. *Sporrong and Lönnroth v Sweden* and *Jacobsson v Sweden* (1989) 12 EHRR 56 were cited as establishing a requirement for fair balance between public interest and individual rights, which was said to be tantamount to a requirement of proportionality. Whether this requires the payment of compensation will depend on the circumstances:

> The right analysis seems to us to be that provided the state could properly take the view that the benefit to the community outweighs the detriment to the individual, a fair balance will be struck, without any requirement to compensate the individual. Should this not be the case, compensation in some appropriate form may serve to redress the balance, so that no breach of article 1 of the First Protocol occurs. (para 58)

14. On the facts in *Trailer and Marina*, evidence that the market value of the claimant's property, and the use that could be made of it, may have been substantially diminished was not sufficient to justify a declaration of legislative incompatibility:

> [G]iven the purpose and genesis of the legislation and the jurisprudence of the European Court of Human Rights, that cannot of itself justify an argument that there has been an infringement of the article 1 of the First Protocol rights of the owner of an SSSI whose value has been substantially diminished as a result of the amendments effected by the 2000 Act. (para 65)

15. Assuming, then, that some form of interference with the respondent's 'possessions' has occurred, the crucial question here remains that of proportionality, and whether this interference struck the required fair balance between Mr Mott's rights and those of others. As Lord Reed set out in *Bank Mellat v Her Majesty's Treasury*

(No 2) [2013] UKSC 39 at [74], there are a number of factors that the English courts will generally take into account when asked to consider the proportionality of a measure: (i) whether its objective is sufficiently important to justify the limitation of a fundamental right; (ii) whether it is rationally connected to the objective; (iii) whether a less intrusive measure could have been used; and (iv) whether, having regard to these matters and to the severity of the consequences, a fair balance has been struck between the rights of the individual and the interests of the community.

16. Counsel for the appellants emphasises the special importance to be attached to the protection of the environment. The impacts of environmental controls are of potentially wide scope and may include, for example, the immediate parties to a given claim, the wider public, future generations, and the rights of non-humans. This does not detract from the need to draw a 'fair balance', nor from the potential relevance of compensation in that context. Indeed, the potential need for compensation is recognised in other parts of the 1975 Act itself.

The Judgments below

17. In the High Court, HHJ David Cooke found the Agency's decision to impose catch limitations to be irrational, in the *Wednesbury* sense that no reasonable authority could have reached this conclusion from the evidence available to it; see *Associated Provincial Picture Houses Ltd v Wednesbury Corporation* [1948] 1 KB 223. The judge's reasoning on this, and his willingness to enter into analysis of the reliability of the scientific evidence presented, were criticised in the Court of Appeal, and we must proceed on the basis that the decision complained of was one that was open to a reasonable decision maker. However, it is clear that this finding also influenced the judge's view on proportionality.

18. On A1P1, it was accepted by the parties that the lease was a 'possession'. The judge considered that, whether the restrictions imposed by the Agency amounted to control or a deprivation, the central question was whether the measures pursued a legitimate aim, employed means that were reasonably proportionate to that aim, and, in particular, struck a fair balance between the public interest and individual rights. *Trailer and Marina* was distinguished on the basis that that case involved a challenge to a legislative scheme, rather than a specific executive decision, and did not support a conclusion that any restriction on environmental grounds was permissible without payment of compensation (para 93). It was held that, whether a deprivation or control, the measures could not be described as proportionate as they lacked a reasonable basis. They also imposed an excessive individual burden on Mr Mott. His rights under A1P1 had therefore been breached.

19. The Court of Appeal agreed with HHJ Cooke's finding that, in the absence of compensation, the restrictions imposed an individual and excessive burden on Mr Mott. The environmental purpose of the restrictions alone could not justify

the lack of compensation. The decision in *Trailer and Marina* turned on the principle of the legislation, rather than its specific effects on the claimant. Giving judgment on behalf of the Court, Beatson LJ commented (at para 89) that 'there is no evidence that the Agency considered the extent of the effect of the condition on Mr Mott and his livelihood'. The Agency now appeal against this judgment.

The Appeal

20. The core questions for determination in this appeal, then, are the following:

1. Are the catch restrictions capable of constituting a qualifying interference with the respondent's property rights, whether amounting to a deprivation or as a control on use?
2. If so, were the measures proportionate, and in pursuit of a legitimate aim?
3. In the absence of compensation, do the measures strike the required fair balance between individual rights and public interest?

21. For the appellants, it was argued that the impact of the catch restrictions did not amount to a deprivation. Even where a measure causes a significant reduction in the financial value of an interest, this will only amount to a deprivation in exceptional circumstances. We were referred to *Mellacher v Austria* (1990) 12 EHRR 391, in which rent control legislation that imposed a 'considerable economic burden' (para 198) on the landlords of affected properties was nevertheless found not to have deprived the applicants of the substance of their property interests. It was suggested that the instant case was not comparable to *Papamichalopoulos v Greece* (1993) 16 EHRR 440, in which the appellants had been deprived of all use and value from a large area of valuable land on which a naval base had been constructed without formal expropriation. It is significant that the applicants in that case could no longer dispose of or deal with their interest in land, whereas here the respondent's ability to deal with his interest is not restricted. Moreover, the limitations complained of are temporary in duration, and are variable in accordance with a rational objective (the health of the salmon population).

22. On fair balance, it was submitted that the burden placed upon the respondent must be weighed against the importance of the public interest served by the limitations. As explained in *Depalle v France* (2012) 54 EHRR 17:

> The Court has, moreover, often reiterated that regional planning and environmental conservation policies, where the community's general interest is pre-eminent, confer on the state a margin of appreciation that is greater than when exclusively civil rights are at stake. (at para 84).

23. In *Depalle*, the applicant had purchased a house built without permission on maritime public property. Between 1961 and 1991, the applicant was granted rights of temporary occupancy. In 1993, the applicant was informed that the

temporary occupation rights could not be renewed but was offered an occupation agreement that would allow occupation but prevent sale or transfer of the property. The applicant rejected this offer. An order was subsequently granted for demolition of the property. The ECtHR held that, despite the lack of compensation, the demolition did not amount to an individual and excessive burden upon the applicant. A similar decision was reached in *Hamer v Belgium* (2008) (Application No 21861/03). These decisions illustrate both the weight that may legitimately be placed on environmental protection, and the latitude to be afforded to public authorities in determining how environmental and planning objectives are to be met.

24. For the respondent, it was argued that the restrictions had effectively prohibited Mr Mott's enjoyment of his rights under the lease, and therefore amounted to a deprivation for the purposes of A1P1. Even if the restrictions were regarded as a control on use, their effect was to impose an excessive and disproportionate burden upon the respondent. Although the rationality of the Agency's decision making is no longer the subject of challenge, insufficient consultation had taken place before the catch limitations were imposed. The Agency had not taken into account the individual burden that would be placed on those who earned their livelihood from the heritage fishing installations. It was accepted that the Agency had the power to pay compensation, and it should have done so in this instance.

Discussion

25. It is manifest that the measures complained of significantly restrict the respondent's ability to exercise the rights afforded to him by his lease. The catch reductions mean that it is no longer financially sustainable for Mr Mott to engage in his chosen occupation, giving rise to severe economic and social consequences for him that do not apply to those fishing for leisure. Such restrictions seem obviously capable of amounting to an interference with the right to peaceful enjoyment of possessions that is the essential subject of A1P1's protections. The authorities cited highlight that the distinction between expropriation and control is not always clear-cut, and categorisation is not essential to my analysis in this instance. What follows focuses, therefore, on the purpose of the measures and whether, in the absence of compensation, they can be said to strike a fair balance between individual and public interest.

26. Guidance on factors that may be relevant to the 'fair balance' test can be taken from *R (on the application of British American Tobacco UK Ltd) v Secretary of State for Health* [2016] EWHC 1169 (Admin); [2016] RPC 22 at para 783, in reasoning based on a close reading of *Vékony v Hungary* CE:ECHR:2015:0113JUD006568113 and subsequently approved in the Court of Appeal:

> [T]he importance of the public interest being served in relation to the nature and importance of the private property interest being intruded upon; the economic consequences for the applicant; the existence of transitional protection; the reasonableness of the process by which the rules were introduced.

Purpose and Importance of the Challenged Measures

27. It was put to us in argument that this case could be distinguished from *BAT* and *Trailer and Marina*, in that this court is not being asked to review the overall legislative scheme or object of the measures complained of. Rather, as in *Vékony*, the challenge is at a 'micro' level to the treatment of the respondent within the Agency's scheme, and the extent to which an individual and excessive burden has been placed upon him.

28. Central to our consideration of individual and excessive burden is the impact of the measures on the respondent's livelihood. This cannot, however, be assessed in isolation from the regulatory purpose, which was to conserve the very salmon stocks on which that livelihood depended. The value of the rights conferred under the respondent's lease are entirely dependent on the existence of a healthy estuarine ecosystem. As the European Court of Justice put it in *Booker Aquaculture Ltd (trading as Marine Harvest McConnell) v Scottish Ministers* (Joined Cases C-20/00 and C-64/00) [2003] ECR I-7411, a challenge to a regulatory requirement to slaughter diseased fish without automatic right to compensation, at para 80, 'the measures referred to do not deprive farm owners of the use of their fish farms, but enable them to continue to carry on their activities there'.

29. In the same way that the creditors in *Bäck v Finland* (2005) 40 EHRR 48 were presumed to accept some risk of financial loss, those obtaining their livelihood from fishing must be assumed to bear some of the risks associated with decline in fish stocks, and some of the responsibility for ensuring that populations remain in a healthy state. The fact that one has entered into a lease that entitles one to catch a certain weight of fish cannot be treated as a guarantee that the permitted number will, in fact, be caught.

30. The weight of the interest being pursued is critical to assessment of fair balance (*BAT* at para 791). This is particularly true where the exercise of property rights and economic freedoms is causing social harms (*BAT* at 798). As the European Court of Human Rights explained in *Hamer v Belgium* at para 79:

> The environment is a cause whose defence arouses the constant and sustained interest of the public, and consequently the public authorities. Financial imperatives and even certain fundamental rights, such as ownership, should not be afforded priority over environmental protection considerations, in particular where the state has legislated in this regard.

Economic Consequences and Severity of Individual Burden

31. It is clear that the income from the putcher ranks might be affected by many factors, and in particular by any drop in salmon populations. Indeed, the Agency argues that the very aim of the limitations was to increase salmon stocks and therefore to maintain the long-term viability of fishing in the area. However, on the evidence presented, the impact on Mr Mott's livelihood appears to be severe, in that he was prevented from obtaining his customary living.

32. The measures complained of lasted only one season, and the quota assigned to the respondent could increase if the salmon stocks were shown to be in a healthy state. It is significant that the limitations complained of were renewable on an annual basis. If the salmon populations were deemed healthy, Mr Mott's salmon catch could be adjusted accordingly. This emphasises that the ability to exploit the property interest in question is dependent not only upon permission from the Agency, but the ecological health of the river. Expectation of future livelihood cannot be treated as entirely fixed but must adapt with changing social and environmental conditions.

33. Where infringement of property rights has occurred, compensation would normally be payable based on the value of the loss. The fact that the putcher rank provided a certain income in the past does not, however, guarantee that this could be expected to continue indefinitely. As Mr Justice Green explains in *R (on the application of British American Tobacco UK Ltd) v Secretary of State for Health* [2016] EWHC 1169 (Admin); [2016] RPC 22 at para 798, in reasoning subsequently approved in the Court of Appeal:

> No individual or company can have an expectation that if it produces and supplies a product that is, or becomes recognised as, contrary to the public interest that it will be entitled to continue to produce and sell that product, or that if the State comes to prescribe or curtail the product in issue that it will be entitled to compensation.

34. As things stand, in the case of any deterioration in the status of the River Wye SAC, and in the health of the salmon population, no legal liability would attach to the respondent. However, the financial impact on the respondent's salmon catch might be just as severe as that caused by the restrictions complained of. The putcher rank operation has, over a long period of time, drawn financial benefit from the predictable migration of salmon upriver. It could be argued that it should, therefore, bear a greater share of the cost of preserving the ecosystem on which the operation relies. It is not clear that 'fair balance' requires the public to guarantee the respondent's future income at its historic level, regardless of the environmental risks posed by his activities, as well as by climate change and other factors.

35. When assessing the overall impact on the respondent, a number of other factors are relevant. Although, given Mr Mott's age and long-standing operation of the putcher rank, he is understandably unwilling to contemplate any alternative

means of obtaining an income, he has enjoyed considerable forewarning of the pressure on salmon stocks. We heard evidence that the local authority is keen to develop the heritage tourism industry in the area, and that tours of the putcher rank could be an attractive proposition in this respect. Maintaining the respondent's livelihood through the payment of compensation is not a viable long-term prospect, and it was proper for the Agency to decide that some limit should be imposed on the expenditure of public funds for this purpose. Although the decision to end the payment of compensation undoubtedly had very significant consequences for the respondent, this it is not enough to render it arbitrary or unreasonable.

Existence of Transitional Protection and Process by which the Measures were Introduced

36. At this point, it is relevant to consider the broader context of the respondent's relationship with the Agency, including the degree of forewarning, his opportunities to engage in dialogue with the Agency, and the timescale on which events have unfolded. As in *Trailer and Marina*, there was ample warning that controls over the operation of his fishing operation were likely to increase rather than decrease. Mr Mott's activities took place in the context of a policy to end mixed-stock fisheries dating back to at least 1996. He was aware from at least 2003 of the Agency's wish to restrict operation of the putcher ranks and was in several fishing seasons paid compensation by the Agency not to operate the putcher rank.

37. Further, as set out above, the severity of the individual burden placed on the respondents must be understood in relation both to their ongoing negotiations with the Environment Agency and to the financial benefits that they have obtained (and expect to obtain in future) from exploitation of salmon stocks. The protected property interest here amounts to a claim to future value. As noted above, the Agency has a long-standing policy of restricting mixed-stock fisheries dating back to at least 1996. When the respondent entered into the current 20-year lease in 1998, the risk of a decline in salmon populations and the introduction of conservation measures must have been at least within his contemplation. The existence of uncertainties around future scientific developments and regulation at the time of entering the insurance contracts in *AXA General Insurance* was highlighted by Lord Reed (at para 128) as an important factor in assessing the proportionality of the interference.

38. It is notable that, as in *Depalle v France* (2012) 54 EHRR 17, the Agency had attempted to purchase the respondent's interest by agreement. Negotiations aimed at the termination of the respondent's operation began in 2004. The respondent was well aware of the Agency's concerns about the health of the estuary's salmon populations, and the long-term sustainability of his operations. Mr Mott had the opportunity to challenge the Exeter report, and to put his case to the Agency. The fact that he may not have agreed with the Agency's assessment is not relevant here, as the Agency's conclusions on this are no longer subject to challenge.

39. The fact that the negotiations were not successful, and that the respondent had no wish to transition away from his existing commercial operation, does not negate the fact he had opportunity to adapt his business plans over a number of years, as compared to months in *Vékony v Hungary*. He cannot have assumed that compensation would be paid indefinitely. While it may well be the case that the transition process could have been better managed, the question for consideration here is whether the process adopted fell so far below accepted standards of transparency and fairness that the Agency's decision was in breach of A1P1. No evidence was presented to us that this was the case.

Conclusion

21. Against this background, I am unable to agree with the judges below that the catch limitations did not strike a fair balance. While it is undoubtedly true that the burden borne by Mr Mott was a heavy one, and that the consequences for him were far more severe than for those who pursued salmon fishing as a leisure interest, the effect of unregulated salmon catch might well, within the foreseeable future, prove equally harsh. On the Agency's reasoning, there was simply no basis on which continued commercial exploitation was compatible with the conservation of healthy salmon populations. The temporary nature and important purpose of restrictions means that they are within the margin of appreciation afforded to government when pursuing policies in the public interest. As well as a strong public interest justification, the measure complained of was also the culmination of a lengthy period of negotiation aimed at ending the respondent's operations.

22. I would therefore overturn the decision of the courts below. In doing so, I would emphasise that general principles are of limited assistance in this area, in which each case must turn on its own facts. As has been set out above, the distinction between control of use and deprivation does not detract from the need to demonstrate that a fair balance has been reached between the public interest and individual property rights. The fact that an interference has an environmental purpose, and the absence of compensation are both relevant, but not necessarily determinative factors. In this case, the onus of demonstrating an individual and excessive burden fell on the respondent, and, on the arguments adduced, was not met.

23. I would uphold the appeal.

Commentary

Hannah Blitzer

Human Rights and Earth Law

The original judgment raises pertinent questions for incorporating Earth law principles into UK law. The first is whether human rights help or hinder environmental protection.[18] The commercial impact of the disputed restrictions challenges the power of public bodies to enforce environmental regulations that impact individuals' rights to enjoy their 'possessions'. Undoubtedly, the Environment Agency's powers to control fishing activity had a wider environmental benefit, namely the conservation of the salmon populations and its estuary ecosystem. Nevertheless, the UK Supreme Court supported the reasoning of the lower courts, which established that, where an individual's right to property is subject to significant interference for environmental purposes, restrictions cannot be imposed without compensating the owner for his loss of livelihood.

Mr Mott was found to have been required to shoulder an excessive and disproportionate burden, resulting in severe impacts on his livelihood; the Environment Agency could only prevent this breach through use of its powers to award compensation.[19] The Court noted that national authorities generally have a wide margin of discretion for environmental protection and conservation measures, and that A1P1 gives no general expectation of compensation for adverse effects.[20] As this case demonstrates, where there is a significant impact on livelihood without compensation, the fair balance may tip in favour of property rights. Certain applications of human rights may therefore be at best unhelpful, and at worst antithetical, to environmental protection.

Property Rights: Anthropocentricity, the Subjectification of Humans and the Objectification of the Environment

A1P1 centres the 'natural or legal person … entitled to the peaceful enjoyment of his possessions' on a *human* or a recognised legal person, such as a corporation. Deprivation of property may be lawful if in the public interest and under the general principles of international law, indicating room for less anthropocentric interpretations based on ecological interests and the value of non-human beings. However, the same general principles make clear that any deprivation of possessions must meet certain conditions to comply with A1P1.[21] State interference

[18] Conor Gearty, 'Do Human Rights Help or Hinder Environmental Protection?' (2010) 1 *Journal of Human Rights and the Environment* 7.
[19] *Mott v Environment Agency*, [31], [36].
[20] ibid [30], [37].
[21] *Bäck v Finland* App No 37598/97 (ECHR, 20 July 2004) [52].

with the right must not be excessively burdensome and must strike a fair, proportionate balance between the protection of an individual's fundamental rights and the wider public interest.[22] How this balance is achieved was central to the original decision.

The discussion surrounding fair balance in *Mott* demonstrates that a choice often must be made between the values of rights-holders and ecological values. *Mott* may even go as far as to advance an epistemology of mastery,[23] or a 'right to exploit'. Philosophical speciesism, or human mastery, is entrenched in law and legitimates a world existing outside the human as being inherently incapable of belonging to anything else but the 'possessive individual'.[24] Thus, property rights may have a capacity to reinforce negative environmental identities (ie a possessive individual's un-ecologically informed right to exploit) and disconnection from the rights-holder's ecological responsibilities.

The Supreme Court reasons that the special importance of ecological protection must not detract from the need for fair balance; the extensive interference with Mr Mott's property and livelihood means that compensation must be paid.[25] Although the judgment evidences the capacity of A1P1 to enable rights-holders' participation in socio-ecological decision-making processes, it also demonstrates that liberal human rights, including the right to property, often 'preserve existing structures and arrangements'.[26] This could be seen to reflect the fact that such rights are specifically concerned with the rights that stem from the very nature of being human and the anthropocentric value that emanates from a commercialised conception of 'livelihood'.

Reimagining A1P1

The original judgment opens the question as to whether human rights have the capacity to accommodate ecological responsibility. The rewritten judgment strays from the emblematic anthropocentrism that grounds the right to property. In this respect, there are very clear demarcations between the original and rewritten case. Importantly, the reimagined judgment threads an ecological voice throughout, questioning the undue weight given to commercial livelihood and the existing structures of the right to property.

Like the original judgment, it is not central to the line of judicial reasoning to categorise the possession as either a deprivation or control on use. Notably,

[22] *Hutten-Czapska v Poland* App No 35014/97 (19 June 2006) [167]–[168]; *Sporrong and Lönnroth v Sweden* App No 7151/75 (ECHR, 23 September 1982).

[23] Sam Adelman, 'Epistemologies of Mastery' in Anna Grear and Louis Kotze (eds) *Research Handbook on Human Rights and the Environment* (Edward Elgar, 2015); Lorraine Code, *Ecological Thinking: The Politics of Epistemic Location* (Oxford University Press, 2006).

[24] Gearty, 'Do Human Rights Help or Hinder?', 8.

[25] *Mott v Environment Agency*, [32].

[26] Bonnie Holligan, 'Human rights and the moralities of property: Participation, Obligation and Value in *R (on the application of Mott) v Environment Agency*' (2019) 11 *Journal of Property, Planning and Environmental Law* 176.

though, while the reimagined judgment differentiates between the aims of the Environment Agency (control) and Mr Mott's experience (deprivation), underlining the need for fair balance, it also goes beyond this.[27] Here, the interests of the community, future generations and the rights of non-humans depend on a healthy estuarine ecosystem and the conservation of such ecosystem comes to the fore. Such factors do not automatically undermine the balancing act or delegitimise the provision of compensation for the interference with the present and future value of Mr Mott's putcher rank.[28]

From an Earth law perspective, property rights in anything beyond our own bodies are problematic. The language of the original judgment implies that ownership in a non-human 'object' encompasses an absolute right to destroy it, should that destruction afford commercial livelihood to the right-holder. However, if rights are grounds of duties in others,[29] then a right relating to the other-than-human implies some sort of obligation to those beings or entities. The reimagined judgment accepts the law as it currently exists, but leaves scope for legal imagination for ecological justice through recognition of the value of biodiversity in its own right and also its importance to ecologically embedded human values.[30] Accordingly, this judgment demonstrates that the law may be used to ecologically embed a relational understanding of 'property'.[31]

Nevertheless, practical challenges exist to reconceptualising the liberal-anthropocentric approach to property rights in the United Kingdom to shift the understanding of nature as an object to a subject.[32] The first is the complexity of outlining a just and fair ecological remedy when there is a deprivation of livelihood, given many ecological identities and species exist across the United Kingdom. There is a risk that certain identities, knowledge and values prevail over others. Yet, courts can, and do, assess the individual facts of each case and this obstacle may be resolved through a careful consideration of the parties' embodied, ecological relationships, as opposed to centring on their economic interests.[33]

Second, existing remedies, particularly human rights remedies based on compensation for economic loss, are anthropocentric constructs. Thus, protecting a habitat, and the salmon species that live within it, may only be evaluated through an anthropocentric lens. The reimagined judgment demonstrates that law can accommodate an obligation not to harm, and perhaps even one to protect.

[27] Reimagined judgment [7].

[28] ibid [9].

[29] Joseph Raz, 'On the Nature of Rights' (1984) 93 *Mind* 194.

[30] Reimagined judgment [15].

[31] Margherita Pieraccini, 'Property Pluralism and the Partial Reflexivity of Conservation Law: The Case of Upland Commons in England and Wales' (2012) 3 *Journal of Human Rights and the Environment* 273.

[32] Peter Burdon, *Earth Jurisprudence: Private Property and the Environment* (Routledge, 2014) 102.

[33] ibid 110. Courts can – and in some contexts such as the adjudication of dignity do – consider spatially embedded conceptions of human rights, environmentally constituted humanness and place-based environmental identities: Dina L Townsend, *Human Dignity and the Adjudication of Environmental Rights* (Edward Elgar, 2020).

By highlighting the temporary nature of the restrictions and the point that the recovery of the salmon stocks may eliminate the need for future restrictions on Mr Mott's activities, a fair balance is achieved between anthropocentric (economic/non-economic) and ecological impacts of necessary environmental protection measures.[34] Furthermore, the reimagined judgment's ecologisation[35] of the right to property and remedies for breach posits a right that can only be exploited as far as the ecosystem allows.[36] Consequently, the new judgment introduces a remedy that balances ecological interests and incorporates the possibility of an ecological perspective: environmental harm may be addressed to benefit the interests of the non-human, as opposed to the human being.

[34] Reimagined judgment [12]–[17].
[35] This reasoning may be extended to the interests of future generations (human and non-human) whose interests are temporally valuable and are not presently protected under A1P1 (n 4).
[36] Reimagined judgment [10].

Notes on the Wildlaw Judgment Generator

Jo Lindsay Walton

Outside

The Wildlaw Judgment Generator (bit.ly/Wildlaw) is a generative digital artwork. It concerns a case eerily similar to *R (Mott) v Environment Agency* [2018] UKSC 10, which Bonnie Holligan has reimagined over the previous pages. The Generator emerged through conversations with Bonnie, where we grew interested in folklore and fairytales as tools for exploring Earth law.

Might magic solutions reveal new angles on real legal problems?

Could imaginary talking beasts help to give voice to the more-than-human world?

Might we pluralise our models of justice by eavesdropping on faintly remembered fey entities – on their imprecations, incantations, quests and transmogrifications, which convey moral lessons worn weird by the centuries?

The Wildlaw Judgment Generator lets the reader appeal each judgment through an endless series of courts. The generator's lower courts hew close to the real judgment, Bonnie's rewriting, and Hannah Blitzer's commentary. This is to familiarise the reader with the case, before things start to get strange. There are a few small fluctuations in this phase – does the judgment refer to the fisherman's 'livelihood' or his 'business'? – which probe how subtly different framings might tug our moral instincts differently.

If the reader continues to appeal, things grow more alien. The litigants' names mutate, the facts of the case may waver. Judgments may start to mention tenuously related areas of law and policy, such as employment law and intellectual property. Even though the fisherman is not an employee, perhaps the rules on redundancy could reveal broad benchmarks in relation to disappearing livelihoods. Even though books and ecosystems are not strikingly similar, isn't what they do have in common quite intriguing? Each is nourished by many widely distributed sources, and each can be stewarded in ways that are conservative, generative and/or destructive. Or what about invoking stranded assets – a hot topic as financial markets contemplate major realignment with net-zero goals – to assess the reasonableness of the fisherman's expectations? As one Generator output would have it:

> *Discussion*. Mr Scott's leasehold is an asset that has prematurely lost its value. A simple way to define 'prematurely' is 'well before the end of its anticipated useful life'. Yet this definition raises the question of appropriate due diligence: in some cases the factors determining the devaluation will have already been present, but not yet priced in.

Was Mr Scott prudent in his 1998 leasehold purchase? To the extent that he was, it appears unfair to deny him the benefit he reasonably anticipated. Yet it is also unfair to ask the taxpayer to bear the cost of this asset's recovery, in the form of compensation to Mr Scott. The stranded asset analogy brings clarity; a definite sum can be attached to the stranded asset, and the question now is the proper distribution of this cost across all relevant stakeholders.

Spend more time with the Generator, and things grow stranger still. The fish themselves get more frequently glimpsed: very much the stuff of fairytales, with their extraordinary wayfaring and shocking bodily transformations. As the case moves up through the courts, it becomes less clear whose judgments we are reading. The realm of established human law and policy recedes, and instead scraps of science, poetry and folklore float into the foreground. Interested monsters and immortal animals seem to poke in their snouts and muzzles to adjudicate. Elias Youssef's illustrations add more chaos: in one, Lady Justice Salmon wears a blindfold and carries a sword and scales (Figure 1); in another, a salmon sprouts limbs to clamber out of the trap, clearly hellbent on revenge. Many of the judgments are more-or-less nonsense, unless a reader decides to linger and speculatively construct their own sense. To take an output at random:

> *The Pine Marten Panel of Petitions, R (Potts) v Environment Agency*
>
> 16 Killjester 1343
>
> *Discussion.* Mr Potts is himself climate crisis's backhanded compliment. And as for the salmon? The salmon are all of us.
>
> *Flanks slither and spark up the riverfoam.*
>
> *Decision.* I would dismiss the appeal.

What on Earth could this mean? In this example, a determined exegete might start with 'climate crisis': no one contends that it is only overfishing, let alone overfishing by Mott, that is imperilling fish stocks in the Wye; other factors include higher average water temperatures, making it trickier for salmon to breathe and to spawn. But why should the climate crisis be paying someone 'compliments'? Perhaps to spur us to think about 'paying' and 'repaying' in new ways, invoking the sort of logic anthropologists describe as reciprocity? Or perhaps simply in the sense that crises can reveal virtue, just like sincere and observant compliments can reveal virtue? If so, perhaps Mr Potts is framed here as an emblem of grit and determination, in refusing to back down throughout years of legal conflict. The 'backhanded' nature of this compliment, then, could be a reminder that resilience – usually a positive term in climate discourse – is not always conducive to a rapid and just transition. Sometimes it is precisely through managing their own climate risks that an actor contributes to climate change or degrades the capacity of other actors to adapt for the warmer and more chaotic world.

Figure 1 Illustration of the Wildlaw Judgment Generator (Elias Youssef)

Inside

In other words, the potentials of the Wildlaw Judgment Generator mostly lie 'outside' the Generator – in the minds of willing and imaginative readers. But what about inside the Generator? How does it come up with these judgments in the first place? The Generator was created using Twine, an open-source tool for creating interactive fiction. So it's not artificial intelligence (AI) in the style of ChatGPT – that is, it's not a deep learning model trained on vast text corpora, embedding words as a high-dimensional space and using self-attention mechanisms to adjust weightings during runtime to mimic contextual understanding. We did briefly explore both GPT-2 and ChatGPT, but ended up not using them for several reasons: GPT-2's responses were too chaotic for what we wanted, and ChatGPT's at the time were too cautious and obvious. Also, it did not feel appropriate to deploy a heavyweight AI model, whose environmental implications are complex and contentious, for an environmentally themed artwork.[37]

[37] eg Thomas S Mullaney et al (eds), *Your Computer Is on Fire* (MIT Press 2021); A Shaji George, AS Hovan George and A S Gabrio Martin, 'The Environmental Impact of AI: A Case Study of Water Consumption by Chat GPT' (2023) 1 *Partners Universal International Innovation Journal*, zenodo.org/record/7855594.

So, we used Twine, which is a bit like a programming language for people who can't really program: it does the hard Javascript, HTML5 and CSS parts for you. In 1920, the Dadaist poet Tristan Tzara advised would-be poets to cut out the words from a newspaper article and pull them at random from a hat. That is still the heart of how the Generator works, except that there are many 'hats' (including hats inside hats), and they have been carefully filled up, so that the judgments make some kind of sense. Here is an example of the Twine code, from one of the more dreamlike sections.

> And sometime (either: "I was", "was I") salmon, and sometime hart.
>
> And sometime $mott (either: "hunted", "hunted", "gave chase", "drove me", "knew me"), and sometime $he (either: "fled", "swam", "haunted", "fled", "flew", "fled", "swam", "haunted", "fled", "flew", "sat still", "spoke", "spake", "dreamed too", "fled before me", "sat in judgment", "heard my case", "heard my case, but the words swam away", "heard the bubbles of my case, but not the waters", "did not", "did not", "knew me not").

Once it has entered its main loop, the Generator flits around among a variety of subgenerators, some of which use fine-grained randomness (at the level of word or phrase, as in the example above), others more coarse-grained (at the level of sentence or short paragraph).

Beyond Tzara and Dada, there is a long tradition of experimental writing that uses randomness and algorithms. Sometimes the rationales for these experiments resembled what we tried here: an attempt to augment our patterns of thinking and seeing, to let us glimpse possibilities beyond the frameworks of the imaginable imposed by everyday existence. But this tradition teaches that these glimpses can also be illusive. That is, there is nothing inherently transformative, oppositional or emancipatory about aleatory and constraint-based writing. As I used these methods to reimagine our chosen judgment, I grew aware of how much they allowed me to avoid judgments too, to keep various options hovering in the air, always available. Should I write 'fled' or 'flew'? Why not both? Should I find in favour of Mott or the Environment Agency? Why not both?

The significance of this equivocal logic is itself equivocal. On one hand, the ability to have it both ways (or three ways, or four) can bring you uncomfortably close to exactly the kind of probabilistic thinking that is so spectacularly failing to address our unfolding environmental emergency. Nature becomes nothing but a collection of risks and opportunities to quantify and manage: 'Should I, as a board member governing a large multinational company, prepare for a world that is 1.5 degrees warmer, or 2.0, or 3.0 degrees? Well, why not prepare for all these scenarios, weighted according to our latest models, now fed on bigger data than ever?' Such an approach struggles to acknowledge that, sometimes, preparing for the worst scenarios can increase their likelihood. Even when that's not the case, it may emanate a misleading aura of prudence, despite being profoundly unequal to the dense interconnectivity of global society and climate, and to the rapid non-linear changes of planetary tipping points.

Yet on the other hand, the Generator's deferred and multiplied decisions can feel hauntingly hopeful. Maybe it's to do with defending any space, however small, in which new habits of deciding might be developed. Such habits must include identifying and interpreting appropriate expertise and evidence, since environmental emergency is characterised by a complexity that far exceeds everyday human experience. Of course, we ought to reject the risible consolations of insuring, diversifying and risk-managing our way through climate crisis. But that doesn't mean that we can just revert to a vague ecological reverence which forsakes quantitative tools, methods and data altogether. Perhaps the question posed by *Mott v Environment Agency* is: how should science now manifest within legal and economic decision-making (and other kinds of decision-making)? Science claims special insight into nature, and right now nature is inviting us to rearrange our societies from the bottom up. Science is therefore, unavoidably, reconstructing its forms of neutrality and normativity. Or put differently: who gets to be the expert on who gets to be the expert?

Such questions are as pertinent to the IPCC and to COPs as they are to Mott. Good answers would be those that included, at least, the diversity of scientific knowledge itself (different experts come to different conclusions); the many types of uncertainty that scientists taxonomise and sometimes quantify (caveats which often don't communicate well to policy-makers); anticolonial contestations of scientific authority (especially as it is constellated by the Global North); many other critiques of scientific authority from the edges of mainstream science (eg from within science and technology studies and feminist philosophy of science); and the unequal distribution of access to science across society (including, perhaps, between Mr Mott and the Environment Agency).

Talking Beasts

How does science interface with, or shade into, everything that is not-science? Today science is in search of greater legal, political and economic power, yet also bases its claim to that power upon tried-and-true tales of scientific neutrality. The contradiction between these two things could be quite generative. Whenever a new inconsistency appears, or an existing inconsistency grows more intense, it may create opportunities for new ways of reconciling, excusing, explaining, concealing, mapping, pidginifying, weak-theorising or strong-theorising, or otherwise mediating between the inconsistent things. We might expect the emergence of a new regime of go-betweens, of entities in whom are gathered all the drives and desires that science has needed to discard, in order to go on being science.

When such entities take the forms of talking beasts, or similar, they are also quite real. They may be proxies for scientific practice, but the reverse is also true: scientific practices invoke and construct nature's many voices. Numerous technologies of analysis and communication – everything from simple bar charts, to interactive Bayesian networks, or even the ensemble of climate models used by the IPCC – make expert knowledge of the natural world available to non-experts, often with aspirations to directness or transparency. The rapid rise in the quantity and variety of ecological data collected is raising the possibility of ecosystems exerting greater agency within decision-making processes. It could be worth reflecting on how such processes resemble (a) nature learning to speak our languages, (b) us learning to speak nature's, and, maybe especially, (c) neither. Meanwhile, these developments are paralleled by (and entangled with) AI research seeking to mobilise traditional ecological knowledge in fields such as anticipatory governance for disaster risk reduction.

Taken in sum, such developments are both exciting and scary. Could they be opportunities for marginalised voices to be given their due weight? And/or are they opportunities for more-than-human voices to be cherry-picked, filtered, appropriated for greenwashing, subjected to new forms of disciplinarity, and forced to articulate themselves in alien languages? Any technology mediating among truly diverse stakeholders – maybe even different ontologies – should never be judged merely technocratically, on how accurate, efficient, or user-friendly it is; it is a kind of strange democratic locus, and deserves the attention of a kind of strange jurisprudence.

Where are the persons in all this? Legal personhood has nothing to do with being a 'person' in the everyday sense, and it makes no claim at all about sentience, sapience, capacity to will, feel, dream, desire. Legal personhood for a river would not mean (contrary to some headlines) that a river has human rights. It would have river rights. And, of course, any such rights can be tailored to the type of entity, in the same way that children and adults, or citizens and non-citizens, have different sets of rights. So, there is no anthropomorphism implied in allowing the salmon, or a river ecosystem, to defend their interests in court, through appointed human guardians (or rather, some mediating assemblage of humans and other things).

Or is there? Rights of nature discourse cannot entirely avoid elements of anthropomorphism, and can even simultaneously rely upon and disavow that anthropomorphism. The legal histories that created protections for endangered species, as well as more recent ontological upheavals in Bolivia, Ecuador and New Zealand, contain moments where the designation 'person' carries the implication of 'you know, like you and me, like humans'. Opponents of rights of nature may scoff at the absurdity of treating a tree, a river, a monkey or a dolphin like a human. Proponents of rights of nature, though, face the temptation to frame their counter-arguments around the same anthropocentric question of who or what should be treated as equivalent to human.

In the Twine excerpt above, the dollar signs indicate variables, used to randomly set the fisherman's name and pronouns at the start, and at intervals throughout. 'Mott' is not among the list of possible names; for some reason it felt creatively freeing to not quite use the fisherman's real name. But in the Twine (and the Javascript) the variable is called $mott, so he does remain the invisible figure that casts these visible shadows; 'Mott' was the word I wrote with, and that the prosody of the generated text is often sort of 'injured', in ways that would be mended by that syllable:

> Last night I dreamt I met $mott.
>
> And one year he hunted me. And one year he did not.

The current version of the Generator occasionally makes quite strong points on Mott's side. I think these came from me much more than from Bonnie. I convinced myself they were necessary, supposing they had something to do with dialectics or autocritique, or with owning the limits of my knowledge. Or with the way things in dreams and fairytales can be both true and not true simultaneously. Or perhaps these moments just introduced a bit of rhetorical variety – *paromologia*, *procatalepsis*, something like that. But now I'm less sure. Maybe I included them because I can be a real conflict-adverse bootlicker? And making unmitigated fun of people makes me feel bad? Did I secretly want Mr Mott, and the Environment Agency – *and* the salmon, krill, prawns, capelins, squid etc – to all *like* me?

So what about the salmon's voices? Neither Mott nor the Environment Agency, I think, is a true friend to these fish. The Agency would like more salmon to live so that more salmon can die. Promoting the economic success of fisheries is not exactly its remit, but it would be unlikely to side with the salmon against the fisheries. Is there any version of 'flourishing' where we're not feasting on their flesh? It just isn't really on anyone's agenda.

In a very small, entirely symbolic, way, the Wildlaw Judgment Generator grew into an attempt to technologically fashion an alternative voice for these fish. Of course, the salmon themselves are predators, partial to krill, prawns, capelins, squid, sprats. Salmon are not always on friendly terms with each other either, destroying one another's nests when competition gets intense. Predator–prey relations generally (and not only those that feature humans as the predator) pose a challenge for interspecies justice. Imagining natureculture red not in tooth and claw, but in truth and law, quickly furnishes absurd images: the ladybug's little palps grip the gavel as it arbitrates dispute between spider and bee? Predator or prey: why not both? Perhaps the wolf's teeth closing in the hard light haunches of the hologram deer? There is plenty that is mysterious and debatable about what the salmon might say, what they might want or not want. But there also is plenty that is pretty obvious.

Whenever something gets newly automated, we are likely to see the thing itself in a new light. But we may also see other things in our surroundings anew. We may shift our sense of what could or could not be automated, what should or should not be automated, or what has or has not been automated all along. Corporations and markets have both been described as AI, for example. Of course, all this means that we see automation itself in a new light.

Nature is growing, in a certain sense, more technological. Vast amounts of biodiversity data are being collected, analysed and acted upon, and there are efforts to integrate nature into systems of quantitative value through ecosystem services and related approaches. More of the natural world is being made visible, even as what we witness is increasingly coated by our sensors and systems. The distinction between managed and unmanaged land is blurred by anthropogenic impacts on the entire climate. Likewise, the law itself is also increasingly mediated via technological systems. We can point to developments such as case law research systems, dispute-resolution platforms, robo-litigation, smart legal contracts, chatbots and legal practice management tools, regtech for audit and compliance, and more.

Neither the technisation of nature, nor the technisation of the law, is an inevitable trend. Neither is unopposed. Nonetheless, they are ongoing processes, and they raise questions about what forms they may take, how they might interact, and how they might reshape law and nature considered as a relational whole. These questions in turn imply choices to make about the choices we make: choices about what should be deliberate and what should be automatic, the proper scope and authority we ought to give to diverse legal, ecological, economic, scientific, aesthetic, political, and other modes of considering and reasoning. If nature is filled with automata, perhaps some of those automata are also us. Now might be a time to reflect upon the automatic reasoning we do on behalf of salmon, capelins, ladybugs, wolves and deer – our traditions, our unquestioned assumptions, our quick inferences, our heuristics, our biases, our strategic poetic anthropomorphisms. Perhaps it is not only callous indifference to the more-than-human world that invites greater intentionality. What if many of our noblest ethical impulses – intuitions we use to identify balance, harmony, care, stewardship, justice, flourishing, kin, deferential reverence and connectivity with the more-than-human – are not entirely to be trusted, or at least due a careful audit? How might we better educate these intuitions, refine or reimagine these categories, and link them responsively with the detailed reality of the more-than-human world, populated by experience of ethical subjects, who are all making history, all in circumstances not of their choosing?

PART IV

Harm and Responsibility

9

Corporations and the Duty of Care for Nature? An *Amicus Curiae* for the Case of *Lungowe & Others v Vedanta Resources PLC & Konkola Copper Mines*

SASKIA VERMEYLEN AND JÉRÉMIE GILBERT

Introduction

The case of *Lungowe & Others v Vedanta Resources PLC & Konkola Copper Mines* was examined by the UK Supreme Court in 2019.[1] The case concerns the impact of mining in Zambia and the liability of corporations for human rights violations and environmental damage. The claimants were 1,826 Zambian citizens who brought proceedings against Vedanta, a UK-domiciled multinational company, and its Zambian subsidiary, Konkola Copper Mines (KCM). The case followed the high level of pollution of the watercourse in the area surrounding Nchanga Copper Mine, one of the largest copper mining sites in the world. In their pleadings, the claimants argued that they had suffered loss of income through damage to their land and waterways due to the defendants' toxic effluent discharges. They also claimed that they suffered personal injuries as a result of having to use and consume polluted water.

The claimants sought damages, remediation and cessation of the pollution, which was having a huge impact upon their daily lives. When starting the proceedings in August 2005 in the English Court, both defendants (Vedanta and KCM) contested the authority of the English courts and filed an application seeking a declaration that the English Technology and Construction Court did not have jurisdiction to try the case.[2] In its 2016 judgment, the Court ruled in favour of

[1] *Lungowe & Others v Vedanta Resources PLC & Konkola Copper Mines* [2019] UKSC 20.
[2] The English Technology and Construction Court is a subdivision of the High Court of Justice (King's Bench Division).

England as the most appropriate jurisdiction for the resolution of the claims, which it allowed to proceed. However, both defendants appealed the first-instance decision and their appeals were heard by the Court of Appeal in 2017, which upheld the decision of the lower court. The defendants then appealed to the Supreme Court. After the hearing, which took place in January 2019, the Supreme Court declared that the claimants did have a good arguable case that Vedanta owed them a duty of care, and that the case could be examined by the courts in England.

At the heart of this judgment on the duty of care of parent companies lies the key question of whether Vedanta had sufficiently intervened in the management of the mine (owned by KCM) such that it assumed a duty of care to the claimants. The liability of a UK parent company had been considered in two previous cases by the UK courts,[3] where proceedings were issued in England against the UK parent company for events that occurred in Nigeria and Kenya, respectively. In both cases, it was found that there was no good arguable case that a duty of care existed. The case against Vedanta examined by the Supreme Court highlights the need for multinational companies to be aware that non-UK claimants may be able to bring claims against them in the English courts where they have a UK parent company.[4]

From this perspective, this judgment is at the centre of the ongoing legal battle about ensuring more accountability for multinational corporations acting under the guise of subsidiary companies in countries where the rule of law is less enforceable. A serious gap exists concerning the liability of companies for such extraterritorial environmental harms. Hence, this case is often seen as a breakthrough, opening doors for liability in English courts where arguably some of the most powerful multinational corporations are domiciled or listed, offering potential legal remedies for damage to the environment on a global scale.[5]

Our Approach: Decolonising the Duty of Care Towards Nature

Despite environmental damage and the duty of care being at the heart of the proceedings, the case did not engage with the damage done to the relevant ecosystem. The judgment focused on the technical issue of the duty of care of corporations and did not engage with whether a duty of care was owed to nature. Surfing on

[3] *Okpabi and others v Royal Dutch Shell PLC and another* [2018] EWCA Civ 191; *AAA and Others v Unilever PLC and Unilever Tea Kenya Limited* [2018] EWCA Civ 1532.

[4] For analysis, see Tara Van Ho, '*Vedanta Resources plc and another v Lungowe and others*' (2020) 114 *American Journal of International Law* 110.

[5] Carrie Bradshaw, 'Corporate Liability for Toxic Torts Abroad: *Vedanta v Lungowe* in the Supreme Court' (2020) 32 *Journal of Environmental Law* 139; Samvel Varvastian and Felicity Kalunga, 'Transnational Corporate Liability for Environmental Damage and Climate Change: Reassessing Access to Justice after *Vedanta v Lungowe*' (2020) 9 *Transnational Environmental Law* 323.

this groundbreaking opening by the Supreme Court, we explore how the judgment could have expanded the duty of care of the holding company (Vedanta) towards the claimants into an ethics of care towards nature. We bring to the fore a more ecological theoretical framing of an ethics of care towards nature by integrating African customs and concepts. We use recent approaches recognising legal personality of rivers as a framework to expand the duty of care of the company into an ethics of care that explicitly recognises the Kafue River as a legal entity with rights to hold the company responsible for its actions. This expanded duty of care shifts the attention away from a premise of conflict between opponents to a more relational approach between humans and non-humans which is more in tune with an Earth law perspective.[6] Since the Supreme Court decision was 'only' about establishing the competence of the English courts, instead of rewriting the judgment we have written an amicus curiae brief for a potential future court to propose a less anthropocentric approach to the issues at stake, focusing on the nature–human relationship.

It is uncertain whether there will be a further case on the merits, or whether the issue of damages and remedies could be examined in detail by the English courts in future. Since the decision of the Supreme Court was published, Vedanta has been locked in a protracted dispute with the Zambian government (which owns 20 per cent of KCM through state mining investment firm ZCCM-IH) after the Zambian government handed control of the mine to a liquidator.[7] Moreover, in parallel more than 2,500 Zambian villagers received an undisclosed settlement from Vedanta Resources in respect of their pollution claims.[8] This amicus curiae brief has been written on the basis of a possible future claim on the merits. This could help us understand what might happen if a less anthropocentric and a less Western-centric approach to law was applied in such a judgment.

One argument we want to put forward to the court is the fact that if it were to embrace the language and approach of recognising rights of nature – in this case the polluted river – this could also support a postcolonial recognition of key African approaches to justice. A good example of where ancestral jurisprudence overlaps with eco-jurisprudence can be found across different communities in West Africa. For example, the Gurene community use *Tiŋa* (Earth) as a concept for a legal system that extends subjectivity and agency to multigenerational humans, plants, animals and inanimate things.[9] Our amicus curiae brief explores the interaction between rights of nature and decolonisation of English law by suggesting that the

[6] Kyle Whyte and Chris Cuomo, 'Ethics of Caring in Environmental Ethics' in Stephen Gardiner and Allen Thompson (eds), *The Oxford Handbook of Environmental Ethics* (Oxford University Press, 2016).

[7] 'Zambian Court Denies Vedanta Attempt to Halt Konkola Copper Mines Split', *Reuters News*, 1 February 2021, reuters.com/article/us-zambia-mining-vedanta-idUSKBN2A12IO.

[8] 'Vedanta Mine Settles Zambian Villagers' Pollution Claim', *BBC News*, 19 January 2021 bbc.co.uk/news/world-africa-55725305.

[9] Anatoli Ignatov, 'The Sovereign Order of *Tiŋa*. Enduring Traditions of Earth Jurisprudence in Africa' In Peter Burdon and James Martel (eds) *The Routledge Handbook of Law and the Anthropocene* (Routledge 2023).

English courts could draw upon African legal concepts in the same manner that courts use precedent from Western jurisdictions.

This is not, as the commentator to our amicus curiae rightly points out, without its own problems or indeed a sense of irony that we argue for the English courts to widen their perspective to include and learn from non-Western perspectives. Our suggested approach is based on two facts. First, in this case the claimants could not gain any access to justice in their home country against a very powerful multinational corporation that was headquartered in the United Kingdom.[10] Secondly, despite decades of decolonisation, most legal systems in Africa are still very influenced by Western legal concepts. As the Ugandan scholar Sylvia Tamale highlights, the decolonisation of the legal system is still an issue that needs to be embraced by the judiciary in most African countries even more than fifty years after independence.[11]

Although many African constitutions, including Zambia's, recognise customary law and embrace legal pluralism, most judgments are still dominated by Western – mostly common law – principles. Therefore, despite the irony of arguing for an English court to embrace a postcolonial approach about a case concerning communities in Zambia, we feel that it is important to invite the courts in England to embrace a different approach to the responsibility of these corporations when their action leads to the destruction of ecosystems abroad. As we have argued elsewhere, whether the case were to be heard in an English or Zambian court, similar barriers to justice would exist.[12]

[10] For reflection on this complexity of accessing justice, see Janine Ubink and Joanna Pickering, 'Shaping Legal and Institutional Pluralism: Land Rights, Access to Justice and Citizenship in South Africa' (2020) 36 *South African Journal on Human Rights* 178; Adaeze Okoye, 'Promoting Access to Justice for Corporate Human Rights Violations in Africa: The Role of African Regional and Sub-regional Courts' in Damilola S Olawuyi and Oyeniyi Abe *Business and Human Rights Law and Practice in Africa* (Edward Elgar, 2022).

[11] Sylvia Tamale, *Decolonization and Afro-Feminism* (Daraja Press, 2020).

[12] Saskia Vermeylen, 'Comparative Environmental Law and Orientalism: Reading Beyond the "Text" of Traditional Knowledge Protection' (2015) 24 *Review of European Comparative & International Environmental Law* 304.

Amicus Curiae Brief

Lungowe & Others v Vedanta Resources PLC & Konkola Copper Mines

The aim of this amicus curiae brief is to propose an ecological duty of care that explicitly recognises the Kafue River as a legal entity with rights, enabling the company to be held liable for its actions to the river itself. This less anthropocentric approach recognises that suffering caused by pollution to the river from the Nchanga Copper Mine extends beyond the local communities, and considers how the health of the river is equally impacted. In part 1 of this brief, we argue for recognition that harm has been committed to the riverine ecosystem applying rights of nature principles. In part 2 we explore how the court could and should embrace local African concepts that are relevant to understanding relationships between the local communities and the concerned river.

1. Recognising the Damage Done to the Kafue River and its Communities

The Kafue River is at the heart of this case, yet it has been quasi-invisible in the legal proceedings so far.[13] The Nchanga mine pumps out approximately 75,000 m^3 of water per day, a component of which is derived from inflow through the open pits during the wet months. According to Action for Water and Water Witness International, a 2014 Zambian government report on the impact of copper mining in Zambia stated that:

> KCM's mining operations in Chingola regularly released effluents and discharge that contained copper, cobalt, sulphates, manganese, and other metals and solids that exceeded standard limits. KCM's mining operation has also been found to cause excessive siltation of the Kafue River and its tributary the Mushishima stream, which flows near Chingola, impacting aquatic ecosystems and agriculture in the area.[14]

Despite the river being one of the main victims, the judgment of the Supreme Court only mentions the river in one paragraph:

> The Google satellite images not only show the two parts of the Nchanga copper mine, but they also show the waterways in the area of the mine and in particular the Kafue

[13] The Kafue River is the longest river lying wholly within Zambia at about 1,576 kilometres (979 miles) long. It is the largest tributary of the Zambezi, and one of Zambia's principal rivers. More than 50 per cent of Zambia's population live in the Kafue River Basin.

[14] Water Futures Programme, *Case Study Briefing: The Crisis of Industrial Water Pollution and Poor Quality Water Supply – Evidence from Chingola*, 19 May 2016, cited in Linda Scott Jakobsson, *Copper with a Cost. Human Rights and Environmental Risks in the Mineral Supply Chain of ICT: A Case Study from Zambia* (Swedwatch 2019), 27.

> River, into which the subsidiary waterways flow. It is this river and these waterways which are at the heart of the claimants' claim in these proceedings. (para 17 of the judgment)

Anchoring ourselves on this sentence from Lord Briggs, 'It is this river and these waterways which are at the heart of the claimants' claim in these proceedings', we are suggesting to the Court that it should recognise the legal personality of the Kafue River and its surrounding waterways and its status as a victim in this case. This builds on a growing body of case law and legal academic commentary recognising the legal personality of natural entities. The idea of extending legal personhood to natural entities stems from the work of Christopher Stone who argued in 1972 that for nature to be better protected, law needed to recognise non-human natural entities such as trees as rights-holders, extending legal standing and recognising them as direct beneficiaries of legal redress. He argued that guardians could act on behalf of natural entities, including receiving collective relief that could be used to preserve and restore them.[15] In his famous dissenting judgment in *Sierra Club v Morton* (1972) in the United States, Justice William O Douglas reflected that: 'the river … is the living symbol of all the life it sustains or nourishes. … The river as plaintiff speaks for the ecological unit of life that is part of it.'[16]

Recognising legal personhood of rivers is a reaction to the long-standing propertisation of nature. There is a significant body of academic commentary on the rights of rivers movement in transnational litigation.[17] Here we include a summary of three key case studies where legal personhood and legal standing were extended to rivers: the Vilcabamba River in Ecuador, the Whanganui River in Aotearoa New Zealand, and the Atrato River in Colombia. We present a brief summary of the approaches followed in each case in order to indicate possible pathways to recognising legal personality of the Kafue River in Zambia. For the sake of clarity, we wish to establish at the outset that there has been some conflation between recognising legal personhood of rivers and rights of nature.[18] While

[15] Christopher D Stone, 'Should Trees Have Standing? – Toward Legal Rights for Natural Objects' (1972) 45 *Southern California Law Review* 450.

[16] *Sierra Club v Morton* 405 US 727 (1972) 743, cited in Linda Sheenan, '"Water as the Way": Achieving Wellbeing through "Right Relationship with Water"' in Michelle Maloney and Peter Burdon (eds) *Wild Law – In Practice* (Routledge 2014) 167.

[17] See Craig M Kauffman and Pamela L Martin, 'How Courts Are Developing River Rights Jurisprudence: Comparing Guardianship in New Zealand, Colombia, and India' (2019) 20 *Vermont Journal of Environmental Law*; Stellina Jolly and KS Roshan Menon, 'Of Ebbs and Flows: Understanding the Legal Consequences of Granting Personhood to Natural Entities in India' [2021] *Transnational Environmental Law* 1; Catherine Magallanes, 'From Rights to Responsibilities Using Legal Personhood and Guardianship for Rivers' in Betsa Martin, Linda Te Aho and Maria Humphries-Kil (eds), *ResponsAbility: Law and Governance for Living Well with the Earth* (Routledge, 2019).

[18] See Cristy Clark et al, 'Can You Hear the Rivers Sing? Legal Personhood, Ontology, and the Nitty-Gritty of Governance' (2019) 45 *Ecology Law Quarterly* 787; Erin O'Donnell, 'Re-setting Our Relationship with Rivers: The High Stakes of Personhood' in Yenny Vega Cárdenas and Daniel Turp (eds), *A Legal Personality for the St Lawrence River and Other Rivers of the World* (Éditions JFD, 2023).

both share the belief that new approaches are urgently needed to better protect nature, there are different options available to do this. Here, we mainly focus on attributing legal personhood to rivers. This is part of the rights of nature movement but is by no means a synonym because legal personality confers both rights and responsibilities.

Rights of the Vilcabamba River in Ecuador

In 2008, the Loja provincial government dumped materials that were accumulated when widening the road near the river, causing the river to flood in 2009 and 2010. Two residents from the United States filed a protection action against the provincial government on behalf of the Vilcabamba River.[19] In 2011, the Provincial Court of Loja ruled in favour of the plaintiffs for the river, recognising the 'democracy of the Earth'. Establishing that Nature has rights, the Court stated:

> [T]here are some premises that are fundamental to advance what can be identified as the 'democracy of the earth'; [this requires recognising that]: a) individual and collective human rights must be in a relation of harmony with the rights of other natural communities in the Earth; b) ecosystems have a right to exist and to carry on their vital processes; c) the diversity of life, as expressed in nature, has a value of its own; d) ecosystems have a value independent of their utility to human beings; and e) a legal framework in which ecosystems and natural communities have an inalienable right to exist and flourish would situate Nature at the highest level of value and importance.[20]

The Court concluded that the dumping of materials violated Nature's rights under Article 71 of Ecuador's Constitution as well as the 'right to be restored … apart from the obligation of the State and natural persons or legal entities to compensate individuals and communities that depend on affected natural systems' under Article 72. But while the Court recognised the rights of nature, it also balanced these rights with the needs of humans (ie road widening). As such, the Court missed the opportunity to recognise the rights of Nature beyond the river (ie the provincial government was allowed to uproot trees but not to dump them in the river).[21]

The Whanganui River, Aotearoa New Zealand

In March 2017, the New Zealand Parliament extended legal personhood to the Whanganui River as part of a process of treaty settlement between the Crown

[19] *Wheeler and Huddle v Gobierno Provincial de Loja*, 11121-2011-0010 Provincial Court of Loja, 30 March 2011.

[20] These statements, originally published on the website of the National Constituent Assembly of Ecuador (29 February 2008) were then reproduced in *Peripecias* No 87 (5 March 2008) and cited in Joel Colón-Ríos 'The Rights of Nature and the New Latin American Constitutionalism' (2015) 13 *New Zealand Journal of Public and International Law* 107, 111 as cited in Magallanes, 'From Rights to Responsibilities'.

[21] Magallanes 'From Rights to Responsibilities'.

and Māori iwi (tribes). Iwi regard the river as their *tupuna* (ancestor) which reinforces the idea that the people are inseparable from the river and that iwi and hapū (subtribes/descent groups or clans) have a responsibility to care for and protect the river, expressed as 'Ko au te awa, ko te awa ko au' (I am the River and the River is me).[22] The 2017 Act recognises that 'Te Awa Tupua is a legal person and has all the rights, powers, duties, and liabilities of a legal person.'[23] Acknowledging the Māori principle of *kaitiakitanga*, or guardianship, the Act appointed legal guardians, in the form of a management body known as Te Pou Tupua comprising one Crown and one Whanganui iwi representative to speak on behalf of the Whanganui River and protect its interests.[24] The Act also provides for the development of Te Heke Ngahuru, a whole river strategy that protects the well-being of the river, including a river fund, Te Koroteke o Te Awa Tupua, to support this.[25]

Atrato River, Colombia

The Atrato River ecosystem is one of the most diverse in the world and home to Afro-Colombian and Indigenous communities. There have been numerous environmental and humanitarian crises in this region, many due to the contamination of the river with toxic substances such as mercury and cyanide because of illegal mining operations. In 2015 a number of community organisations filed a motion for protection in the Administrative Tribunal of Cundinamarca on behalf of the affected communities and argued, initially unsuccessfully, that the state had an obligation to remove the mining operations. However, Colombia's Constitutional Court later ruled in favour of the communities' claim and went one step further, recognising the river itself as a legal person with its own rights that needed protection.[26] Three different rights were recognised in the decision: individual, community and biocultural rights. It is particularly the latter that are of importance for our case.

The Court used the concept of biocultural rights that are recognised in Colombia's Constitution to acknowledge the interdependence between nature and local communities:

> Biocultural rights are the precondition for the rights of ethnic and indigenous communities to exercise territorial autonomy in accordance with their own laws and customs. This includes the right of communities to administer the natural resources in the territories in which they have developed their culture, traditions and their special relationship with the environment and biodiversity.[27]

[22] Te Awa Tupua (Whanganui River Claims Settlement) Act 2017, s 69(3).
[23] ibid s 14(1).
[24] ibid ss 18–19.
[25] ibid s 57.
[26] *Tierra Digna v Republic of Colombia* (10 November 2016), Constitutional Court, T-622 of 2016, translated by and quoted in Magallanes 'From Rights to Responsibilities'.
[27] ibid 133.

The Court ordered the establishment of a Commission including two guardians – one from the local community and one from the government – and an advisory panel of experts, similar to the New Zealand model in the Te Awa Tupua Act. The Court also ordered the government and other specified research institutes, and non-governmental and community organisations to collectively implement a plan to clean the river and combat mining activities.[28]

Synthesis

Most current environmental laws regulate how much destruction nature can cope with, based on a perception of ecosystems, including rivers, as property. Recognising legal personhood of rivers means that they are no longer perceived as property but as rights-bearing entities. This means that local communities are also given legal authority to enforce and defend the river's rights, and damages may be awarded for violations of the river's rights, including full restoration of the river's pre-damaged status. A key element of recognising the legal rights of rivers is in highlighting connection and relationality between ecosystems and local communities. Living entities are relatives not resources. Attributing legal personality to a river implies that the river can have legal relations with other subjects. This is reflected in the concept of kincentric ecology, which refers to the idea that 'humans are part of an extended ecological family that shares ancestry and origins',[29] putting the emphasis on relationality between humans and nature.[30] In recognising the legal personality of the Kafue River it is important that this element of relationality should not be overlooked, especially in this Zambian context where local communities have their own relationships with nature. Here we are inviting the Court to embrace a relational approach that recognises the entanglements between nature and humans.

2. Decolonial Restorative Justice

In African contexts law is not just derived from common law, but also from laws of the Earth within African customary law. As Ng'anga Thiong'o testifies:

> In Africa we have a cosmovision of where there are no objects within the context of customary law. Everything is living. The sky is part of us, so is the Earth, air, water, the plants and the animals. We have to keep the balance between all these aspects for the community to survive. The community is not just human community. It is a community

[28] Craig M Kauffman and Pamela L Martin, *The Politics of Rights of Nature: Strategies for Building a More Sustainable Future* (MIT Press, 2021) 195–98.

[29] See eg Enrique Salmon, 'Kincentric Ecology: Indigenous Perceptions of the Human–Nature Relationship' (2000) 10 *Ecological Applications* 1327.

[30] Justine Townsend et al, 'Right for Nature: How Granting a River "Personhood" Could Help Protect It', *The Conversation*, 3 June 2021, theconversation.com/rights-for-nature-how-granting-a-river-personhood-could-help-protect-it-157117.

> with many other subjects. Customary law is a source of law that contains all these principles, these have stood the test of time, since time immemorial, and they have been transmitted from one generation to another.[31]

There are multiple ways of relating to a river and these must be taken into consideration in restoration. Restoring the river requires first and foremost acknowledging the special relationship that exists between communities and the river. In Aotearoa New Zealand restoration of the Whanganui River has not just been about improving an ecological process; it is also about healing and restoring the relationship between people and the river.[32] In the words of Robin Wall Kimmerer, 'we need acts of restoration, not only for polluted waters and degraded lands, but also for our relationship to the world'.[33] This requires extending the duty of care of the corporation and the government towards the local communities to an ethics of care that includes the more-than-human.

In the context of Zambia, a similar relationality can be found amongst the Lamba (*AŴalamb*) people. Although the Lamba comprise a small percentage of the total population in Zambia, the whole of the Copperbelt province is on Lamba land (*Ilamŵa*). Due to copper mining, *Ilamŵa* is now urbanised and many other groups, of which the Bemba people form a significant part, have moved to the area. Despite this influx, the Lamba people have continued to nurture deep cultural roots to the area and their culture is still anchored in traditional education and values.[34]

For the Lamba, the great source for their law is *Lesa*, the creator of all things, of the people and everything else that lives in the realm of the *Lesa*. *Lesa* first created the sun before the moon, and then the stars. *Lesa* also arranged the whole country: rivers, mountains, anthills, grass, trees and lakes.[35] For the Bemba, *Lesa* is also the creator of all things, including heaven and Earth, and is considered both male and female. Before Christianity *Lesa* was seen as Mother-Earth, but with the arrival of Christianity became the Father-Sky God.[36] In addition to *Lesa*, other spirits also play an important role in Zambian cosmologies. For example, an important spirit for the Bemba people is *ngulu* who are considered the early inhabitants of the lands and residing in waterfalls, rocks, trees and anthills. Other spirits are *imipashi*, or the ancestral spirits, who are associated with the fertility of the bush and the gardens, and the lineage of the clan.[37]

[31] Ng'anga Thiong'o, 'Earth Jurisprudence in the African Context?' in Peter Burdon (ed), *Exploring Wild Law: The Philosophy of Earth Jurisprudence* (Wakefield Press 2011) 174.

[32] Jacinta Ruru, 'Listening to Papatūānuku: A Call to Reform Water Law', (2018) 48 *Journal of the Royal Society of New Zealand* 215; Linda Te Aho, 'Te Mana o Te Wai: An Indigenous Perspective on Rivers and River Management' (2019) 35 *River Research and Applications* 1615.

[33] Robin Wall Kimmerer, *Braiding Sweetgrass: Indigenous Wisdom, Scientific Knowledge, and the Teachings of Plants* (Milkweed Editions, 2015).

[34] Rosemary Kalenga, 'The Lambas of the Copperbelt/Zambia's Behaviours and Taboos before Colonisation and Christianisation: A Literature Review to Accommodate Research in the Indigenous Realm' (2015) 14 *Indilinga – African Journal of Indigenous Knowledge Systems* 185, 187.

[35] ibid 186.

[36] Thera Rasing, 'Female Initiation Rites as Part of Gendered Bemba Religion and Culture: Transformation in Women's Empowerment' (2017/2018) 7 *Zambia Social Science Journal* 55, 58.

[37] ibid 59.

Given the importance placed on relationships with the creator god, the spirits and the ancestors in Zambian societal organisation and structures, polluting the Kafue River is seen as a provocative act that may aggrieve the ancestors, who are, after all, the ultimate arbiters and judges in Zambia's religions and cultures. Instead of seeing the river as a commodity or property belonging in trust to the state, it is important that the river is seen as belonging to a spiritual world that cannot be owned, let alone spoiled or polluted. This would, according to local communities' beliefs, equate to disrespecting gods, spirits and ancestors, which ultimately may have repercussions for the people themselves as this may create bad luck and hardship.

Taking these local cosmologies into consideration, future mining operations undertaken by Vedanta and its subsidiary in Zambia, KCM, must, in our view, incorporate ethics of care that respect the moral and spiritual relationships between local communities and the river. Instead of imposing a neocolonial moral framing, this ethics of care can be structured as an African moral obligation to care for the environment as an expression of interconnectedness between people, the biophysical world and the spiritual world. Using this approach to manage the future relationship between Vedanta, its subsidiary and the community living along the Kafue River, Vedanta and its subsidiary would have an obligation of care towards the community, its wider biophysical environment, and the creator gods, spirits and ancestors. For the Lamba people, human beings are always in close relationship with everything around them and are seen to play just a small part in the wider natural and spiritual world.[38] Ancestral and many other spirits live in the forests along the Kafue River, and are responsible for the welfare of the Lamba people. Destruction to the Kafue River and its surroundings results in people being cut off from their relationship with the deities and their spiritual worlds which can result in catastrophic consequences.[39] From this perspective, it is important that future relations between Vedanta and its Zambian subsidiary, and the community and the environment should recognise the importance of embracing different worldviews and spiritualities and be guided by these overarching local principles of relationality and relatedness.

Relationality requires taking into account how harms done to both the communities and the river create a cumulative effect of environmental harm. We refer the Court to arguments made by Chief Judge of the Land and Environment Court in New South Wales, The Hon Justice Brian J Preston that environmental statutes should take into account these cumulative environmental effects, especially in the case of waterways where activities/pollution should not be assessed in a self-contained manner.[40] Once it is acknowledged that part of the harm committed was to

[38] Lackson Chibuye and Johan Buitendag, 'The Indigenisation of Eco-theology: The Case of the Lamba People of the Copperbelt in Zambia' (2020) 76 *Teologiese Studies/Theological Studies* a6067.

[39] ibid.

[40] Brian J Preston, 'Internalizing Ecocentrism in Environmental Law' in Michelle Maloney and Peter Burdon (eds) *Wild Law – In Practice* (Routledge 2014).

the Kafue River itself, remediation requires a more holistic and restorative approach than only compensating the local river communities for the harm they suffered due to the river being polluted. We posit, taking into account African philosophy, local cosmologies and customary justice, that restoring the river must not just be conceptualised as an ecocentric right but also, importantly, include a sense of responsibility for '*restoring* [our emphasis] any damage and/or the cost of protecting the land and its resources from any harm'.[41] The example of Te Awa Tupua provides insights into how to repair these intergenerational, multispecies social–environmental relations, through paying respect to the cultural values underpinning relationships between humans and non-humans. As Hikuruo et al argue, restoring a river requires not only the recognition of legal pluralism or indeed acknowledging in this case the Māori's cultural legal norms and practices, but also fluvial pluralism, which can be best described as valuing rivers as 'holistic, historical, and cultural agents with lives and rights of their own'.[42] Learning from river communities in this way can create spaces 'for thinking about rivers pluralistically'.[43]

These principles should also form the basis of the remedies that are sought in this case, and we are of the opinion that these can be best achieved through a restorative justice conference. In Justice Preston's view restorative justice provides the right framing to broaden the identification of victims of environmental harm beyond the community and avoid harms being replicated in the future.[44] This also recognises that remediation will take many generations, particularly as the harm caused affects natural resources that cannot be replaced, and consequently, intergenerational relationships between humans and non-humans.

To achieve restoration of the river ecologies, the river must also be represented in the process of restorative justice. As Justice Preston confirms, rivers can indeed be successfully represented by a surrogate victim at restorative justice conferences. To paraphrase Justice Preston, by giving the river a voice and recognising and healing it as a victim, humanity's relationship with the river is also transformed.[45] The Court should therefore allow for the community that is dependent on the river for its subsistence and well-being to represent both the river and the community as victims of the harm caused. There is relevant common law precedent here. In the New Zealand case of *Waikato Regional Council v Huntly Quarries Ltd and Ian Harrold Wedding*,[46] the river was represented by the chairperson of the Waikato

[41] Nicole Graham 'Owning the Earth' in Peter Burdon (ed), *Exploring Wild Law: The Philosophy of Earth Jurisprudence* (Wakefield Press 2011) 266.

[42] Dan Hikuroa et al, 'Restoring Sociocultural Relationships with Rivers: Experiments in Fluvial Pluralism Restoring Sociocultural Relationships with Rivers' in Bertrand Morandi, Marylise Cottet and Hervé Piégay (eds), *River Restoration: Political, Social, and Economic Perspectives* (Wiley 2021), 67.

[43] ibid 67.

[44] Brian Preston, 'The Use of Restorative Justice for Environmental Crime' (2011) 35 *Criminal Law Journal* 136. Article based on a paper that was delivered to the EPA Victoria Seminar on Restorative Environmental Justice 22 March 2011, Melbourne.

[45] ibid.

[46] *Waikato Regional Council v Huntly Quarries Ltd and Ian Harrold Wedding*, Auckland District Court (McElrea DCJ) 30 July 2003 and 28 October 2003.

River Enhancement Society at a restorative justice conference to expose the harm that was committed through the illegal dumping of sediment-laden stormwater discharged from the offender's quarry, affecting the river quality of the Waikato River. The reason why we refer to this case is because it demonstrates the potential for restorative justice conferencing to address both the past and future behaviour of an offender. It allows for making reparations to victims for the harm caused both to humans and non-human biota such as the riverine ecosystem. We are of the opinion that restorative justice conferences are more in tune with this local African context where the Earth itself is a great source of law.

We invite the Court to recognise the concern of the applicants that undertakings may not be given legal effect and enforced under current Zambian environmental legislation. Therefore, restorative justice conferencing is the preferred route to come to an agreement about the future behaviour of the company. The company's promises obtained in the restorative justice conferencing could be incorporated into the orders made by a sentencing court and we recommend that the court follows the approach to restorative justice outlined by Justice Brian Preston and provide that the offending company must:

- Prevent, control, abate and mitigate harm to the riverine ecosystem caused by the activities of the company;
- Pay the costs for the restoration of the harm caused;
- Pay compensation for the loss of income, and damage to the natural and cultural environment of the communities living along the river;
- Carry out and pay for the restoration and enhancement of the environment along the river for the benefit of the communities;
- Adapt their practices in order to prevent the continuance or recurrence of the offences;
- Carry out and pay for the environmental audit of activities of the company.

The moral principles that have framed the restorative justice conferencing should also be applied through this ruling to the future management of the natural resources. This means that:

- According to the beliefs of the community, past, present and future generations are all part of the moral community that set out the rules of engagement for the behaviour and management practices of the company and its subsidiary;
- The fundamental relatedness of beings includes a relatedness with other natural entities.

It is timely for this Court to express its opinion that the healing for past and current colonial and neocolonial mercantile practices should be guided by acknowledging African worldviews that are not guided by separatism between humans and nature. To conclude our amicus curiae, we would like to quote the great Zimbabwean writer and illustrator Credo Mutwa:

> In old Africa we … believe that we had nature within and beyond ourselves. By making us believe that the highest gods were part animal and part human being, we were taught to look upon animals with great reverence, love and respect. … The native people of Africa regarded them as a blessing from the gods – as something unbelievably sacred and vital for the continued existence of human beings. Black people believed that animals were the blood of the earth and that as long as there were migrations criss-crossing the country, human existence on Earth was guaranteed.[47]

[47] Credo Mutwa, *Isilwane: The Animal* (Struik, 1996) 13–15, cited in Kai Horsthemke '*Isilwane: The Animal – Ubuntu, Ukama* and Environmental Justice' in Rainer Ebert and Anteneh Roba (eds), *Africa and Her Animals: Philosophical and Practical Perspectives* (Unisa Press, 2018), 4.

Commentary

Felicity Kayumba Kalunga

Introduction

The amicus brief proposes two main innovations in approaches to environmental litigation. First, the authors advance an ecocentred duty of care that includes ethics of care owed to nature, in this case the Kafue River. The second key contribution is a decolonial restorative justice perspective that emphasises the restoration of the river, over and above compensatory relief to the people affected by the acts of the corporation. The authors develop their arguments, discussing the rights of nature using various sources including Zambian traditional and customary norms. The second argument emphasises the value of restorative justice as an appropriate remedy in instances involving damage to nature. At first glance, these innovations appear problematic in the context of a case involving the exercise of jurisdiction by English courts over torts committed on foreign soil by a foreign defendant. It may seem ironic to advocate for a decolonial approach to conceptualising the duty of care within the context of transnational litigation which typically symbolises neocolonial practice. It also appears difficult to imagine how a restorative justice order would be implemented in the context of transnational litigation against a defendant domiciled in England due to the difficulties of enforcing foreign judgments that issue non-monetary orders.

A Decolonial Concept of the Duty of Care

The apparent irony in the proposed approach seems to stem from the fact that instituting claims in an English court for torts committed in Zambia by both Vedanta Resources and KCM seemingly perpetuates a neocolonial approach to litigation that esteems English courts over their Zambian counterparts. Critics of existing principles governing the application of foreign law in English courts have faulted English courts for presenting English legal principles as superior to foreign ones when developing rules to guide the admission of foreign law, which is admitted as evidence rather than law.[48] English courts are cognisant of this criticism and therefore approach cases involving foreign competing jurisdiction with caution. For instance, the trial judge in the case of *Lungowe and Others v Vedanta Resources Plc & Konkola Copper Mines* cautioned that 'I am conscious that some of the foregoing paragraphs could be seen as a criticism of the Zambian legal system. I might even be accused of colonial condescension. But that is not the intention or

[48] Anthony Gray, 'Choice of Law: The Presumption in the Proof of Foreign Law' (2008) 31 *UNSW Law Journal* 136, 139.

purpose of this part of the judgment.'[49] With this background, one might wonder what value could be gained from the arguments presented in this chapter in favour of a decolonial concept of a duty of care owed to rivers which incorporates African customary and religions norms. Would the case not best be resolved in Zambia where courts would be more inclined to apply customary norms as law?

The above concerns notwithstanding, transnational litigation remains of tremendous value in securing access to justice for victims of environmental violations by multinational corporations in countries with weak access to justice. In any event, there is no guarantee that a Zambian court is more likely to apply a decolonial concept of the duty of care, chiefly on account of the legacy of colonialism on the development of law in Zambia. Zambian courts, like their English counterparts, would potentially apply a duty of care based on propertisation of rivers. A previous and similar case decided by Zambian courts, in which liability was established, was overturned on appeal on account of failure by the claimants to prove both causation and loss and to value their loss. The case is illustrative of the approach taken by courts establishing liability and loss in such cases.[50] This is what makes the arguments presented in this brief compelling as it challenges our conception of the duty of care, which is key in establishing liability in environmental rights claims. The novel arguments advanced in the brief are admissible in English courts within the existing legal principles governing reception of foreign law as I demonstrate below.

Courts in England and Wales have long entertained cases of torts occurring in foreign jurisdictions against defendants domiciled in England and Wales or in a foreign country. Where such cases are admitted, the court would ordinarily apply the law of the foreign state. In *Vedanta Resources Plc and Another v Lungowe and Others*, Lord Briggs stated that 'the level of intervention in the management of the mine requisite to give rise to a duty of care upon Vedanta to persons living, farming and working in the vicinity is (as is agreed) a matter of Zambian law'.[51] English courts ordinarily accept foreign law as evidence to be proved in court but not as law.[52] Where foreign law is not proved, the courts have historically applied English law or would presume that the foreign law is the same as the forum law.[53] Anthony Gray argues that this assumption that the law of the foreign country is the same as English law is a legacy of imperialism and colonialism and need not continue in the current age.[54] This colonial conception of the superiority of English law and its attendant principles must pave the way to the reality of legal pluralism, including

[49] *Lungowe and Others v Vedanta Resources Plc and Konkola Copper Mines Plc* [2016] EWHC 975 (TCC) para 198.

[50] *Nyasulu and 2000 Others v Konkola Copper Mines Plc* [2015] ZMSC 33.

[51] *Vedanta Resources Plc and Anor (Appellants) v Lungowe and Others (Respondents)* [2019] UKSC 20, para 17.

[52] Gray 'Choice of Law', 143.

[53] Jack Wass, 'The Court's In Personam Jurisdiction in Cases Involving Foreign Land' (2014) 63 *ICLQ* 103, 107.

[54] Gray, 'Choice of Law', 140.

by modifying key concepts such as the duty of care as is argued here, to admit other normative perspectives.

In addition to the arguments on a flexible concept of the duty of care that have been advanced by the arguments in this brief, the decolonial concept of the duty to the river can also be deduced from Zambian statutory law which recognises customary law norms. For instance, section 4 of the Environmental Management Act 2011 which provides for the right to a clean, safe and healthy environment, states that the right includes 'the right of access to the various elements of the environment for recreational, education, health, spiritual, cultural and economic purposes'. This law can be relied upon to support a claim by people who depend on the Kafue River for their spiritual well-being to seek restorative remedies on behalf of the river. Another example of Zambian environmental legislation which recognises customary norms is section 5(2) of the Water Resources Management Authority Act 2011 which requires authorities to ensure that 'traditional practices as recognised in customary areas and which are beneficial to water resource management are taken into account in the management of water resources'. Further, the conception of statutory liability under Zambian law should give effect to the constitutional morality of Zambian law under which customary law is recognised and respected.

Enforceability of Restorative Justice Orders

The amicus brief proposes that in addition to awarding compensation to the communities who have suffered damages, the court should include restorative justice as an important element in the case, both as a way to deal with the harm committed to the community and the river, and importantly to include provisions that avoid harms being replicated in the future. The argument proposes a format that the order could take, drawing on the arguments by Justice Brian Preston on restorative environmental justice. The proposal is progressive. However, some of the examples of such restorative justice orders bear the characteristics of injunctive relief. The problem here stems from the challenges of enforcing non-monetary orders in a foreign country. Elena Merino Blanco and Ben Pontin argue that compared to a monetary judgment that can be enforced on the assets of a defendant within the jurisdiction of the determining court, a non-monetary remedy such as an injunction would put a defendant in a stronger position to oppose the jurisdiction of English courts on grounds of comity and exorbitant jurisdiction because it is difficult to enforce such a judgment on foreign soil.[55]

The authors here suggest an innovative way to address challenges of enforcement by proposing a restorative forum drawn from the example of the case of

[55] Elena Merico Blanco and Ben Pontin, 'Litigating Extraterritorial Nuisances under English Common Law and UK Statute' (2017) 6 *Transnational Environmental Law* 285, 305.

Waikato Regional Council v Huntly Quarries Ltd.[56] Such a forum can be structured so that the restorative orders issued by that forum are in the form of an agreed to judgment similar to a consensual judgment such as the one reached in the case of *The Bodo Community and Others v Shell Petroleum Development Company of Nigeria Ltd*[57] in Nigeria. The restorative conferencing forum could then be conducted in Zambia by parties and other experts who would take on the interests of the river from a customary and religious perspective.

[56] *Waikato Regional Council v Huntly Quarries Ltd and Ian Harrold Wedding*, Auckland District Court (McElrea DCJ) 30 July 2003 and 28 October 2003.

[57] *The Bodo Community and Others v Shell Petroleum Development Company of Nigeria Ltd* [2014] EWHC 1973 (TCC).

10

Ecocide in the International Criminal Court: *The Prosecutor v Mr X (Reparations Order)*

RACHEL KILLEAN

Introduction

My contribution to this collection explores the reparative possibilities of an international crime prohibiting ecocide being included in the mandate of the International Criminal Court (ICC). While momentum behind ecocide's criminalisation has grown exponentially in recent years, there is currently no such crime. As such, this is not a rewritten version of an ICC judgment. Rather, it is a fictionalised judgment drawn from real-life facts; the environmental destruction wrought by oil exploitation in Ogoniland, Nigeria provides the well-documented and devastating backdrop for this creative judgment-writing exercise. The harm experienced by Ogoniland's human inhabitants described below is also very real, and my primary motivations in writing this judgment have been to both shine a spotlight on the interconnected harms experienced in Ogoniland and to imagine what it might take to redress those harms. I want to acknowledge up front that there were a range of procedural and substantive aspects that would normally feature in an ICC reparations order that there was simply no room to discuss. I prioritised the issues that I felt were most interesting for the purpose of exploring reparations for ecocide. To any readers coming to this chapter with expertise in international criminal law and the practice of reparations – I ask for your indulgence. The rest of this brief introduction outlines some of the challenges I faced in putting this judgment together and explains some of the choices made along the way.

One key challenge related to defining ecocide. As anyone with an interest in ecocide will know, the Stop Ecocide's Independent Expert Panel definition has fast gained prominence as the definition de rigueur.[1] However, early in the drafting

[1] 'For the purpose of this Statute, "ecocide" means unlawful or wanton acts committed with knowledge that there is a substantial likelihood of severe and either widespread or long-term damage to the environment being caused by those acts.' Independent Expert Panel for the Legal Definition of Ecocide: Commentary and Core Text, June 2021.

process I found myself turning away from this definition and returning to the 2010 definition offered by Polly Higgins.[2] There are four reasons for this. First, in common with others,[3] I am not convinced that the panel has created a definition that is workable in practice. The requirement that acts be illegal or 'wanton' (with reckless disregard for damage which would be *clearly excessive* in relation to the social and economic benefits anticipated), when coupled with the requirement that the accused knows that there is a substantial likelihood of damage to the environment, may pose a barrier to a successful prosecution. Second, I value Higgins's explicit inclusion of 'omissions' as well as 'acts' in her proposed definition. The ICC does not refer to a general omission liability beyond Article 28 (superior responsibility) and some specific crimes (eg starvation). Yet, 'crimes of omission' can have severe environmental consequences[4] (as demonstrated below) and their criminalisation has been identified by many proponents of ecocide as crucial to creating a duty of care and responsibility for preventing environmental catastrophe.[5] Third, I appreciate Higgins's centring of not only ecological and climate-related consequences but also cultural loss.[6] As green criminologists, genocide scholars and Indigenous legal scholars have demonstrated, crimes against nature are often also crimes against culture,[7] with some using the 'genocide–ecocide nexus' to describe the interconnected nature of the destruction of nature and the loss of cultural identity.[8] Fourth, and I will freely admit this is not an 'academic' reason, I wanted to pay tribute to Higgins's dedicated work on pursuing accountability for ecocide, which was abruptly cut short following her death in 2019.

Another challenge was selecting a case study through which to explore reparations for ecocide. As the Order would be appearing alongside judgments drawn from the United Kingdom's legal systems, I wanted to focus on crimes with some connection to the UK. The actions and omissions of fictionalised individuals employed by Shell to engage in oil extraction in Ogoniland were an obvious choice. Oil was discovered

[2] Polly Higgins, *Eradicating Ecocide: Laws and Governance to Prevent the Destruction of our Planet*, 2nd edn (Shepheard-Walwyn, 2015) 61–69.

[3] Kevin Jon Heller, 'The Crime of Ecocide in Action', *Opinio Juris*, 28 June 2021, opiniojuris.org/2021/06/28/the-crime-of-ecocide-in-action.

[4] Ronald Kramer, 'Climate Change: A State-corporate Crime Perspective' in Toine Spapens, Rob White and Marieke Kluin (eds), *Environmental Crime and its Victims: Perspectives within Green Criminology* (Ashgate, 2014) 23–41.

[5] See Mark Allan Gray, 'The International Crime of Ecocide' (1996) 26 *California Western International Law Journal* 215; Polly Higgins, *Earth Is Our Business: Changing the Rules of the Game* (Shepheard-Walwyn, 2012); and also Giovanni Chiarini, 'Ecocide and International Criminal Court Procedural Issues', UCC Centre for Criminal Justice and Human Rights Legal Working Paper Series, November 2021; Rob White, 'Ecocide and the Carbon Crimes of the Powerful' (2018) 37 *University of Tasmania Law Review* 95.

[6] The Independent Expert Panel also lists grave impacts on 'cultural resources' within its definition of 'severe', but I find this somewhat diluted by the requirement that it be either irreversible or experienced by a 'large number of human beings'.

[7] Lauren J Eichler, 'Ecocide Is Genocide: Decolonizing the Definition of Genocide' (2020) 14 *Genocide Studies and Prevention* 104; David R Goyes et al, 'Genocide and Ecocide in Four Colombian Indigenous Communities: The Erosion of a Way of Life and Memory' (2021) 61 *British Journal of Criminology* 965.

[8] See eg Damien Short and Martin Crook (eds), *The Genocide–Ecocide Nexus* (Routledge, 2022).

in the Niger Delta region in 1958. At that time, Nigeria was a British colony and oil exploration commenced through an agreement between Shell and the colonial government. Following Nigeria's independence in 1960 Shell continued to extract oil, in the midst of emerging evidence on the harmful effects of oil exploration and extraction on the local populations. Government interventions from the 1970s failed to address the environmental and social impacts of the industry, and by the 1990s Shell had been named in more than 500 environmental lawsuits filed in Nigeria.[9] Shell ceased extractive activities in 1993. Nevertheless, an extensive network of pipelines criss-crosses Ogoniland, and oil spills and fires continue to devastate the natural environment. Attempts to draw attention to these harmful impacts have historically led to violence perpetrated against protestors and community organisers.[10]

The 'extreme harms to the environment' by Shell – a British-registered public limited company – have been acknowledged by many.[11] The harms caused to the Niger Delta ecosystem have been described as a 'textbook ecocide'[12] and have been systematically documented by a range of human rights and environmental organisations.[13] Recent years have seen concerted and successful efforts to hold Shell liable for these harms in the English and Dutch court systems.[14] As such, I thought it would be interesting to explore the alternative pathways to accountability and repair that might have opened had the Rome Statute included a crime of ecocide at the time the harms occurred. However, I have not used Shell's name in the wording of the judgment, as neither the parent company nor its subsidiaries have, to date, been held internationally criminally accountable for their acts and omissions in the Niger Delta. I also want to be clear that this judgment is not written with a particular accused person in mind. I do not have access to the type of detailed information that would be needed to trace harmful acts and omissions to specific people. I have chosen specific sites for the purposes of exploring the nature of the harm, but I have anonymised them somewhat to avoid unintentionally implicating any particular individual. What is interesting to me is not determining liability of

[9] Jedrzej George Frynas, *Oil in Nigeria: Conflict and Litigation between Oil Companies and Village Communities* (Transaction, 2000).

[10] Center for Constitutional Rights and Earth Rights, 'Fact Sheet: The Case Against Shell', available at wiwavshell.org.

[11] Alex Lawson, 'Shell Consultant Quits, Accusing Firm of Extreme Harms to the Environment', *The Guardian*, 23 May 2022, theguardian.com/business/2022/may/23/shell-consultant-quits-environment-caroline-dennett.

[12] Eva Sevrin, 'Hot Times for Ecocide (II): The Belgian Proposal', *Leuven Public Law*, 25 March 2022, leuvenpubliclaw.com/hot-times-for-ecocide-ii-the-belgian-proposal.

[13] See Amnesty International, *Petroleum, Pollution and Poverty in the Niger Delta* (2009); United Nations Environment Programme, *Environmental Assessment of Ogoniland* (2011); Amnesty International; and CEHRD, *The True 'Tragedy': Delays and Failures in Tackling Oil Spills in the Niger Delta* (2011); Friends of the Earth and Amnesty International, *No Progress: An Evaluation of the Implementation of UNEP's Environmental Assessment of Ogoniland, Three Years On* (2014); Amnesty International and CEHRD, *Clean it Up: Shell's False Claims about Oil Spill Response in the Niger Delta* (2015); Amnesty International, *No Clean-Up, No Justice: An Evaluation of the Implementation of UNEP's Environmental Assessment of Ogoniland, Nine Years On* (2020).

[14] *Okpabi and others (Appellants) v Royal Dutch Shell Plc and another (Respondents)* [2021] UKSC 3; *Fidelis Ayoro Oguru and others (MD et al (plural)) vs Shell Petroleum (case a) and Royal Dutch Shell PLC and Shell Petroleum Development Company of Nigeria (Ltd)*, The Hague Court of Appeal, 29 January 2021, Case numbers: 200.126.804 (case a) + 200.126.834 (case b).

individuals, but exploring the aftermath of a finding of liability, and the opportunities it presents for repair.

A significant challenge was deciding how much of the ICC's Rome Statute to change. In the end, the parallel universe I created mirrors our own apart from the inclusion of ecocide in the Rome Statute's original mandate. I debated whether to introduce corporate liability and to put the company itself on trial, or its Nigerian subsidiary rather than the fictionalised defendant in this hypothetical case. Considering the scale of the harm and the reparations required, and the role of the company's profit-driven logics in facilitating ecocide, prosecuting a corporation rather than individuals had its appeal.[15] I also considered extending the definition of victimhood to encompass other-than-human victims of harm (eg the mangroves themselves). As I have explored elsewhere, engaging with other-than-human harm and access to reparation in its own right is arguably a crucial part of recognising the inherent value of the natural world.[16] Nor is it an outlandish concept – recent moves to grant reparative rights to nature can be found in the practice of Colombia's Jurisdicción Especial para la Paz[17] for example. However, in the end I decided to stay largely within the confines of the Rome Statute as it is. While seeing value in a multitude of other approaches of varying degrees of creativity, I was interested in seeing how the Court's reparation mandate might stretch to hold and respond to the harms of ecocide should such a crime be introduced without any other adjustments being made. The results of this attempt are as follows.

[15] On the value of introducing corporate liability, see eg Marco Colacuri, 'The Draft Convention Ecocide and the Role for Corporate Remediation' (2021) *International Criminal Law Review* 1.

[16] Rachel Killean, 'Environmental Restorative Justice in Transitional Settings' in Brunilda Pali, Miranda Forsyth and Felicity Tepper (eds), *The Palgrave Handbook of Environmental Restorative Justice* (Palgrave MacMillan, 2022) 247–73.

[17] See the website of Jurisdicción Especial para la Paz, jep.gov.co/JEP/Paginas/Jurisdiccion-Especial-para-la-Paz.aspx.

International Criminal Court

Trial Chamber I

The Prosecutor v Mr X (Reparations Order)

1 June 2023

A. Procedural History

In January 2018 the Situation in the Niger Delta was referred to the International Criminal Court by the Federal Government of Nigeria. Investigations opened in March 2018, with a focus on alleged crimes of ecocide under Article 8 ter perpetrated since 1 July 2002 (when the Rome Statute entered into force). The regional focus was identified as encompassing Ogoniland, a kingdom which covers 1,050 square kilometres in Rivers State, southern Nigeria. Ogoniland has over 1 million inhabitants. It is also home to both the third largest mangrove ecosystem in the world and one of the largest surviving rainforests in Nigeria.

On 1 October 2021 the Trial Chamber I found Mr X guilty of the crime of ecocide, meaning 'acts or omissions committed in times of peace or conflict by any senior person within the course of State, corporate or any other entity's activity which cause, contribute to, or may be expected to cause or contribute to serious ecological, climate or cultural loss or damage to or destruction of ecosystem(s) of a given territory(ies), such that peaceful enjoyment by the inhabitants has been or will be severely diminished (Article 5(1)(e) and Article 8 ter)'.

These convictions relate to the convicted person's acts and omissions during his time as a senior employee of the Petroleum Development Company (Nigeria) Ltd ('The Company'). He is found liable under the principle of superior responsibility, for: (i) the repeated failure to decommission and make safe facilities in Ogoniland following the cessation of active oil extraction in 1993; (ii) the failure to adequately and speedily respond to oil spills that have taken place between 2009 and 2015; (iii) inadequate and incomplete clean-ups of severe land and water contamination in Ogoniland; and (iv) the unethical action of channelling oil into Ogoniland's waterways. On the 20 October 2021 Mr X was sentenced to twenty years' imprisonment for these crimes.

The Chamber has received submissions on the reparations process from the Trust Fund for Victims, the Legal Representatives of Victims, the Defence for Mr X, and the Office of the Prosecutor. It has also received observations from the Federal Government of Nigeria, the United Nations Environment Programme (UNEP), the World Health Organization (WHO), the International Union for the Conservation of Nature (IUCN), Friends of the Earth Nigeria and Europe, the Centre for Environment, Human Rights and Development (CEHRD), Center for Constitutional Rights and Earth Rights (CCRER), Amnesty International and Milieudefensie. The Chamber notes that 2,000 victims of the ecocide perpetrated in Ogoniland participated in the trial proceedings. Their views and concerns have been considered throughout the proceedings.

As established by this Court's practice, a reparation order must: (i) be directed against the convicted person; (ii) establish and inform the convicted person of their liability for the reparations; (iii) provide reasons for the type of reparation ordered; (iv) define the harm caused to victims as a result of the crimes perpetrated, and appropriate modalities of reparations; and (v) identify those victims eligible or set out eligibility criteria.

B. Scope of the Case

This Reparations Order relates to acts and omissions perpetrated by the accused, causing ecological, climate and cultural loss in four sites across Ogoniland.[18] The repeated failure to decommission and make safe facilities in Ogoniland following the cessation of active oil extraction in 1993 has resulted in ecological loss through the widespread contamination of water, including wells, creeks and estuaries in these areas. The failure to adequately respond to spills has caused the contamination of surface soil to seep into sediments, swamp land and groundwater – significantly harming vegetation and mangrove and forest ecosystems. Oil spills in land have caused fires, making recovery much more difficult. The channelling of oil into waterways and the contamination of land and water have impacted wildlife and aquatic life. The destruction of mangroves has been particularly devastating for many fish species, while the loss of habitat and frequency of fires has impacted land animals and bird species.

The destruction of mangroves has further resulted in climate loss, being one of the key ecosystems, alongside rainforests, in need of protection and repair if we are to prevent catastrophic global heating. The frequency of gas flaring sites has also had climate impacts, turning Nigeria into one of the highest emitters of greenhouse gases on the African continent.[19]

Finally, the failure to make facilities safe, the frequency of oil spills and the failure to clean them up has resulted in cultural loss for the Ogoni people. The land has been stripped of many of its natural resources, destroying the long-standing subsistence farming and fishing-based economy of the local indigenous population, and bringing an end to the intergenerational transmission of their culture.

[18] See eg, Amnesty International, *Petroleum, Pollution and Poverty in the Niger Delta* (2009); UNEP, *Environmental Assessment of Ogoniland.* Nairobi, Kenya: United Nations Environment Programme (2011); Amnesty International and CEHRD, *The True 'Tragedy': Delays and Failures in Tackling Oil Spills in the Niger Delta* (2011); Friends of the Earth and Amnesty International, *No Progress: An Evaluation of the Implementation of UNEP's Environmental Assessment of Ogoniland, Three Years On* (2014); Amnesty International, *No Clean-Up, No Justice: An Evaluation of the Implementation of UNEP's Environmental Assessment of Ogoniland, Nine Years On* (2020).

[19] GR Ana, 'Air Pollution in the Niger Delta Area: Scope, Challenges and Remedies' in M Khallaf, *The Impact of Air Pollution on Health, Economy, Environment and Agricultural Sources* (Intechopen, 2011).

The implications of these losses are detailed below in the description of the victims' harms.

C. Principles of Reparations

Reparations fulfil two main purposes that are enshrined in the Court's Statute. First, they oblige convicted persons to repair the harm they have caused. Second, reparations aim, to the extent possible, to relieve victims' suffering by addressing the consequences of criminal acts committed by the convicted person, deterring future violations, and delivering a sense of justice through accountability.

Principles of reparations are general concepts which are to be distinguished from the order for reparations. Principles can be formulated considering the circumstances of a specific case, but can also be applied, adapted or expanded upon by future trial chambers.[20] The present Chamber adopts the principles established by previous chambers of the Court, and particularly notes those requiring gender sensitivity; consultation with victims; recognition of transgenerational harm; the need for reparations to be appropriate, adequate, proportionate, prompt, and self-sustaining wherever possible; the liability and rights of the accused; and the importance of State cooperation in the enforcement of reparations.[21] However, as this is the first Reparations Order relating to ecocide, the Chamber has also identified the following principles to reflect the specific circumstances of the case.

1. Recognising Interconnected Human and Other-than-Human Harm

Pursuant to rule 85 of the Court's Rules of Procedure and Evidence, only natural and legal persons who have suffered or sustained physical, material, psychological and/or moral harm as a result of a crime for which the defendant was convicted may qualify as victims. Natural persons may be direct victims of the crimes, or indirect victims who have suffered harm as a result of the commission of a crime against another person. Legal persons may include 'inter alia, nongovernmental, charitable and non-profit organisations, statutory bodies including government departments, public schools, hospitals, private education institutes … , companies, telecommunications firms, institutions that benefit members of the community … and other partnerships'.[22]

[20] For the methodology applied to identify new principles, see, inter alia, International Law Commission, *First Report on General Principles of Law*, 5 April 2019, A/CN.4/732.

[21] *The Prosecutor* v. *Thomas Lubanga Dyilo*, Amended Reparations Order, ICC-01/04-01/06-3129-AnxA, paras 1–49; *The Prosecutor* v. *Germain Katanga*, Reparations Order, ICC-01/04-01/07-3728, paras 29–30; *Prosecutor* v. *Ahmad Al Faqi Al Mahdi*, Reparations Order, ICC-01/12-01/15-236, paras 26–50; *Prosecutor* v. *Bosco Ntaganda*, Reparations Order, ICC-01/04-02/06, para 30.

[22] Lubanga Amended Reparations Order, para 8; Al Mahdi Reparations Order, para 41; Ntaganda Reparations Order, para 32.

The Rules' framing of victimhood notably excludes all the other-than-human natural entities that have suffered harm as a result of the crimes perpetrated by the convicted person. While environmental destruction can be a feature of any of the core crimes,[23] this exclusion naturally has particularly pronounced implications in cases concerning ecocide, a crime premised on the destruction of the natural world. Although natural entities are precluded from being beneficiaries of reparation measures, it is their destruction that has caused the physical, material, psychological and/or moral harm experienced by victims. It is therefore appropriate that when deciding the types and modalities of reparations in cases of ecocide, the Court ensures that particular attention is paid to the interconnected nature of human and other-than-human harm and repair, and the potentially beneficial role of environmental restoration and repair for victimised individuals and communities. Adopting such an approach will facilitate reparations that can better address the root causes of the suffering experienced by human beneficiaries.

2. *Eco-sensitivity and Do No Harm*

The Court shall expand its 'do no harm' principle to encompass a new principle of 'eco-sensitivity'. Adapted from the practice of conflict-sensitivity[24] (which is already implemented by the Court's Trust Fund for Victims),[25] an eco-sensitive approach is one that: (i) attempts to understand how reparations may interact with environmental damage through the use of environmental impact assessments; (ii) monitors, evaluates and mitigates against any unintended environmental effects, and (iii) positively influences environmental sustainability wherever possible. An eco-sensitive approach requires the Chamber to centre biological diversity and ecological integrity and incorporate an awareness of the possible long-term and intergenerational impacts of reparative projects. The Chamber notes that this approach could be applied to all future reparation orders, regardless of the crime perpetrated. However, it is crucial in cases concerning ecocide.

This principle should have application at each stage of reparation design and delivery. This will require initial environmental impact assessments of the effects likely to arise from a proposed reparation or assistance project. This should feature both consultation with local experts and victim participation as integral aspects to ensuring reparations proceed in an eco-sensitive manner.[26] Ongoing monitoring

[23] M Gillett, 'Eco-Struggles: Using International Criminal Law to Protect the Environment During and After Non-International Armed Conflict' in C Stahn, J. Iverson, and JS Easterday (eds), *Environmental Protection and Transitions from Conflict to Peace* (OUP, 2017).

[24] Adapted from 'Conflict-Sensitive Approaches to Development, Humanitarian Assistance and Peace Building: Resource Pack' conflictsensitivity.org/key_reading/conflict-sensitive-approaches-to-development-humanitarian-assistance-and-peacebuilding-resource-pack/.

[25] Trust Fund for Victims, 'Strategic Plan 2014–2017' (August 2014) trustfundforvictims.org/sites/default/files/imce/1408%20TFV%20Strategic%20Plan%202014-2017%20Final%20ENG.pdf.

[26] S Jay et al, 'Environmental Impact Assessment: Retrospect and Prospect' *Environmental Impact Assessment Review* (2007) 27: 287–300.

and evaluation will be required as reparation projects progress, with flexibility built in to enable adjustments as necessary.

3. *Dignity, Non-discrimination and Non-stigmatisation*

The Court has long held that reparations should address underlying injustices and avoid replicating discriminatory practices or structures that predated the commission of the crimes.[27] In cases involving ecocide, the application of this principle will require consideration of those structural inequalities which may shape who is able to access and use natural resources, and recognition that disadvantaged groups may suffer disproportionately from environmental degradation and unequal distribution of natural resources. For victims from marginalised groups, ecocide may have been accompanied by and facilitated by a long-term lack of input into how the natural world is used and protected. Furthermore, the aftermath of ecocide may not signal an end to unsustainable resource exploitation, environmental degradation and/or lack of protection for the environment. The Court shall consider these potential vulnerabilities and processes of marginalisation and unsustainable extraction. At minimum, the Court should avoid reinforcing harmful practices of exclusion, while aiming to further equitable access to and protection of the natural environment. A gendered lens is important here, as women and girls may face gender-specific risks, challenges, and discrimination in gaining access to, using and protecting their natural environment.[28]

D. Order for Reparations against the Convicted Person

1. *Victims*

Victims are those natural and legal persons that can prove on the balance of probabilities that they have suffered harm with a causal link (using a 'but for' standard of causation) to the crimes perpetrated by the convicted persons, and the convicted person could have reasonably foreseen that his crimes and the conduct underlying the conviction could cause such harm.[29] The relevant crimes are as follows:

> Count 1: ecocidal omissions in **Site A**, including: the failure to make safe a pipeline; failure to remediate an oil spill; consistent failure to clean up adequately and completely ongoing contamination resulting from three oil spills, leading to severe contamination in land and waterways.
> Count 2: ecocidal omissions in **Site B,** including: failure to make safe a manifold, failure to respond to two oil spills, resulting in a fire, failure to clean

[27] Lubanga Amended Principles, para 17.
[28] Adapted from Al Mahdi Reparations Order, para 34.
[29] Adapted from Lubanga Amended Reparations Order, para 59; Al Mahdi Reparations Order, para 44.

up adequately and completely the severe land and water contamination, enabling contamination to spread through residential areas; failure to engage in cleanup activities following the fire; failure to prevent oil channelling into waterways.

Count 3: ecocidal omissions in **Site C,** including: failure to make safe and secure a remediation site, resulting in a spill; failure to clean up adequately and completely extensive and severe soil contamination close to community water supplies; failure to prevent oil channelling into waterways.

Count 4: ecocidal omissions in **Site D,** including: failure to make safe a product line, resulting in an oil spill close to residential areas, agricultural land, drinking water wells, and sacred forest; failure to clean up adequately and completely severe soil and water contamination, including the contamination of drinking water.

In its Judgment, the Chamber concluded that ecocide affected not only the direct victims of the crimes, namely the Ogoni people living in the above areas, but people throughout Nigeria and the international community. This conclusion is reflective of the specific ecological and climate-related harms caused by ecocide. This Chamber acknowledges these harms, while also recognising that the people of Ogoniland have suffered disproportionately more harm as a result of the convicted person's crimes. The Chamber notes that it has only received requests for reparations from members of the Ogoni community, and moreover observes that addressing these harms presents a means of addressing the broader harms experienced by the Nigerian and international community. The following section therefore limits its assessment of harm to those experienced by the people of Ogoniland.

2. *The Types of Harm Suffered by the Victims and Appropriate Modalities of Reparation*

The widespread and severe nature of the harms caused by ecocide are such that victims have suffered multidimensional harms, encompassing physical, material, psychological and moral harm. Reparations for these harms can be individual or collective and can be awarded concurrently. Modalities can include restitution, compensation, rehabilitation and symbolic measures. The Chamber stresses that in reaching its decision on appropriate modalities, it particularly took into account the victims' wish not to be granted symbolic reparations unless they serve practical purposes, and their wish to receive awards aimed at supporting sustainable and long-term livelihoods and well-being, rather than simply addressing their needs on a short-term basis.

i. Physical Harm Caused by Environmental Destruction

The natural systems of air, water and land have been massively damaged by the convicted person's crimes.[30] Ogoni communities that have lived and continue to live in the vicinity of the spills, oil discharges and fires detailed above have suffered physical harms as a result. These communities are exposed to air pollution, polluted water from drinking wells, dermal contact with oil through bathing and washing, and oral exposure through eating foods that have been contaminated by petroleum hydrocarbons.[31] UNEP has noted that the ability of petroleum hydrocarbon to migrate means that every water well within the vicinity of contaminated waterways is likely to be contaminated.[32] The scale of the harm is also heightened by the reliance on agriculture and fishing in Ogoniland, both of which increase the risks of exposure to pollutants.[33] Oil pollution has also had a direct impact on victims' ability to access healthy food, due to the impact on agricultural land and fisheries.[34] This harm intersects with other forms of harm: the lack of access to fresh fish means communities have turned to buying frozen or dry fish to consume, raising the cost of living while interrupting traditional ways of living.

Victims have been forced to continue using polluted water sources due to the lack of alternatives. This has resulted in health issues ranging from dermatitis to water-borne illnesses.[35] Victims complained about a range of breathing problems, skin lesions and gastrointestinal problems. While victims told the Court that they had found it difficult to obtain accurate information about how these issues relate to pollution, expert evidence from UNEP, WHO, Amnesty International and CEHRD has clearly illustrated that these harms relate to oil pollution. Expert evidence has also demonstrated that residents living close to Site D have been exposed to benzene, a known carcinogen, in their water supplies and air supply. This exposure is at levels over 900 times above WHO guidance and has led to excess lifetime cancer risks. The Chamber notes that the average life expectancy in Ogoniland is less than 50 years, highlighting the impacts of chronic oil pollution.[36]

The Chamber is satisfied that the convicted person's crimes are the proximate cause of this harm and that he is therefore liable for the physical harms experienced by victims through their exposure to pollutants. Two forms of reparation are necessary to address these harms: environmental restitution and physical rehabilitation.

[30] JK Nduka and OE Orisakwe, 'Water-Quality Issues in the Niger Delta of Nigeria' *Environmental Science and Pollution Research* (2011) 18:237–246; T Bodo and B Gimah, 'The Pollution and Destruction of the Niger Delta Ecosystem in Nigeria: Who Is To Be Blamed?' *European Scientific Journal February* (2020) 16(5): 161–182.

[31] UNEP (2011), p. 198.

[32] *Ibid*, p. 188.

[33] *Ibid*, p. 183–184.

[34] Amnesty International and CEHRD (2015), 11.

[35] LK David and T Bodo, BG Gimah, 'Petroleum Pollution and Decrease Neuroplasticity in Brain Development of the Ogoni Children in Rivers State, Nigeria' *Journal of Advances in Medicine and Medical Research* (2007) 29: 1–13.

[36] UNEP (2011) p 10.

The destruction of the natural environment lies at the heart of this case. Victims have asked for reparations to restore, maintain and protect the natural environments impacted by the convicted person's crimes. The Chamber considers that a range of specific environmentally restorative modalities will be required, in keeping with the principles of interconnected harm and eco-sensitivity. These may include measures to address land-based contamination, for example through manual cleaning and low-pressure water jetting. Rehabilitation of waterways will be crucial, and priority should be given to clean-ups in areas where communities continue to rely on contaminated wells for drinking water. Measures may also involve establishing local nurseries, so that healthy, indigenous plants will be available to regenerate heavily impacted ecosystems, such as damaged mangroves and forest areas.[37]

Mr X's crimes have also had harmful impacts on the global climate, meaning environmentally restorative projects will benefit the wider victimised community. Attention should be paid to the transformative potential of reparations in this context, and to the particular importance of guarantees of non-recurrence. Restitution of the environment may be accompanied by measures designed to protect the environment from future harm, whether through the designation of protected areas or through other initiatives undertaken to improve environmental protection more generally. Such measures should be taken to the extent possible and following consultations with government authorities, victims, and local communities as necessary. While the Company and its subsidiaries are not subject to the jurisdiction of this Court, it may be that other guarantees of non-recurrence could be established through consultation with the Company, such as improved policies and practices regarding safeguarding pipelines and responding to leaks.

In addition, specific measures of rehabilitation are needed to address the physical harms experienced through exposure to pollutants in the victimised communities' air, water and soil. Priority should be given to those who are suffering acute physical symptoms, but the Chamber acknowledges that the physical harms caused by exposure to pollutants may continue to emerge over time. Measures of rehabilitation may include a range of preventative, curative and rehabilitative services designed to address the multitude of harmful impacts experienced by victims.

ii. Material Harm, Economic Loss and Related Harms

Material harms encompass the uncompensated destruction of personal property, including boats, fishing nets, other fishing and agricultural equipment and in some cases dwelling buildings destroyed by spills. Further material harms result from the loss of natural resources, including fresh and affordable food (fish and farming produce), building materials for dwellings and boats (wood), and traditional

[37] *Ibid*, p. 13.

medicines (plants).[38] In some instances, victims have lost other financial assets, including those who had invested in farms and/or fish farms. Some victims have lost their entire life's savings and have been forced to close businesses, leading to secondary harms such as unemployment within communities.

Material harms also include lack of income. More than 60 per cent of people living in the region depended to some degree on the natural environment for their livelihoods, whether through farming and foraging, fish farming, shellfish harvesting or fish trading.[39] The damage caused by pollution has been both immediate and long-term, causing ongoing material harms through the destruction of these livelihoods.[40] These harms are gendered in nature; women in particular have traditionally relied upon mangrove swamp fisheries for sources of income through collecting shellfish and gathering mangrove wood to sell.[41] Some victims spoke of local markets shutting down due to pollution and the lack of economic activity in the area. This has meant that those who have been able to keep a living have been forced to travel further to sell their wares, a harm that is discussed further below. This loss of income has transgenerational impacts: one of the most immediate consequences of the loss of income has been families pulling their children out of school to avoid fees.[42]

The loss of income-generating activities has led to family and community separation and disruption caused by involuntary migration in search of alternatives sources of income.[43] Many victims spoke of lacking skills to rely upon when farming and fishing became impossible, and of being torn between the need to make a living and their attachment to their community and home. The harms caused by the loss of income are gendered in nature. Women reported having to travel far from home to gather or purchase food to sell in their communities, disrupting their family and community lives. Many women spoke of combining these periods of travel with caring responsibilities in their communities, voicing frustration at being both unable to migrate and unable to make a living in their home village. Men reported being unable to marry due to lacking the money to pay for the bride-price. Victims of all genders also revealed that families were unable to pay for the burial of their loved ones and the associated customary reception, with some bereaved victims leaving family members in the morgue for over two years.[44]

[38] S Pegg and N Zabbey, 'Oil and Water: The Bodo Spills and the Destruction of Traditional Livelihood Structures in the Niger Delta' *Community Development Journal* (2013) 48(3): 391–405, 392.

[39] UNEP (2011) p.175.

[40] AI/CEHRD (2011), pp. 15–18.

[41] OK Adeyemo, OE Ubiogoro and OB Adedeji, 'Oil Exploitation, Fisheries Resources and Sustainable Livelihood in the Niger Delta, Nigeria' *Nature & Fauna* (2009) 24(1): 56–58, 59; A Fentiman and N Zabbey, 'Environmental Degradation and Cultural Erosion in Ogoniland' *The Extractive Industries and Society* (2015) 2:615–624.

[42] Pegg and Zabbey (2013) pp. 391–405.

[43] CO Opukri and IS Ibaba, 'Oil Induced Environmental Degradation and Internal Population Displacement in the Nigeria's Niger Delta' *Journal of Sustainable Development in Africa* (2008) 10(1): 173.

[44] Fentiman and Zabbey (2015), p. 622.

The Chamber is satisfied that the convicted person's crimes are the proximate cause of this harm and that he is therefore liable for the material, economic and related harms experienced by victims through the destruction of natural resources. These harms will require individual awards of compensation and collective measures of economic rehabilitation.

Individual compensation will be required for those victims who have lost personal property as a direct result of the convicted person's crimes. Business owners may also qualify for compensation, where the loss of their business is directly attributable to the crimes included in the judgment. More broadly, the Chamber considers that collective measures of economic rehabilitation should be awarded to address the collective harm caused by the convicted person's crimes. These measures may include community-based programmes designed to enhance victims' skills, return/resettlement programmes for those forced to migrate for work, a 'microcredit system' that would assist the population to generate income, or other cash assistance programmes to restore some of Ogoniland's lost economic activity.[45]

It is likely that the rehabilitation of the Ogoni people's natural environment will take years to complete, precluding them from returning to their traditional modes of income generation in the near future. Emphasis should therefore be placed on sustainability rather than short-term projects in order to create long-term opportunities for victimised communities to flourish. In recognition of the principles of interconnected harm and eco-sensitivity, priority should also be given to eco-sensitive and environmentally sustainable skills programmes and income-generating opportunities. It may be that modalities of reparation can be designed that train and empower victims to engage in environmentally regenerative and protective projects, such as restoring mangroves, regenerating protected natural areas and developing eco-tourist initiatives. In keeping with the principle of non-discrimination, such measures should avoid replicating any patterns of marginalisation that might risk excluding groups or individual victims from benefiting from income-generating opportunities.

Given the broader climate-related harms perpetrated by the convicted person, attention should be paid to the transformative potential of such measures. It may be that the development of environmentally restorative or protective income-generating activities could have longer and more international positive impacts. This is particularly important in the Ogoniland context, where lack of other income-generating opportunities has resulted in victims and other community members turning to oil bunkering and illegal refining to survive.

iii. Psychological and Moral Harm

The contamination of soil and water has resulted in the loss of intangible cultural heritage, defined by the Court as 'traditions, customs and practices, knowledge, vernacular or other languages, forms of artistic expression and folklore'.[46] For the

[45] Adapted from Al Mahdi Reparations Order, para 83.
[46] Al Mahdi Reparations Order, para 15.

Ogoni, waterways and aquatic resources are sacred and intricately tied to community life,[47] 'representing an all-important aspect of their history and identity'.[48] Victims described beliefs associated with waterways, of hosting festivals to pay tribute to spirits and practicing healing practices and spiritual rituals in community creeks believed to have spiritual protective powers.[49] They explained how pollution had made these activities impossible due to the harmful health impacts of bathing in polluted waters. Victims also spoke of a belief that water spirits had been directly affected by the oil pollution, either leaving communities for unknown places or acting in ways that were harmful to the community.[50]

Victims also highlighted the loss of culturally relevant income-generating activities such as communal fishing practices (referred to by the Ogoni as *dor bon*) and cooperative farming practices, both of which had traditionally been accompanied by song and oral history customs designed to pass on community knowledge. They described how the loss of income had restricted their ability to participate in cultural life, such as singing and dancing associations, and how the pollution of woodland had diminished the raw materials necessary to build masks, instruments and other artefacts needed for traditional plays and performances.[51]

Victims noted that there were no longer safe places for children to play, and that as a result children were not developing the 'local knowledge' that usually came from living in the natural environment, such as the names of plants and trees, methods of fishing and farming, and the history of the community.[52] In the past, this 'local knowledge' provided a decent quality of life, this possibility has been eroded by the convicted person's crimes. Expert witnesses described how this combination of challenges has led to centuries of Ogoni customs and practices being abandoned and forgotten.[53]

These harms have impacted victims' psychological well-being, diminishing opportunities for social interaction, and creating profound feelings of disconnection. Parents spoke of their children feeling angry and disillusioned, and fearing for their future. Victims of all genders and ages have suffered disruption to their life plans, meaning 'the lack of self-realisation of a person who, in light of their vocations, aptitudes, circumstances, potential, and aspirations, may have reasonably expected to achieve certain things in their life'.[54] Accompanying these harms is a pervasive sense of hopelessness expressed by victims; victims spoke of having their sense of purpose eroded by the scale of the pollution and its impacts on their lives.[55]

[47] K Saro-Wiwa, *Genocide in Nigeria: The Ogoni Tragedy* (Saros, 1992), p. 12.
[48] UNEP (2011), p. 175.
[49] Fentiman and Zabbey (2015), pp. 619–621.
[50] *Ibid*, 620–621.
[51] *Ibid*, 619–620.
[52] PI Igbara and B Keenam, *Ogoni in Perspective: An Aspect of Niger Delta History* (Onyoma Research Publications, 2012).
[53] Pegg and Zabbey (2013) p. 401.
[54] Ntaganda Reparations Order, para 72.
[55] Fentiman and Zabbey (2015), 620–621.

The Chamber is satisfied that the convicted person's crimes are the proximate cause of this harm and that he is therefore liable for these psychological and moral harms. The Chamber considers that collective reparations are required to address these harms, including psychosocial rehabilitation and symbolic measures.

Access to psychosocial rehabilitation is required in recognition of the harms caused by the disruption to victims' life plans, their cultural, community and family life, and social interactions. This might involve access to psychiatric care for those suffering mental health issues, as well as psychological support for those experiencing behavioural disorders. Trauma-based counselling may play an important role for those suffering psychological harm, while help with addiction may be required for those who have turned to substance use as a coping strategy. Measures of psychosocial rehabilitation may also encompass social services and community and family-oriented assistance and services, designed to promote social well-being within the community.[56]

Symbolic reparations may include initiatives and events designed to commemorate, celebrate and reinvigorate communities' heritage. They might also include measures such as the establishment of a memorial designed to publicly recognise the psychological and moral harms of ecocide. Furthering the principles of eco-sensitivity and interconnected harm, and in recognition of the harms perpetrated through the loss of space to play and be in community, a memorial might be in the form of restored and protected park land to be enjoyed as both a commemorative and recreational space.

Mr X may also contribute to measures of satisfaction by way of a voluntary apology to the victims of his crimes. However, such a measure would require consultation with victims to determine whether an apology would be welcomed and appropriate, and if so, in what manner. Finally, it may be that the publication of this Order, which contains an assessment of the types of harm experienced by the community, could have value as a means of raising awareness about the extent of the damage.[57] Measures should be taken to ensure that victims are provided with information about this Order and its contents.

3. *Costs and Liability of the Accused*

Mr X is liable to repair the harm caused to victims who have 'suffered harm as a result of the crime' for which he was convicted.[58] Reparation orders are intrinsically linked to individual criminal liability and must be proportionate to the harm caused. This Order is therefore made against the convicted person.[59] While the ICC has no power to make a Reparations Order or recommendations against a

[56] Ntaganda Reparations Order, para 203.

[57] Lubanga Amended Reparations Order, para 43.

[58] Rule 85a: 'Victims' means natural persons who have suffered harm as a result of the commission of any crime within the jurisdiction of the Court.

[59] Lubanga Amended Reparations Order, para 21.

state, it notes that state parties have the obligation to cooperate with Reparation Orders and that this order is made without prejudice to the state obligations to repair victims' harm.

Following financial investigations conducted by OTP and requests submitted to the United Kingdom and the Federal Republic of Nigeria pursuant to Article 93(1)(k) of the Rome Statute, substantial property and financial assets belonging to the convicted person has been identified, frozen and seized. Following Article 75(2) of the Statute and rule 98 of the Rules of Procedure and Evidence, the Trust Fund for Victims may use the convicted person's resources for reparation awards as determined by the stipulations and instructions set out in this Order. In line with the Rule 98(5) of the Rules and Regulation 56 of the Trust Fund's Regulations, the Trust Fund may use other resources to supplement the resources collected from the convicted person.[60]

The Chamber determines that the convicted person is liable to repair in full the harm suffered by the victims of the crimes for which he has been convicted.[61] Costs have been estimated following consultation with and evidence by the Registry, the Trust Fund for Victims, relevant experts (including experts in environmental restoration) and the parties, and in light of previous jurisprudence by the Court. The Chamber notes that victims will have experienced different kinds of harm, that victims will therefore require access to varying measures of the reparations awarded, and that the cost to repair the harm for each victim may therefore vary significantly. However, in line with the Appeals Chamber jurisprudence and bearing in mind the rights of the convicted person to legal certainty, the Chamber has made conservative estimates on the average costs per victim. Following consultation with relevant experts, the Chamber has estimated the total number of victims potentially eligible for reparations as being 120,000 individuals across the four crime sites.

Estimates are as follows:

(i) Measures of environmental restitution including clean-up of waterways and land contamination and the restoration and rehabilitation of forest and mangrove ecosystems: USD 22,500,000 per site, per year for five years. Additional clean-up of carcinogens in the Site D water supply: USD 50,000,000 per year for five years.[62] **Total:** USD 500,000,000 (five hundred million dollars).

(ii) Measures of physical rehabilitation for health issues including breathing problems, skin lesions, gastrointestinal problems: USD 1,500 for 20,000 victims per crime site (80,000 in total: USD 120,000,000). Additional healthcare for victims who are suffering from cancers reasonably attributable to exposure to water-based carcinogens in Site D: USD 3,000 per victim for an estimated 50,000 victims (USD 150,000,000). **Total**: USD 270,000,000 (two hundred and seventy million dollars).

[60] Lubanga Amended Reparations Order, para 271.
[61] Ntaganda Reparations Order, para 221.
[62] UNEP (2011) p. 227.

(iii) Compensation for pecuniary damages including the loss of property and assets: USD 1,500 (on average) per victim for an estimated 10,000 victims in each crime site (40,000 in total). The USD 1,500 average is based on the following monetary values for material harm: USD 500 for boats or agricultural vehicles, USD 250 for fishing or agricultural equipment, USD 500 for fishing or agricultural buildings, and USD 250 for building materials and natural resources. **Total:** USD 60,000,000 (sixty million dollars).

(iv) Collective measures of economic rehabilitation across the four crime sites including community-based programmes designed to enhance victims' skills, return/resettlement programmes for those forced to migrate for work, a 'microcredit system' that would assist the population to generate income, or other cash assistance programmes to restore some of Ogoniland's lost economic activity: USD 180,000 per crime site for the first year. **Total:** USD 720,000 (seven hundred and twenty thousand dollars).

(v) Psychosocial rehabilitation including psychiatric care for those suffering mental health issues, psychological support for those experiencing behavioural disorders, trauma-based counselling, addiction support, social services, and community and family-oriented assistance and services: USD 1,500,000 per crime site for the first year. **Total:** USD 6,000,000 (six million dollars).

(vi) Symbolic measures including initiatives and events designed to commemorate, celebrate, and reinvigorate communities' heritage: USD 60,000 per crime site for the first year. **Total:** USD 240,000 (two hundred and forty thousand dollars).

(vii) **Total cost of reparations**: USD 836,960,000 (eight hundred and thirty-six million, nine hundred and sixty thousand dollars).

E. Conclusion

For the foregoing reasons, the Chamber hereby:

Issues an Order for Reparations against Mr X.

Orders individual and collective reparations to be awarded to the victims of the crimes for which Mr X is liable.

Assesses the convicted person's liability as:

Mr X: USD 836,960,000.

Requests that the Trust Fund for Victims submit its implementation plan by 9 September 2023.

Commentary

Damien Short

Rachel Killean's case study is a welcome and timely contribution to thinking through the possibilities of an international crime prohibiting ecocide, how it could function and its remedial prospects. While currently no such crime exists, there is growing social and political momentum for ecocide to be established in law. Killean's ICC judgment is hypothetical but based on an infamous and appalling example of human rights violations and widespread long-term and devastating ecological destruction in Ogoniland, Nigeria. For many years following Polly Higgins's early definition of ecocide there were competing civil society and academic definitions in circulation, making it difficult for a focused lobbying campaign for state backers to attempt to amend the Rome Statute and include a form of ecocide as an international crime in its own right. Recently, however, the Stop Ecocide Foundation's Independent Expert Panel definition has become the 'go to' definition of ecocide and, to an extent, assuaged many, if not all, of the prior dissenting voices and objectors.[63] Even so, I have considerable sympathy with Rachel Killean's decision to utilise the prior Higgins's[64] formulation as this case really does highlight the utility of a configuration which explicitly includes acts of 'omission', particularly as 'crimes of omission' can have severe environmentally destructive consequences.[65] As Killean notes, the extreme harms caused to the Niger Delta ecosystem are a 'textbook' case of ecocide.[66]

Apart from the inclusion of ecocide, this hypothetical judgment envisaged an unchanged Rome Statute – without the inclusion of 'corporate liability' – meaning that putting the corporation responsible on trial was impossible. That said, piercing the 'corporate veil' to target responsible individuals has significant appeal since, historically, responsible individuals (CEOs, managers and the like) have been shielded by the veil, getting away with criminal liability themselves. Moreover, historically large numbers of multinational corporations have simply added criminal fines to their balance sheet debit column, ultimately continuing the harmful practice if it still produces considerable shareholder profit.[67]

[63] 'For the purpose of this Statute, "ecocide" means unlawful or wanton acts committed with knowledge that there is a substantial likelihood of severe and either widespread or long-term damage to the environment being caused by those acts.' Independent Expert Panel for the Legal Definition of Ecocide: Commentary and Core Text, June 2021.

[64] Polly Higgins, *Eradicating Ecocide: Laws and Governance to Prevent the Destruction of Our Planet*, (Shepheard-Walwyn, 2010).

[65] Ronald Kramer, 'Climate Change: A State-corporate Crime Perspective' in Toine Spapens, Rob White and Marieke Kluin (eds), *Environmental Crime and its Victims: Perspectives within Green Criminology* (Ashgate, 2014) 23–41.

[66] Eva Sevrin, 'Hot times for Ecocide (II): The Belgian proposal' *Leuven Blog for Public Law*, 25 March 2022, leuvenpubliclaw.com/hot-times-for-ecocide-ii-the-belgian-proposal/.

[67] Joel Bakan, *The Corporation: The Pathological Pursuit of Profit and Power* (Free Press, 2004). For an indicative list of corporate criminality and the standard fines see globalexchange.org/ten-top-corporate-criminals-of-2018/.

Rachel Killean's interest was in seeing how the ICC's reparation mandate might extend and respond to the potential criminal harms of ecocide. In her hypothetical judgment the Chamber concluded that ecocide affected the direct victims of the crimes, the Ogoni people and also noted other victims throughout Nigeria and the internationally community, reflecting the widespread ecological and climate-related harms caused by the offences. Even so, the Chamber only considered reparations from members of the Ogoni community, which was the only feasible route to take for this exercise, and likely the most plausible approach an ICC chamber would take if this were a real case. The ultimate determination held the convicted person jointly and severally liable to repair, in the fullest way possible, the harms suffered by the victims. Conservative estimates on the average costs per victim were made following 'consultation with relevant experts'. This is an entirely plausible way of handling such a difficult task. It was estimated the total number of victims potentially eligible for reparations was 120,000 individuals across the four crime sites, making the sums of monetary reparations the Chamber ultimately awarded in this hypothetical judgment considerable.

Assuming both the individual concerned and the Trust Fund had sufficient monies to discharge these damages, there remains the classic concern that monetary compensation can never fully restore that which has been lost. Many ecosystems and lives were destroyed in Ogoniland. Monetary reparations cannot repair ecologically induced cultural loss that has been ongoing for decades. Yet, cultural revitalisation may well be easier following a proper clean-up and once the recurring spills have been stopped. Were the crime of ecocide to be practiced and enforced by the ICC as Killean has envisaged here, all may not be lost for the Ogoni people and the natural environment of Ogoniland.

PART V

Knowledges

11

On Windfarms and Whimbrel: *Sustainable Shetland v Scottish Ministers*

SIR CRISPIN AGNEW OF LOCHNAW BT KC

Introduction

Sustainable Shetland is an unincorporated association that aims to support social, environmental and economic sustainability in the Shetland Islands. It sought judicial review of a decision by Scottish Ministers to grant planning permission and consent under section 36 of the Electricity Act 1989 for construction of a development comprising 103 wind turbines on Mainland island, Shetland.[1] A fuller account of the background to the case can be found in the Outer House decision given by Lady Clark of Calton (24 September 2013).[2] The consent was challenged on the grounds that the Scottish Ministers' decision not to hold a public inquiry was unreasonable and unlawful. The scheme was also argued to be incompatible with the Ministers' obligations under the Directive 2009/147/EC of the European Parliament and of the Council on the conservation of wild birds (Wild Birds Directive 2009), due to its effects on whimbrel. Whimbrel are migratory wading birds, 95 per cent of the UK population of which live on Shetland. The author of this reimagined judgment was Senior Counsel for Sustainable Shetland.

Background Issues

The case raises a number of issues for practitioners concerned about the rights of third parties considering a rights of nature challenge to a decision with environmental implications.

First, Shetland Islands Council was a participant in the Viking windfarm proposal through its Shetland Trust, of which the councillors were also trustees.

[1] *Sustainable Shetland v Scottish Ministers* [2015] UKSC 5.

[2] *Sustainable Shetland v Scottish Ministers* [2013] CSOH 158. The case was then heard in the Inner House, reported at [2013] CSIH 116, before appeal to the Supreme Court.

Despite the authority officers advising that the Council should object to the proposed development because it is contrary to policy GDS1 of the Shetland Structure Plan (2000), the Council decided not to object. Attempts to challenge this on the grounds of conflict of interest were unsuccessful. The consequence of the Council not objecting to the application for section 36 of the Electricity Act 1989 consent to the construction of generating stations (wind turbines) was that the Scottish Ministers did not have to order a public inquiry – paragraph 2 of Schedule 8 of the 1989 Act. Therefore objectors, like Sustainable Shetland, were limited to a judicial review challenge on legal grounds only, arising from issues raised in the decision letter and so factual issues could not be challenged as they might have been in an inquiry. This raises the question of the lack of third-party rights of appeal when consent is granted for this type of infrastructure project. Only the developer may appeal a refusal of a planning application and require a public inquiry. A third-party objector cannot appeal a grant but can only judicially review the decision to grant the application, which could be seen as a limitation on the ability to participate in environmental decision-making.[3]

Secondly, the application for consent for the operation of a 127 (reduced from 150) turbine windfarm was made in isolation from applications for consent for closely associated projects. At the time of the litigation, there was no subsea interconnector cable to transmit power generated by the windfarm from Shetland to the mainland. Ofgem would only consider whether or not to authorise an interconnector if sufficient generating capacity had been authorised in Shetland and it was not approved until 2020. While the Viking windfarm would provide a substantial part of that capacity, other windfarms would probably need consent before there was sufficient capacity in Shetland to justify a Shetland interconnector. This meant that there was no overall strategic environmental assessment of the plan to provide an interconnector to Shetland with sufficient windfarm consents to provide the necessary generating capacity to warrant consent for the interconnector. This was not an issue that could be challenged in the Viking windfarm application. The extent to which environmental impact assessments can or should consider cumulative or downstream effects of energy development projects is the subject of ongoing judicial consideration. For example, there has been recent discussion in *R (on the application of Substation Action Save East Suffolk Ltd) v Secretary of State for Business, Energy and Industrial Strategy* [2022] EWHC 3177 (Admin), Ground of Appeal 5 'Cumulative effects' and in *R (on the application of Finch) v Surrey County Council*.[4]

Thirdly, the judgment raises the core ethical question of why some wildlife should be sacrificed for the benefit of humans, ie the whimbrel that will be killed

[3] See Aarhus Convention Compliance Committee (ACCC) reference ACCC/C/2013/90 from Northern Ireland and J Peter Clinch 'Third Party Rights of Appeal: Enhancing Democracy or Hindering Progress?' (2006) 7(3) *Planning Theory & Practice* 327.

[4] At the time of writing, the Supreme Court's decision in this case is pending: www.supremecourt.uk/cases/uksc-2022-0064.html.

or displaced by the windfarm or the hooded crows that were to be killed as part of the management plan to give some protection to whimbrel. This is not an issue that can be explored fully in the context of current Scottish and UK legislation but is an ethical consideration for some under the consideration of the rights of nature. The reimagined judgment draws on the Universal Declaration of Rights of Mother Earth (UDRME) to suggest that such conflicts should be resolved in a way that maintains the integrity, balance and health of Mother Earth.

The Supreme Court
Sustainable Shetland v Scottish Ministers
9 February 2015

Lord Agnew

Introduction

1. The appellants, Sustainable Shetland, are an unincorporated association concerned in the protection of the environment of the Shetland Islands. By these proceedings they challenge a consent granted on 4 April 2012 by the Scottish Ministers for the construction of a windfarm. The consent was under s 36 of the Electricity Act 1989 and was accompanied by a direction that separate planning permission was not required (Town and Country Planning (Scotland) Act 1997, s 57(2)). Although the appellants' objections in earlier exchanges had related to the impact of the development on the environment generally, the focus of their challenge in the courts has related to the alleged failure of the Ministers to take proper account of their obligations under the Birds Directive, in respect of the whimbrel, a protected migratory bird. Their challenge was upheld by the Lord Ordinary (Lady Clark of Calton) on other grounds which are no longer in issue, but she indicated that she would if necessary have upheld the challenge also under the directive. The Ministers' appeal was allowed unanimously by the Inner House.

2. The proposed windfarm was on a very large scale. In its amended form it would have had 127 turbines (reduced from 150), located in three areas (Delting, Kergord and Nesting), covering a total area of some 13,000 hectares (50 square miles), of which some 232 hectares would be physically affected. Associated infrastructure would include 104 kilometres of access tracks, and anemometer masts, and borrow pits. The original application was made in May 2009. It was accompanied by an environmental statement, as required by the Electricity Works (Environmental Impact Assessment) (Scotland) Regulations 2000 (SSI 2000/320).

3. The whimbrel population of the Shetlands is highly significant in national terms, representing (at 290 pairs on the basis of a 2009 survey) around 95 per cent of the total UK population. Of this, some 56 pairs breed in the central mainland area, where the windfarm would be sited; 23 pairs within the development site; and 31 pairs breed in the Fetlar Special Protection Area. Between 72 and 108 adult whimbrels from the Shetlands die annually from existing causes. The 2009 survey showed a decline in the Shetlands region over the previous 20 years of 39 per cent overall, but with wide variations across the region. The decline in

Central Mainland was only 6 per cent, compared to between 54 per cent and 80 per cent in the Fetlar SPA.

4. The potential impact on the whimbrel population emerged as an important issue in early objections from, among others, Scottish Natural Heritage (SNH). There followed a series of detailed exchanges between SNH and the developers on both the assessment of the likely impact of the development on the whimbrel population and mitigation measures. It is unnecessary to do more than summarise some of the main points. In response to the SNH objection, the developers revised their environmental statement by submitting a new addendum, including a chapter 'A 11 Ornithology', which dealt in detail with the likely effects on whimbrel. It was said to be based on more than eight years of study, which gave 'considerable confidence in the robustness of these assessments'. It was acknowledged that the population processes of Shetland whimbrel were 'poorly understood', and that, in the absence of previous windfarm developments in areas with breeding whimbrel, the likely impact had to be inferred from knowledge of responses of other related wader species, such as the curlew. It predicted that operational disturbance would result in the long-term displacement of 1.8 pairs, which might be able to resettle elsewhere, and a collision mortality rate of 2.1 whimbrel per year.

5. The addendum included a habitat management plan (HMP), which contained detailed assessment of the factors affecting the whimbrel population, and proposed habitat management actions. For example, the 'single most important action' to increase whimbrel breeding success was said to be the control of the likely main nest predator, the hooded crow, over sufficiently large areas during the nesting season. The HMP was said to have 'a high likelihood of more than offsetting any adverse effects of the windfarm and a reasonable likelihood of causing the Shetland whimbrel population to partially and possibly fully recover over the lifetime of the Viking Wind Farm'.

6. Although the revised proposals led SNH to withdraw some of its objections to the proposals, those in respect of whimbrels were maintained. In its letter of 11 February 2011, SNH referred to a 'high likelihood of a significant adverse impact of national interest'. SNH made specific reference to the EU Birds Directive: 'Whimbrel are subject to certain general provisions of the EU Birds Directive which apply to all naturally occurring birds in the wild. These include Articles 2, 3(1), 3(2)(b) and the last sentence of Article 4(4). Achieving and maintaining favourable conservation status of the national population is in line with these provisions and obligations. In this case our advice is that the proposed Viking windfarm is highly likely to result in a significant adverse impact on the conservation status of the national population of whimbrel.'

7. SNH expressed doubts as to the likely success of the HMP, given the 'unproven and experimental' nature of some of the proposed mitigation measures, and the 'scale and location of the project' which were not comparable to other mainland

restoration sites. In later correspondence, SNH described the ornithological assessment as 'associated with a high degree of uncertainty in several critical respects'. It disagreed with the predicted collision mortality rate, which it put at 4.2 for 127 turbines, or 3.7 if the Delting turbines were removed. SNH welcomed the HMP as offering 'the possibility of significant biodiversity benefits' and as 'an excellent opportunity to explore various habitat management methods' as yet untested in the Shetlands; but advised that it contained a 'qualitative assurance which cannot be relied on with certainty to significantly mitigate these impacts'. It regretted that, in spite of the significant efforts made in co-operation with the developers, it had been unable to resolve all their concerns.

8. The Scottish Ministers gave their decision by letter dated 4 April 2012. They recorded the representations of various consultees, statutory and non-statutory (including those of SNH and RSPB, relating to effects on birds). They also noted the receipt of a total of 3,881 public representations, of which 2,772 were objections and 1,109 were in support of the development; the objections 'raised concerns on a number of subjects including habitat, wildlife, visual impact and infrastructure'. In view of the 'apparently insurmountable aviation issues' associated with the 24 turbines in the Delting area, it would not be appropriate for those to be included in any consent, but there remained the option of granting consent for the remaining 103 turbines.

9. The letter stated that the Ministers had had regard to 'their obligations under EU environmental legislation' and to 'the potential for impact on the environment, in particular on species of wild birds'. It noted that the peatland ecosystem was in serious decline, and that the restoration proposed by the HMP would 'offer benefits to a whole range of species and habitats'. It was 'far more ambitious and expansive' than plans accompanying previous windfarm proposals encompassing an area in total of 12,800 hectares and had been welcomed by SNH as offering the possibility of significant biodiversity benefits.

10. In a section headed 'Whimbrel', the letter discussed the respective submissions and the supporting evidence on this subject. The SNH estimate of 3.7 collision deaths per year was regarded as 'very small' when considered in the context of the 72–108 annual deaths from other causes. Of the view of SNH and others that the development would result in a 'significant impact of national interest', the letter commented: '[M]inisters are not satisfied that the estimated impact of the development on whimbrel demonstrates such a level of significance. In addition, ministers consider that the potential beneficial effects of the Habitat Management Plan (HMP) can reasonably be expected to provide some counterbalancing positive benefits.'

11. It was accepted that the beneficial effects of the HMP could not be predicted with certainty, for the reasons given by SNH, but the letter continued:

> [M]inisters note that the HMP will take one-third of the UK population of whimbrel under active management, and will target some 100 whimbrel 'hotspots'. Based on the

> detailed environmental information provided in the environmental statement and addendum, ministers are satisfied that the measures proposed by the HMP are likely to have a positive value to the conservation status of the whimbrel. These measures include a variety of management techniques, including predator control, habitat restoration, protection and management. Ministers are satisfied that an HMP which includes significant predator control from the outset, as well as ongoing habitat restoration, protection and management, is likely to counteract the relatively small estimated rate of bird mortality. Further reassurance is gained from the commitment to ongoing development and improvement built into the HMP as understanding of its effect improves, and from the fact that this commitment will be required by condition.
>
> In any case, if, despite the implementation of the HMP, the estimated negative impact on the species were to remain, ministers consider that the level of impact on the conservation status of the whimbrel is outweighed by the benefits of the project, including the very substantial renewable energy generation the development would bring and the support this offers to tackling climate change and meeting EU Climate Change Targets.
>
> The whimbrel is in decline on Shetland. Ministers consider that the HMP represents an opportunity – currently the sole opportunity – to try to improve the conservation status of the species. Without the Viking Windfarm HMP, there currently appears to be no prospect of any significant work being undertaken to reverse the decline of the whimbrel in the UK.

12. It was considered that conditions on the consent would ensure comprehensive monitoring of the effects of the development and the success or otherwise of the mitigation measures, which work would also 'inform ongoing initiatives for the conservation of whimbrel'. The letter went on to consider other issues, under the headings 'Landscape and visual', 'Economic and renewable energy benefits' and 'Other considerations', before concluding that 'environmental impacts will for the most part be satisfactorily addressed by way of mitigation and conditions, and that the residual impacts are outweighed by the benefits the development will bring', and that consent should therefore be granted.

Statutory Requirements and the Birds Directive

13. By paragraph 1 of Schedule 9 of the Electricity Act 1989, developers are required in formulating their proposals to have regard to 'the desirability … of conserving flora, fauna and geological or physiographical features of special interest', to 'do what [they] reasonably can to mitigate any effect' which the proposals would have on such flora, fauna or features; and, in considering their proposals, the Ministers are required to have regard to the extent of compliance with those duties. There is no allegation in this appeal of non-compliance with these duties by the developers or the Ministers.

14. In addition, as is common ground, the Ministers were required to take due account so far as relevant of the obligations of the United Kingdom under the Birds Directive. The directive currently in force, which dates from 2009 (2009/147/EC),

was a codification of provisions originally found in the 1979 Directive (79/409/EEC) with subsequent amendments. As such they have been discussed in a number of cases in the European Court of Justice. Detailed analysis can be found in the opinions of Advocate General Fennelly in C-44/95 *R v Secretary of State for the Environment, Ex p Royal Society for the Protection of Birds* [1996] ECR I-3805 ('the Lappel Bank case') and C-10/96 *Ligue Royale Belge pour la Protection des Oiseaux ASBL v Région Wallonne* [1996] ECR I-677.

15. As has been seen, SNH drew particular attention to 'Articles 2, 3(1), 3(2)(b) and the last sentence of Article 4(4)'. To understand the arguments here and in the courts below, it is necessary to set these in their context. By Article 1, the directive applies to 'the conservation of all species of naturally occurring birds in the wild state in the European territory of the Member States to which the Treaty applies'. Article 2 requires Member States to take similar measures for regularly occurring migratory species which correspond in particular to ecological, scientific and cultural requirements, while taking account of economic and recreational requirements. Article 3(1) requires Member States '[i]n the light of the requirements referred to in Article 2' to take the requisite measures 'to preserve, maintain or re-establish a sufficient diversity and area of habitats for all the species of birds referred to in Article 1'; such measures to include (Article 3(2)(b)): '(b) upkeep and management in accordance with the ecological needs of habitats inside and outside the protected zones.'

16. Article 4(1) requires 'special conservation measures' to be taken in respect of the species mentioned in annex I of the directive, 'in order to ensure their survival and reproduction in their area of distribution', and requires Member States to 'classify in particular the most suitable territories in number and size as special protection areas' for the conservation of these species. Article 4(2) requires 'similar measures' for regularly occurring migratory species not listed in annex I. It is common ground that whimbrel, though not listed in annex I, are subject to the requirement for 'similar measures' for migratory species under Article 4(2). The Fetlar special protection area (SPA) was designated pursuant to this duty.

17. It was established by the European Court in the Lappel Bank case that, notwithstanding the reference in Article 2 to 'economic and recreational requirements', such factors were not relevant in choosing or defining special protection areas under Article 4. The precise relevance of such factors to the scope of the duties under Article 2 is a matter of debate. In C-247/85 *Commission v Belgium* [1987] ECR 3209, para.8, the European Court observed: 'Article 2 of the directive … requires the Member States to take the requisite measures to maintain the population of all bird species at a level, or to adapt it to a level, which corresponds in particular to ecological, scientific and cultural requirements, while taking account of economic and recreational requirements and from which it is therefore clear that the protection of birds must be balanced against other requirements, such as those of an economic nature.' However, in the later Lappel Bank case, the Advocate

General ([1997] QB, pp 238–239, para 57) took the view that this balance was relevant under Article 2, not to the level at which the population of the particular species was to be maintained, but only to the measures required to achieve it. The Court did not express a view on that point, confining itself to ruling on Article 4.

18. In the same passage SNH made reference to the aim of achieving 'favourable conservation status' for a relevant species. This expression does not appear in the Birds Directive itself. The concept is taken from the Habitats Directive (92/43/EEC), and is of direct application to the obligations of states in relation to the European network of special areas of conservation under Article 3 of that directive ('Natura 2000'). For this purpose, Article 1(i) defines the 'conservation status' of a species as 'the sum of the influences acting on the species concerned that may affect the long-term distribution and abundance of its populations within the territory'. Conservation status is taken as 'favourable' when:

> population dynamics data on the species concerned indicate that it is maintaining itself on a long-term basis as a viable component of its natural habitats, and
>
> - the natural range of the species is neither being reduced nor is likely to be reduced for the foreseeable future, and
> - there is, and will probably continue to be, a sufficiently large habitat to maintain its populations on a long-term basis.

19. There are links between the two directives. By Article 3 of the Habitats Directive, special protection areas designated under Article 4 of the Birds Directive were also included in the Natura 2000 network, and (by Article 7) such areas were subject to the same obligations in respect of conservation measures as defined by Article 6 of the Habitats Directive. However, there appears to be nothing in either directive to link the concept of 'favourable conservation status' as such to the general obligations under Article 2 of the Birds Directive, which apply to all wild birds, not just those defined for special protection under Article 4 or otherwise.

The Courts below

20. On 24 September 2013, the Lord Ordinary gave judgment reducing the Ministers' decision on the grounds (apparently first raised by the court itself) that, in the absence of a licence granted under s 6 of the Electricity Act, the Ministers had no power to grant consent. That ground of decision was not supported by these appellants or any other party to the present proceedings, and it was not followed by Lord Doherty in a later case: *Trump International Golf Club Scotland Ltd v Scottish Ministers.* The Inner House (2014 SLT, p 811, para 19) agreed with his reasoning. It is unnecessary to consider the point further.

21. The Lord Ordinary held in the alternative that the Ministers had failed to take proper account of their obligations under the Birds Directive. She criticised the Ministers for failing to 'address explicitly legal issues arising out of the [directive]

and explain their approach to decision making' (para 239). In a long section (paras 245–291) she undertook her own detailed interpretation of provisions of the directive, followed by a discussion of their application to the facts of the case. Without disrespect, I hope it is sufficient to highlight what appear to be the key points in the discussion.

22. She identified what she understood to be the respective positions of the parties:

> [257] In summary, the fundamental dividing line between the interpretation put forward by the petitioners compared with that advanced on behalf of the respondents and interested party is that the petitioners maintain that Article 2 sets down a common standard which requires to be met that the population of the species, in this case whimbrel, are to be maintained at a level which corresponds in particular to ecological, scientific and cultural requirements and that obligation rests on the State. … There is discretion in how Article 2 is to be implemented but not discretion as to whether it is to be implemented or not.
>
> [258] In contrast, the respondents submit that the reference to maintaining the population in Article 2 is subject to other considerations … [which] at a minimum included economic and recreational requirements. It is a balancing exercise. … The final position of the respondents was to say in effect that windfarm energy production contributing to climate change targets out-balanced or outweighed 'the obligation' of maintaining the population of whimbrel to the level specified in Article 2.

23. In resolving that issue, she attached particular weight to the opinion of Advocate General Fennelly in the Lappel Bank case (see above) as to the limited role of economic and recreational requirements even under Article 2 (paras 259–263). She also attached weight to the obligation of the state in respect of migratory species under Article 4(2). The accepted position was that, despite the existence of the Fetlar SPA, whimbrel were not in 'favourable conservation status' in the Shetlands or the United Kingdom. This raised the question as to whether the designation of that area was fulfilling the obligations of the United Kingdom under that article, and if not 'what the implications of that were for the decision making in this case'. It was necessary for the decision maker to give 'some indication that they have addressed the issues as envisaged in the Directive'. Taking account of 'the problems with the existing conservation status of whimbrel', there was no reasoning to explain why the Fetlar SPA site provided sufficient protection and exhausted their obligation under Article 4(2) of the directive (para 272).

24. As to the HMP, there was no explanation as to why the Ministers, departing from the view of SNH, and 'in a situation where it is not disputed that the reasons for the whimbrel decline are not known and the habitat management plan is untried and untested in Shetland in relation to whimbrel', were able to conclude that the HMP would provide 'some unspecified level of mitigation' (para 285). Further, in her view, there was 'the fundamental difficulty' that the Ministers had failed to take the directive as 'the starting point' for consideration of the facts.

Article 2 imposed an obligation to take requisite measures to maintain whimbrel at 'an appropriate level', which, in her opinion, would involve 'addressing the issue of what is required by Article 2 in respect of whimbrel in this case'. These were not pure questions of fact, but 'matters of mixed fact and law'. The Ministers had failed to address these issues, except by way of a 'balancing exercise' taking account of the benefits of the project in relation to meeting EU climate change targets – an exercise which in her view was not permitted by the directive (paras 285–288).

25. On appeal, the approach of First Division was radically different. In the single opinion of the court, delivered by Lord Brodie, they criticised the Lord Ordinary for addressing the wrong question:

> The question which should have been the focus of the Lord Ordinary's attention was whether the grant of consent by the Scottish Ministers had been a lawful decision, once due account was taken of, inter alia, the Wild Birds Directive. Instead, the Lord Ordinary applied herself to the rather different question as to whether the Scottish Ministers, in their decision letter, had demonstrated that they had fully understood and complied with their ongoing obligations under the directive in respect of the United Kingdom population of whimbrel, irrespective of the likely effect on it of a consent to the development. (para 26)

26. Whether the development was likely to have a materially adverse effect on the bird populations protected by the directive was 'an entirely factual question' for the Ministers to determine. They had concluded that increased mortality was unlikely but in any event were not satisfied that, even without mitigation by virtue of the HMP, the impact was of significance in relation to the conservation of the species. In the view of the court: 'Once that conclusion was arrived at, the Wild Birds Directive, and any associated problems of interpretation and application, fell out of the picture as far as this proposal was concerned' (para 27). Although, the decision letter had not referred expressly to the directive, it was clear to an informed reader that the decision had been made having regard to SNH's assessment which referred to specific provisions of the directive (para 29). The Lord Ordinary's criticism of the Ministers' reasoning in relation to their duties under Article 4(2) reflected the erroneous view that they were required to satisfy themselves as to their performance of those duties as a preamble to consideration of the application (para 30). Once they had decided that 'the development would have no significant adverse impact, and might possibly be beneficial', the issue of what was required by Article 2 in respect of the whimbrel was 'one that it was unnecessary to explore' (para 31).

The Issues in the Appeal

27. Notwithstanding the approach taken in the courts below, which concentrated on the issues arising under the Wild Birds Directive and the advice of SNH that the 'Viking windfarm is highly likely to result in a significant adverse impact

on the conservation status of the national population of whimbrel', the argument developed in this court was that the Scottish Government had failed to give sufficient weight to the rights of the whimbrel, a species that was to be displaced from parts of the development site and which would be affected by a significant mortality rate caused by the wind turbines. It was argued, for Sustainable Shetland, that the obligations in the Birds Directive such as that in Article 2 'to take the requisite measures to preserve, maintain or re-establish a sufficient diversity and area of habitats for all the species of birds referred to in Article 1' and Article 4(1), which requires 'special conservation measures' to be taken in respect of the species mentioned in annex I of the directive, 'in order to ensure their survival and reproduction in their area of distribution', are compatible with a rights of nature approach to the protection of species. This is supported by the definition of favourable conservation status in Article 1(e) the Habitats Directive (Council Directive 92/43/EEC). This EU approach reflects similar rights in the Universal Declaration of Rights of Mother Earth (UDRME), which, although not binding in the United Kingdom and not an international treaty, can be considered in reaching a decision on the rights of the whimbrel. There is a presumption that domestic law should be read consistently with international law and domestic decision makers are entitled to take international obligations into account and have done so increasingly; Lord Mance, 'International Law in the UK Supreme Court', Speech given at King's College, London, 13 February 2017, paras 8 and 11.b. We consider that same approach should apply to the UDRME.

28. Articles 1 and 3 of UDRME recognise that humans and other beings, which includes whimbrel, have effectively equal rights, which have to be respected by humans, and in particular humans have to 'respect, protect, conserve and where necessary, restore the integrity, of the vital ecological cycles, processes and balances of Mother Earth'. Article 2(1)(a) recognises that the whimbrel have '(a) the right to life and to exist' and the right '(c) … to continue its vital cycles and processes free from human disruptions'. These rights are incompatible with the expectation that the windfarm will have a mortality rate of between 2.1 and 4.2 and, per SNH, 'is highly likely to result in a significant adverse impact on the conservation status of the national population'. Article 3(1)(i) requires the establishment of 'precautionary and restrictive measures to prevent human activities from causing species extinction, the destruction of ecosystems or the disruption of ecological cycles'. If there was the risk of a significant adverse impact on the conservation status of the whimbrel, as identified by SNH, then the precautionary principle would require the development consent to be refused, because there is a risk of extinction in Scotland as the principal area occupied by whimbrel in the United Kingdom.

29. Sustainable Shetland accepted that Article 1(7) recognised that '(7) The rights of each being are limited by the rights of other beings and any conflict between their rights must be resolved in a way that maintains the integrity, balance and health of Mother Earth.' They argued that the Scottish Ministers had not undertaken this balancing exercise. It could only be undertaken at a full hearing on

all the evidence in a public inquiry, particularly in this case where the Scottish Ministers' adviser opposed the development.

30. The Scottish Ministers and Viking argued that if the court could have regard to the rights of nature and the UDRME, which they did not accept, then Scottish Ministers had struck an appropriate balance. Climate change was, itself, a significant danger to humans and to many species including whimbrel in Scotland and the United Kingdom. Therefore, the drive to obtain renewable energy, which would help to protect the Earth, humans and species justified in the balance the impact on whimbrel because it helped maintain 'the integrity, balance and health of Mother Earth'.

31. In response, Sustainable Shetland argued that the balancing exercise of competing scientific and other evidence was so important in reaching a decision that maintained the integrity, balance and health of Mother Earth that it could not be carried out in house by the Scottish Ministers where their scientific adviser, SNH, had objected to the proposal. In a Scottish parliamentary answer, the Scottish Ministers had admitted that they had no in-house scientific advisers and relied on the regulators such SNH for such scientific advice (Response of Paul Wheelhouse MSP to question S5W-08415, 4 May 2017). Such a balancing exercise could only be undertaken at a full hearing on all the evidence at a public inquiry, particularly as the Scottish Ministers had no separate advisers other than SNH (who also objected to the grant of the application).

Discussion

32. In this case, we accept that Sustainable Shetland should be allowed to introduce its rights of nature argument at this stage, although that is unsatisfactory as we have not had the views of the lower court on this argument. We have allowed it because of the importance of the issues, which have not been argued before in the UK court and because it does not raise any new factual issue.

33. We accept that, even though the UDRME is not an international treaty and has not been incorporated into national law, it is an approach to which we should have regard. It represents the considered views of people with expertise in this area of law; *cf* Lord Mance. Further, rights of nature have been given recognition in the constitutions of some states, such as the constitutions of Ecuador and Brazil and that some courts have recognised the rights of nature – see Judgment T-622/16 *(The Atrato River Case)*, Constitutional Court of Colombia (2016).

34. In the US Supreme Court, Mr Justice Douglas, in a dissenting judgment, suggested that natural objects such as rivers and species should have legal personality, so that interested parties could pursue actions to protect nature – *Sierra Club v Morton* 405 US 727 [1972] at pp 741–743. The idea that the interests of nature should be heard in environmental decision-making has been given effect by the

UNECE Convention on Access to Information, Public Participation in Decision-making and Access to Justice in Environmental Matters (Aarhus Convention). The United Kingdom is a signatory and it is introduced into UK law by the Environmental Impact Assessment (EIA) Directive (2011/92/EU as amended by 2014/52/EU). The Aarhus Convention gives the (human) public a right to participate and make representations about developments that might have significant effects on the environment (Article 6) and also standing to raise or take part in proceedings challenging developments in a process that is not to be prohibitively expensive (Article 9).

35. There is some similarity in approach in the Birds Directive for Article 1 and 2 species, including the whimbrel, which require special protection. For example, Article 4(1) requires 'special conservation measures' to be taken in respect of the species mentioned in annex I of the directive, 'in order to ensure their survival and reproduction in their area of distribution'. The latter requirement to ensure their survival is akin to the UDRME rights that all species have the right to exist and to their life cycles. While not directly equivalent, in that the UDRME gives all beings the rights and that is a different approach, the EU directives direct that particular species should be protected, albeit without recognising their inherent rights of nature. We consider that the UDRME should be taken into account in reaching the decision on whether or not the windfarm should have been authorised.

36. Further, we accept that if the UDRME is taken into account, that under Article 7(1) any conflict between rights must be resolved in a way that maintains the integrity, balance and health of Mother Earth. We accept that it can be argued that the Scottish Ministers did undertake this balancing exercise by considering the impact on whimbrel and the need to address climate change. However, we consider that this complex balancing exercise, which must be based on scientific and other evidence, could not be carried out by the Scottish Ministers alone based on representations of the developers, where the Scottish Ministers' scientific adviser, SNH was against the proposal. We consider that there should have been at least a public inquiry, where the evidence could be tested, because of the importance of the rights of nature in seeking to resolve a conflict in a way that maintains the integrity, balance and health of Mother Earth. The evidence should cover the overall impact on all species and ecosystems, including humans and not only whimbrel, given that crows were also to be killed as part of the whimbrel management plan. This should be balanced against the actual benefits for climate change and how climate change in Scotland might itself impact beneficially or adversely on nature. It is the whole impact on the integrity of Mother Earth that has to assessed. The approach taken in the lower courts reflected only the impact on whimbrel, and that was subordinated to the needs to address climate change without any overall analysis.

37. While it was not argued in the courts below, we consider that Sustainable Shetland is right to argue that without an inquiry the Scottish Ministers do not have the expertise to carry out this important balancing exercise required by

Article 7(1) UDRME. This is particularly so where the Scottish Ministers, in the parliamentary answer, accepted that they did not have in-house expertise, and relied on the statutory regulators such SNH, who in this case opposed the application on the grounds of its impact on whimbrel. We consider that there ought to have been a public inquiry, and, in so far as the Scottish Ministers had a discretion to decline to order one, that that decision was unlawful.

Decision

38. We therefore allow the appeal and remit to the Scottish Ministers to hold a public inquiry to consider the scientific and other evidence that is necessary for them to reach an informed decision on the balancing exercise that must be carried out under Article 7(1) UDRME. We hold that UDRME is a relevant consideration and should be taken into account in the balance that needs to be struck between rights of nature, the impact of climate change and to achieve a balance that that 'maintains the integrity, balance and health of Mother Earth'.

39. It is not a matter of considering the rights of whimbrel in isolation, but the balancing exercise requires to be of the rights of all natural beings, including ecosystems in the wider area set against the impacts or benefits of the windfarm in the context of maintaining the integrity, balance and health of Mother Earth.

Commentary

Malcolm Combe

The judgment of the UK Supreme Court in the Sustainable Shetland case paved the way for a windfarm on the largest island in Shetland. For those not au fait with the place, Shetland is the northernmost archipelago of the United Kingdom of Great Britain and Northern Ireland (over 200 kilometres away from the Scottish mainland), and is rather windy. Shetland's location also saw it playing an important role in an earlier energy moment driven by the discovery of fossil fuels, namely the development of the North Sea oil and gas sector. A pivot towards renewable energy infrastructure might have a certain innate attraction in comparison to the hydrocarbon infrastructure that preceded it. As Agnew's very selection of this case for an Earth law reworking demonstrates, it is decidedly not that simple.

Agnew's introduction raises several points that are themselves worthy of further comment. In the first place, Agnew bemoans that the appellants, an association known as Sustainable Shetland, were restricted to the backstop, administrative law remedy of a judicial review to try to prevent this large windfarm development, with all its associated implications for the environment and in particular the whimbrel population of Shetland. In Scotland, judicial reviews can only be raised at the Court of Session (a civil court based in Edinburgh). There are practical and access to justice issues for anyone channelled down this route (in any context),[5] not to mention the particular geographic considerations in the case of litigants from Shetland. These barriers exist despite the Aarhus Convention in the context of environmental matters and access to justice and Article 13 of the European Convention on Human Rights on the right to an effective remedy.[6] Even where judicial review affords local activists a chance to scrutinise important decisions at the highest level,[7] there may be questions around the extent to which anyone instigating a review is representative of the whole community.

Agnew also raises the ethical question about why any wildlife should be sacrificed for the benefit of humans, introducing a deontological rather than consequentialist analysis. When ostensibly clean and renewable energy schemes are in play, this might seem particularly challenging to balance, but there are other legal

[5] See eg Jon Kiddie, 'Homelessness & Judicial Review: A Missed Opportunity for Reform' (2020) *1 Smeal Review* 66, also at https://smeal.org/article/homelessness-and-judicial-review-missed-opportun.

[6] There are obvious financial implications when litigating in Scotland, as discussed in Ben Christman and Malcolm M Combe, 'Funding Civil Justice in Scotland: Full Cost Recovery, at What Cost to Justice?' (2020) 24(1) *Edinburgh Law Rewiew* 49. Particular environmental concerns also arise across the UK, including in Scotland, which is evidenced by the United Nations Economic Commission for Europe Decision VII/8s concerning the United Kingdom (this and related documentation is available at https://unece.org/env/pp/cc/decision-vii8s-concerning-united-kingdom). All of this can make it difficult for communities (such as the community affected in Shetland by this development) to have their voices heard.

[7] Consider *Walton v The Scottish Ministers* [2012] UKSC 44.

spheres where wider public interests can lose out to narrower interests (perhaps in relation to measuring a particular private law nuisance[8] or when unqualified human rights are in play).

The introduction further notes the eventual approval in 2020 by the energy regulator Ofgem of an interconnector to link Noss Head in Caithness and Weisdale Voe in Shetland. This interconnector forms an important piece of the overall jigsaw for the export of energy from Shetland to the Scottish mainland and in turn the UK national electricity grid. On 14 April 2023, the energy company SSE published an update on its website to report that the first of its Vestas 117 turbines was installed at its Viking site (at South Midfield, west of Kergord). This is not a site I can claim any knowledge of, although it feels familiar to me having read about an area slightly to the south of it in a book by a Shetland author.[9] The landscape affected by this development also brings to mind a book written by a Lewisman now resident in Shetland.[10] On my only trip to Shetland to date, I was struck by certain similarities between some of the places I visited and the Isle of Lewis (a place I know well, being where my mother belongs to). Such similarities go beyond proximity to the sea and ocean, by way of the peaty landscape, the Norse place names, and the crofting system of land tenure that is a feature of the north and west of Scotland (now governed by the Crofters (Scotland) Act 1993).[11]

Lewis has also had various windfarm proposals and developments in recent years, which some people have campaigned against and others have sought to use legal devices to advance alternative schemes.[12] It is evident windfarms – especially a scheme involving over 100 wind turbines, as is the case for the Shetland scheme under discussion – raise many questions, which may involve the interaction a development will have with existing land uses, not to mention the multifarious impact it may have on the customs and culture of a locality. This may be a particular concern in what might be characterised as rural or indeed peripheral areas, especially if they feel overly burdened by a development and when they are all too aware of an interconnector carrying energy to more populous areas. Such renewable energy schemes will also have an impact on the local ecosystem.

[8] *Ben Nevis Distillery (Fort William) Ltd v North British Aluminium Co Ltd* 1948 SC 592.

[9] Malachy Tallack, *60 Degrees North: Around the World in Search of Home* (Polygon, 2015).

[10] Donald S Murray, *The Dark Stuff: Stories from the Peatlands* (Bloomsbury, 2018).

[11] Anyone wishing to read more about crofting might refer to Crispin Agnew, *Crofting Law* (T & T Clark, 2000).

[12] eg *Stornoway Wind Farm Ltd v Crofters Having Rights in the Common Grazings of Aignish, Melbost & Branahuie, Sandwick North Street and Sandwick & Sandwick East Street* 2017 SLCR 178 and related cases involved an attempt to use provisions of the Crofters (Scotland) Act 1993. For analysis of debates in Lewis, see Joseph Murphy and Adrian Smith, 'Understanding Transition – Periphery Dynamics: Renewable Energy in the Highlands and Islands of Scotland' (2013) 45(3) *Environment and Planning A: Economy and Space* 691, and Annabel Pinker, 'Debating Energy Futures on Lewis: Energy Transitions, Emergent Politics, and the Question of the Commons' (2019) https://www.hutton.ac.uk/blogs/debating-energy-futures-lewis-energy-transitions-emergent-politics-and-question-commons-0. On the legal aspects of windfarm development and crofting tenure, see Stephanie Hepburn, 'Unlocking the Potential of Wind Power in Scotland's Crofting Counties' (2023) 185 *Property Law Bulletin* 4.

This takes us back to the topic at hand: the whimbrel, a little bird which (in a UK context) is largely found in Shetland. It played a central role in the litigation that navigated two stages at the Court of Session (being the original judicial review at the Outer House and then an appeal to the Inner House) and at the UK Supreme Court. Ultimately, the absolute protection of whimbrel was not on the winning side of the scales in terms of the balancing exercise made in accordance with the Electricity Act 1989 (the statute under which consent for the windfarm was granted). This weighing exercise involved consideration of the Birds Directive, but there was no hallowed place for birds beyond that. As acknowledged at the outset, our Earth law judge was an advocate (the Scottish terminology for barrister) for Sustainable Shetland. In the Earth law judgment, there are no sour grapes evident. Instead, Agnew makes his ruling based on something novel and not argued in the original litigation.

After largely tracking the first twenty-seven paragraphs of Lord Carnwath's opinion in the UK Supreme Court (albeit with the original paragraph 18 deleted), the device deployed by Agnew (starting at paragraph 27) is to characterise the obligations found in the Birds Directive plus the definition of favourable conservation status in the Habitats Directive as factors which bring the UDRME into play. This allows the UDRME to be considered in reaching a decision on the rights of (in this case) the whimbrel.

There is then an allusion to the not at all simple issue of whether a drive towards renewable energy was something that contributed to the integrity, balance and health of Mother Earth (paras 30–31), before the 'Discussion' section. This begins by proficiently dealing with the civil procedure point that might have prevented Mother Earth-related arguments being aired at the top of the judicial hierarchy when they were not considered in the courts below (para 32). Agnew then draws on emerging comparative jurisprudence, together with the Aarhus Convention, to explain why the Scottish Ministers – as original decision-makers – should indeed have taken the UDRME into account (paras 33–34). In terms of what the decision would actually have been had this been factored into the equation, this is not something that is definitively ruled upon – an understandable sidestep in the context of an appellate judgment.

Rather, matters are remitted back to a public inquiry, on the basis that the Scottish Ministers would not have been able to engage in what was now the appropriate balancing exercise simply with input from the developers, especially when the statutory body charged with looking after Scotland's natural heritage was against the proposal (para 35) and possessed expertise that Scottish Ministers did not (para 36).[13] Given the above-mentioned limitations of judicial review as compared to a public inquiry, and with a judgment such as this laying the necessary groundwork for it, it seems at least plausible that a public inquiry would afford

[13] This body now goes by the name NatureScot, but at the time of the litigation it still used its statutory name, Scottish Natural Heritage.

a better opportunity for the interests of parties affected by this development to be suitably represented. It may even be worth considering whether such public inquiries could be shaped in some way so as to be better informed by local human communities, in the hope that this might bring further environmental benefits.[14] This would be consonant with Scotland's recent manoeuvres towards land reform and community empowerment.[15]

This Earth law judgment does not quite go so far as to absolutely prioritise the rights of the whimbrel. Accordingly, even in the Earth law counterfactual, it remains possible that a consequentialist analysis would have ultimately been adopted in a way that allowed a renewable energy development to proceed and in turn some long-term displacement of or collision mortality for a small number of whimbrel (notwithstanding any habitat management plan instigated by the developer). This may not be a completely hard-line approach to the rights of nature, but it seems a pragmatic approach. Such an approach would at least have allowed for a proper stress test of the overall development proposals in a manner that was not constrained by the parameters of a judicial review action, whilst ensuring suitable weight was given to the interests of whimbrel in any balancing exercise that followed.

[14] For an indication of the challenges in this area, see Maria Lee et al, 'Public Participation and Climate Change Infrastructure' (2013) 25(1) *Journal of Environmental Law* 33.

[15] It is not possible in this short commentary to quantify whether and to what extent such involvement would have a positive effect in relation to a local ecosystem or indeed the whimbrel that were at issue in this case, but for an overview of the potential impact of some land reform measures on the environment, see Malcolm M. Combe, 'The Environmental Implications of Redistributive Land Reform' (2016) 18(2) *Environmental Law Review* 104 and more recently Bobby Macaulay and Chris Dalglish, 'Community Landowners and the Climate Emergency, Research Report for Community Land Scotland' (2021) available at https://www.communitylandscotland.org.uk/resources/community-landowners-and-theclimate-emergency/. On community ownership of renewable energy infrastructure, see Aileen McHarg, 'Community Benefit through Community Ownership of Renewable Generation in Scotland: Power to the People?' in Lila Barrera-Hernández et al (eds), *Sharing the Costs and Benefits of Energy and Resource Activity: Legal Change and Impact on Communities* (Oxford University Press, 2016) 297.

12

On the Issuing of Traffic Regulation Orders in the Lake District National Park: *Stubbs (on behalf of Green Lanes Environmental Action Movement) v Lake District National Park Authority & Ors*

JULIA AGLIONBY

Introduction

In August 2020, the High Court issued a judgment in an application for judicial review by the Green Lanes Environmental Action Movement (GLEAM) against the Lake District National Park Authority (LDNPA).[1] GLEAM claimed the LDNPA had erred in law in its decision not to recommend consulting on a Traffic Regulation Order (TRO) to limit the use of mechanised four-wheel-drive vehicles on two green lane routes between Little Langdale and Coniston in the Lake District. A 'green lane' is a lay term for an unclassified unmetalled and unsealed highway or byway open to all traffic (BOAT); they are often grassed over, hence the name.

The route passes through a landscape that to many epitomises the beauty and special qualities of the Lake District National Park with multiple scattered farmhouses, barns and green valley floors leading up to the open fells and commons. These farms are working businesses that sustain traditional fell flocks and hill farming practices. The area was also significant in the development of the early conservation movement as key players such as GM Trevelyan and Beatrix Potter invested in farms to avert further development and transferred these to the National Trust. Mining was historically important, but no longer occurs. The quarrying of slate continues to this day in nearby Elterwater.

[1] *Stubbs (on behalf of Green Lanes Environmental Action Movement) v Lake District National Park Authority & Ors* [2020] EWHC 2293 (Admin).

While road transport has a long history as a connector between the west coast and Ambleside, the scale and nature and frequency of vehicle usage over metalled roads has changed over time with visits to the Lakes now exceeding 20 million per year. Most of the sealed road network is now unsuitable for walkers as the frequent passing of cars makes the highways too busy, and sometimes unsafe, to enjoy the tranquillity of the National Park. This is one reason why pressure has been put on the LDNPA to restrict vehicular use on these green lanes as there is a conflict between recreational users – for instance those on foot or bicycle and those in recreational four-wheel-drive vehicles – as well as between local farmers and recreational motor vehicles. Over time, the surfaces of the green lanes have been damaged by increased recreational usage, though this has been addressed to a large degree via a maintenance programme.

What remains in dispute is whether the current, and potentially increasing, recreational use by four-wheel-drive vehicles is consistent with conserving the special quality of the Lake District National Park relating to beauty. A TRO can be imposed '[f]or the purpose of conserving or enhancing the natural beauty of the area, or of affording better opportunities for the public to enjoy the amenities of the area, or recreation or the study of nature in the area'.

Surveys undertaken by the LDNPA indicated 75 per cent of users of U5001 at Tilberthwaite would prefer the use of recreational motorised vehicles to be prohibited.

The application by GLEAM for judicial review was brought on three grounds:

1. The LDPNPA in making its decision failed to properly interpret and apply section 11A(2) of the National Parks and Access to the Countryside Act 1949, as modified by section 62 of the Environment Act 1995. This enacts the 'Sandford Principle':

   > In exercising or performing any functions in relation to, or so as to affect, land in a National Park, any relevant authority shall have regard to the purposes specified in subsection (1) of section five of this Act and, if it appears that there is a conflict between those purposes, shall attach greater weight to the purpose of conserving and enhancing the natural beauty, wildlife and cultural heritage of the area comprised in the National Park.

2. It also failed to discharge the duty upon it under section 122 of the Road Traffic Regulation Act 1984 and failed to make a decision based upon the relevant mandatory considerations.
3. It misdirected the Members in relation to the test for consultation under regulation 4 of the National Park Authorities Traffic Orders (Procedure) (England) Regulations 2007.

The judge in the original case dismissed all three claims for the following reasons:

1. The test for the implementation of the Sandford Principle requires there to be an irreconcilable conflict between the interests of conservation and public enjoyment rather than simply a conflict, ie all other ways should be explored

to resolve a conflict before the Authority should prioritise conservation and ban public enjoyment – in this case the usage of motorised vehicles on these unsealed roads.

2. The Assessment Report (AR) was not a report to resolve whether to issue a TRO or not: it was to look at all the possible options for resolving the conflict, and, as such, the Authority was not bound by the requirements of section 122 of the Road Traffic Regulation Act 1984.
3. The AR provided to the members of the LDNPA gave sufficient information to the Planning Committee and the members were not seriously misled. There was no error of law in the defendant not providing the full range of consultation options that may have been possible.

As a result of this decision, the extensive use of recreational four-wheel-drive vehicles continued to cause public concern. The objectors considered this an egregious breach of the purpose of a National Park to conserve the natural and cultural heritage of protected landscapes and to offer opportunities for quiet enjoyment. It was also considered to threaten the Outstanding Universal Value of the Lake District World Heritage Site.

Many people expressed their disappointment at the judgment that justice for this iconic place had not been served and continued to back the campaign for a TRO in Little Langdale. Breaking this down, justice, in this case, can be considered to have been failed on two grounds. Firstly, justice did not serve nature by failing to protect the beauty of the site. In a National Park, it can be argued that peace and tranquillity should have primacy over the interests of a small number of adventure enthusiasts and the businesses that serve them. Secondly, the framework for determining whether to consult on a TRO focused on process not outcomes. The TRO creation procedures are positive rather than normative and do not embrace the statutory duty of the LDNPA to conserve the special qualities of the site.

Why is it that the LDNPA appeared caught up in a narrow interpretation of administrative guidance framing specific procedural decisions that precluded them from agreeing to consult on a TRO? Was it the fear of significant objections to a TRO by the motorised vehicle users? In deciding how to tackle this reimagined judgment, there was a choice in approach. Is the law at fault in not allowing a conclusion that would support the imposition of a TRO, or is it the interpretation of the existing law by the judge that is erroneous? Furthermore, at the time of writing, three years after the original judgment, National Park purposes are a policy topic in which significant development has occurred.

On reviewing the submissions of the parties and the underlying statutes and statutory instruments, I concluded that there was scope for reinterpretation within the existing law in a way that supports and upholds the conservation of the special qualities of the site. What has evolved over time and even in the three years since the original judgment is the policy context and societal values as regards nature, tranquillity and beauty. These set the framework within which current law is interpreted in the reimagined judgment. This is possible legally because the text of the primary legislation is broad, so there was no need to create new narratives or imagine alternative legislation. Rather, it was relatively straightforward within the existing legal orders to arrive at a different conclusion. The work of the Yorkshire Dales National Park Authority was useful in demonstrating that a different framing of the challenge for resolving conflicts over the recreational motorised vehicles was possible without being overly authoritarian.[2]

The outcome of the case hinged on whether the Sandford Principle had been correctly applied. Key differences between the original judgment and mine are as follows:

1. Mr Justice Dove did not take section 11A(2) of the Environment Act 1995 at face value but interpreted it in the light of the Sandford Principle as quoted in the LDNPA Assessment Report in paragraph 1.10.1.[3] This quote, while often used, differs from the words in the actual Sandford Report, which has no reference to the word 'irreconcilable'.[4] The Sandford Report uses the word 'acute' and I disagree with Mr Justice Dove that irreconcilable and acute are interchangeable words.
2. Requiring an 'irreconcilable' conflict sets a high bar that is neither in the legislation nor in any statutory instruments. It gives equal weight to the two purposes of beauty and enjoyment and ignores the LDNPA's statutory duty to conserve and enhance the special qualities of the site which, in my view, are at risk.
3. Mr Justice Dove gives less weight to the Road Traffic Regulation Act 1984, which through section 22(2), recognises in law that, where the beauty of a National Park is at risk due to traffic, there are grounds for consulting on a TRO. I agree with Mr Justice Dove that the balancing act set out in section 122 of the Road Traffic Regulation Act 1984 is only to be undertaken after the consultation. It appears to me that the LDNPA sought to undertake this balancing act in advance of the consultation.
4. Mr Justice Dove takes equality of the purposes of National Parks as a starting point, relying on section 5 of the 1949 Act. I disagree with this as it is inconsistent with current law and relevant policies that are material. For example, the conclusions of the Sandford Report that give greater weight to beauty and nature have regularly been echoed in further policy documents and acts: for example, the Environment Act 1995, the Glover Review 2019 and Defra's

[2] For policies on 'green lanes' in the Yorkshire Dales National Park, see www.yorkshiredales.org.uk/things-to-do/get-outdoors/where-can-i-go/green-lanes/green-lanes-management/.

[3] Lake District National Park Authority, Assessment Report for the Rights of Way Committee Report on 8th October 2019. Available at www.lakedistrict.gov.uk/__data/assets/pdf_file/0020/151742/Committee-Report-Assessment-Paper.pdf.

[4] Report of the National Parks Policies Review Committee (Sandford Report) (HMSO, 1974).

2022 response to Glover.[5] This policy direction is also required by UNESCO to secure the attributes of the World Heritage Site, which it considers are at risk due to the failure to manage the use of green lanes by recreational vehicles.

Overall, my judgment was able to reach a different conclusion to that of Mr Justice Dove by focusing on the legislation and interpreting that in the light of current government policy and statutory duties. My view is there is more than enough evidence from third parties and the LDNPA's own policies to demonstrate the necessity to consult on a TRO.

[5] Julian Glover and Department for Environment, Food and Rural Affairs, *Landscapes Review: National Parks and AONBs* (2018); Department for Environment, Food and Rural Affairs, *Landscapes review (National Parks and AONBs): Government Response* (2022).

In the High Court of Justice
Kings Bench Division
Administrative Court

Patricia Stubbs (on behalf of Green Lanes Environmental Action Movement) v Lake District National Park Authority and Others

2 June 2023

Mrs Justice Aglionby

1. The Claimant, Green Lanes Environmental Action Movement, contends that the defendant, the Lake District National Park Authority, has failed to properly interpret and apply s 11A(2) of the National Parks and Access to the Countryside Act 1949, and to prioritise the statutory purpose of the Lake District National Park, by deciding not to consult on a Traffic Regulation Order closing High Tilberthwaite unsealed highway (U5001) for use by recreational four-wheel-drive vehicles.

2. The judgment is arranged in three parts. I first examine the facts of the usage over time of the unsealed highway U5001 including the impacts of that usage. Secondly, I turn to the defendant's obligations under English law with particular attention to the Sandford Principle as enshrined in s 11A(2) of the National Park Act 1949. Finally, I consider further obligations on the defendant deriving from the defendant's commitments as expressed in international treaties, including the European Landscape Convention and UNESCO's World Heritage Site guidance and specific recommendations for this site. These collectively inform the decision I reach.

The Facts and the Framework for Assessing the Facts

3. The use of motorised vehicles for recreational use on High Tilberthwaite road (U5001) has increased over time and the condition of the road had declined, particularly on the unsealed section. This has caused difficulties for agricultural users from nearby farms and resulted in a conflict with other non-motorised amenity users, such as walkers and cyclists. As a result, an amenity group, Save the Lake District, made a request in 2017 to the Lake District National Park Authority (LDNPA) to impose a Traffic Regulation Order (TRO) to restrict the use of recreational four-wheel-drive motorised vehicles on this unsealed road.

4. There is no disagreement that High Tilberthwaite is a public highway and has been for many years. It was recognised as an 'Ancient Highway' in an 1857 Enclosure Award. The length of the unsealed section is 2.5 km which comprises 2.1 per cent of the network of unsealed roads open to motorised traffic and 0.09 per cent of the total unsealed rights of way network in the Lake District National Park area.

5. It is also agreed that, as a National Park Authority, the LDNPA has the legal powers to consult on and issue a TRO for a range of reasons as set out under s 1 of the Road Traffic Regulation Act 1984, including, as set out in s 22(2) of that Act, for 'the purpose of conserving or enhancing the natural beauty of the area, or of affording better opportunities for the public to enjoy the amenities of the area, or recreation or the study of nature in the area'.

6. The National Park Authorities' Traffic Orders (Procedure) (England) Regulations 2007 came into effect on 1 October 2007. Defra provided guidance in 2007 to National Park Authorities for making TROs. This guidance draws attention to the test for assessing natural beauty as a framework to assess whether the natural beauty is being negatively affected by the use of the public highway and, if so, whether a TRO is appropriate. The tests set out are:

a) Landscape quality (ie condition, that is the intactness of the landscape, the condition of its features, its state of repair, and the absence of incongruous elements);
b) Scenic quality (ie appeal to the visual senses, for example due to important views, visual interest and variety, contrasting landscape patterns, and dramatic topography or scale);
c) Relative wildness i.e. the presence of wild (or relatively wild) character in the landscape due to remoteness, and appearance of returning to nature;
d) Intrusiveness (ie freedom from undue disturbance. Presence in the landscape of factors such as openness, and perceived naturalness);
e) Natural heritage features i.e. habitats, wildlife and features of geological or geomorphological interest that may contribute strongly to the naturalness of a landscape;
f) Cultural heritage features (ie archaeological, historical and architectural characteristics or features that may contribute to the perceived beauty of the landscape);
g) Associations (ie connections with particular people, artists, writers, or events in history that may contribute to perceptions of beauty in a landscape or facilitate understanding and enjoyment). (Guidance, page 5)

7. The LDNPA officers prepared an Assessment Report (AR) during the period 2017–2019, which was presented to the Rights of Way Committee of the LDNPA on the 8 October 2019. The report's recommendation was that a TRO should not be consulted on as all other opportunities to resolve the matter had not been exhausted. The Rights of Way Committee decided to follow the advice of its officers and it was decided to ask Cumbria County Council to improve and maintain the surface of the road and to establish a partnership management group to look at achieving consensus on future use of the unsealed highway.

8. The reasons for the request for a TRO by Save the Lake District as reported in the AR are:

a) Increasing vehicular usage over the last 15+ years;
b) Levels of use are damaging the surface of the roads;
c) Damage is such that farming is becoming unviable, and the local farmer(s) can no longer access their land easily or safely;
d) Levels of use (and an increase in use) have a negative impact on the amenity, natural beauty, and tranquillity of this area;
e) Levels of use (and an increase in use) negatively impacts the ability of most users to enjoy this area of the National Park;
f) The levels of use are impacting upon the Outstanding Universal Values for which the Lake District has been designated a World Heritage Site;
g) MPV usage create conflict between types of user;
h) This conflict with vehicular use contravenes the Sandford Principle. (AR para 1.5.1)

9. Save the Lakes was unhappy with the LDNPA's decision and worked with the national campaign group Green Lanes Environmental Action Movement (GLEAM) to challenge the decision.

Grounds for Review

10. Leave has been granted to challenge the decision on the following grounds: the defendant, in making their decision not to consult on a TRO, failed to properly interpret and apply s 11A(2) of the 1949 Act, which amended the original Act to give legal status to the Sandford Principle. The grounds of challenge are, in summary, that the defendant erred in not giving greater weight to the statutory purpose of conserving and enhancing the natural beauty, wildlife and cultural heritage when conflict arose between that and opportunities for enjoyment from the use of four-wheel-drive vehicles for recreation.

Purposes and Qualities of the Lake District National Park

11. The AR explains that 'Amenity and Beauty' is a statutory term derived from s 5(2) of the National Parks and Access to the Countryside Act 1949 (as amended and as informed by ss 59 and 99 of the Natural Environment and Rural Communities Act 2006). It is one of the two principal criteria for designating National Parks, the other being opportunities for open-air recreation (see below). A National Park landscape is considered to have exceptional natural beauty of national or international importance.

12. The special qualities of the Lake District National Park are defined by the Environment Act 1995, which the LDNPA is required to conserve and enhance

under the statutory purposes of a National Park. The LDNP 2015–2020 Partnership Management Plan defines the special qualities as:

a) A world class cultural landscape
b) Complex geology and geomorphology
c) Rich archaeology and historic landscape
d) Unique farming heritage and concentration of common land
e) The high fells
f) Wealth of habitats and wildlife
g) Mosaic of lakes, tarns, rivers, and coast
h) Extensive semi-natural woodlands
i) Distinctive buildings and settlement character
j) A source of artistic inspiration
k) A model for protecting cultural landscapes
l) A long tradition of tourism and outdoor activities
m) Opportunities for quiet enjoyment

13. The Outstanding Universal Value of the World Heritage Site (WHS) is based on the three themes of identity, inspiration and conservation and is well summarised in the International Council on Monuments and Sites (ICOMOS)'s technical review in 2016 as 'a landscape of exceptional beauty that has been shaped by persistent agro-pastoral traditions, that has inspired artistic and literary movements, generating ideas of global influence about the notion of landscape that have left physical marks, and a landscape that catalysed the development of landscape protection at the national and international levels'. More formally, the inscription was accepted on the basis of WHS criteria (ii), (v) and (vi).

14. The National Trust, which owns 20 per cent of the Lake District National Park and including the land surrounding the High Tilberthwaite road, supports the call to impose a TRO. Its statement, made at the LDNPA Rights of Way Committee in October 2019 was in the following terms:

> We believe that MPV use is damaging and should be regulated by a Traffic Regulation Order (TRO) at Tilberthwaite and High Oxen Fell. … In particular, we think that:
>
> 1. The most recent technical expert advice was not followed in carrying out the assessment of the impact on Outstanding Universal Value.
> 2. The Sandford Principle says if there is a conflict between protecting the environment and people's enjoyment of it, that can't be resolved by management, then protecting the environment is more important.
> 3. Describing these remote valleys as honey pot sites – on a par with Windermere and Bowness, shows a lack of understanding of Landscape Character.
>
> … And we think that this activity is at odds with what people want from their national parks in the 21st century – to tackle climate change and champion sustainable transport – cornerstones of the emerging Partnership and Local Plans.

> We fully understand that managing a national park is challenging but where conflict can't be resolved by management, protecting the environment is more important.
>
> We can't support the Lake District National Park's current recommendation, and we're asking them to defer the decision until a more comprehensive impact assessment is done, which we would be happy to support.

15. In May 2019, ICOMOS, as technical advisor to UNESCO on World Heritage Sites, issued a report on the situation on those Green Lanes in which it noted the ten-fold increase in vehicles between 2002 and 2017. It noted that the LDNPA has the statutory authority to introduce TROs and that the tests for introducing TROs were met. It advised the state party – the UK Government – to:

> a) Introduce Traffic Regulation Orders (TROs) on green roads in the property;
> b) Avoid linking the sustainability of farms with income from 4×4 vehicle activities;
> c) Set out a clearer and more detailed articulation of physical attributes of Outstanding Universal Value in future Heritage Impact Assessments and based these on a more integrated landscape approach;
> d) Strengthen the interaction between the recreational community and local communities of farmers, residents and NGOs. (ICOMOS, *Technical Review: The English Lake District*, May 2019)

The Decision not to Consult on a TRO

16. The LDNPA relies heavily in reaching its recommendation on its assessment of a survey of visitors and the results of online surveys. It draws on these views when deciding whether or not the use of recreational vehicles is compatible with the special qualities of the National Park and whether or not their use threatens the Outstanding Universal Value (OUV) of the World Heritage Site.

17. The AR adopts a mechanistic approach to assessing the facts, looking carefully at issues such as noise pollution, tranquillity indices, etc. In assessing all these, it conclude that the banning of recreational four-wheel-drive vehicles would not make a significant difference to these indices. The AR does acknowledge in paragraph 14.8.23 that:

> [I]t is beyond doubt that removing recreational MPV traffic from the roads would change the experience for those meeting the traffic whilst on the roads themselves. The question then is really 'by how much', and is the impact on other users' so great that MPV traffic needs to be prohibited.

The AR throughout seeks to balance the existing legal rights of all vehicles to use U5001 against the Lake District's special quality of quiet enjoyment. There is no reflection in the AR process that, while all vehicles are currently entitled in law to use U5001, rights of using a highway are not without limit nor that government policies may evolve over time. Rights for unconstrained vehicle usage under current laws were granted when the situation on the ground was very different.

18. Considerable space in the AR is given to assessing the appropriateness or inappropriateness of four-wheel-drive recreational driving with reference to mechanical vehicles from 1913 onwards and the AR seeks to make a case that there is a cultural history associated with road driving, while accepting that in the 1960s recreational car driving on U5001 was only occasional. Furthermore, the AR argues that no one is seeking to ban use of cars on tarmacked roads so why should the rules for unsealed roads be any different? This is a surprising argument, given that an unsealed road is a materially different type of highway to a sealed or tarmacked road and no one would expect the same nature of usage on unsealed roads as on a tarmacked road. More importantly, the Authority is making a strong case for sustainable transport systems for the National Park and repeatedly seeks to encourage visitors to avoid the use of private cars, recognising the public highways of the Lake District are not fit for increasing numbers of visitors.

19. The cultural heritage of the Lake District has been considered in great detail by many learned landscape scholars and has been subject to considerable scrutiny over the past three decades as the National Park repeatedly sought World Heritage Status. In 2017, the Lake District was finally inscribed by UNESCO as a WHS Cultural Landscape. At no point in this period or in the WHS nomination documents was the recreational use of four-wheel-drive vehicles considered as a contributing part of the cultural landscape or to its Outstanding Universal Value. Policy VE6 of the WHS Management Plan states: 'Our strategy is to transform visitor movement to, from, and in the Lake District focussing on changing the travel choice visitors make.' The same document says the vision for addressing climate change measures in the Lake District includes offering sustainable transport options. Nowhere is there an ambition to encourage or maintain the current use of recreational four-wheel-drive vehicles.

The Application of the Sandford Principle

20. National Parks in the United Kingdom are formed by the application of the National Parks Act 1949, which defines their purposes:

> s 5(1) The provisions of this Part of this Act shall have effect for the purpose –
> (a) of conserving and enhancing the natural beauty, wildlife and cultural heritage of the areas specified in the next following subsection; and
> (b) of promoting opportunities for the understanding and enjoyment of the special qualities of those areas by the public.

21. Over the following decades, as more National Parks came into being, local councils increasingly grappled with how to balance these two purposes to such a degree the Government formed a National Parks Policies Review Committee chaired by Lord Sandford to address this and other key issues of governance. The committee reported in 1974.

22. The Sandford Principle arises from the report of the National Parks Policies Review Committee where the tension between the two purposes in clause 5 are reflected on. At paragraph 2.25 the report states:

> [2.15] The first purpose of national parks, as stated by Dower and by Parliament – the preservation and enhancement of natural beauty – seems to us to remain entirely valid and appropriate. The second purpose the promotion of public enjoyment – however, needs to be re-interpreted and qualified because it is now evident that excessive or unsuitable use may destroy the very qualities which attract people to the parks. We have no doubt that where the conflict between the two purposes, which has always been inherent, becomes acute, the first one must prevail in order that the beauty and ecological qualities of national parks may be maintained.

23. In the conclusion to the report this is restated as 'finding No 12':

> [12] But there have also been uncertainties and differing views about the purposes of a national park, which stem from the ambiguities of the statute, which gives equal weight to the preservation and enhancement of natural beauty on the one hand, and the promotion of public enjoyment on the other. The apparent assumption that any conflict between the purposes could be easily resolved has been disproved by experience, which shows that public use of the parks can be of such a kind and on such a scale as to be destructive of their environment qualities. Good management can protect the parks and cater for visitors with diverse inclinations by providing opportunities and facilities for differing kinds of public enjoyment in different parts of each park, according to the varying qualities and circumstances. By developing the capacity of suitable areas to absorb greater numbers of the more gregarious visitors, pressures may be diverted from the wilder and more sensitive areas. But where it is not possible to prevent excessive or unsuitable use by such means, so that conflict between the dual purposes becomes acute, the first one must prevail in order that the beauty and ecological qualities of the National Parks may be maintained.

24. In addition to this well-known principle, it is helpful to consider the more detailed commentary at the time in the Sandford Report and the Hansard record of the debate in the House of Lords on the 2 July 1974, in particular the opening speech of Baroness White. Already at that time it was being proposed that the purposes be revised and strengthened to note that the term 'natural beauty' does not fully cover the need for ecological conservation. The lack of clear government policy on the matter was bemoaned. Three separate excerpts from Baroness White's 1974 speech on the Sandford Report exemplify that the conflict between the natural beauty and enjoyment by the public has already been recognised by 1974;

> Because of these increasing pressures and because deterioration is so hard to reverse we believe that the statutory purposes of the parks should be restated. …
>
> It is the second purpose … that needs qualification; and they repeat: 'We recommend that the statute be amended to make it clear that their enjoyment by the public shall be in such manner and by such means as will leave their natural beauty unimpaired for the

> enjoyment of this and future generations'. There the dilemma, the conflict of interest, is very clearly stated. …
>
> This precept would set the acceptable limit to wear and tear caused by human pressure on the living environment.

25. There has been no restatement of the purposes of National Parks since 1949 but the Sandford Principle, via s 62 of the Environment Act 1995, was inserted into the National Parks Act 1949 as follows:

> Section 11A(2) In exercising or performing any functions in relation to, or so as to affect, land in a National Park, any relevant authority shall have regard to the purposes specified in subsection (1) of section five of this Act and, if it appears that there is a conflict between those purposes, shall attach greater weight to the purpose of conserving and enhancing the natural beauty, wildlife and cultural heritage of the area comprised in the National Park.

26. A seventieth-anniversary Review of England's National Landscapes was commissioned by Defra and undertaken by an independent panel chaired by Julian Glover, which reported in 2019. The report made clear recommendations about reviewing the purposes to strengthen the role of our national landscapes in nature recovery and also to re-energise the purposes to better engage people with our national landscapes. Glover proposed that the reworded purposes should apply to both National Parks and Areas of Outstanding Natural Beauty (AONBs) and be as follows:

> 1. Recover, conserve and enhance natural beauty, biodiversity and natural capital, and cultural heritage.
> 2. Actively connect all parts of society with these special places to support understanding, enjoyment and the nation's health and wellbeing.

Glover's Review reaffirmed that the Sandford Principle should continue to apply.

27. In January 2022, Defra responded to the Glover Review's proposals (*Landscapes Review (National Parks and AONBs): Government Response*, 2022). On the matter of the purposes, Defra stated that it agreed with the intention of the Review's proposals on the purposes and commented that it intended to amend the purposes to reflect that a core function of protected landscapes should be to drive nature recovery. In November 2023, Defra published its action plan *(Consultation Outcome: Implementing the Landscapes Review,* 2023*)* and changed its approach, commenting in its response to Consultation Question 7:

> We consider that strengthening the intent of this proposal [to amend the purposes] has instead been delivered by the commencement of the Environment Act biodiversity duty and will be enhanced by additional duties through the Levelling Up and Regeneration Act. This will focus relevant authorities on delivery. We will continue to track progress to inform whether additional policies or activities are needed.

28. Defra's 2022 *Response* clarifies that it intends the Sandford Principle to remain in force. It also states that it will consider enhancing the powers of National Parks to manage green lanes through the expansion of enforcement powers. By the time that the Consultation Outcome was published in November 2023, however, Defra had decided it would not amend the legislation and that green lanes could be adequately protected by existing provision for TROs. This appears to have been prompted by many negative responses from motorised vehicle users to the consultation question: 'Should we legislate to restrict the use of motor vehicles on unsealed, unclassified roads for recreational use, subject to appropriate exemptions?'

The Need for an 'Irreconcilable' Conflict?

29. At the heart of this judgment is whether the LDNPA properly applied the Sandford Principle in deciding not to consult on a TRO. The claimant's case focuses on the application of the word 'irreconcilable' in regard to the conflict between the two purposes. The LDNPA relied heavily in their AR on asserting that only if the conflict between the interests was unreconcilable is it appropriate to consult on and issue a TRO. The word 'irreconcilable' is not in statute nor in chapter two of Lord Sandford's report, 'Three Purposes Examined' but relates to some other statement from Lord Sandford that has then been used in Government Circulars and then has become the de facto legal bar despite having no formal legal standing.

30. The claimant, GLEAM, argues that the word irreconcilable does not appear in s 11A(2) of the Environment Act 1995 and therefore is the wrong test. Attention is drawn to the only other case that reached the courts concerning the application of the Sandford Principle, *R (Harris and another) v Broads Authority* [2016] EWHC 799 (Admin); [2017] 1 WLR 567. In that case Holgate J said at paragraph 75 of his judgment: 'Section 11A(1) of the 1949 Act imposes relatively broad duties, which are largely dependent upon the value judgments made by a National Park Authority from time to time.' Section 11A(1) is concerned with the duty to foster the economic and social well-being of local communities in addition to the purposes. The point made by Holgate J is important as it reminds us of the need for judgment by National Park Authorities and implies that such judgment may vary over time.

31. Management Planning for the Lake District National Park has evolved over its seventy years of existence to address internal challenges such as increasing visitor numbers and external challenges such as changes in funding to farming and the climate change and biodiversity crises. The management policies of the Lake District National Park are decided through the Lake District Partnership; these have recently been reviewed and reissued in the Partnership's *Management Plan for the Lake District 2021–2025* adopted on 20 October 2021. There are five key

outcomes, one being sustainable travel and transport. The documents and associated films make clear that providing low-carbon options for travel is critical both for those arriving in the park and so that visitors can leave their cars at their base and use sustainable means to travel around the park.

32. Furthermore, the *Management Plan* in Annex 7 recognises the need to monitor the use of unsealed roads to secure three attributes of the World Heritage Site Outstanding Universal Value: extraordinary beauty and harmony, agropastoral system and landscape conservation.

33. The growing emphasis on sustainable travel by the LDNPA is especially important in light of the increase in number of visitors to the National Park to over 20 million in 2022. The road infrastructure has stayed the same except for a few bypasses. A tension therefore arises between encouraging the National Park to be open to all and retaining the other special qualities of the Lake District National Park, including quiet enjoyment.

34. Focusing on U5001, it is also worth reminding ourselves that the specific location of this road is in an intact small scale farmed landscape of immense beauty, not in a 'honey pot' area such as Ambleside or Keswick. ICOMOS advised the state party (the UK Government) to ensure that the impact of recreational driving on landscape character was more comprehensively examined through a more thorough Heritage Impact Assessment.

35. In 2007, the UK Government ratified the European Landscape Convention agreed in Florence in 2000. The aims of the Convention are: 'To promote landscape protection, management and planning, and to organise European co-operation on landscape issues.' Landscape Protection is defined in Article 1d as: 'actions to conserve and maintain the significant or characteristic features of a landscape, justified by its heritage value derived from its natural configuration and/or from human activity'.

36. In January 2022, the LDNPA issued a position statement on unsealed roads: LDNPA, *Position Statement on Unsealed Roads* (2022). This makes clear the risk that the LDNPA considers can arise to the special qualities of the National Park and the attributes of the WHS from the recreational usage of vehicles on unsealed roads. The LDNPA acknowledges the impact on tranquillity of vehicle usage and will work with all stakeholders to mitigate the impact of green lane vehicle usage, recognising that usage of green lanes is legal and preceded the inscription of the WHS. They will seek to introduce TROs where there is unequivocal evidence of harm to the WHS or special qualities of the Lake District National Park in line with Defra guidance and the law.

37. In 2023, the World Heritage Site Committee reported on the state of the English Lake District and on the matter of unsealed roads:

> Vehicular access to unsurfaced roads is an issue that continues to be reported by third parties and has been subject to ICOMOS Technical Reviews. The LDNPA's Right of Way

Committee established the Tilberthwaite Partnership Management Group to monitor the usage and condition of unsealed roads. In 2021, the LDNPA did not consider that sufficient evidence of harm to OUV had emerged from the use of the Tilberthwaite road to justify a ban on the activity. In 2022, LNDPA's Position Statement on unsealed roads was adopted. It aims at sustainable and responsible use of unsealed roads and provides a context for management and decision-making in this regard. No update has been provided in 2023.

38. I have considered the 2019 AR and conclude that the LDNPA assessment of appropriateness of consulting on a TRO is flawed and did not fully take into account the integrity of the OUV. It failed to properly consider the question of appropriateness of a TRO in the light of:

a) the Lake District Partnership Management Plan, both the 2015–20 version and the newly adopted 2021–25 version;
b) the agreed special qualities of the LDNP;
c) the commitment to maintain the OUV and integrity of the WHS;
d) the landscape character of the location of U5001;
e) the LDNPA's long standing policy ambition for more sustainable travel to alleviate congestion and address the climate crisis;
f) the European Landscape Convention;
g) The LDNPA's 2022 position statement on unsealed roads.

39. The National Trust, the Friends of the Lake District and ICOMOS all requested the LDNPA to impose a TRO to prevent the use of recreational motor vehicles on U5001. No one is contesting the current legal rights of vehicles to use the road, but, in landscapes of the highest designation, where the volume and nature of usage increases and causes harm, changes in what activity is lawful are to be expected to maintain the integrity of National Parks.

40. It is my view that the LDNPA in 2019 erred in accepting the recommendations of the AR that repairing the surface and a partnership management group would be sufficient to meet their obligations to the site. The AR spends considerable length drilling down into the minutiae of surveys but fails to consider these details within the context of the national and international designations of the Lake District and their statutory duties under s 11A(2) of the 1949 Act. The AR gives preference to motorised vehicles over pedestrians or bicycles with an almost insurmountably high bar set for the removal of the current rights of recreational drivers and the imposition of a TRO.

41. The question should instead be asked is: 'Is the use of four-wheel drive vehicles for recreational purposes on an unsealed road U5001 an appropriate activity given the sensitive nature of that specific site and landscape and land use for which this area is designated nationally and internationally and our obligations to address the climate crisis?'

42. I note that there is evidence of significant public concern on this issue. The claimants point to the fact that almost 390,000 people have signed a petition to end the use of off-road recreational vehicles on green lanes in the Lake District. UNESCO via its advisor ICOMOS has asked the Lake District to consider banning recreational off-road vehicles due to the impact on the World Heritage Site. Further, s 62 of the Environment Act 2023 requires a greater weight to be given to conserving and enhancing the natural beauty over promoting enjoyment of National Parks. Since the 2019 AR, the LDNPA has considered the matter of usage of unsealed roads more strategically in the context of the special qualities of the National Park and the attributes of the World Heritage Site. Through its 2022 Position Statement, the LDNPA now explicitly recognises a TRO should be consulted on where there is unequivocal evidence of harm to the site as a result of continuing and potentially increasing recreational usage of unsealed roads. This is a move away from the requirement for irreconcilable conflict applied in the LDNPA's original decision.

Conclusions

43. The claimant's case is therefore upheld and the LDNPA is required to consult on a TRO for U5001. The TRO consultation process allows a number of options to be presented and requires a balancing process of interests. While any eventual imposition of a TRO may result in a legal challenge by existing users, that is not a reason for the defendant not to meet its statutory duty to protect the site's special qualities.

Commentary

Chris Rodgers

Context for the Decision: Balancing Landscape and Recreation in Decision Making in Protected Landscapes

This case raises several important questions about the way in which the 'environmental' interest is protected in decision-making based on public law models of the kind widely used in English law. Many of the protections applied in English law to preserve and enhance protected landscapes are introduced through the medium of planning law and development control. In this context, all decisions on development control in the planning system are essentially 'balancing' exercises between different 'material considerations' relevant to a proposed development; albeit one in which the development plan has priority in the decision-making matrix. Many restrictions on changes in land use are applied in National Parks, and these give special status to landscape protection in the balance struck by the various National Park Authorities when making decisions on development control. But there is a wide range of other contexts where this balance must also be drawn, and this case – which concerned an application for a TRO – is illustrative of one of them.

Little attention has been given in public policy discourse as to how decision-makers are to balance increased public access to the countryside on the one hand, with the protection of sensitive natural habitats and landscapes on the other. The exception (with which this case is concerned) is the need to balance these in the management of National Parks. In its original form the Sandford Principle was advisory but it was amended and given statutory force in the Environment Act 1995. This now states that where there is a conflict between the purposes for which its regulatory or other powers in relation to a National Park are exercised, a National Park Authority must 'attach greater weight to the purpose of conserving and enhancing the natural beauty, wildlife and cultural heritage of the area comprised in the National Park'. The statutory embodiment of the Sandford Principle, therefore, stresses (i) the nature of the balancing function to be carried out in weighing the different objectives sought in a National Park, while (ii) also making it clear that the conservation of its natural beauty, wildlife and cultural heritage must be given precedence over public recreational access in decision-making where there are conflicts as to land use. This is one of very few instances where legislation gives clear guidance to decision-makers as to how and where the balance is to be drawn between different material considerations relevant to decisions by the National Park Authorities when exercising their management functions – for example when deciding applications for planning consent, when licensing access for fishing, or for camping and other recreational activities.

It might be argued that the Sandford Principle is a rare example of Earth law principles being applied in contemporary environmental law, in that it prioritises natural beauty and landscape preservation over other human-centric concerns. The extent to which it does so in practice, however, depends very much on how it is applied in individual instances. And this, in turn, will be conditioned by judicial guidance on the way in which the balance between competing interests is to be drawn in individual cases where the Sandford Principle is invoked.

Patricia Stubbs v Lake District National Park Authority

The facts in *Stubbs* are set out more fully in Mrs Justice Aglionby's introduction. The High Court gave a restrictive interpretation of the Sandford Principle. It held that the principle requires there to be an irreconcilable conflict between the interests of conservation and public enjoyment before the balancing principle should apply to give preference to considerations of landscape and nature conservation over public recreational access. It will not be brought into play simply because these factors are in conflict. The Court ruled, therefore, that all other steps should be taken and considered to resolve a conflict before the National Park Authority could place conservation first and prohibit public enjoyment. The Authority's own officers had produced an AR in October 2019 considering the impacts of four-wheel-drive vehicle use on unsealed roads, and this had proposed several solutions to encourage dialogue and agreement between user groups. In the Court's view, the LDNPA was entitled to adopt recommendations in the AR and it was accordingly held that it had not applied the Sandford Principle inappropriately.

The reinterpretation presented here, using Earth law principles, emphasises that the judgment (and the approach to the balancing exercise that it represents) reflected the positive nature of legislative rights in English law. It is also characteristic of the rather conservative approach to statutory interpretation adopted by courts in the common law tradition, ie that established rights (especially, but not solely, property rights) should not be impugned by the courts when interpreting statutes – unless the statutory language is clear and displays an intention to do so. The approach in the *Stubbs* case ignores a more normative approach to legal principles that would focus on adapting them to achieve outcomes in line with public policy.

The reinterpretation of the judgment in this chapter adopts a normative approach to interpreting the balancing function required by the 1995 Act. In so doing it emphasises the potential for judicial review of decisions by public bodies to ensure that they appropriately balance conservation and recreational interests. This has been achieved by drawing attention to the latitude that the LDNPA had when considering the weight to be given to different factors, and by identifying and adjusting them accordingly. If we adopt an Earth law-centred approach that redraws this balance, then we can say – as Mrs Justice Aglionby does – that the LDNPA was in error in accepting the recommendations of the AR that repairing the road surface and establishing a partnership management group would be sufficient to address the conflict in land use. The decision to refuse a TRO was therefore open to judicial review, in that the LDNPA (i) considered irrelevant considerations and (ii) incorrectly attached the wrong weight to them when applying the balancing process required by the Sandford Principle. If we put Earth law at the centre of the judgment, this is the question that they should have asked themselves. As Mrs Justice Aglionby highlights, this meant that they applied the wrong test and asked themselves the wrong question. The question that should instead be asked is whether the use of four-wheel-drive vehicles for recreational purposes is an appropriate activity in the Lake District National Park given the landscape and land use for which this area is designated nationally and internationally, and with additional reference to our obligations to address the climate crisis.

Conclusion

The redrawing of the judgment presented here illustrates that this type of Earth law-centric approach could be adopted in many public law cases where decision-makers are required to carry out a balancing exercise, and this could be achieved without changes in the relevant legislative framework. A more radical and far-reaching solution to the problems raised in this case would, on the other hand, require that the weight to be given to the environmental interest (which here included not only nature conservation, but also landscape conservation and cultural interests) be more clearly defined. This would restrict the discretion of decision-makers to ignore environmental concerns where a conflict arises. The only other case in which the courts have given guidance on the application of the Sandford Principle is *R (on the application of Harris) v Broads Authority*.[6] This was another restrictive decision, the High Court holding that the principle did not apply to the Norfolk Broads – which is not formally designated as a National Park but is instead constituted and administered under the Norfolk and Suffolk Broads Act 1988. It was here held that the Sandford Principle would not apply by extension to an area that was not formally governed by the National Parks legislation. This limits the geographical reach and scope of the Sandford Principle to National Parks, and it will not therefore apply to prioritise landscape protection in decisions made by bodies administering other areas of high landscape value – for example AONBs or national nature reserves.

The restrictive legislative interpretations adopted in both the *Stubbs* and *Harris* cases illustrate that, if we are to improve the protection of fragile and valuable landscapes, we must give greater protection to a wider range of landscapes with cultural significance. It would be beneficial for the scope of the Sandford Principle to be both extended and strengthened by legislation. This would enable its application to give priority to conservation values in decision-making and the management of all protected landscapes, and not solely National Parks.

[6] *R (on the application of Harris) v Broads Authority* [2016] EWHC 799 (Admin).

13

To Open Up: A Performative Rewriting of *Pendragon v United Kingdom*[1]

LUCY FINCHETT-MADDOCK AND ANDREAS PHILIPPOPOULOS-MIHALOPOULOS

Opening Up

Pendragon v United Kingdom (1998) 27 EHRR CD179 has been 'opened up' at a time where questions of belonging, rights to roam, trespass and access to land have never felt so raw. Its tendrils, its stutterings, its legacy, feel as present today as if standing at those very stones in 1995 alongside Arthur Pendragon, the claimant who took this case to the European Court of Human Rights (ECtHR) a year later.

Arthur Pendragon, of the Glastonbury Order of Druids, performed a summer solstice ceremony at Stonehenge along with around forty others, and was subsequently arrested for trespassing under the Public Order Act 1986. The Stonehenge monument is known as an ancient calendar tracking the Earth's move around the sun; its stones align with sunrise on the longest day of the year and sunset on the shortest day. It has been a site of worship for Druidic cultures referring to solar and lunar movements as part of their faith for centuries. Pendragon brought a complaint to the ECtHR, citing the infringement of his rights to religious freedom, freedom of expression and assembly under Articles 9, 10 and 11 in turn of the European Convention on Human Rights (ECHR). The case is immediately important in thinking about the nature of public access to heritage sites, access to land and freedom of assembly. And yet, as we will see through an immersive rereading and rewriting of the case text, *Pendragon* opens up complex histories of power and inequality: forms of expression, resistance and aesthetics, within and beyond the English countryside.

The reading of the case is performative. By this we mean that it both took the form of a double performance; and that the rewriting performs the case as much as simply imagining a better judgment. We feel that conventions of academic

[1] The companion video to this text is available at: andreaspm.com/show/to-open-up-a-rereading-of-pendragon-v-uk-1998.

writing do not serve when rewriting judgments from the perspective of marginalised groups, objects and practices, considering it has only been something of an occurrence since recent times even to consider those who sit outside of the legislative class. How can we even take the perspective of the Earth in the first place? In performing and performatively writing the case, we have decided to take the law's materiality to heart. We built on Philippopoulos-Mihalopoulos's work in critical environmental law,[2] which seeks to expose the injustices of environmental law, with a concern for its spatial and physical realities, and how these may affect legal outcomes and legal ontologies;[3] and Finchett-Maddock's work on the nexus between law and art as an epistemic necessity.[4]

We also took our cues from the art practices of both authors in order to work outside the text of the law.[5] We were inspired by, and indeed form part of, the new materialist movement emanating from a feminist questioning of the porosity of the body,[6] and the philosophical order of 'object-oriented-ontology' as inculcated by Graham Harman.[7] Both new materialism and speculative philosophy of objects look to non-human relations in the world and how we are always already entangled in them. In this sense, our work here is concerned with accounting for the enmeshed material environment of law and how law affects its determination in lived 'reality'.

00:11 of the Summer Solstice 1995

Arthur Pendragon was arrested at 00:11 am on the morning of the summer solstice 1995 and charged a few hours later with taking part in a prohibited assembly contrary to section 14A (5) of the Public Order Act 1986 (as amended by section 70 of the Criminal Justice and Public Order Act 1994). In the preceding

[2] See specifically for work on environmental law, Andreas Philippopoulos-Mihalopoulos (ed), *Law and Ecology: New Environmental Foundations* (Routledge, 2011); Victoria Brooks and Andreas Philippopoulos-Mihalopoulos (eds), *Research Methods in Environmental Law: A Handbook* (Edward Elgar, 2017); Andreas Philippopoulos-Mihalopoulos, 'Critical Environmental Law as Method in the Anthropocene' in Philippopoulos-Mihalopoulos and Brooks (ibid) 131–58.

[3] See Andreas Philippopoulos-Mihalopoulos, *Spatial Justice: Body, Lawscape, Atmosphere* (Routledge, 2013) for work on spatial understandings of law.

[4] Lucy Finchett-Maddock, 'Forming the Legal Avant-Garde: A Theory of Art/Law' (2023) 19 *Law, Culture and the Humanities* 320.

[5] These include a confluence between law and art as practices that take form in performance art (often in the form of performance lectures) but also in more traditional artistic practices such as painting, installation art and sculpture.

[6] See works of Karen Barad, *Meeting the Universe Halfway: Quantum Physics and the Entanglement of Matter and Meaning* (Duke University Press, 2007); Rosi Braidotti, *The Posthuman* (Polity Press, 2013); Elizabeth Grosz, *Towards a Corporeal Feminism (Theories of Representation and Difference)* (Indiana University Press, 1994); and Jane Bennett, *Vibrant Matter: A Political Ecology of Things* (Duke University Press, 2010).

[7] See Graham Harman, *Immaterialism: Objects and Social Theory* (Polity Press, 2016); Graham Harman, *Object-Oriented Ontology: A New Theory of Everything* (Pelican, 2018).

months, the Chief Constable of Wiltshire had applied to the Salisbury District Council for an order to stop anyone gathering within four miles of the monument between 11:59 pm, 17 June and 11:59 pm, 21 June 1995. Pendragon had sought to challenge the authority of the order and its impact on those who wished to assemble to observe their religious rights, bringing judicial proceedings in the local Salisbury court. The challenge was rejected with assembly on a public highway being considered a civil wrong, citing the order as a proportionate measure to limit more non-peaceful gatherings.

Not only Druids, but those of the New Traveller communities and other New Age spiritual groups accessed the site. On 8 May 1995 and again on 1 June, alleged 'mass trespass' took place at Stonehenge.[8] Although Pendragon's activities were separate, he was removed along with members of these other communities under the auspices of the order that he previously had challenged. He took his challenge to his arrest and charge to the ECtHR, which, at the time, required an initial application to the (now defunct) European Commission of Human Rights. He complained that his rights under Articles 9, 10 and 11 of the Convention had been violated, and that UK law had failed to protect his rights to observe his religion. In barring public access to the site for solstice celebrations the order had violated Article 14 by disproportionately discriminating against Druids. He argued there was no means available in UK law to challenge the order contravening the right to an effective remedy under Article 13 ECHR.

In the event, the order was deemed by the Commission to be a proportionate measure, balancing Pendragon's rights with those of the public and the protection of the site. The Commission noted that the powers exercised by the police under the Public Order Act 1986 were principally with limitations on certain types of assembly; and therefore dealt with the case only under Article 11 of the Convention (following *Chappell v the United Kingdom*[9] which we will come back to later), whilst having regard to Articles 9 and 10.[10] The order was deemed as a proportionate measure in balancing the protection of the site, considering interference with the applicant's right to freedom of assembly reasonably regarded as 'in a democratic society … for the prevention of disorder' within the meaning of Article 11, paragraph 2 of the Convention.[11] The case was dismissed.

Even in this very brief account of the case, one can perhaps discern something of a chink to the events – through description, metaphor, the relaying of facts through lexical repetition and extension. And yet within the use of text, there are other methods and means of relaying history and legal intervention, of embodying, spatialising and materialising the law, that are left outside.

We move on to the rereading.

[8] *Pendragon v United Kingdom* (1998) 27 EHRR CD 179, p 10.
[9] *Chappell v the United Kingdom* Appl No 12587/86 (1987) 53 DR 241.
[10] *Pendragon v United Kingdom*, 7.
[11] ibid 8.

Stutterings

The elements are pouring out:

stone

air **breaths**

body (animate)

body (inanimate)

time (of day/of year) **time (historical)** **time (immeasurable)**

space (sacred) **space (public)** **space (liturgical)**

space (of the body) **space (of the case)**

We collect these elements in their assemblage tenuously tied together by the law. We change the order, we mix them with the ahistoricity of spatial justice, the withdrawal of material justice, and the roundness of planetary justice; and we place them onto a plinth, a Jenga-like structure of fragility and certain atmospheric seduction.

This is a judgment for a future openness.

We turn to the first performative rewriting offered by Philippopoulos-Mihalopoulos, drawing on his performance 'To Open Up / A Rereading of *Pendragon v UK*'.[12] The performance, delivered online during COVID-19, tries to give body and voice, immersion and atmosphere, to the crisp and almost two-dimensional pages of the case report. A performative reading seemed to be a fitting iteration from the perspective of the Earth: a rereading etched with atmosphere and body, where the case is spoken, drawn and 'sounded' as opposed to written down. There is a textual outline of the enacted rereading: even this is akin to pavement poetry, where the words are etched across almost reimagined bars on a score, evincing a mysticism, and musicality evocative of the Druidic faith (similarly present in classical music playing and recordings of chanting within the background of the footage).

Following Gilles Deleuze, we have called this rereading a 'stuttering',[13] giving way to gaps through which the case never closes, never concludes, remains open here in the present and emanating in the past, shifting between recountings. This stuttering gives way to a spatial determination of law, an echoing in the cavity of the mouth and the swirling circling word of the law that trips and

[12] 'To Open Up / A Rereading of Pendragon v UK 1998', found at andreaspm.com/show/to-open-up-a-rereading-of-pendragon-v-uk-1998.

[13] Gilles Deleuze, 'He Stuttered' in Constantin V Boundas and Dorothea Olkowski (eds), *Gilles Deleuze and the Theater of Philosophy* (Routledge, 1994) 23–29.

hops until it eventually falls off the lips of the utterer. Orality, in place of writing, echoes the ahistoricity and transtemporality that the Stonehenge megaliths conjure in their capacity for transmitting deep time. Stuttering also practices critical environmental law, interjecting itself between the utterance of the actual wording of the original judgment. We refer to this understanding of environmental law as an 'assemblage', one interwoven with other areas of law, implying a disciplinary crossing over from public to private, to criminal, and beyond. The description of critical environmental law as assemblage takes us to the writings of Deleuze and Félix Guattari, the philosophy of which underpins Philippopoulos-Mihalopoulos's thoughts. Assemblages are mixtures and compositions, an arrangement of networks, nodes and movements that move horizontally across space, as if like 'war machines'. This understanding allows us to think of the presence of law, as a composite or with capacity and potential across time and space, and the environment.[14]

The performance embodies the invocation that all beings are interconnected and interwoven through shared networks and ecologies. This became even more evident in the second performative reading of the case, a live portrayal by Lucy Finchett-Maddock. This second performance follows on and enhances the first, playing along the concept of practice of *assemblant* (as a more-than-human assemblage of law, stones, words, gestures, animate and inanimate bodies) and *assembly* (in the service held by the applicant, there were about twenty people present), and seeking to connect the online experience with those in person at the UK Earth Law Judgments Project Workshop, Middle Temple, December 2021. While a video of the first performance was replayed on screen, the performer, dressed in attire not dissimilar to a druidic robe, painstakingly starts tying participants, objects and spaces within the room together with one long piece of string. Everybody was made participant in this slow weaving in of the narrative; playthings in a cosmic bondage that brought together human bodies, chairs, tables, screens, rugs (Figure 2). As each stretch of fibre cross-hatched from one to the next, a web was created, as if it were a breaking down of atomic materiality – a reminder of the encircling and networking life force of ecological systems and their entwined laws. The performances mirrored each other, and both mirrored the text of the judgment, bringing forth the idea that utterings and declaratory acts are always performative, with law one of the most obvious examples of language. Performance and text, 'like a switch that breaks the natural link between sensorial experience and conscious elaboration'.[15]

[14] See Gilles Deleuze and Félix Guattari, *A Thousand Plateaus: Capitalism and Schizophrenia* (Bloomsbury, 2013).

[15] Paulo Virno, *La Negazione in Franco 'Bifo' Berardi, And Phenomenology of the End* (Aalto University Publication Series, 2014) 14.

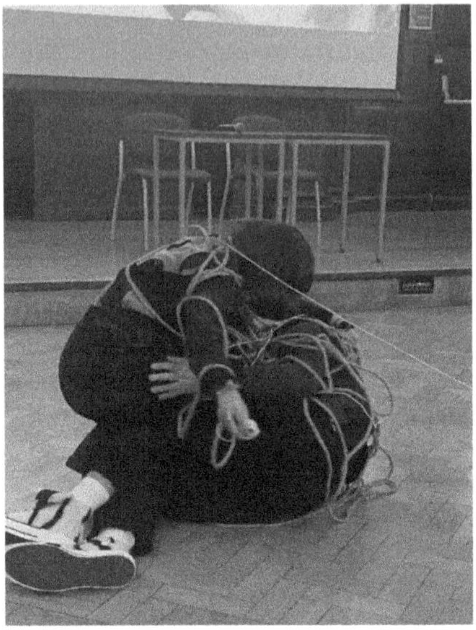

Figure 2 Performance of 'To Open Up' at Law as Performance Workshop, Westminster Law and Theory Lab, November 2023, with Andreas Philippopoulos-Mihalopoulos and Lucy Finchett-Maddock

Stonehenge, the focus of the re-etching, the geometry of which compels the sun to shine through the 4,500-year-old stone circle, our solar orb viewable just to the left of the outlying Heel Stone as it rises on midsummer's day. This very stone, although one of the sarsen stones, sits on the edge of the circle, and was the place where Pendragon sought to conduct Druidic ceremonial rituals on the midsummer evening of 20 June and the morning of 21 June 1995. It is the geographical and geometrical determinations of law's usage to circumvent Pendragon's activities that day that come through within the rereading, and the extent to which law has always been 'Earthbound'.[16]

Going back to the online performance, Philippopoulos-Mihalopoulos draws a circle citing Stonehenge as a 'hyperobject' and our desire for it to mean something, or to be 'part of' something. A hyperobject, according to philosopher Timothy Morton, is an all-inclusive, all-absorbing object whose narrative power endures beyond our spatial and temporal understanding of it, allowing it thus to exist in a new regime of knowledge where we can either understand these objects, or no longer understand them at all.[17] Philippopoulos-Mihalopoulos renders out loud this spatial determination:

[16] Taking from considerations of aesthetics, Earth systems science and law, law as 'Earthbound' has been elaborated on by Daniel Mathews, *Earthbound: The Aesthetics of Sovereignty in the Anthropocene* (Edinburgh University Press, 2020).

[17] Timothy Morton, *Philosophy and Ecology after the end of the World* (Minnesota University Press, 2013).

We want narrative, we create it

We want law, we create it.

We want narrative: the law creates us.

The performance questions not just the meaning of the case, but the grander meaning of law and its narrative intervention. The law made those stones in a certain way, but which law? The law of the Druids and common law clashing on the mossy surface of the monument like two different solar systems projecting themselves on it at the same time. Where do we turn? Why is your law better than mine? Why is placing a highway next to the monument more respectful than staging a solstice ceremony there? Why should capitalist logic trump pagan logic in the determination of the stones? Why must the narrative projected on the monument be monolithic?

The performance attempts also to consider how one relates to one's environment, and in particular how megaliths such as Stonehenge act as an elixir for that search for meaning – spirituality, identity and expressions of power through material forces and objects – for better or worse. In the performance, we hear:

law as an object,

law as whiteness,

Stonehenge as whiteness.

I belong, I'm a Celt, I sing

This immediately brings us to the seat of colonialism that finds itself within the predominantly white countryside. The English idyll emerges through centuries of enclosure and engrossment, whereby the proceeds of racial domination are fixed as capital, as the country estate, as vast swathes of individually owned aristocratic property feeding understandings of class-based ownership across the land.[18] As Ben Pitcher in his definitive study of Stonehenge writes:

> In the corporeal logic of nationalism – even a nationalism apparently accommodated to a multicultural present – the rural landscape belongs most securely to those who are racialised as white, and the experience of visiting rural landscapes reinforces the entitlement and belonging of these subjects. Racialised minorities may be welcome visitors, but rural Britain is not symbolically 'theirs' in quite the same way.[19]

Yet, not all is lost. Pitcher discerns a true potential in Stonehenge's rather hazy (as opposed to easily appropriable) origins and connecting function to a broader planetary ontology:

> On the occasions of solstice and equinox when visitors to Stonehenge are permitted to touch the stones, such immersive, embodied, sensual engagements transform Stonehenge from a dead object. … By framing witness of the rising sun, almost the

[18] Corinne Fowler, *Green Unpleasant Land: Creative Responses to Rural England's Connections* (Peepal Tree, 2020) for an intellectual history of the role of race and power within rural Britain.

[19] Ben Pitcher, *Back to the Stone Age: Race and Prehistory in Contemporary Culture* (McGill-Queen's University Press, 2022) 136.

> oldest thing that anyone will ever look at, Stonehenge can animate planetary finitude, questions of human survival, and the terms on which it occurs. Rather than serving as the frontispiece to British history, Stonehenge can be thought of as an extraordinary generative device for unpicking nationalism's hold and prominence.[20]

This critique and – at the same time, hope – is also reflected in the aesthetics of the performance: the image is somewhat opaque and obscured, green-screened on a background of a large black Murano glass piece, discarded by the glassblowers on the island of Murano as something that no longer serves them, that came out wrong. The shiny, rough-cut surface of the glass belies its human intervention, just as Stonehenge belies its human provenance. Performing green screen against a background of the mineral, or the 'inhuman' as Yussof calls it,[21] means that the face and body of the performer become enmeshed with the inhuman, the expressions mediated by the reference to the monolithic as skin. The result is an obfuscation of the performer and an immersion that demonstrates a ghostly presence, or a 'shape left by the absence', as a reminder of Avery Gordon's account of haunting and colonial injustice and the remaining spectres of those once removed violently through the use of law and its force.[22]

Closing Up

Moving in between concepts of *assemblant* and *assembly*, *Pendragon* seems to be promising the preservation of a space open and accessible: this is a public good, a common narrative of inclusive Englishness, a welcoming tourist sight, history etched in stone. And yet this very case annuls this access, despite the subsequent 'managed access' status of the monument which enabled even Pendragon to return and perform druidic ceremonies.[23] There is a paradox here between public and private, for if the land itself were of a public nature, then surely there would not have been the question of trespass? There are a number of cases that point us in the direction of what the 'public' really means.[24] Once again, perhaps these are more questions of *who* may have access: who has rightful access to the countryside, particularly that of the Englishman's castle? This was exposed into white British consciousness as questions of belonging, race and identity came to the fore after the years of the pandemic, where the vast majority of those living in city spaces did not have such access.[25]

[20] ibid 152.

[21] Kathryn Yussof, *A Billion Black Anthropocenes or None* (University of Minnesota Press, 2019).

[22] Avery Gordon, *Ghostly Matters: Haunting and the Sociological Imagination* (University of Minnesota Press, 1997).

[23] Steven Morris, 'Summer Solstice: Thousands Descend on Stonehenge to Greet Longest Day' *The Guardian* 21 June 2013.

[24] *Aston Cantlow PCC v Wallbank* [2003] UKHL 37. See also Lucy Finchett-Maddock, *Protest, Property and the Commons: Performances of Law and Resistance* (Routledge, 2016).

[25] Artists in recent times have meditated on this question of race, nomadism and cultural construction within the British countryside, such as Jeremy Deller, Damian Le Bas and Ingrid Pollard (2022

Questions of access, protest and assembly have similarly been live movements within political and legislative architectures in the United Kingdom in recent times. We have seen the Police Crime Sentencing and Courts Act 2022 closing in on protest rights through the statutory redefining of public nuisance under section 78, making the previous common law offence of public nuisance much broader, limiting demonstration noise levels and time limitation, with protestors now facing a criminal offence where they did not before. Criminal damage to memorials was raised from a £5,000 fine and six months to ten years imprisonment under section 50 of the same act.[26] These legislative interventions moved in after the powerful waves of protest of Black Lives Matter and Extinction Rebellion, and the iconic toppling of the Edward Colston statue; which brings us full circle to monument, heritage, power and legality found within the materiality of Stonehenge, and the statues around the United Kingdom commemorating those of slavery and colonial wealth.[27]

Pendragon is immersed in its material chronology and precedent. At least when it comes to the line of reasoning that the decision followed, the claims made for religious rights of practice and observance of the Druidic faith regarding access to Stonehenge had previously been ruled as inadmissible by the European Commission of Human Rights in *Chappell v the United Kingdom*.[28] Nevertheless, this case allows for a greater understanding of not just the assemblages of public order, but also those of heritage and administrative law that give legal charge to specific sites of significance.

Rewriting and performing the case as an *opening* embodies this networked and nomadic nature of the resistances that had preceded the presence of Arthur Pendragon in 1995 attempting to practice his faith. There are webs of resistance and legality, through public order, antisocial behaviour, as well as heritage. The legislative authority of the Ancient Monuments and Archaeological Areas Act 1979 gave, under section 19, access to the public to any monument under the ownership or guardianship of the Secretary of State. Subsection 2 provides that the Secretary of State or local authority may control the times of normal public access to the monument deemed in the interests of safety, or for the maintenance or preservation of the monument. It is under section 34 of the National Heritage Act 1983 that English Heritage was given charge of looking after the monument, and in February 1986 it decided to close the site over the summer solstice.

The material circumstances of what happened in *Pendragon* that very evening prior to the summer solstice in 1995 is a culmination of legal and resistant sediments that stretch back hundreds of years, with resonance from the 1960s, and regarding legal intervention, the 1980s onwards. The case reverberates with two

Turner Prize shortlist), for their work on environment, landscape and cultural identity, most recently demonstrated in retrospective 'Carbon Slowly Turning' (MK Gallery, 2022).

[26] Amending the Magistrates' Courts Act 1980, s 22 and Sch 2 para 1.

[27] For a geographical determination, see the UCL Centre for the Study of the Legacies of British Slavery, found at ucl.ac.uk/lbs/maps/britain.

[28] *Chappell v the United Kingdom* Appl No 12587/86 (1987) 53 DR 241.

eras of resistance, one in 1985 and another in 1992. *Chappell* takes us back in time to the Stonehenge Free Festival, held 1972–1984. In 1985, a four-mile exclusion zone around Stonehenge was set up, bringing to a close an era of free partying that ignited the burgeoning electronic rave scene, with the nomadic New Age Traveller communities who had set out on the road with their countercultural ways of life since the 1960s. The Romani Gypsy communities are also intertwined, present in their movement for many hundreds of years: the Romanichal diaspora arrived in the United Kingdom by the sixteenth century, with origins in Rajasthan in India; a reminder of the histories of non-white British ruralism. Although the New Age Traveller communities and those of Romani are distinct, their nomadism remains a common defining feature that, when joined with the ravers of the late 1980s and early 1990s, gave rise to sound-system collectives. Some of these sound-system and road-based collectives became more and more present as part of the free party scene around Stonehenge, the Peace Convoy being one of the best known from 1983 to 1985,[29] with a flashpoint culminating in 'The Battle of the Beanfield' in 1985 between festival goers and police. According to *Chappell*, the Peace Convoy was one of the main reasons that Stonehenge was closed in 1985, due to their more violent and threatening behaviour which became evident that same year. Yet when checking other sources, it seems that various injunctions used to close Stonehenge were not communicated to those planning to attend, with the battle becoming somewhat of a self-fulfilling prophecy.[30]

The second moment of rural resistance precedes *Pendragon*. In 1992 a large-scale week-long rave took place at Castlemorton Common, starting on the late May spring bank holiday. Not long after, the Criminal Justice and Public Order Act 1994 was drafted, outlawing outdoor illegal electronic music events playing music that 'emitted a series of repetitive beats' (section 63), adding to many other legal impositions faced by those connected with the traveller movement.[31] This outlawing of a way of life is a reminder of the recently repealed Vagrancy Act 1824, which sought to remove and hide those who have emigrated to the cities from their rural agricultural backgrounds.[32] These are just some examples of a series of repeated exclusions of any nomadic way of life that does not fit a fixed state of property, any rhizomatic and *assemblant* thinking; as well as of movements that seek the right to connect spiritually, aesthetically and in political solidarity with the megalith site itself.

At the end of the second performance, the whole room is covered in a spider's web of lines. The intention behind these is to throw into matter the connections

[29] Kevin Hetherington, *New Age Travellers: Van Loads of Uproarious Humanity* (Cassell, 2000) 11.

[30] See Christopher Partridge, 'The Spiritual and the Revolutionary: Alternative Spirituality, British Free Festivals, and the Emergence of Rave Culture' (2007) 7 *Culture and Religion* 41.

[31] See Chris Ashford and Mark O'Brien, 'Counter-cultural Groups in the Age of Covid: Ravers, Travellers and Legal Regulation' (2022) 86 *Journal of Criminal Law* 241, for the impact of recent COVID restrictions on the alternative rave scene.

[32] Cristy Clarke and John Page, 'The Lawful Forest: A Critical History of Property, Protest and Spatial Justice' [2022] *Edinburgh Critical Studies in Law, Literature and the Humanities* 110.

amongst the various participating bodies, human and non-human. Yet, we discover that these lines and circles also place us in specific positions. No one can move easily. Not even the performer can enter the space: she has to confine herself to the edge of the web; the only free-moving, black-cladded, spider-like presence, yet herself imprisoned by her own lines of connection. These connections, like anything we do and we become, are mere *dispositifs*, tools for good or for bad, gestures of presence that denote nothing more than that. What counts is what we do with them, how we become *with* them, how we mobilise them. Who plucks on the line, who attempts to connect, who travels the line across the room, who is included, who not. Nothing is decided for ever.

In the first performance, we hear that *the body of the case is still pulsing*. It is a vector between temporalities. We are taken back through the pages of precedent, transported through the realms of ancient and contemporary forms of the sacred, where deep time brings us face-to-face with the call for meaning and apprehension of what it means to be in the world; in between lines that might or might not connect, that might pull us in this or that direction. Our work of poetic undoing is never done. We carry on rereading, reiterating, reenacting, re-embodying, back to Earth, back to precedent, back to life – the case will be pulsing for some time further.

14

Afterword: Changing Legal Cultures

HELEN DANCER, BONNIE HOLLIGAN AND HELENA HOWE

Aim of the Chapter

The aim of this final chapter is to highlight practical opportunities for using the judgments to develop Earth law. We reflect upon how the transformations in legal cultures proposed by the reimagined judgments might be brought about through changes within legal professions, new pedagogic practices and creative public outreach.

Transforming Legal Professions

Responsibility

The ethical framework in which legal professionals operate is one facet of legal culture. This slippery concept describes the norms that govern the structures and functioning of the legal system, within which lawyers and adjudicators must take responsibility and exercise judgment.[1] Professional ethics constitute a core part of vocational training and practice for lawyers, all of whom are bound by codes of conduct, or in the case of adjudicators, a set of core principles.[2] While such codes and principles are focused largely on duties and processes, the entire ethical framework in which lawyers operate is underpinned by the normative principle of the rule of law.[3] Yet, what about the culture in which the professional legal self is created? As James Boyle argues, the entire project of becoming a practitioner

[1] Justice Brian Preston, 'The Many Facets of a Cutting-edge Court: A Study of the Land and Environment Court of New South Wales' in Elizabeth Fisher and Brian Preston (eds), *An Environmental Court in Action: Doctrine, Function, Process* (Hart Publishing, 2022).

[2] In the UK these include: *BSB Handbook Part 2: Code of Conduct for Barristers*; *SRA Code of Conduct for Solicitors, RELs and RFLs*; and *Guide to Judicial Conduct* for judges, tribunal members, coroners and magistrates.

[3] Tom Bingham, *The Rule of Law* (Penguin, 2011).

amounts to a constitution of the social subject by the structure of their discipline.[4] If the constitution of legal subjectivity lies 'in the creation and maintenance of the "purified" fantasy persona who confronts and receives knowledge', Boyle asks: 'How is the professional self that we construct shaped by a reified set of functions we imagine ourselves having to fulfil?'[5]

In ethical terms, the constituting of these functions is becoming increasingly contested. How can, for example, legal professionals navigate the perceived tensions between the interests of justice encapsulated in concepts such as the 'cab rank rule' for barristers, and the context of the climate crisis?[6] Practising lawyers, as Steven Vaughan acknowledges, are active in the shaping of environmental laws but also deeply implicated in the creation of environmental harms.[7] Yet, he argues, lawyers' professional obligations do not prevent them from taking, and indeed often require them to take, an environmentally responsible stance when faced with clients seeking their assistance to cause those harms.[8] Ethical practice requires the exercise of integrity, in the sense of not taking unfair advantage or knowingly inflicting harm on another,[9] as well as acting in the 'public interest.'[10]

The reimagined judgments affirm both the value of those responsibilities and the inclusion of the more-than-human within those harms and that 'public'. Although a commitment to the rule of law is also fundamental, lawyers may often find themselves with significant discretion in their interpretation of laws, especially confronting the complex, dynamic and open-textured rules in the environmental context.[11] In this respect, the judgments provide a more holistic conception of both procedural and substantive justice that may assist lawyers to exercise that discretion and advise their client in a more Earth-sensitive manner. In giving a sense of the potential arenas of future liability, the project may help lawyers to fulfil their obligation to act in a client's best interests.[12] This may involve avoiding future charges of ecocide (Rachel Killean) or tortious liability (Karen Morrow; Saskia Vermeylen and Jérémie Gilbert), to guide them towards actions that truly fulfil their obligations of corporate social responsibility. To the extent some of the judgments present imaginaries that are too radical for immediate transposition, they may, nevertheless, contribute to an intellectual and moral climate that makes it easier for lawyers to take an ethical stand.

At a time of increasing divergence of legal professional training from university education, the Earth law judgments may also contribute to much-needed

[4] James Boyle, 'Is Subjectivity Possible? The Postmodern Subject in Legal Theory' (1991) 62 *University of Colorado Law Review* 489, section D.

[5] ibid.

[6] Michael Harwood, 'Cab Rank in the Current Climate', *Counsel*, 12 June 2023.

[7] Steven Vaughan, 'Existential Ethics: Thinking Hard About Lawyer Responsibility for Clients' Environmental Harms' (2023) 76 *Current Legal Problems* 1.

[8] ibid.

[9] ibid 14.

[10] ibid 19–20.

[11] ibid 15–18.

[12] ibid 18–19.

capacity-building within clinical legal education and continuing professional development, to ensure that decision-making is supported by the necessary expertise.[13] The Earth law judgments offer a speculative version of the 'visible models of justice' described by Hope Babcock.[14] They could, for example, form the basis of mooting exercises for trainee legal professionals, and/or contribute to enriching continuing professional development of lawyers or the judiciary. As illustrations of judicial opportunity for reinterpreting existing doctrines and process, the judgments may help foster the development of new animating principles[15] to ensure that the courts – or other decision-makers – can protect the interests of the more-than-human.

Activist and Cause Lawyering

Across the globe, activist lawyers are asking courts to interpret laws to recognise and protect the interests of the more-than-human. Sometimes, they reach judges who are willing to push at the boundaries of traditional legal thought to develop rights of nature,[16] extend legal subjectivity to non-human animals,[17] or require governments to be held accountable for their responsibilities to address climate change.[18] The reimagined judgments are an act of celebration and solidarity, as well as contribution to the toolkit. Those judgments which provide such plausible interpretations of existing principles that they would cause barely a murmur (Bonnie Holligan, Julia Aglionby) could be drawn on by all lawyers when faced with a similar claim in future. Those which also involve closely reasoned alternatives to current law but which, by including beings and entities within existing categories or approaches not usually found there, exhibit a more speculative dimension (Helen Dancer, Joe Wills), could assist lawyers with more radical ambitions of challenging anthropocentrism. Inspiration for more fundamental recalibration of the system is provided by those judgments which introduce new forms of liability (Rachel Killean) or multisensory interaction with the claim (Lucy Finchett-Maddock and Andreas Philippopoulos-Mihalopoulos).

[13] Elizabeth Fisher and Eloise Scotford, 'Climate Change Adjudication: The Need to Foster Legal Capacity: An Editorial Comment' (2016) 28 *Journal of Environmental Law* 1, 4.

[14] Hope Babcock, 'Environmental Justice Clinics: Visible Models of Justice' (1995) 14 *Stanford Environmental Law Journal* 3.

[15] Similar arguments have been made in respect of feminist judgments. See Kate Fitz-Gibbon and JaneMaree Maher, 'Feminist Challenges to the Constraints of Law: Donning Uncomfortable Robes?' (2015) 23 *Feminist Legal Studies* 253.

[16] An action for protection of the rights of Los Cedros forest in Ecuador was a constitutional world first: Collateral Review Case Ruling 1149-19-JP/21, Constitutional Court of Ecuador, 10 November 2021.

[17] Constitutional Court, no 253-20-JH (Estrellita), 27 January 2022, translation available at animal.aw.harvard.edu/wp-content/uploads/Final-Judgment-Estrellita-w-Translation-Certification.pdf.

[18] eg, in Europe, the groundbreaking case of *The State of the Netherlands (Ministry of Economic Affairs and Climate Policy) v Urgenda* ECLI:NL:HR:2019:2007.

Because the reimagined judgments lack the authority (and violence)[19] of 'real' judgments, their contribution to establishing a new legal order is inevitably limited. Nevertheless, the judgments may act as worked examples of ways in which disputes involving the more-than-human could be approached, building on existing theoretical discussion on how ecocentric and wild approaches might be put into practice.[20] By normalising the inclusion of marginalised beings and entities in judicial deliberations, the judgments propose an enhanced role for the courts in protecting and honouring the more-than-human. In so doing, they also contribute to the integration of more-than-human interests into legal doctrine. As Fisher and Scotford note in the context of climate change: 'By adjudicating on such cases, the complex problem of climate change is incorporated into the legal order.'[21] This process of assimilation is likely to be fraught and contested, but the judgments provide an entry point for environmental and Earth justice concerns that can be built on by activists and social movements. This could be through public interest environmental litigation,[22] legislative reform efforts[23] or the creation of new forums, both formal and informal, in which Earth law principles can be applied.[24]

Earth Law Judging as a Form of Critical Pedagogic Practice

Chapter two identified three central features of the Earth law judgments' approach to legal knowledge: recognition of diversity and multiplicity, understanding of knowledge as embodied and relational, and engagement with epistemological ethics and politics. These commitments serve also as inspiration and guidance for pedagogic practice.

Diversity in the Legal Curriculum

There is an established tradition of using critical judgment writing as a means of expanding and diversifying the legal curriculum.[25] The line between creative

[19] See Nicole Rogers, 'Performance and Pedagogy in the Wild Law Judgment Project' (2017) 27 *Legal Education Review* 5, 11.

[20] eg Michelle Maloney and Peter Burdon (eds) *Wild Law – In Practice* (Routledge, 2014).

[21] Fisher and Scotford, 'Climate Change Adjudication', 4.

[22] An option discussed in the Australian context by Brendan Sydes, 'The Challenges of Putting Wild Law into Practice', in Maloney and Burdon, *Wild Law*, 58.

[23] Such as the Ecocide Bill that, at the time of writing, had just been introduced into the House of Lords: Ecocide HL Bill (2023–24) 21.

[24] See here Karen Morrow, 'Peoples' Sustainability Treaties at Rio+20' in Maloney and Burdon, *Wild Law*, 45; and Samuel Alexander, 'Wild Law from below' in Maloney and Burdon, *Wild Law*, 31.

[25] See eg Rosemary Hunter, 'Introduction: Feminist Judgments as Teaching Resources' (2012) 46 *The Law Teacher* 214; Jennifer Koshan et al, 'Rewriting Equality: The Pedagogical Use of Women's Court of

thinking and wishful thinking is a fine one. Elizabeth Fisher counsels against enabling students in 'wishful thinking': the self-indulgent and unrealistic embrace of simple utopias, in which law is used to cure all environmental ills.[26] This could be seen as a risk with such a project. Yet such projects can also be seen as offering the possibility of helping students to develop what Fisher describes as a 'legal imagination': an ability to reason towards possible futures, grounded in the complex reality of environmental problems and located within a shared understanding of the way law operates.[27] Judgments projects arguably work well here: they are exercises in which scholars explore alternative legal futures, not as individuals on a flight of wholly disconnected fancy, but as a pluralist, relational activity in conversation with other understandings and perspectives.

The judgments in this collection can be approached as a contribution to theoretical literature on Earth law. Reading Earth law judgments written by others offers a means of exploring the variety of Earth law perspectives and strategies. The judgments also serve as substantive contributions across the legal curriculum, offering a means of 'mainstreaming' Earth law thinking.[28] Across the core curriculum, the judgments in the collection encourage reflection on the possibilities and limitations of tort law (Morrow and Howe), judicial review (Agnew, Aglionby and Dancer) and human rights law (Wills and Holligan). At the same time, they disturb traditional taxonomies, supporting an 'integrative pedagogy' that draws attention to connection between existing legal categories, and between the 'legal' and 'non-legal'.[29]

Beyond reading, judgment writing suggests a range of possible student activities. The rewriting of judgments (or part of judgments) provides a means of sharpening students' argumentative and analytical skills, while exposing the practice of judging, and the kind of judicial writing produced in common law systems, to scrutiny.[30] The imagining of alternatives reveals legal doctrine to be the product of a creative process, rather than a natural artefact.

The employment of alternative judgments as a means of pursuing systemic transformation is not without risk. As Anna Grear acknowledges, there is a danger that acceptance of existing doctrinal logics and rationalities will reinforce, rather

Canada Judgments' (2010) 4 *Canadian Legal Education Annual Review* 121; Bridget J Crawford et al, 'Teaching with Feminist Judgments: A Global Conversation' (2020) 38 *Law and Inequality Scholarship*, law.umn.edu/cgi/viewcontent.cgi?article=1623&context=lawineq; and Rogers, 'Performance and Pedagogy'.

[26] Elizabeth Fisher, 'Legal Imagination and Teaching' in Lavanya Rajamani and Jacqueline Peel (eds), *The Oxford Handbook of International Environmental Law* (Oxford University Press, 2021) 140.

[27] ibid 144–48.

[28] On the need to incorporate wild judging across all areas of the curriculum, see Rogers, 'Performance and Pedagogy', 16–17.

[29] Kate Galloway and Nicole Graham, 'Learning Ecological Law' in Peter D Burdon and James Martel (eds), *The Routledge Handbook of Law and the Anthropocene* (Routledge 2023) 330.

[30] See eg Rogers, 'Performance and Pedagogy', 15–16; Crawford et al, 'Teaching with Feminist Judgments', 4.

than disrupt, dominant paradigms.[31] Judicial diversity presents a special difficulty for Earth law. The challenges of bringing non-human voices into legal systems outlined in chapter two are equally present in the classroom. Not only are students and scholars faced with the gaps in the legal record,[32] but the means of filling these gaps may simply not exist. Institutional constraints can play a constructive role here in inculcating epistemic humility. In many ways, the value of the Earth judgment is in its own limits, or rather, in its ability to accept and explore these limits.[33]

Embodied and Relational Practice

The ethical and epistemological commitments of Earth law predispose the Earth judge to working across boundaries: disciplinary, institutional, jurisdictional.[34] The judgments encourage the opening up of pedagogic practices to ecological embeddedness, and the sensitisation of law students to new kinds of knowledge. This may lead in various directions but suggests in general a need for interdisciplinarity and the forging of new collaborations within and outside of academia.[35] One fruitful avenue might be an interdisciplinary module offering a variety of perspectives on the same case or scenario.

Legal education should further support the creation of space for collaboration beyond the human with a wider world of 'interdependent, communicative normativities'.[36] This is likely to require material and experiential as well as abstract reasoning. Legal scholars can learn here from environmental education practices that foreground connection with the more-than-human, for example, Forest school.[37] The opening up of different juridical possibilities mirrors the broader epistemic and ontological uncertainties of a world characterised by climate crisis. Rather than the transmission of facts, uncertain pedagogies involve listening to students, cultivating responsible engagement and learning to live with the possibility of more than one answer.[38]

[31] Anna Grear, 'Learning Legal Reasoning while Rejecting the Oxymoronic Status of Feminist Judicial Rationalities: A View from the Law Classroom' (2012) 46 *The Law Teacher* 239, 242.

[32] Crawford et al, 'Teaching with Feminist Judgments', 51.

[33] ibid 32.

[34] See Nicole Graham, 'Learning Sacrifice: Legal Education in the Anthropocene' in Kirsten Anker et al (eds), *From Environmental to Ecological Law* (Routledge, 2020) 209.

[35] See eg Stephen Bunbury and Andreas Philippopoulos-Mihalopoulos, 'The Law School Degree Show: Law, Materiality, Decolonization and Authentic Assessment' (2023) 57(2) *The Law Teacher*, 187; Isabelle Giraudou, 'Environmental Legal Education as if Earth Really Mattered: A Brief Account from Japan' (2021) 8 *Asian Journal of Legal Education* 7.

[36] Anna Grear, 'Legal Imaginaries and the Anthropocene: "Of" and "For"' (2020) 31 *Law and Critique* 351, 363.

[37] Helena R Howe, 'Making Wild Law Work – The Role of "Connection with Nature" and Education in Developing an Ecocentric Property Law' (2017) 29 *Journal of Environmental Law* 19.

[38] Perpetua Kirby and Rebecca Webb, 'Conceptualising Uncertainty and the Role of the Teacher for a Politics of Climate Change Within and Beyond the Institution of the School' (2023) 75 *Educational Review* 134. See also comments in Crawford et al, 'Teaching with Feminist Judgments', 35.

Responsibilities

The Earth law judgments speak to the responsibilities of educators to ecological and human communities. The act of (re)imagining has here a civic and public function, in the cultivation of what, drawing on Martha Nussbaum's work, has been characterised as an 'ethical imagination'.[39] The versions of Earth law presented in the collection share a commitment to the situated and the embedded. As with other alternative judgment projects, they suggest endpoints that are 'local and activist in nature'.[40] Each of the judgments provides fodder for conversations beyond academia on topics such as the legacies of extractive industry (Morrow), decision-making around energy development (Agnew), and sewage pollution and worker activism (Zbyszewska). Some, in particular Killean's judgment on ecocide, suggest immediate law reform objectives. As these dialogues move beyond the university classroom, they will likely benefit from the diverse and creative avenues for engaging with the judgment content discussed below.

It was argued above that Earth judging has potential to contribute to the development of ethical agency in future legal professionals. The reading of alternative judgments serves to sensitise students to the contingency of existing legal rules, and, more importantly, to who and what has been excluded from consideration.[41] The gap between formal law and justice is explicitly recognised.[42] This recognition may help to open law, and the legal professions, to previously marginalised voices; as one academic explains in the context of feminist judging, '[the students] see themselves and their possibilities'.[43] This has particular value in the context of the commodification of university education, and a legal profession that does not necessarily value university legal studies, as a means of repoliticising the classroom.[44]

Creative Practice and Public Engagement

The Judgment Project Itself

Alternative judgment projects are themselves creative acts, pushing the boundaries of established legal reasoning. However, Earth law judgments are perhaps particularly creative because they often look beyond existing legal forms, cultural

[39] See Sharon Cowan's comments in Crawford et al, 'Teaching with Feminist Judgments', 42, drawing on the work of Martha Nussbaum. Martha C Nussbaum, 'Poets as Judges: Judicial Rhetoric and the Literary Imagination' (1995) 62 *The University of Chicago Law Review* 1477, 1519.

[40] Crawford et al, 'Teaching with Feminist Judgments', 53.

[41] ibid 30.

[42] ibid 3.

[43] ibid 29.

[44] Helen Carr and Nick Dearden 'Research-led Teaching, Vehicular Ideas and the Feminist Judgments Project', (2012) 46 *The Law Teacher*, 268.

values and even conventional approaches to time, as part of their contribution to a paradigm shift in judging, towards more-than-human relationality and subjectivity. Nicole Rogers and Michelle Maloney observe that as performative and creative acts, Wild, or Earth law, judgment projects share much in common with the activities of the International Rights of Nature Tribunal that was established by the Global Alliance for the Rights of Nature in 2014 as a platform for activism and for marginalised voices to be heard. While the tribunal has no formal legal recognition, it serves as a global forum 'for people from all around the world to speak on behalf of nature, to protest the destruction of the Earth … and to make recommendations about Earth's protection and restoration'.[45] Like the Rights of Nature Tribunal, both the Australian and the UK Earth law judgment projects constitute a means of 'performing or inventing a form of law which has no legitimacy within existing legal systems'.[46]

Using the Arts in Envisioning Earth Law

Inviting different artistic ways of knowing and sensing the world into the realm of environmental decision-making can generate cross-cultural, ethical and emotional insights into environmental and legal problems that cannot be achieved through established forms of rational and scientific enquiry.[47] Indeed, while environmental art is taking an increasingly prominent position in galleries and exhibition centres,[48] Earth law approaches to judging suggest that there is no reason why artistic and literary works of all kinds – soundscapes, music, short film, painting and photography – could not find a place in courtrooms of the future. In this respect, the project is part of a broader conversation in legal and political theory about law beyond text,[49] and the role of imagination in bringing more just legal pasts and futures into being.[50]

Expanding law's media may be particularly valuable in helping decision-makers respond sensitively to the causes and consequences of ecological destruction.[51]

[45] See the website of the International Rights of Nature Tribunal: rightsofnaturetribunal.org.

[46] Nicole Rogers and Michelle Maloney, 'The Australian Wild Law Judgment Project' (2014) 39 *Alternative Law Journal* 173, 174.

[47] Benjamin J Richardson, *The Art of Environmental Law: Governing with Aesthetics* (Hart Publishing, 2019); Justice Brian Preston, 'Changing How We View Change: The Artist's Insight' (2022) *IUCN Academy of Environmental Law Colloquium*, 15 July 2022, QUT Brisbane.

[48] eg 'Our Time on Earth', Barbican, London, 5 May–29 August 2022; 'The Shape of a Circle in the Mind of a Fish', Serpentine Gallery, London, ongoing, and, local to the authors, the ONCA gallery, Brighton: onca.org.uk. On the need to link creative ambition with activist praxis, see Marv RecInto, 'Eco Exhibitions Won't Save Us', *Art Review*, 18 July 2023.

[49] Zenon Bankowski, Maksymilian Del Mar and Paul Maharg, *The Arts and the Legal Academy: Beyond Text in Legal Education* (Routledge, 2013).

[50] Peter Goodrich and Thanos Zartaloudis (eds), *The Cabinet of Imaginary Laws* (Routledge, 2021).

[51] Preston, 'Changing How We View Change', 17–24 (see eg the sonograms of bird song created by John Wolseley, 24).

Creative practice can add new means of representation, while exposing the instability inherent in legal knowledges and subjectivities. Melding Bob Dylan's lyrical truism that 'the times they are a-changin', with Elizabeth Fisher's call for environmental law to become 'hot law' in order to deal with ever-evolving 'hot situations', Justice Brian Preston proposes that art can bring to the attention of legal decision-makers a broader range of knowledges and voices, thereby improving their decision-making under conditions of constant flux.[52] In this collection, Jo Walton's Wildlaw judgment generator exemplifies the capacity of art to open up law to the fluidity and complexity inherent in decision-making about ecosystems.

Like many judgments in the UK legal tradition, the majority of the reimagined versions in this collection are, in effect, short stories. As such, they both benefit from and illustrate the capacity of narrative to engage emotion, ignite passion and include marginalised voices.[53] Wills takes the narrative device even further, drawing on imagery from fiction and folklore to represent an alternative cultural perspective on the fox. Even those judgments that do not directly employ art forms still present space and opportunity for incorporating creative practices into their deliberative processes. Creative practice could provide methods for the inclusion of unheard voices and emotion that is advocated for in the chapters by Agnew, Aglionby and Dancer, enabling local communities to express their relational connection with the land or species, and perhaps even offering avenues for those creative expressions to become integrated into the decision-making process.

The performance works that comprise the judgment of Finchett-Maddock and Philippopoulos-Mihalopoulos, alongside the text, stand out for having escaped the confines of the written form. In so doing, they illustrate how art may transcend the limits of supposedly rational or scientific approaches to enable a concept or emotion to be expressed that is not reducible to cognitive 'knowing'. Elsewhere, Justice Brian Preston has employed painting to convey multitemporal and multi-spatial landscapes that capture the perception of indigenous peoples of the Andes that time is non-linear.[54] By comparison, Finchett-Maddock and Philippopoulos-Mihalopoulos's performance of visual and aural stuttering and an 'opening up' of elements of earth, air, space, time and body in their assemblage tenuously tied together by law speaks to Anna Grear's call for a legal imaginary that means 'opening law, and certainly opening legal theoretical work, to the sensory organs of the arts – with their unique capacity to dislodge and to re-invent imaginaries, their unrivalled ability – along with plural indigenous lifeways'.[55]

[52] ibid 2–5.

[53] Chris Hilson, 'The Role of Narrative in Environmental Law: The Nature of Tales and Tales of Nature' (2022) 34 *Journal of Environmental Law* 1.

[54] Preston, 'Changing How We View Change', 13–16.

[55] Grear, 'Legal Imaginaries and the Anthropocene', 360.

Earth Law Judgments as Invitation to Public Dialogue

The Earth law judgments provide opportunities for a wide variety of public engagement activities and events, including for publicly staged recreations of the claims that incorporate other voices and perspectives, in the vein of the mock animal trials staged by the lawyer turned artist Jack Tan.[56] In a work inviting us to 'reconsider our understanding of the position of humans in relation to animals and the environment',[57] Tan turned Leeds Town Hall into the fictional Department of Animal Justice where barristers brought claims on behalf of – and against – animal clients. Whilst the judgments in the collection featuring animals (Wills, Howe, Holligan and Agnew) present obvious opportunities for similar productions, those representing unheard human voices – both present and future (Dancer, Morrow, Vermeylen and Gilbert, Aglionby) – and even rivers (Vermeylen and Gilbert, Killean), provide material for powerful performative (re)imaginings. The collection extends an invitation to conversation, collaboration and creative and political practice. Transformation of legal cultures must involve the judge, and the courtroom, but it does not end there.

[56] Jack Tan, *Four Legs Good*, jacktan.wordpress.com/art-work/four-legs-good/.
[57] ibid.

INDEX

www.ingramcontent.com/pod-product-compliance
Ingram Content Group UK Ltd.
Pitfield, Milton Keynes, MK11 3LW, UK
UKHW020244290926
15470UKWH00002B/722

9 781509 970858